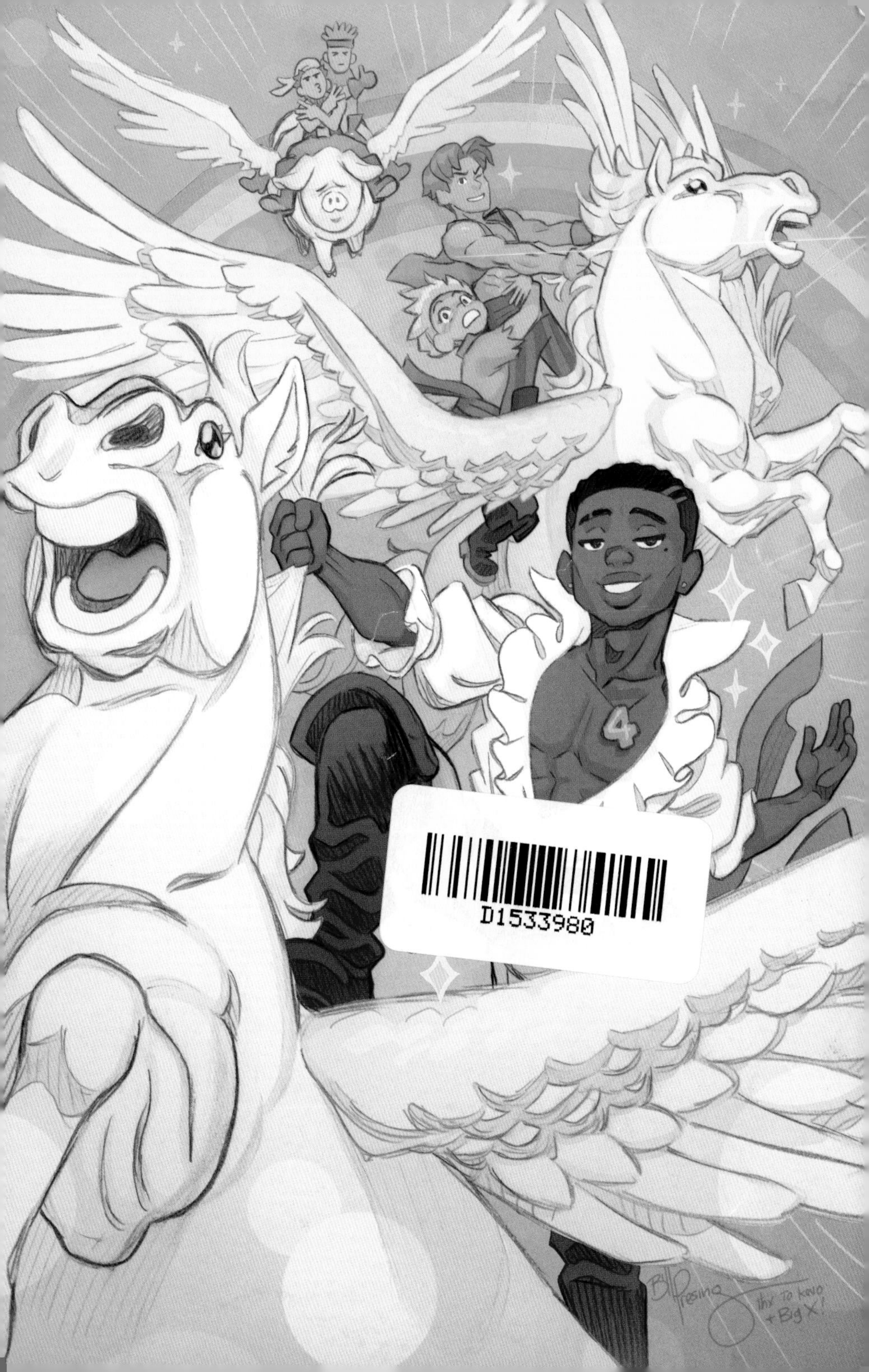
4
Bill Presing
thx to kavo + Big X!

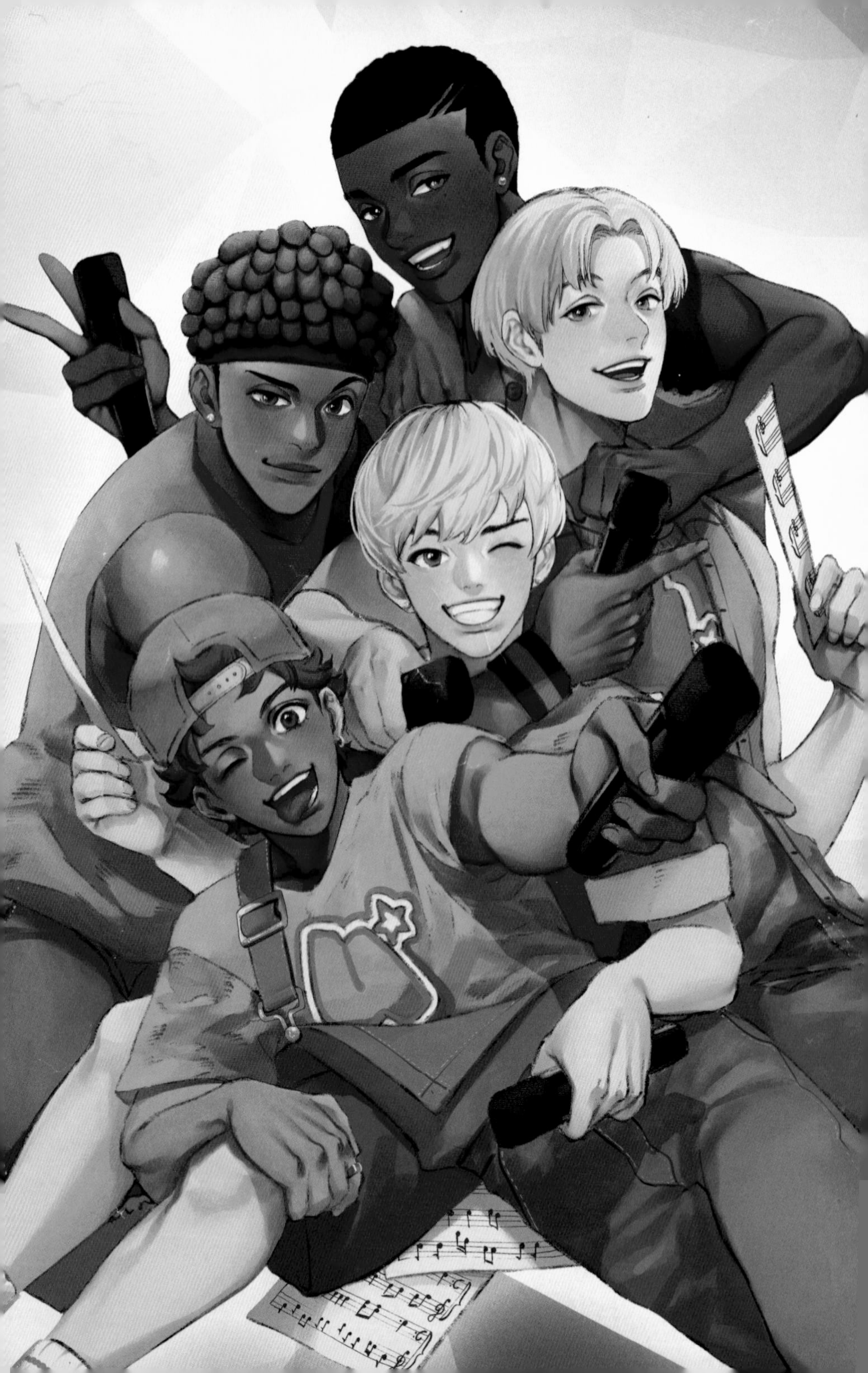

Disney · PIXAR

TURNING RED

4*TOWN 4*REAL

HOT

yeah!

4town 4ever

VIZ MEDIA

4★TOWN
IN CONCERT

Date		Location
May 18	....	Toledo, OH
May 25	....	Toronto, ON
June 2	....	Kitchener, ON
June 9	....	Edmonton, AB
June 18	....	New York, N
June 25	....	Pittsburg, P

WORLD TOUR '02

Tickets on Sale Call (416) 555-0155 and at the Box Office. Get yours today!

POSTER INSID

Tween beat

4★TOWN
ANNOUNC
NEW TOU

Disney · PIXAR

TURNING RED

4✦TOWN 4✦REAL

Story by
Dirchansky

Pinup illustration by
Bill Presing

Art by
Kaifee

VIZ MEDIA

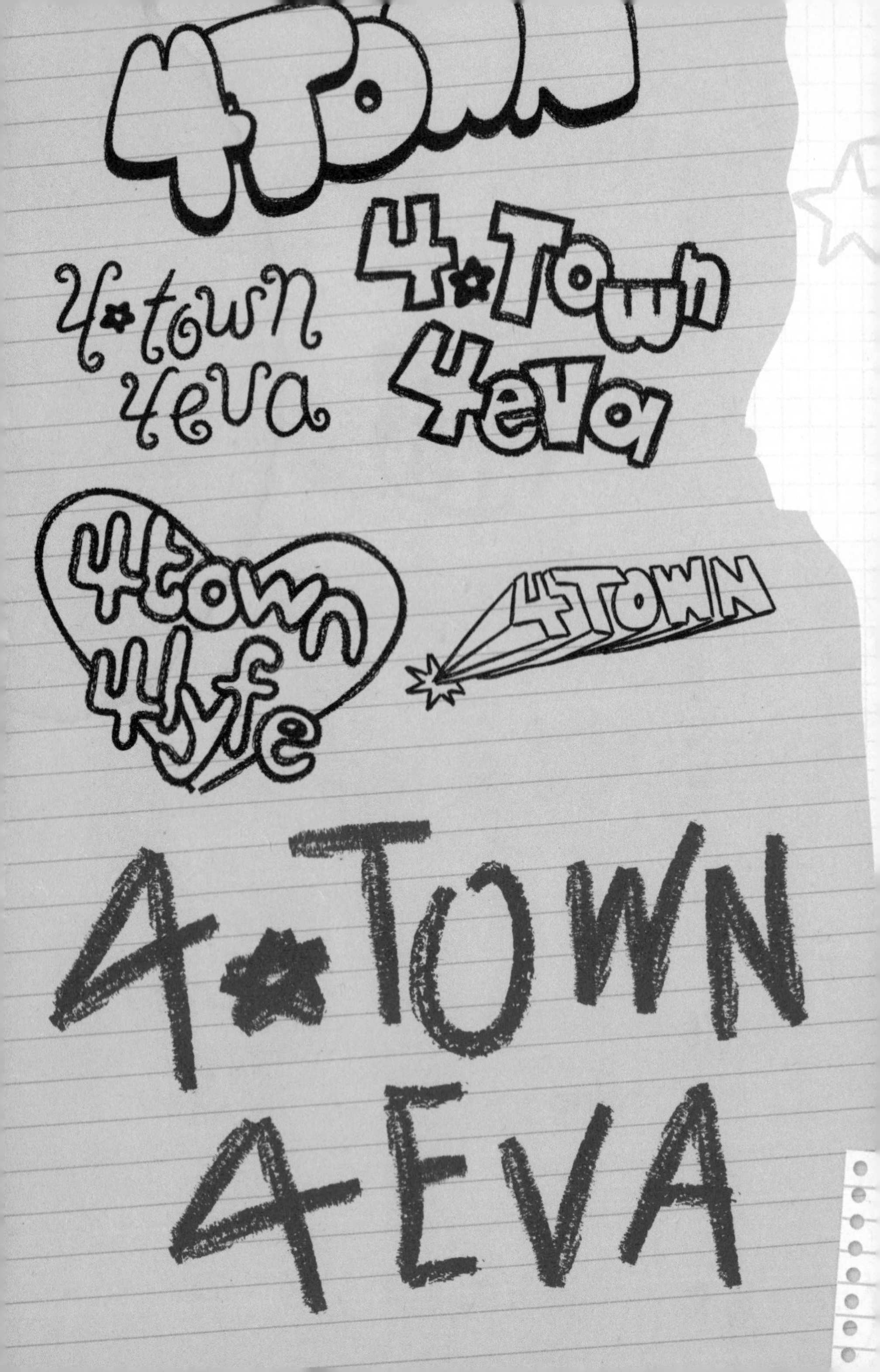
4TOWN
4town
4eva
4Town
4eva
4town
4lyfe
4TOWN
4TOWN
4EVA

4★Town
'99 Australian Tour

4★Town

4town
4ever

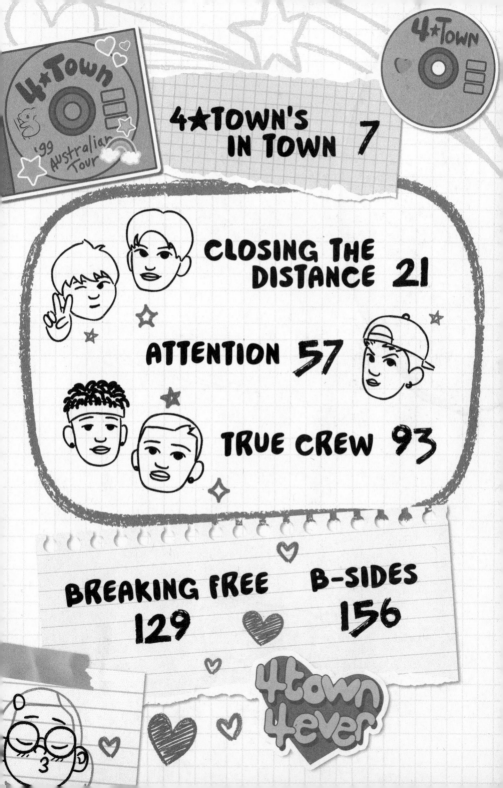

4★TOWN
Hottest Band
of the Year!

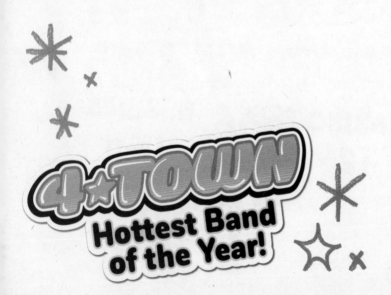

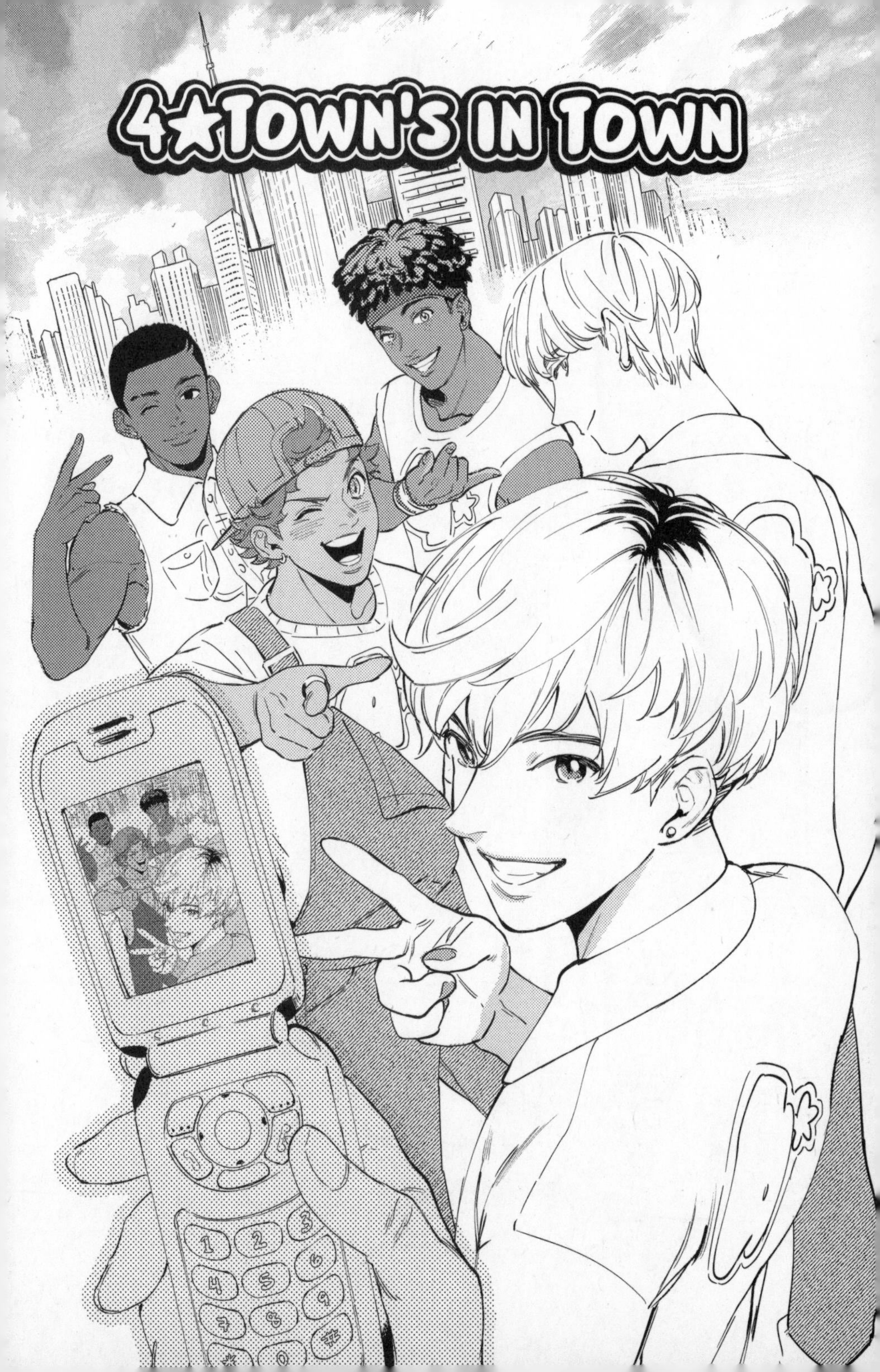
4★TOWN'S IN TOWN

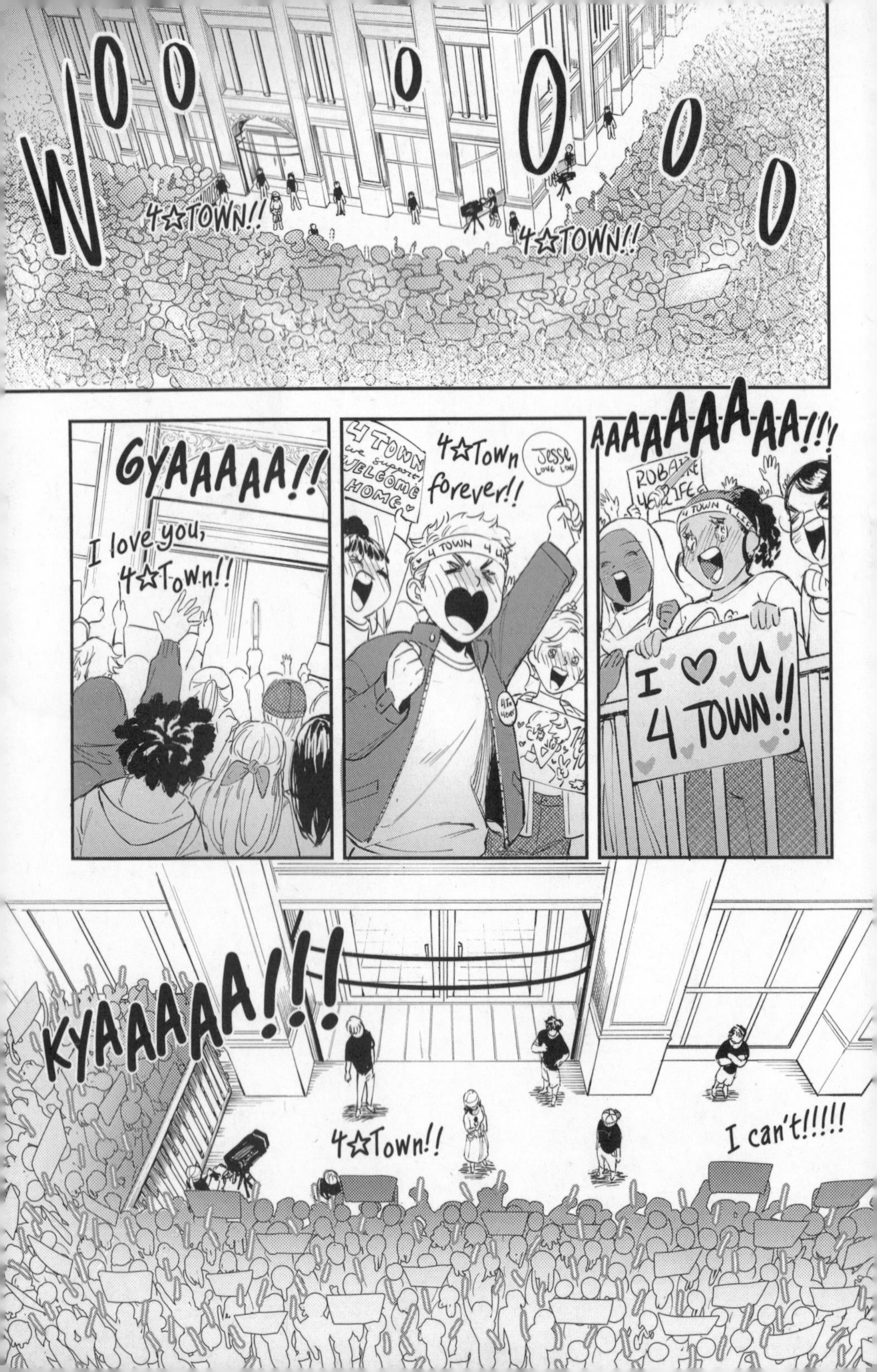
WOOOOOOO
4☆TOWN!!
4☆TOWN!!
GYAAAAAA!!
I love you, 4☆Town!!
4 TOWN
we support
WELCOME HOME
4☆Town forever!!
Jesse
LOVE LOVE
AAAAAAAAA!!!
I ♥ U 4 TOWN!!
KYAAAAA!!!
4☆Town!!
I can't!!!!!!

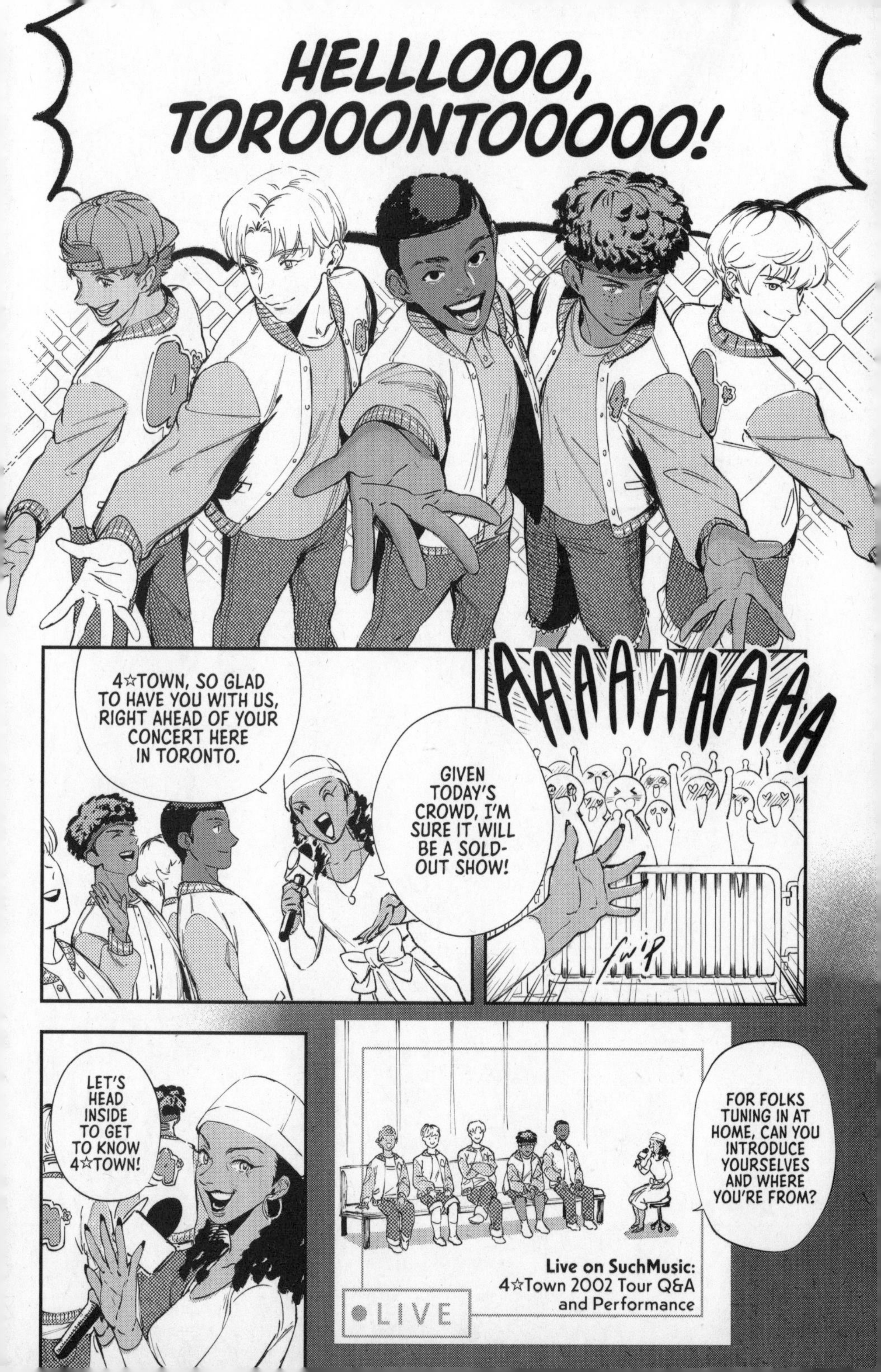
HELLLOOO, TOROOONTOOOOO!
4☆TOWN, SO GLAD TO HAVE YOU WITH US, RIGHT AHEAD OF YOUR CONCERT HERE IN TORONTO.
GIVEN TODAY'S CROWD, I'M SURE IT WILL BE A SOLD-OUT SHOW!
AAAAAAAAA
fwip
LET'S HEAD INSIDE TO GET TO KNOW 4☆TOWN!
FOR FOLKS TUNING IN AT HOME, CAN YOU INTRODUCE YOURSELVES AND WHERE YOU'RE FROM?
Live on SuchMusic: 4☆Town 2002 Tour Q&A and Performance
LIVE

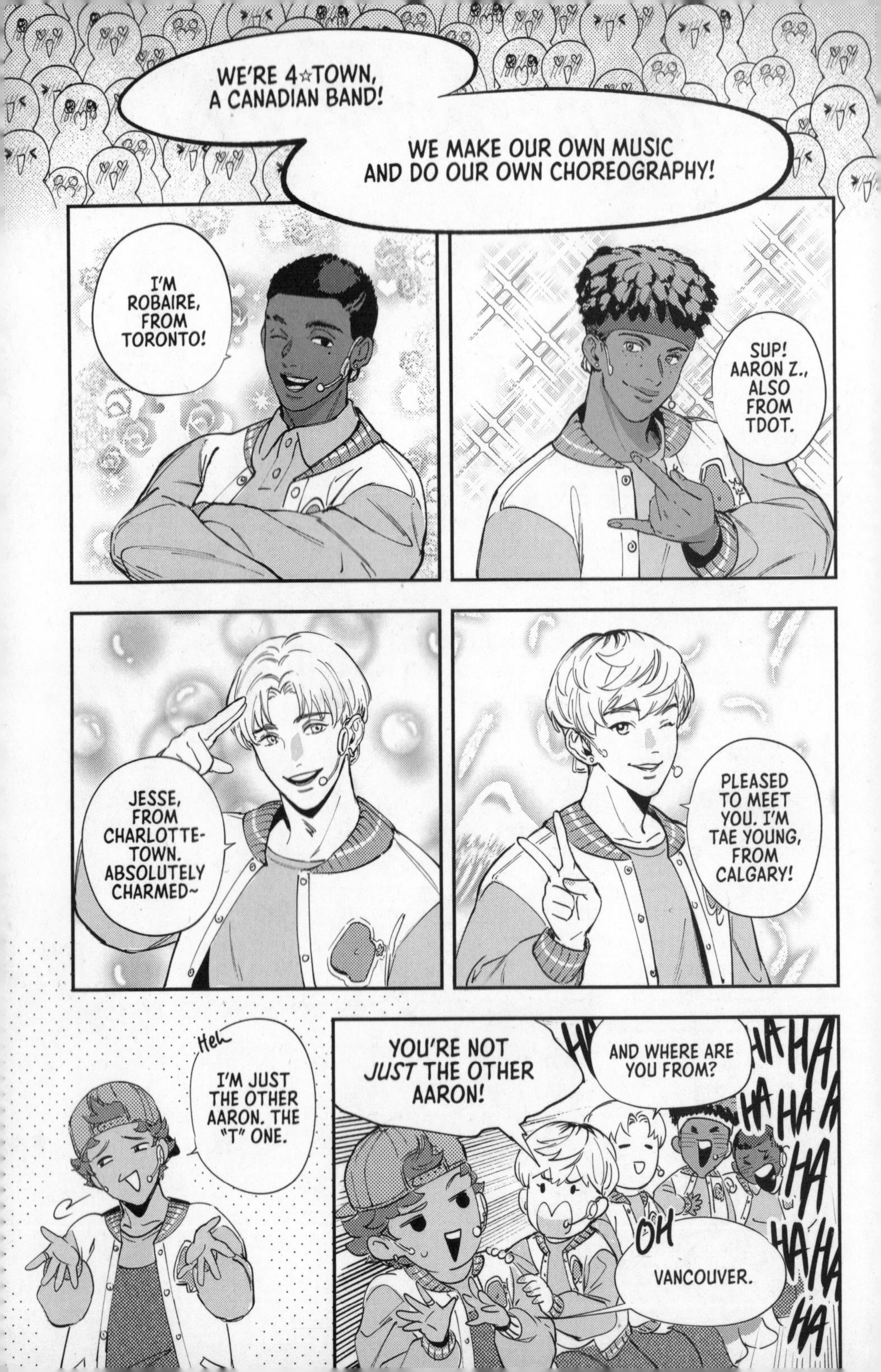
WE'RE 4☆TOWN, A CANADIAN BAND!
WE MAKE OUR OWN MUSIC AND DO OUR OWN CHOREOGRAPHY!
I'M ROBAIRE, FROM TORONTO!
SUP! AARON Z., ALSO FROM TDOT.
JESSE, FROM CHARLOTTE-TOWN. ABSOLUTELY CHARMED~
PLEASED TO MEET YOU. I'M TAE YOUNG, FROM CALGARY!
Heh
I'M JUST THE OTHER AARON. THE "T" ONE.
YOU'RE NOT JUST THE OTHER AARON!
AND WHERE ARE YOU FROM?
HA HA HA HA HA HA HA HA HA HA HA
OH
VANCOUVER.

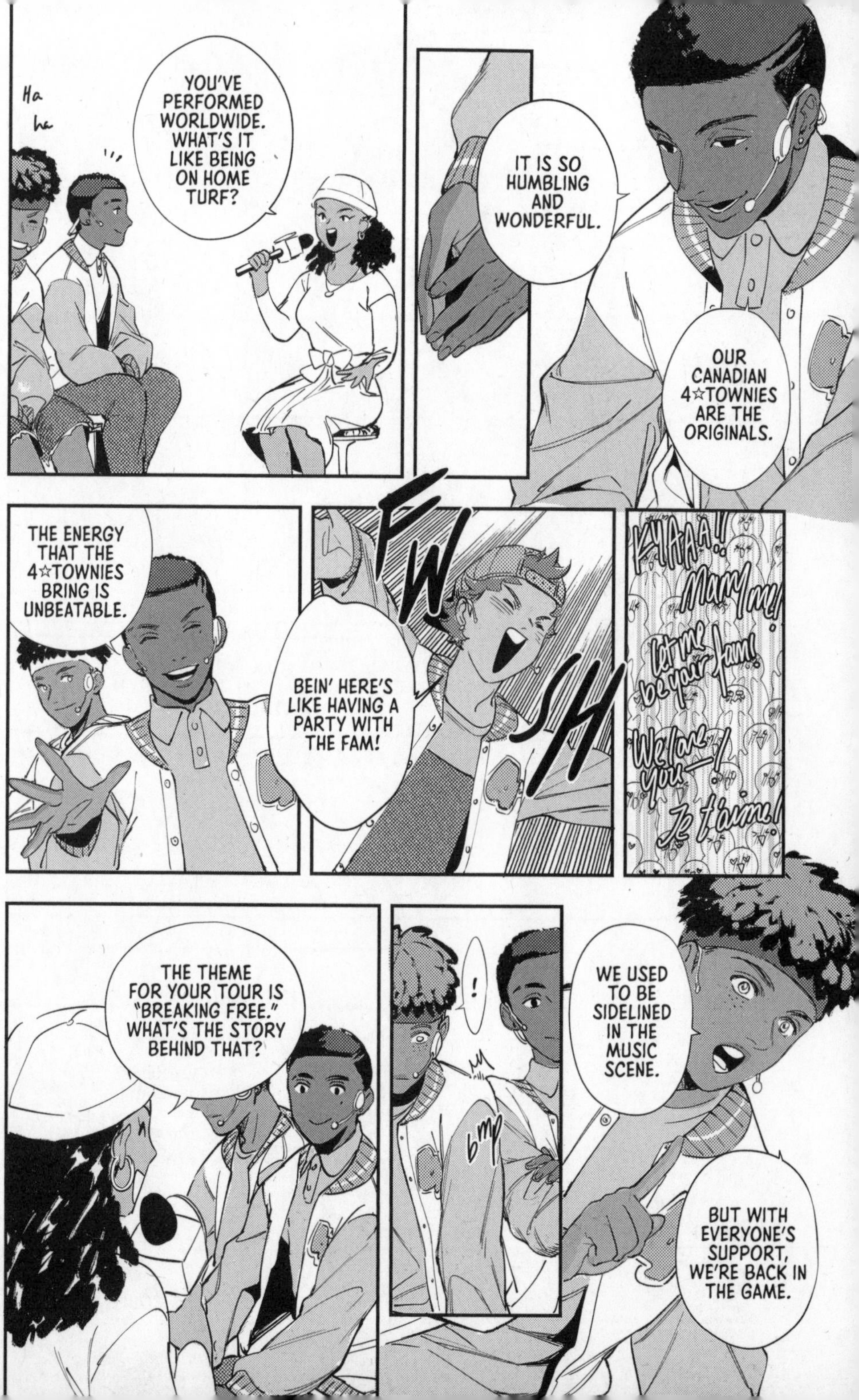

Ha ha
YOU'VE PERFORMED WORLDWIDE. WHAT'S IT LIKE BEING ON HOME TURF?
IT IS SO HUMBLING AND WONDERFUL.
OUR CANADIAN 4☆TOWNIES ARE THE ORIGINALS.
THE ENERGY THAT THE 4☆TOWNIES BRING IS UNBEATABLE.
FWSH
BEIN' HERE'S LIKE HAVING A PARTY WITH THE FAM!
KYAAA!!
Marry me!
Let me be your fam!
We love you—!
Je t'aime!
THE THEME FOR YOUR TOUR IS "BREAKING FREE." WHAT'S THE STORY BEHIND THAT?
!
bmp
WE USED TO BE SIDELINED IN THE MUSIC SCENE.
BUT WITH EVERYONE'S SUPPORT, WE'RE BACK IN THE GAME.

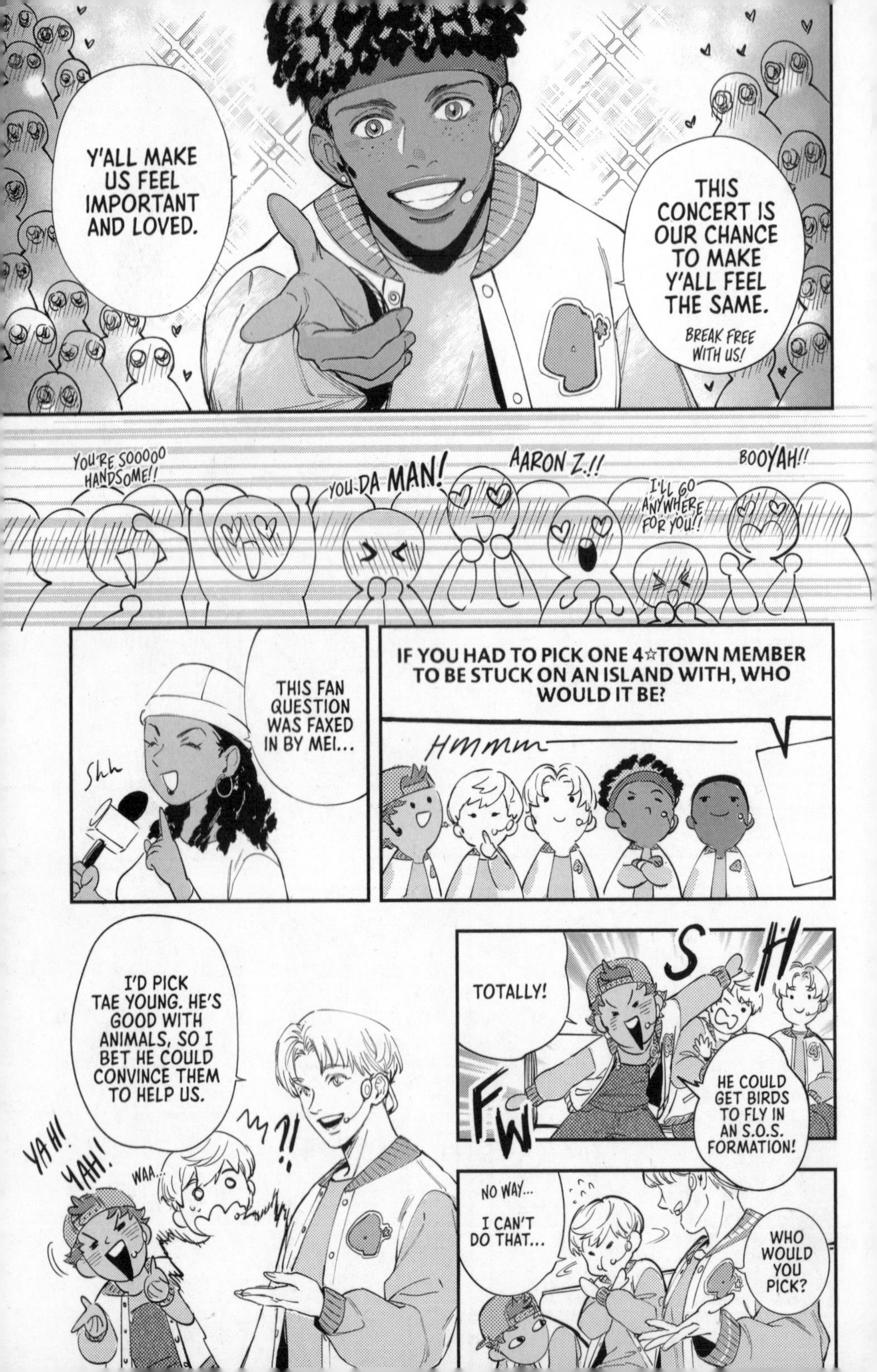
Y'ALL MAKE US FEEL IMPORTANT AND LOVED.
THIS CONCERT IS OUR CHANCE TO MAKE Y'ALL FEEL THE SAME.
BREAK FREE WITH US!
YOU'RE SOOOOO HANDSOME!!
YOU DA MAN!
AARON Z!!
I'LL GO ANYWHERE FOR YOU!!
BOOYAH!!
Shh
THIS FAN QUESTION WAS FAXED IN BY MEI...
IF YOU HAD TO PICK ONE 4☆TOWN MEMBER TO BE STUCK ON AN ISLAND WITH, WHO WOULD IT BE?
HMMM
I'D PICK TAE YOUNG. HE'S GOOD WITH ANIMALS, SO I BET HE COULD CONVINCE THEM TO HELP US.
YAH! YAH!
WAA...
?!
TOTALLY!
SH
FW
HE COULD GET BIRDS TO FLY IN AN S.O.S. FORMATION!
NO WAY...
I CAN'T DO THAT...
WHO WOULD YOU PICK?

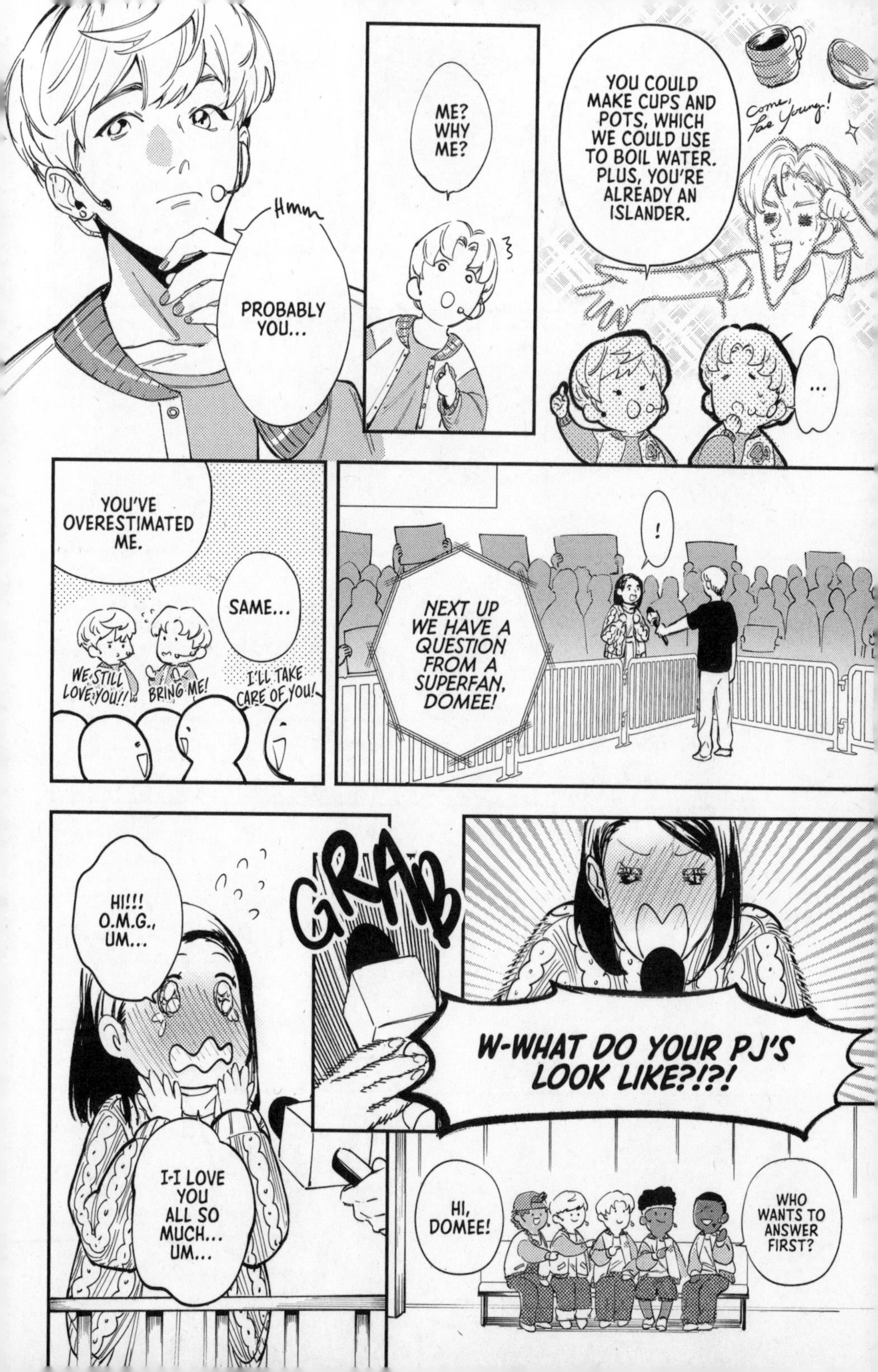

Hmm
PROBABLY YOU...
ME? WHY ME?
YOU COULD MAKE CUPS AND POTS, WHICH WE COULD USE TO BOIL WATER. PLUS, YOU'RE ALREADY AN ISLANDER.
Come, Tae Young!
...
YOU'VE OVERESTIMATED ME.
SAME...
WE STILL LOVE YOU!!
BRING ME!
I'LL TAKE CARE OF YOU!
!
NEXT UP WE HAVE A QUESTION FROM A SUPERFAN, DOMEE!
HI!!! O.M.G., UM...
I-I LOVE YOU ALL SO MUCH... UM...
GRAB
W-WHAT DO YOUR PJ'S LOOK LIKE?!?!
HI, DOMEE!
WHO WANTS TO ANSWER FIRST?

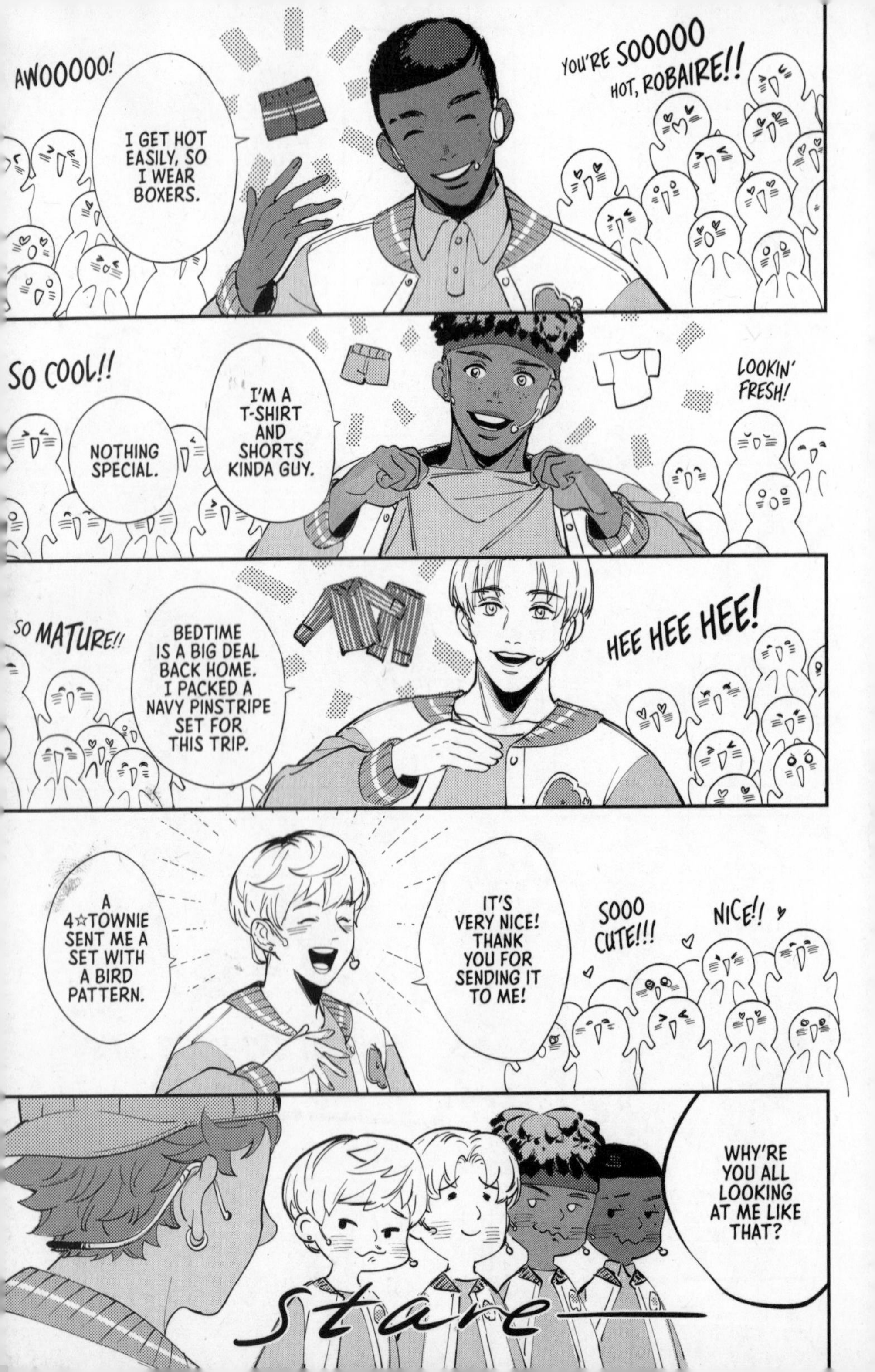
AWOOOOO!
I GET HOT EASILY, SO I WEAR BOXERS.
YOU'RE SOOOOO HOT, ROBAIRE!!
SO COOL!!
NOTHING SPECIAL.
I'M A T-SHIRT AND SHORTS KINDA GUY.
LOOKIN' FRESH!
SO MATURE!!
BEDTIME IS A BIG DEAL BACK HOME. I PACKED A NAVY PINSTRIPE SET FOR THIS TRIP.
HEE HEE HEE!
A 4☆TOWNIE SENT ME A SET WITH A BIRD PATTERN.
IT'S VERY NICE! THANK YOU FOR SENDING IT TO ME!
SOOO CUTE!!!
NICE!!
Stare
WHY'RE YOU ALL LOOKING AT ME LIKE THAT?

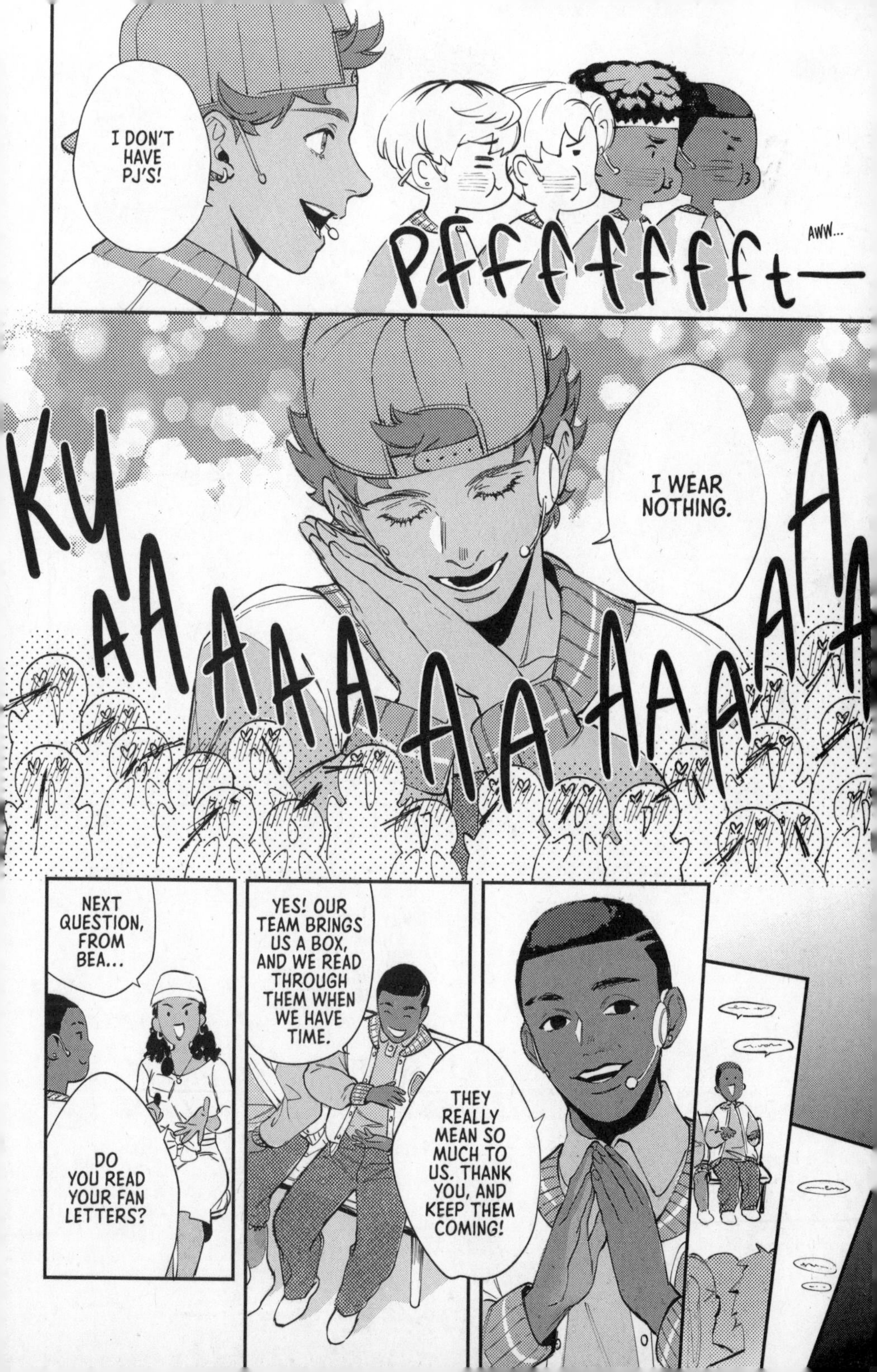
I DON'T HAVE PJ'S!
Pfffffffft—
AWW...
KyAAAAAAAAAAAAAA
I WEAR NOTHING.
NEXT QUESTION, FROM BEA...
DO YOU READ YOUR FAN LETTERS?
YES! OUR TEAM BRINGS US A BOX, AND WE READ THROUGH THEM WHEN WE HAVE TIME.
THEY REALLY MEAN SO MUCH TO US. THANK YOU, AND KEEP THEM COMING!

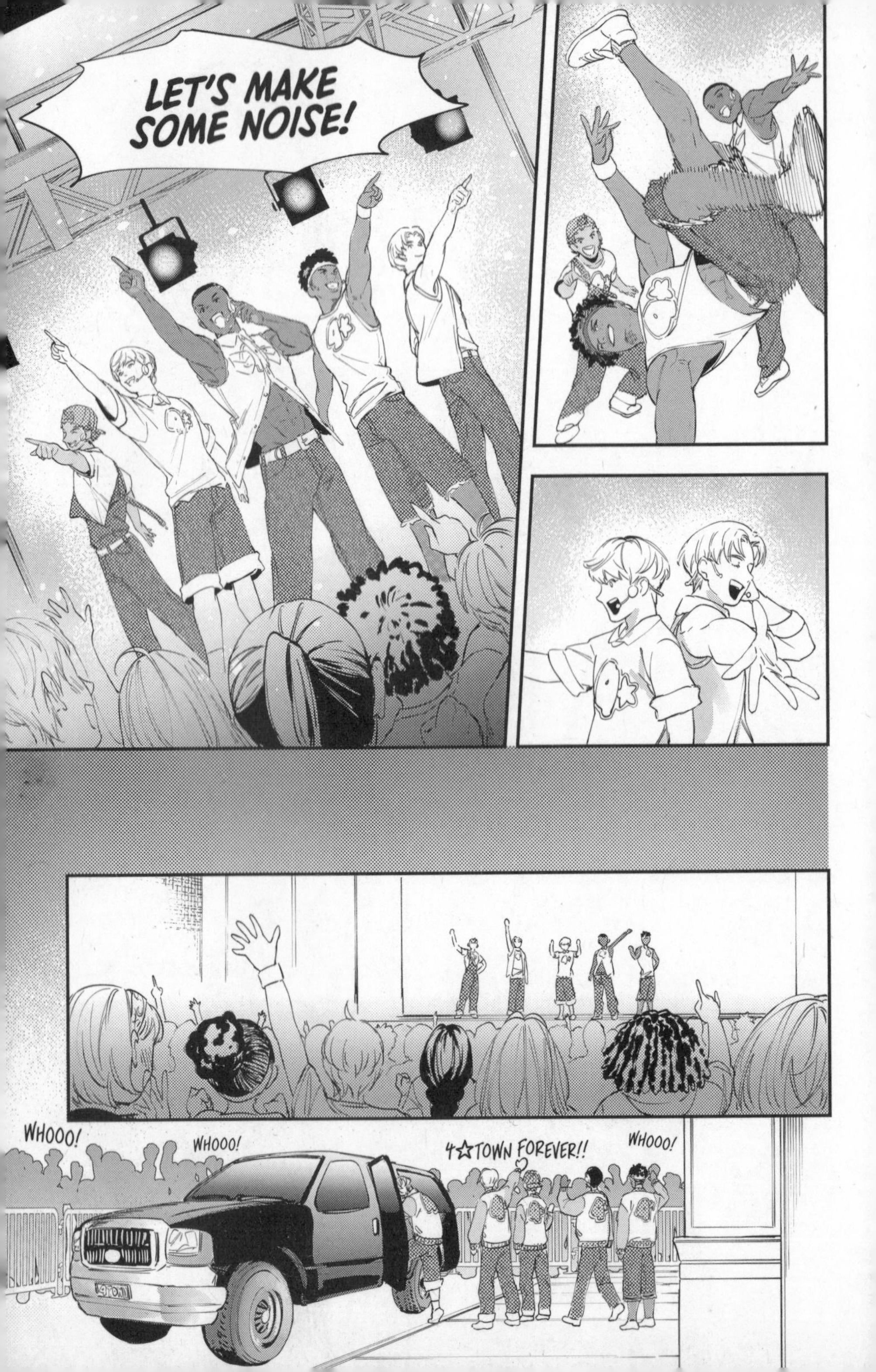
LET'S MAKE SOME NOISE!
WHOOO!
WHOOO!
4☆TOWN FOREVER!!
WHOOO!

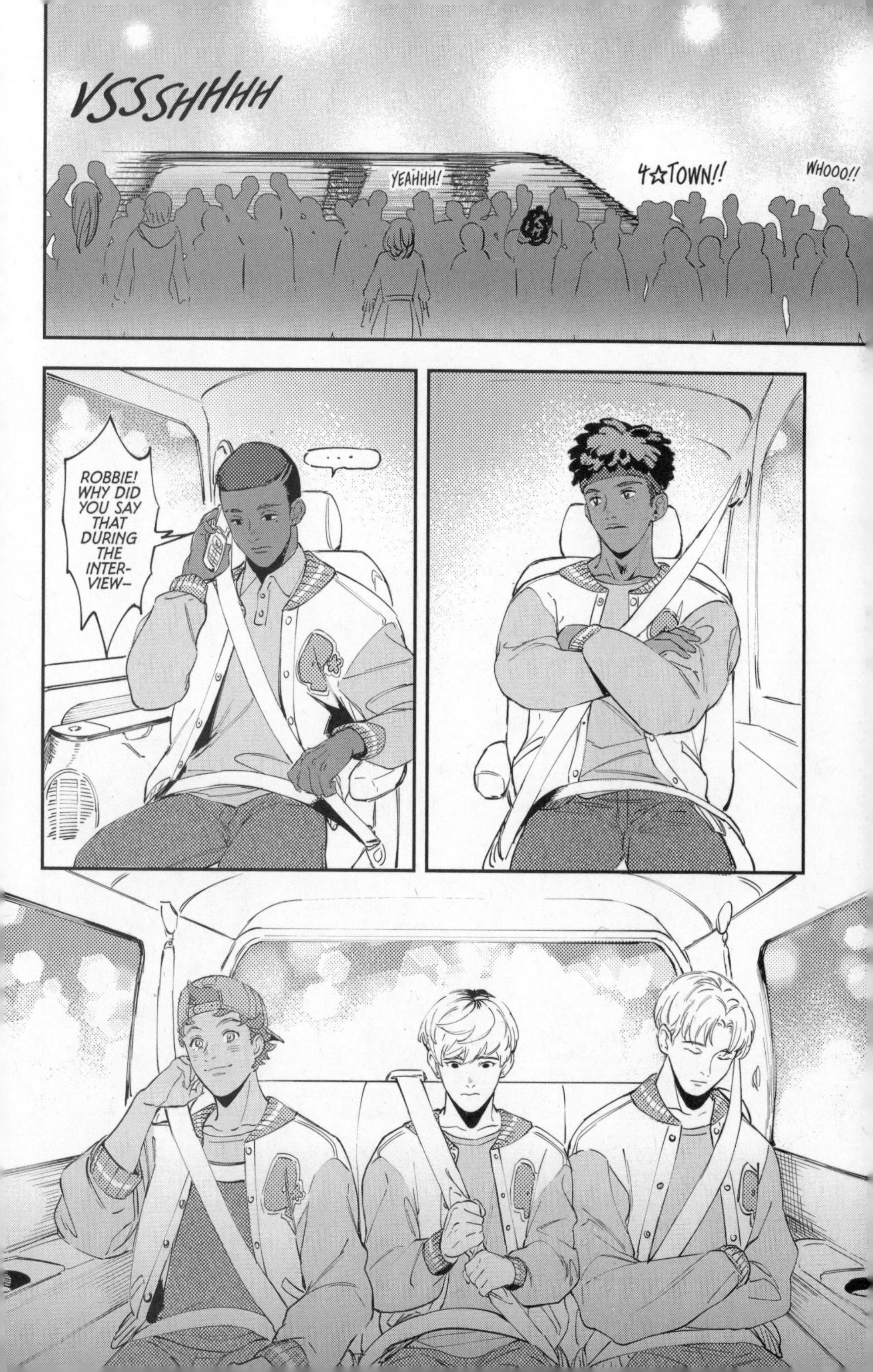
VSSSHHHH
YEAHHH!
4☆TOWN!!
WHOOO!!
ROBBIE! WHY DID YOU SAY THAT DURING THE INTER-VIEW—
...

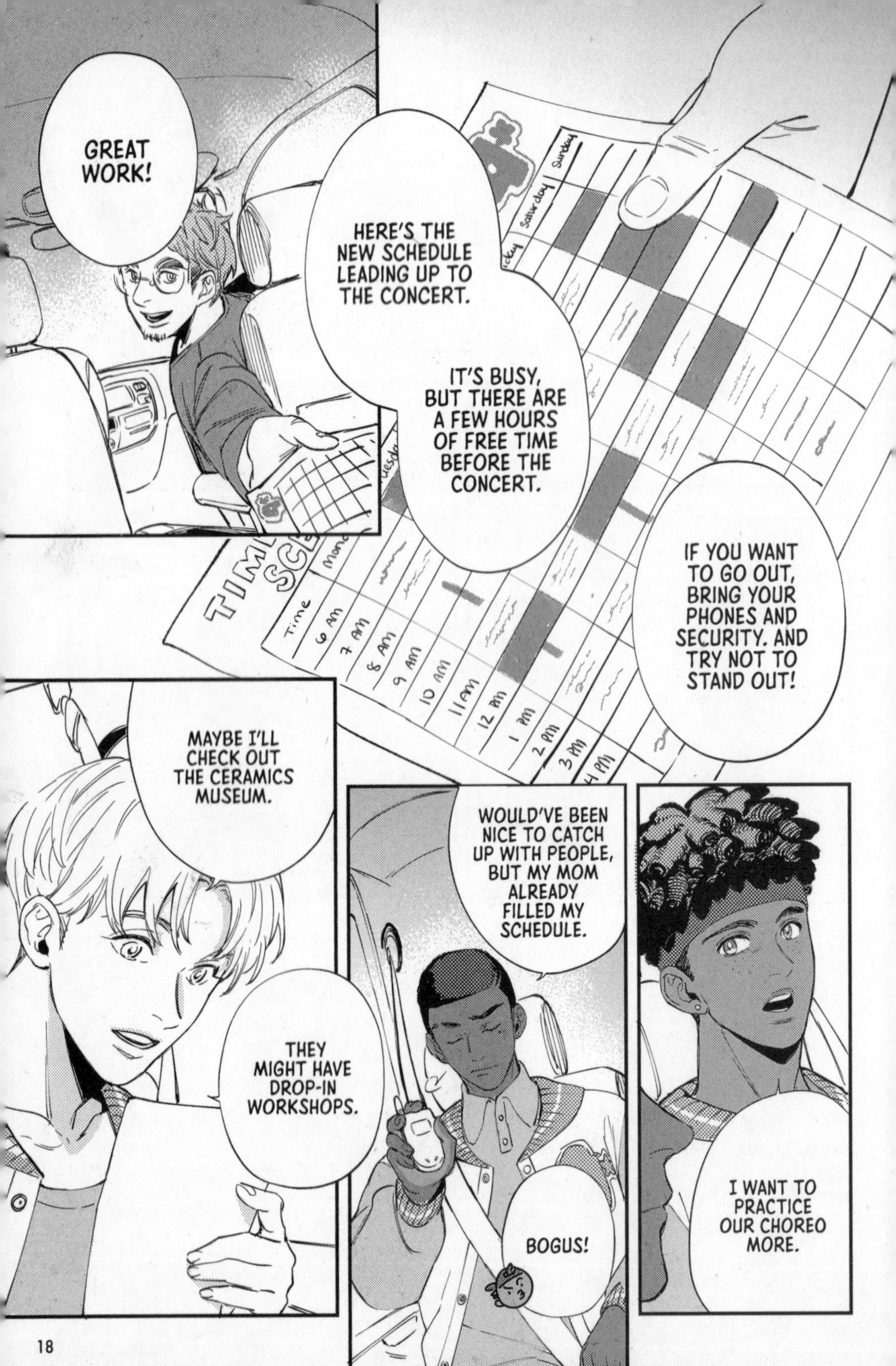
GREAT WORK!
HERE'S THE NEW SCHEDULE LEADING UP TO THE CONCERT.
IT'S BUSY, BUT THERE ARE A FEW HOURS OF FREE TIME BEFORE THE CONCERT.
IF YOU WANT TO GO OUT, BRING YOUR PHONES AND SECURITY. AND TRY NOT TO STAND OUT!
MAYBE I'LL CHECK OUT THE CERAMICS MUSEUM.
THEY MIGHT HAVE DROP-IN WORKSHOPS.
WOULD'VE BEEN NICE TO CATCH UP WITH PEOPLE, BUT MY MOM ALREADY FILLED MY SCHEDULE.
BOGUS!
I WANT TO PRACTICE OUR CHOREO MORE.

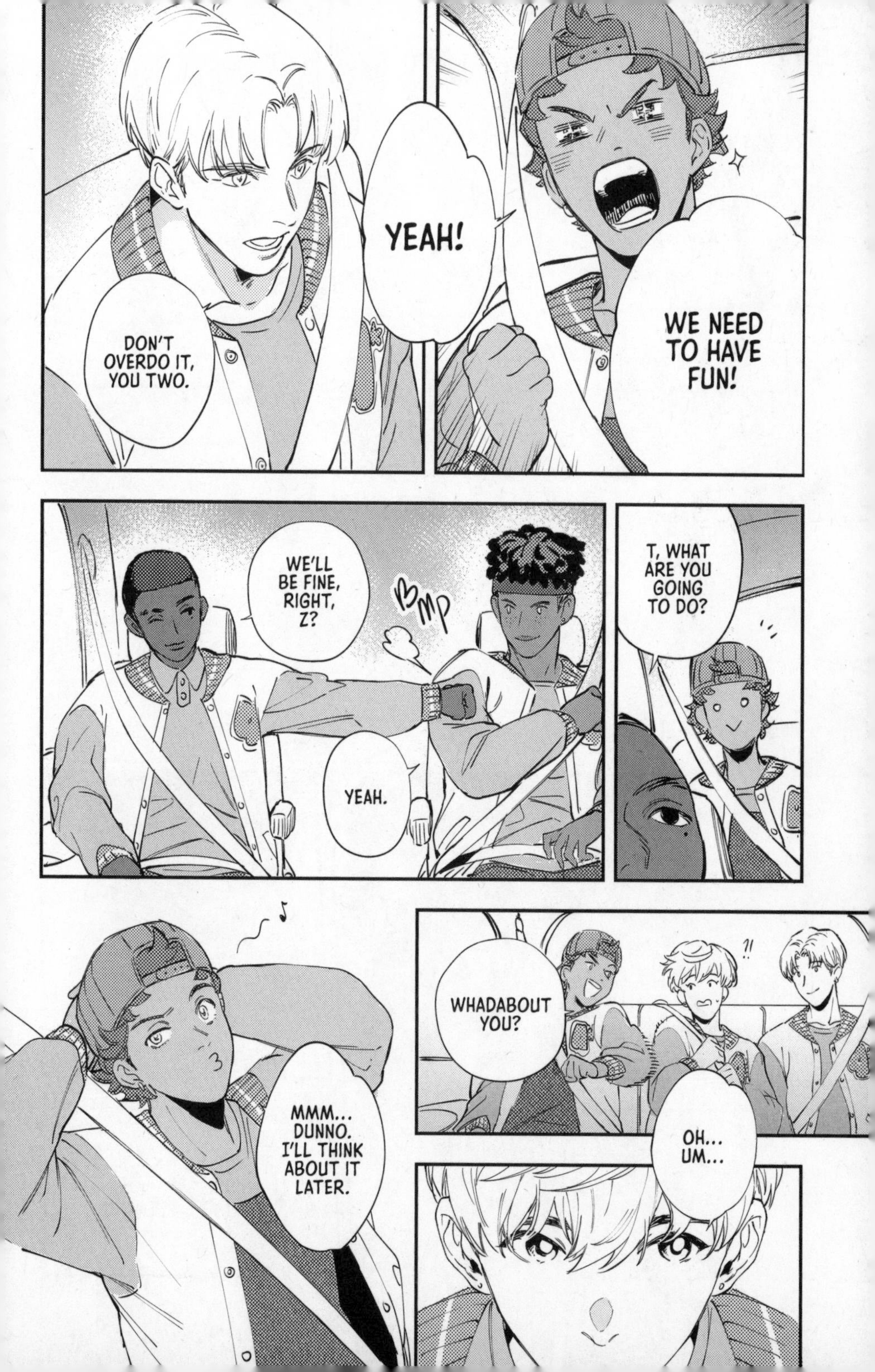
DON'T OVERDO IT, YOU TWO.
YEAH!
WE NEED TO HAVE FUN!
WE'LL BE FINE, RIGHT, Z?
BMP
YEAH.
T, WHAT ARE YOU GOING TO DO?
MMM... DUNNO. I'LL THINK ABOUT IT LATER.
WHADABOUT YOU?
OH... UM...

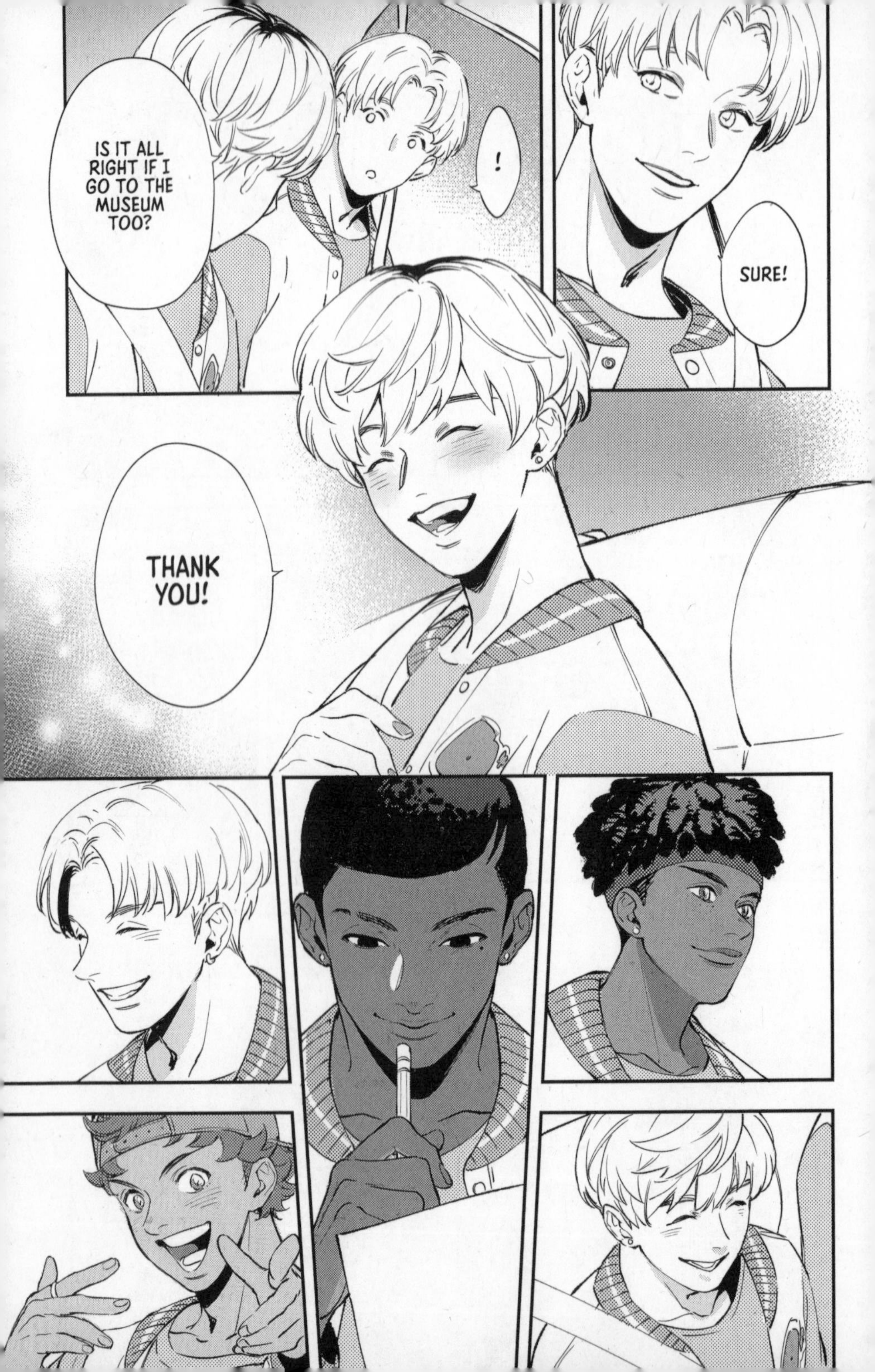
IS IT ALL RIGHT IF I GO TO THE MUSEUM TOO?
!
SURE!
THANK YOU!

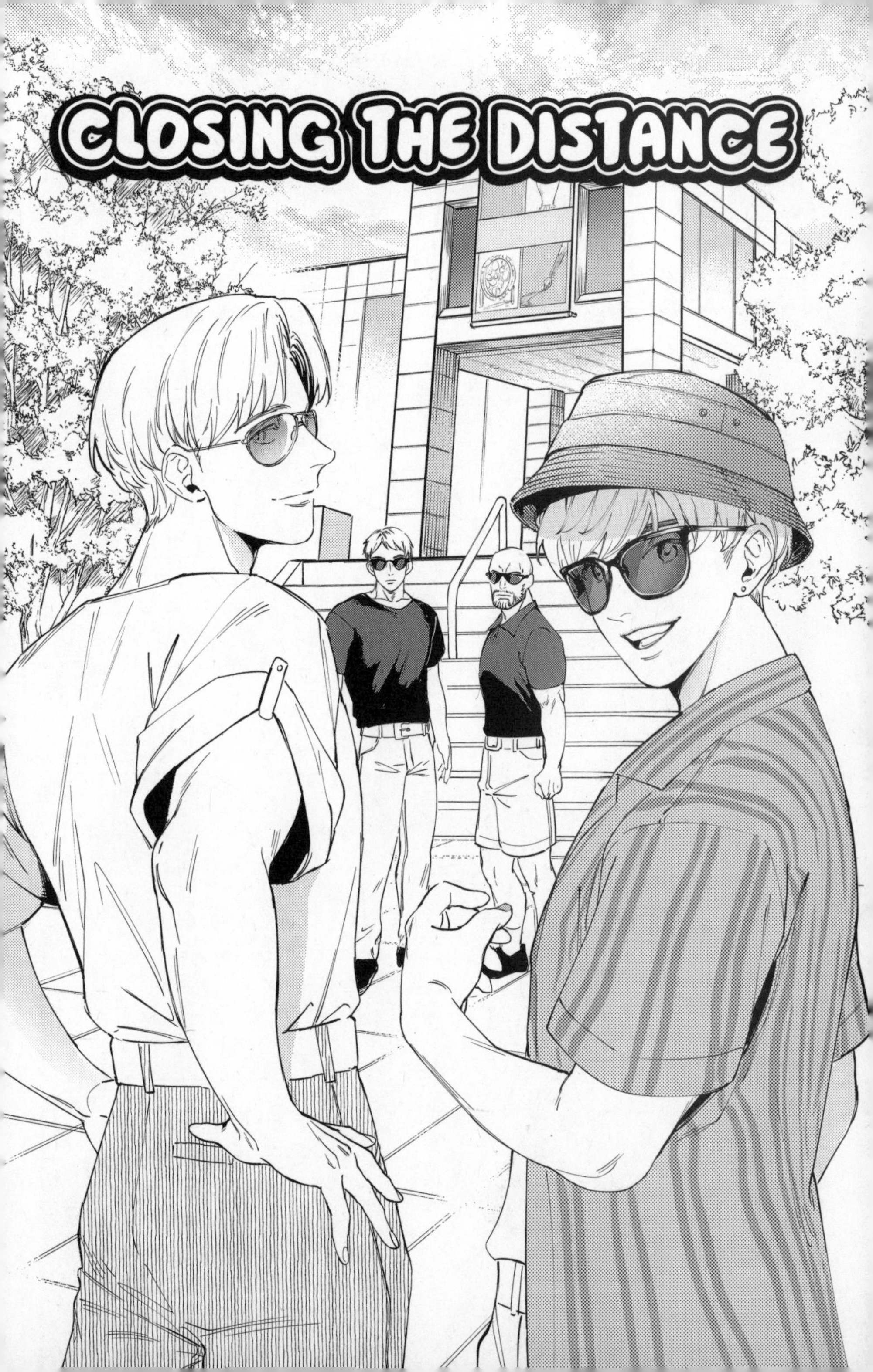
CLOSING THE DISTANCE

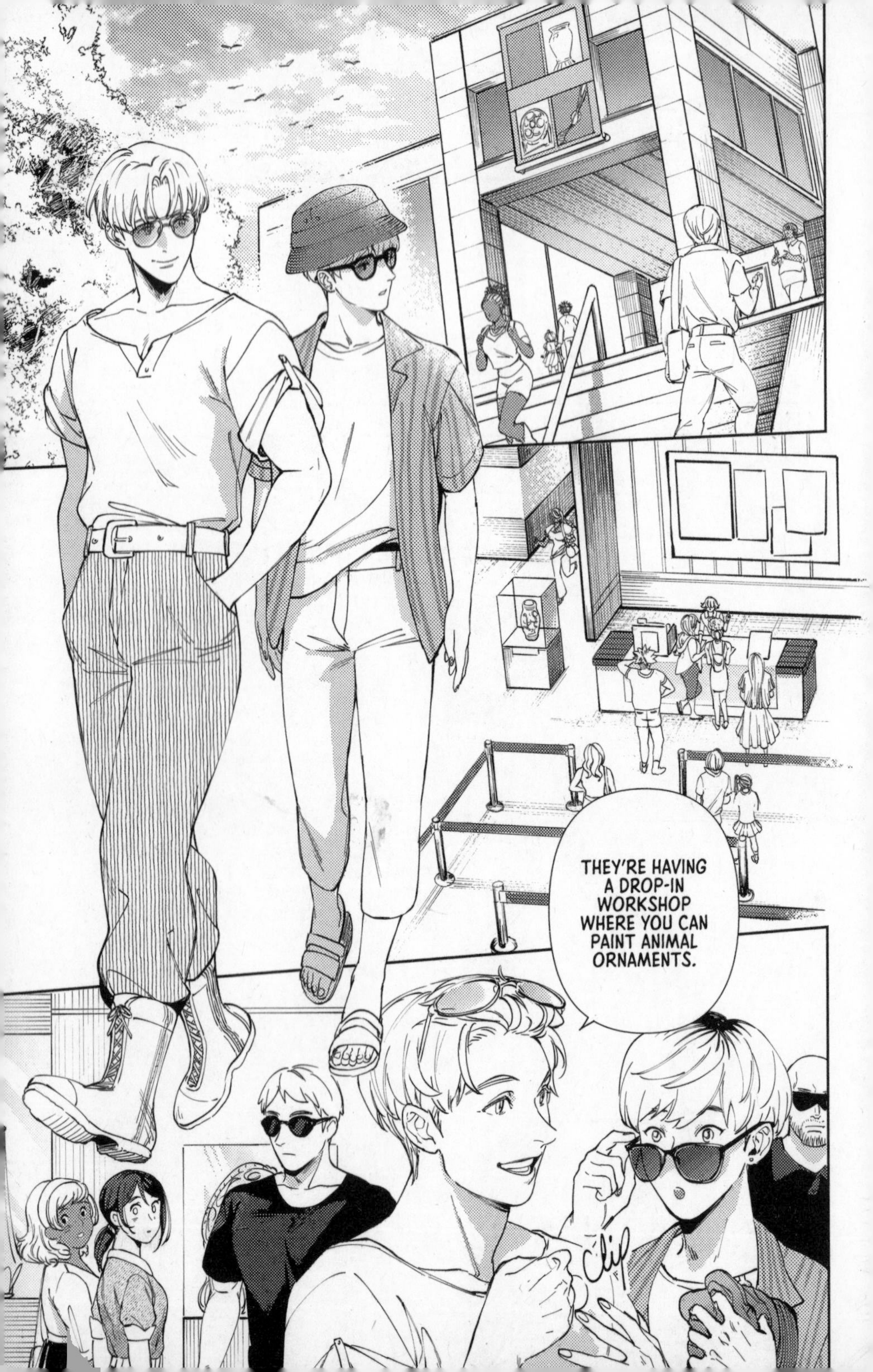
THEY'RE HAVING A DROP-IN WORKSHOP WHERE YOU CAN PAINT ANIMAL ORNAMENTS.

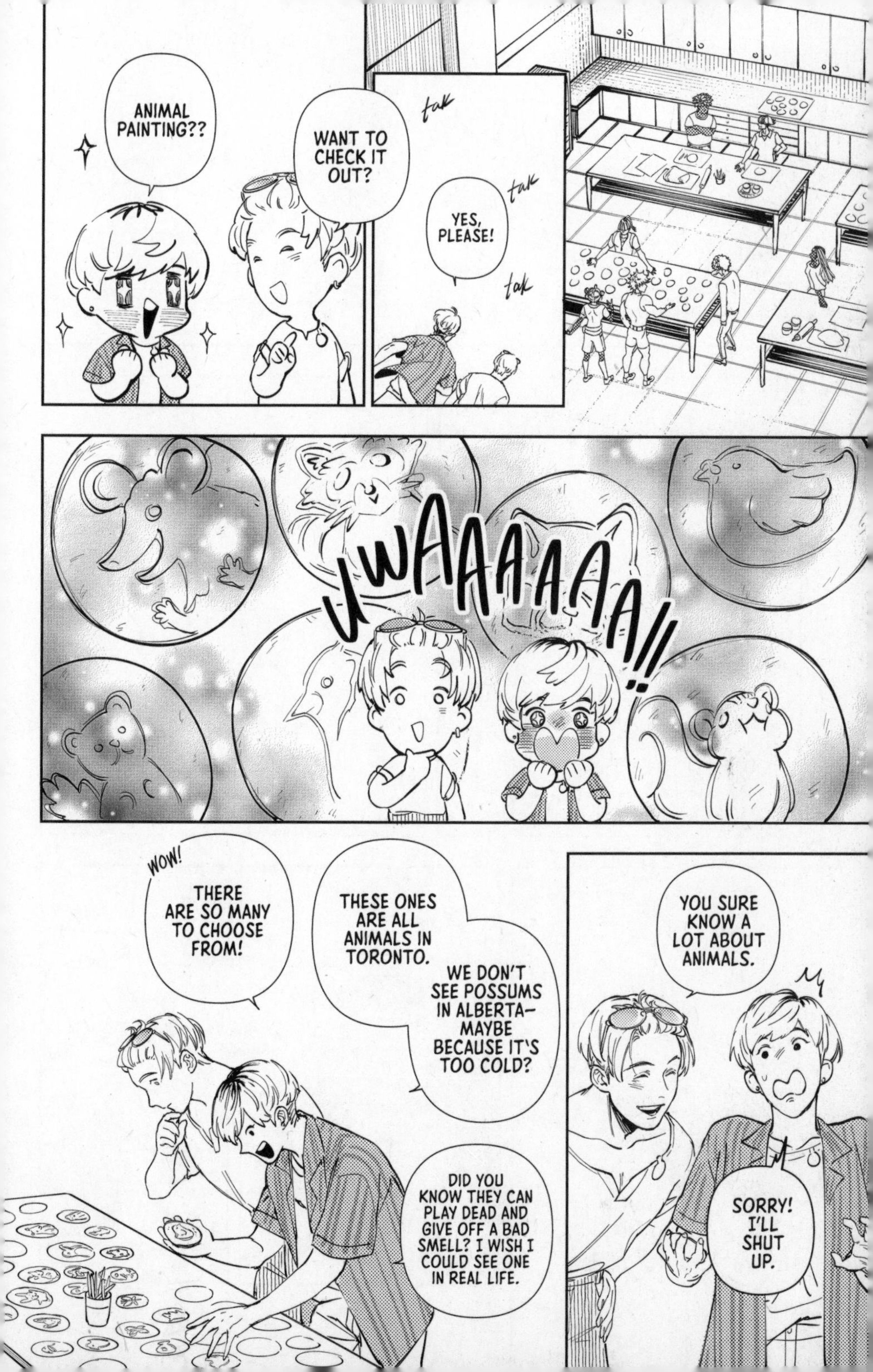
ANIMAL PAINTING??
WANT TO CHECK IT OUT?
tak
YES, PLEASE!
tak
tak
UWAAAAAAA!!
WOW!
THERE ARE SO MANY TO CHOOSE FROM!
THESE ONES ARE ALL ANIMALS IN TORONTO.
WE DON'T SEE POSSUMS IN ALBERTA—MAYBE BECAUSE IT'S TOO COLD?
DID YOU KNOW THEY CAN PLAY DEAD AND GIVE OFF A BAD SMELL? I WISH I COULD SEE ONE IN REAL LIFE.
YOU SURE KNOW A LOT ABOUT ANIMALS.
SORRY! I'LL SHUT UP.

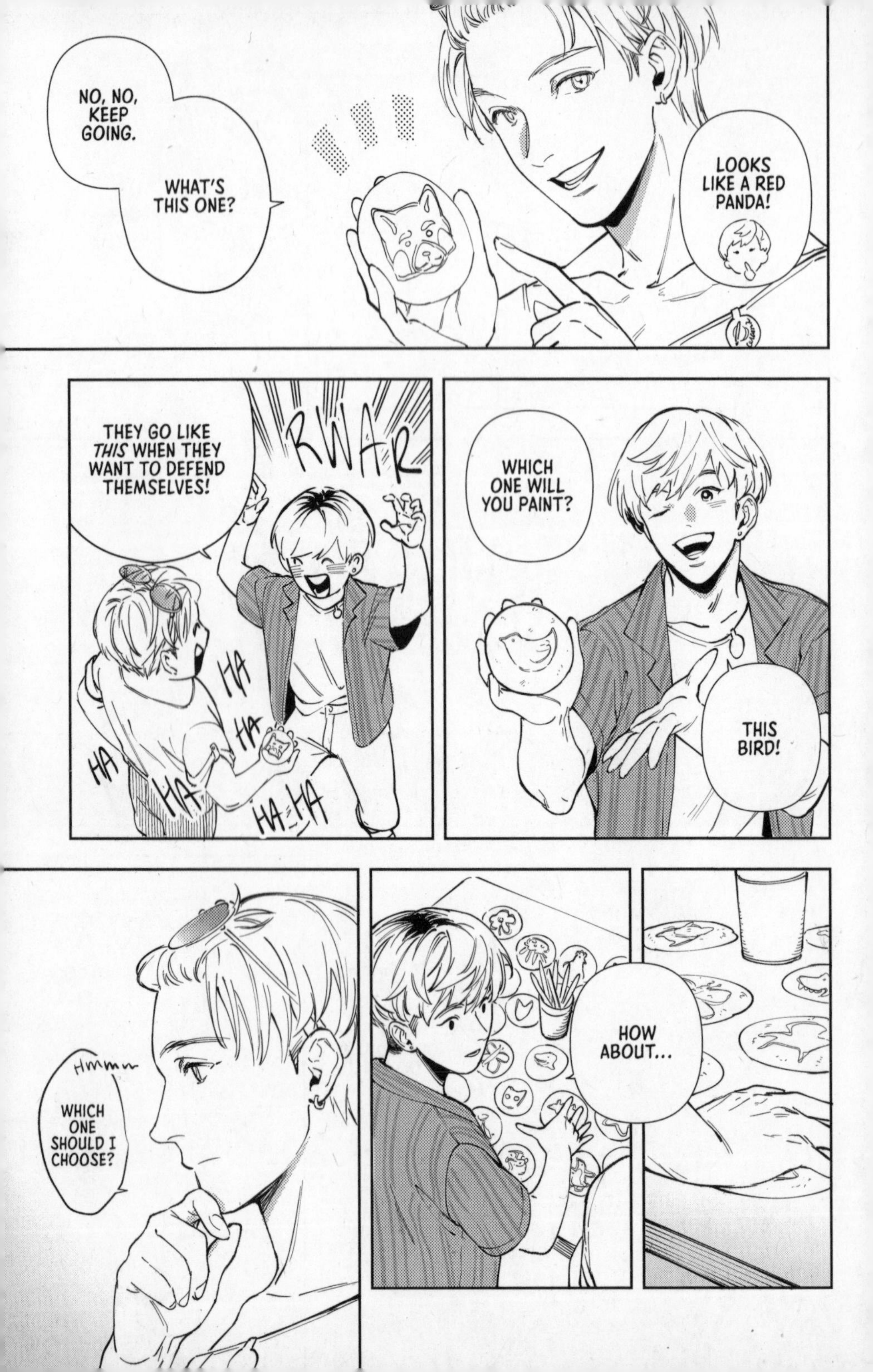
NO, NO, KEEP GOING.
WHAT'S THIS ONE?
LOOKS LIKE A RED PANDA!
THEY GO LIKE *THIS* WHEN THEY WANT TO DEFEND THEMSELVES!
RWAR
HA HA HA HA HA HA
WHICH ONE WILL YOU PAINT?
THIS BIRD!
Hmmm
WHICH ONE SHOULD I CHOOSE?
HOW ABOUT...

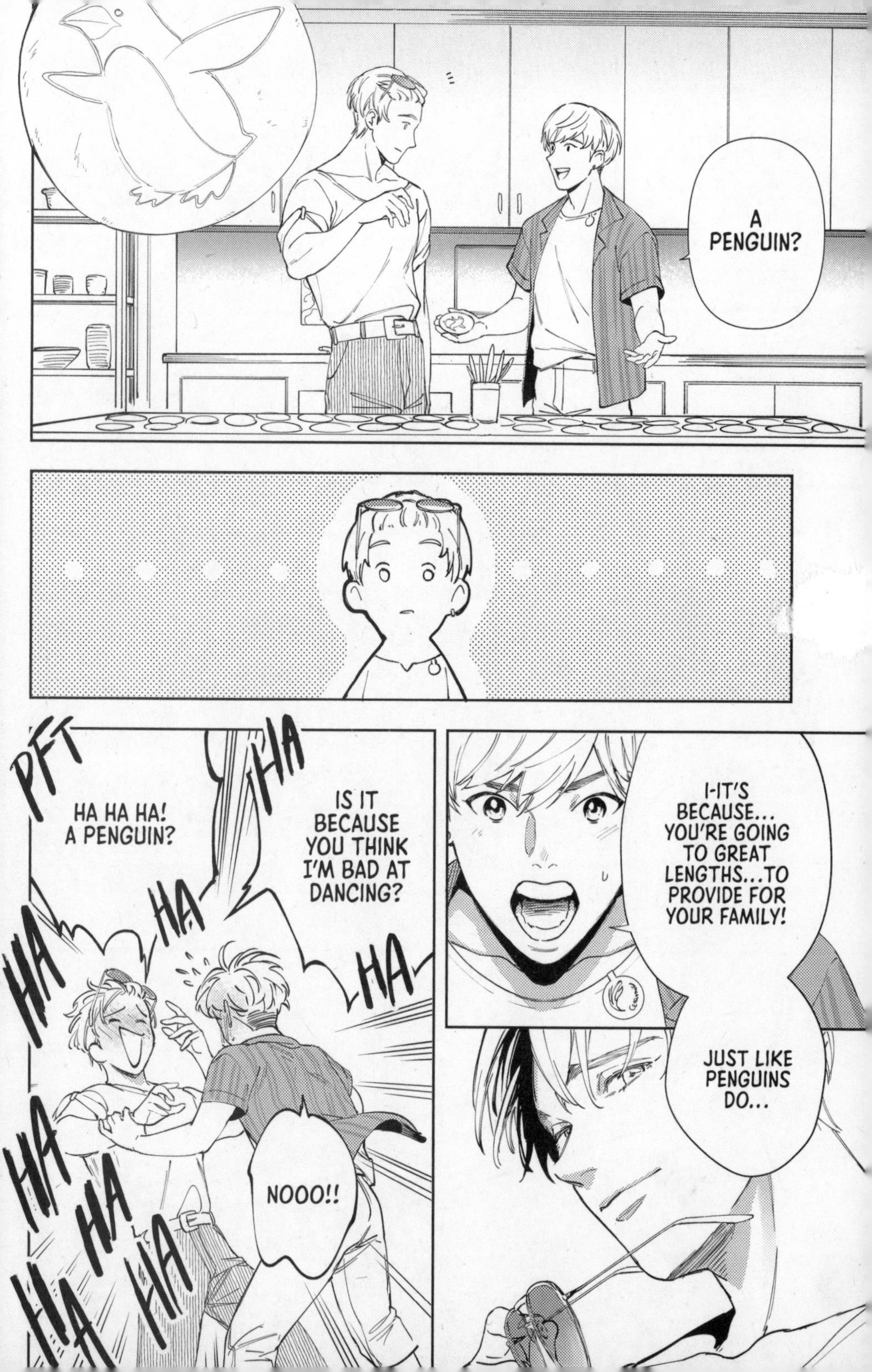
A PENGUIN?
. . . .
PFT
HA HA HA! A PENGUIN?
HA
IS IT BECAUSE YOU THINK I'M BAD AT DANCING?
HA
HA
HA
HA HA HA HA HA HA
NOOO!!
I-IT'S BECAUSE... YOU'RE GOING TO GREAT LENGTHS...TO PROVIDE FOR YOUR FAMILY!
JUST LIKE PENGUINS DO...

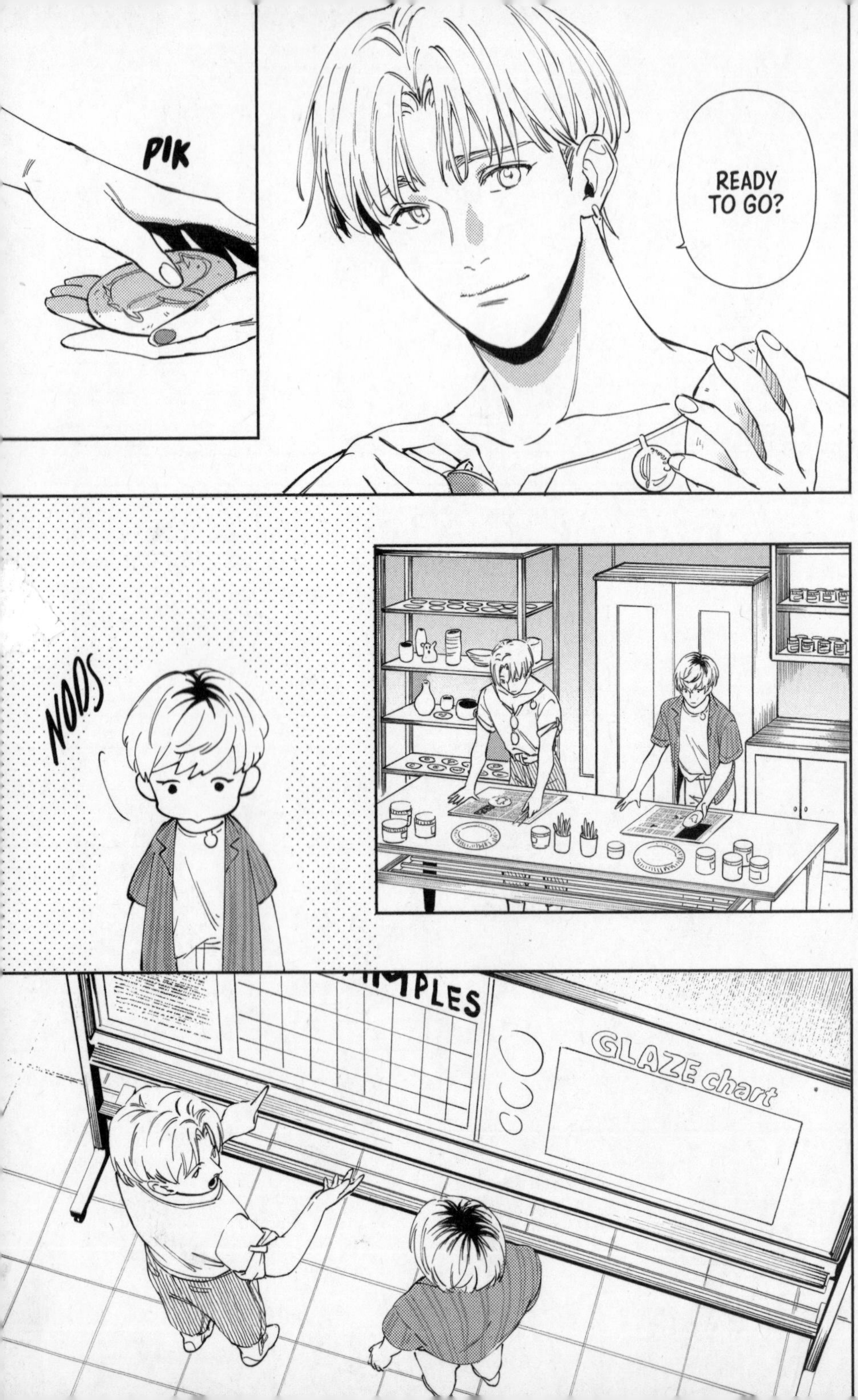
PIK
READY TO GO?
NODS
GLAZE chart

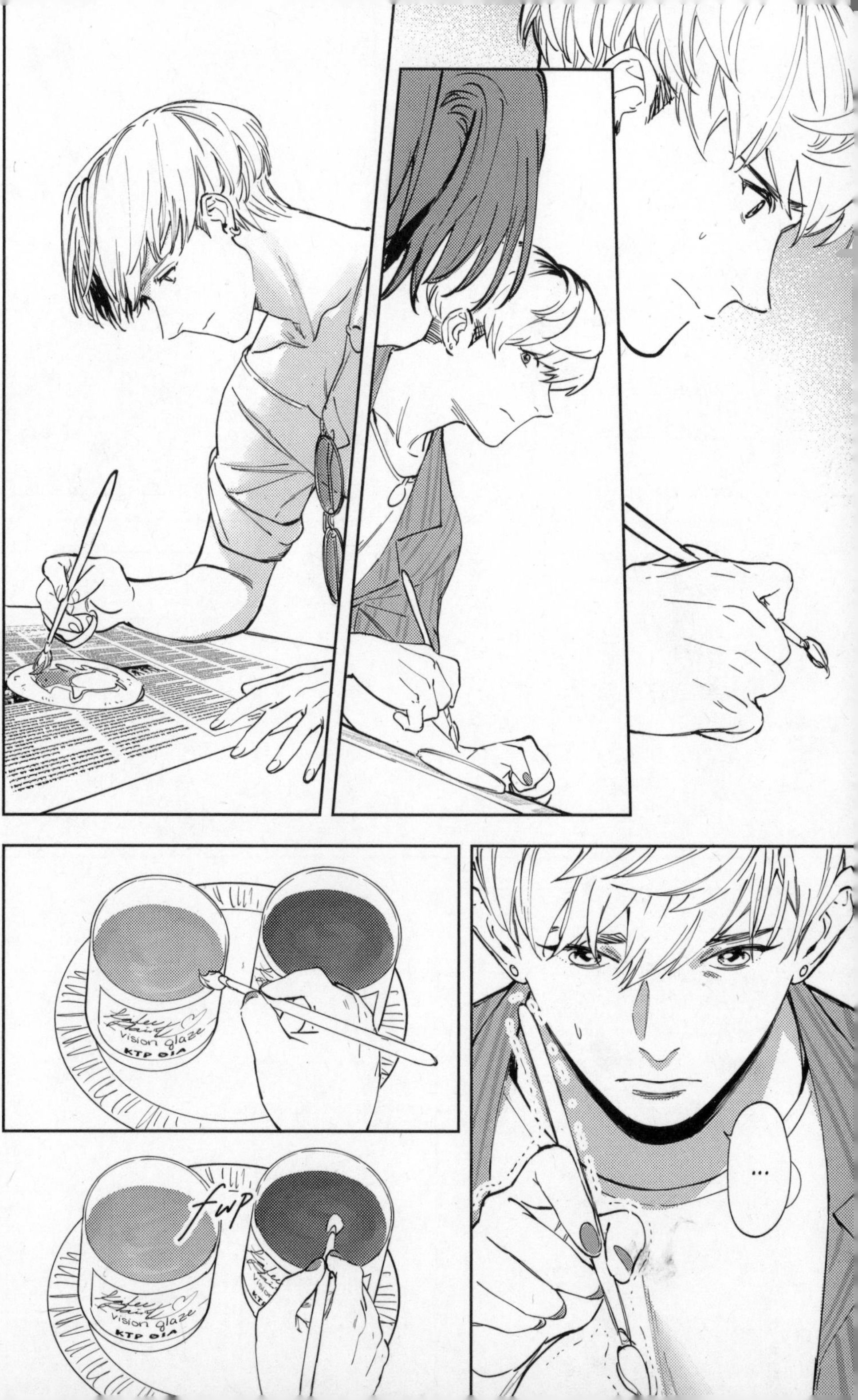
vision glaze
KTP ΘIA
fwp
vision glaze
KTP ΘIA
...

HOW'S IT GOING, BUD?

NO NEED TO BE SHY!

!!

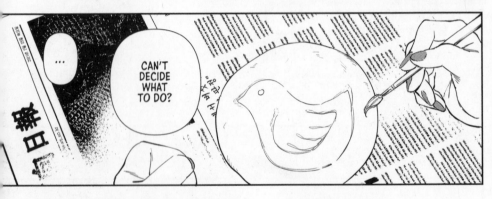

...

CAN'T DECIDE WHAT TO DO?

YOU COULD PAINT MORE REALISTICALLY...

...OR GO WITH SOMETHING MORE ABSTRACT.

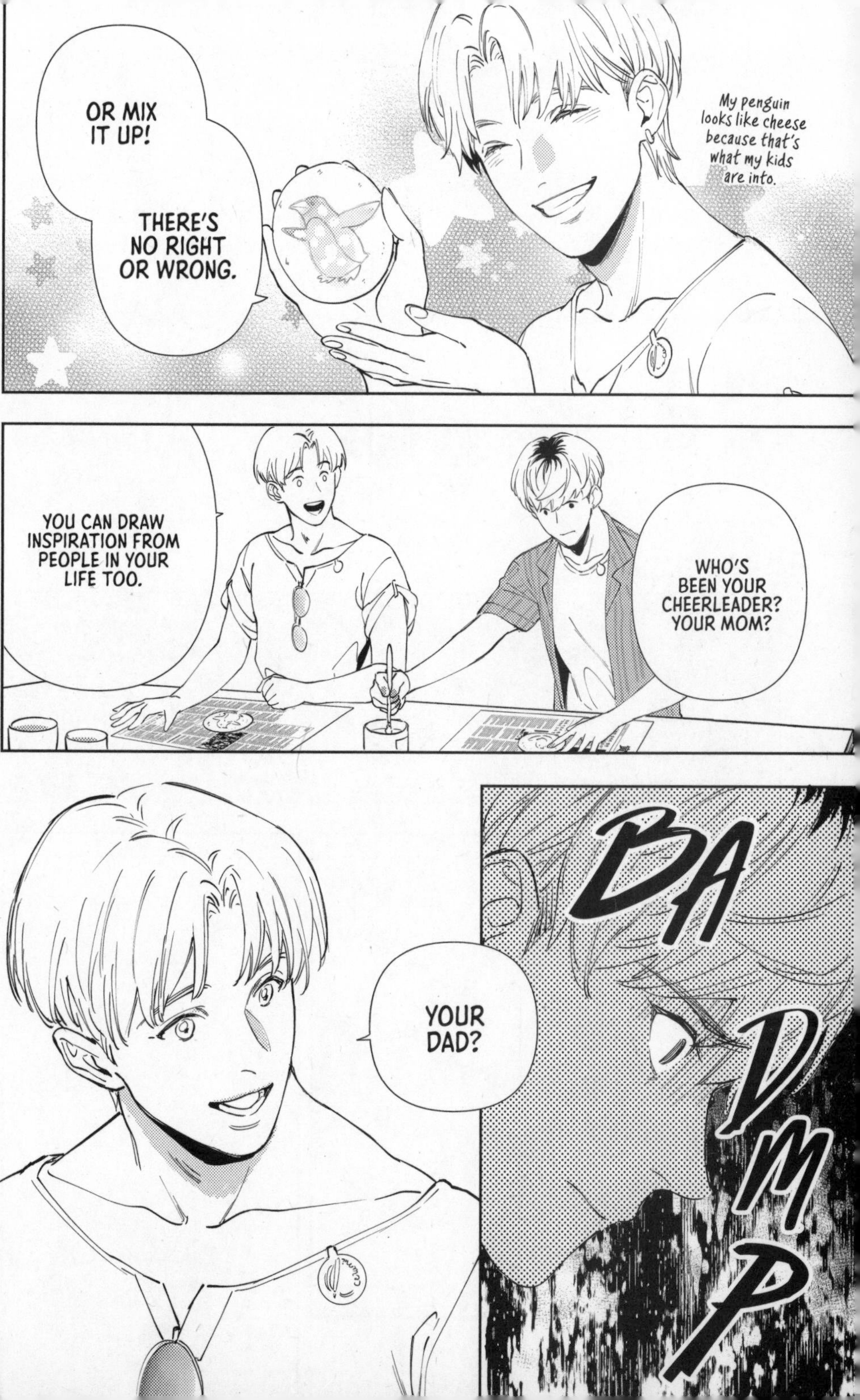
OR MIX IT UP!
THERE'S NO RIGHT OR WRONG.
My penguin looks like cheese because that's what my kids are into.
YOU CAN DRAW INSPIRATION FROM PEOPLE IN YOUR LIFE TOO.
WHO'S BEEN YOUR CHEERLEADER? YOUR MOM?
YOUR DAD?
BA DMP

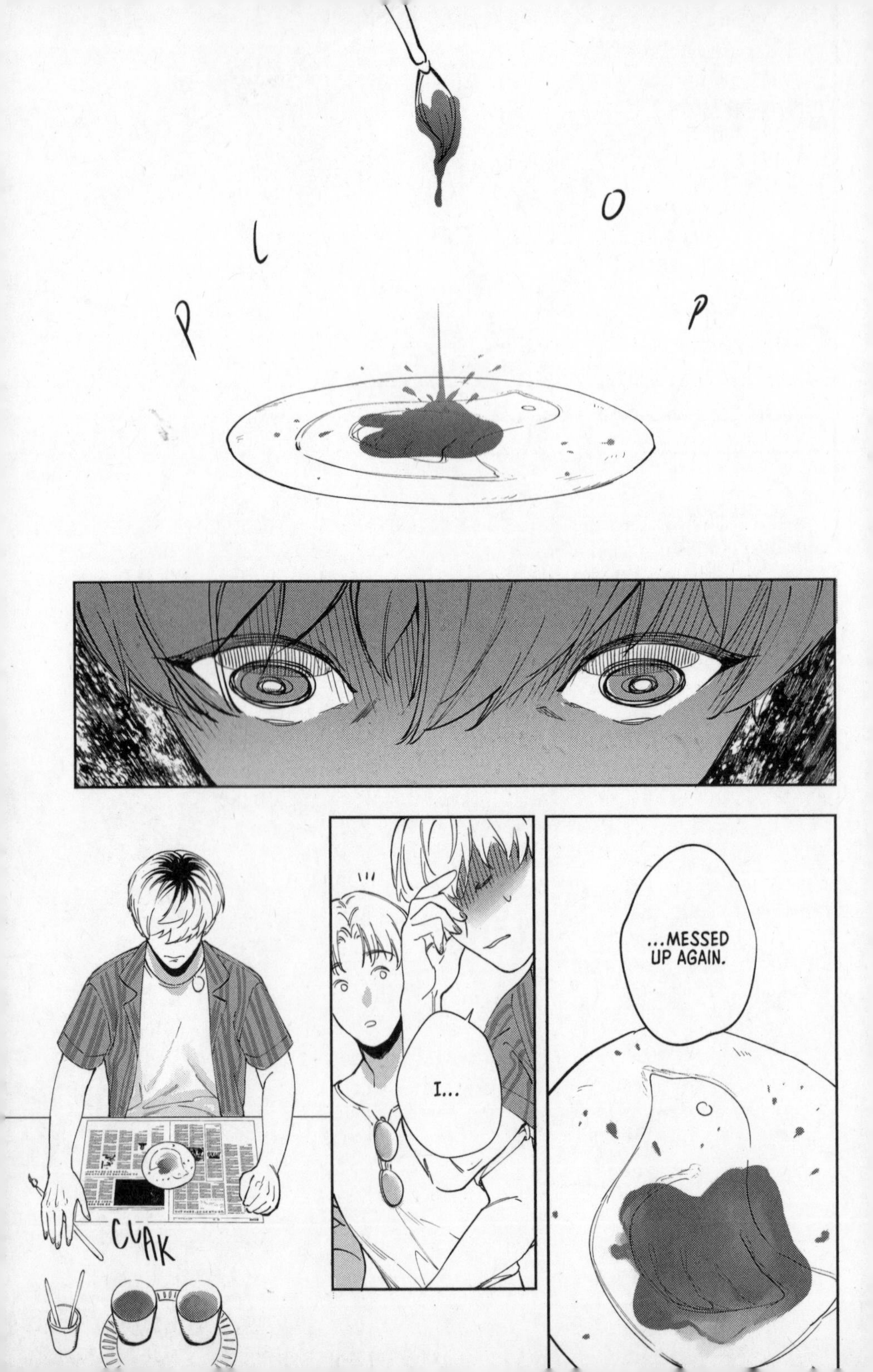
PLOP
CLAK
I...
...MESSED UP AGAIN.

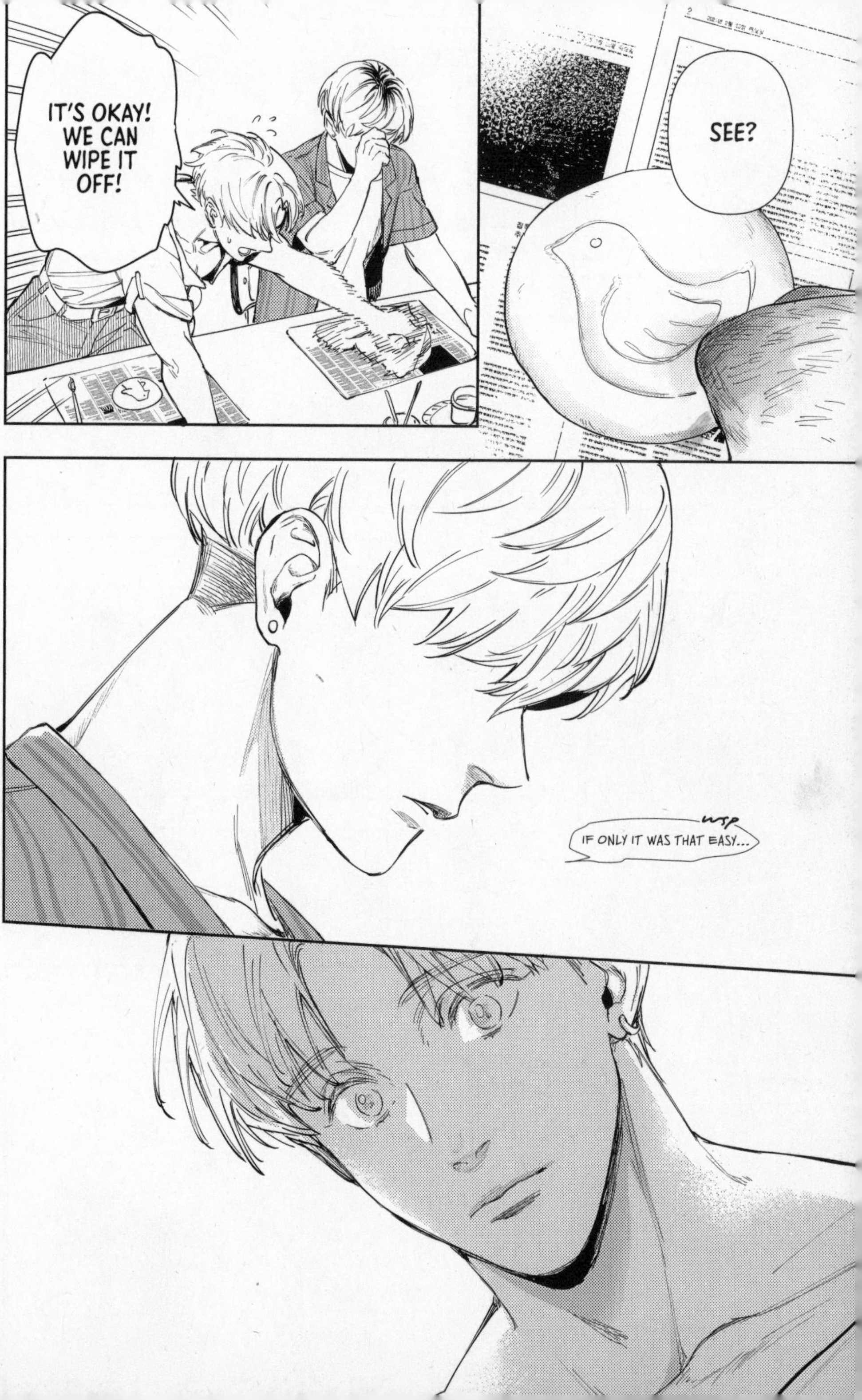
IT'S OKAY! WE CAN WIPE IT OFF!
SEE?
IF ONLY IT WAS THAT EASY...

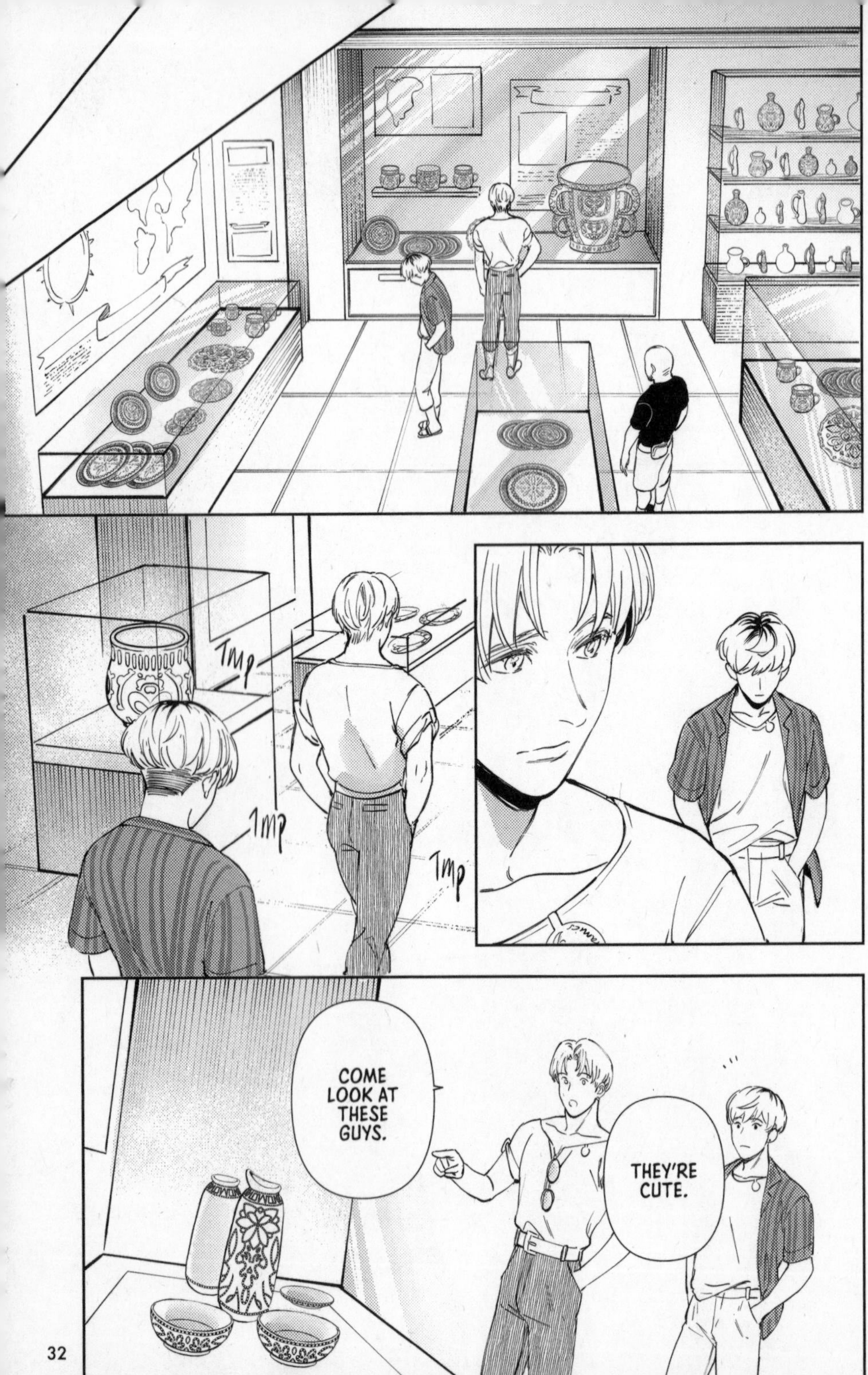
Tmp
Tmp
Tmp
COME LOOK AT THESE GUYS.
THEY'RE CUTE.

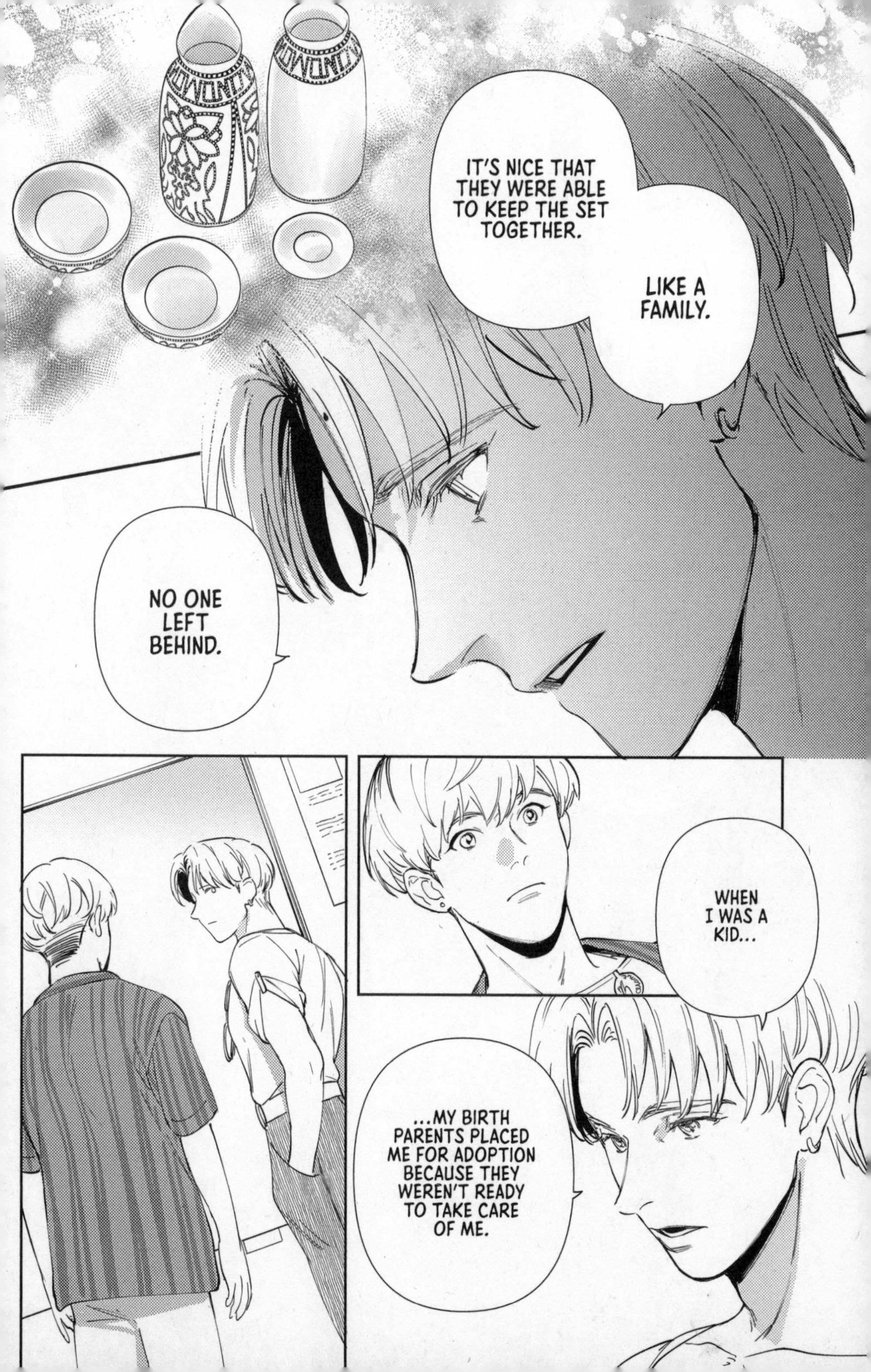
IT'S NICE THAT THEY WERE ABLE TO KEEP THE SET TOGETHER.
LIKE A FAMILY.
NO ONE LEFT BEHIND.
WHEN I WAS A KID...
...MY BIRTH PARENTS PLACED ME FOR ADOPTION BECAUSE THEY WEREN'T READY TO TAKE CARE OF ME.

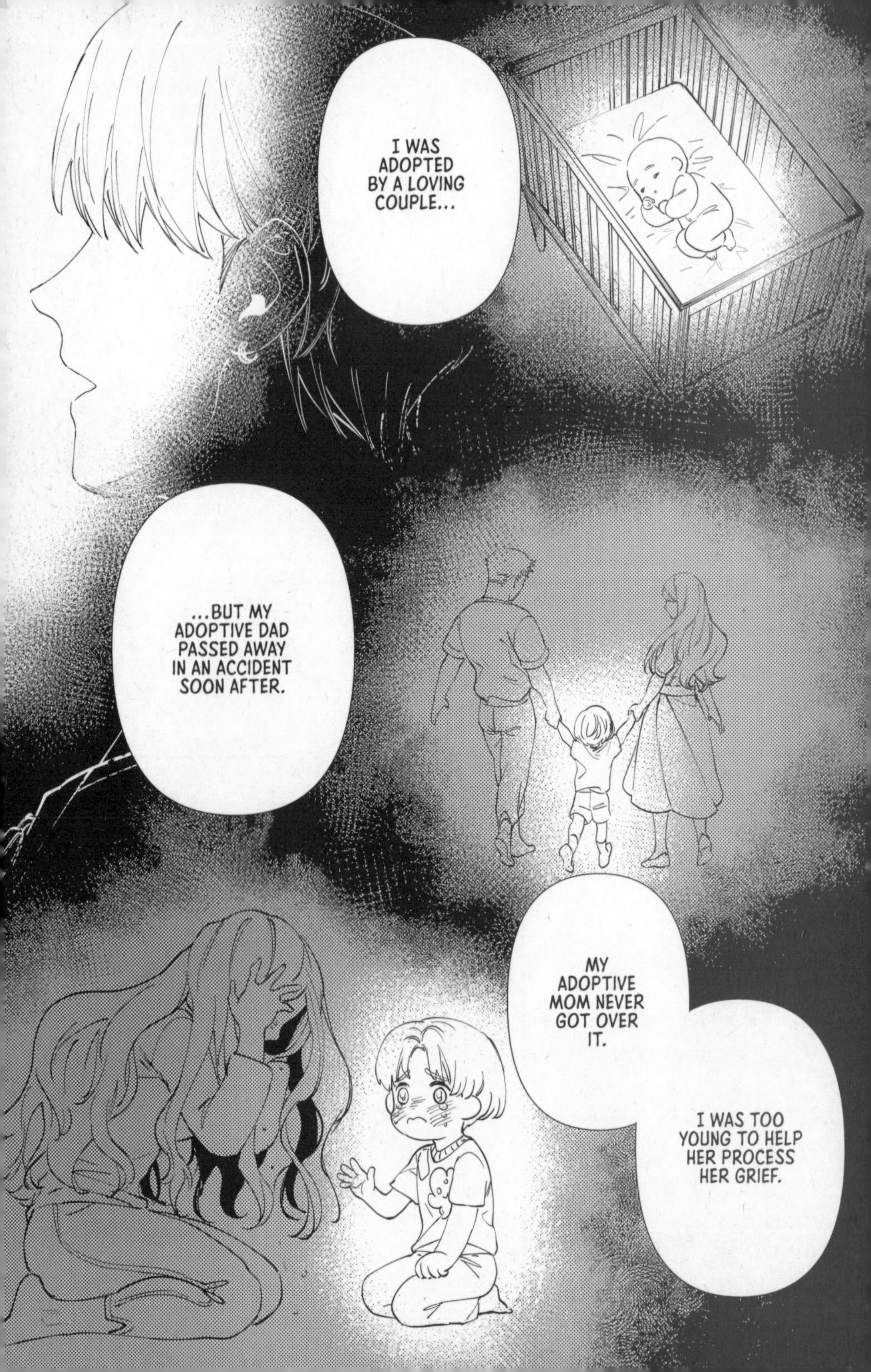
I WAS ADOPTED BY A LOVING COUPLE...
...BUT MY ADOPTIVE DAD PASSED AWAY IN AN ACCIDENT SOON AFTER.
MY ADOPTIVE MOM NEVER GOT OVER IT.
I WAS TOO YOUNG TO HELP HER PROCESS HER GRIEF.

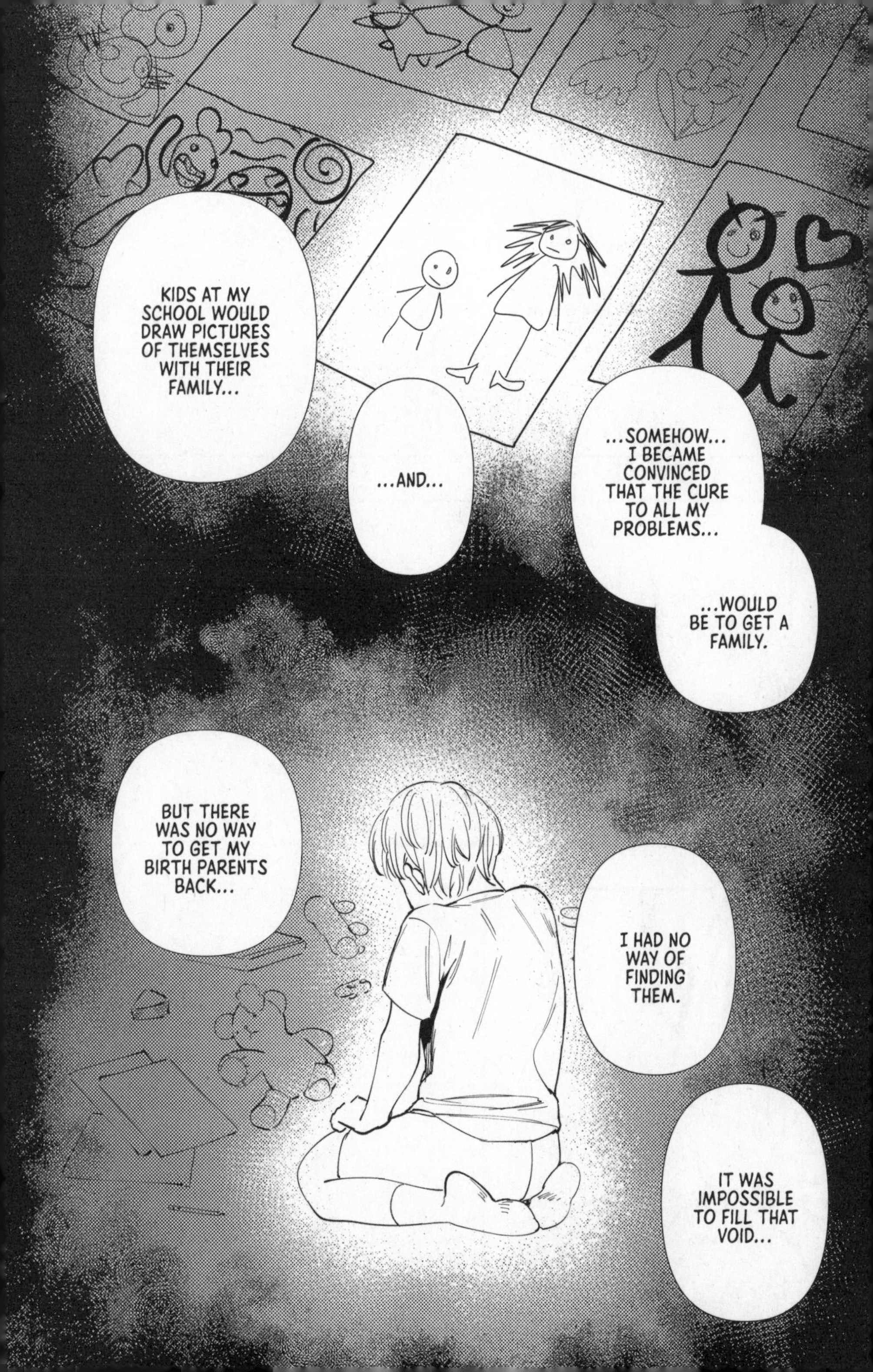

KIDS AT MY SCHOOL WOULD DRAW PICTURES OF THEMSELVES WITH THEIR FAMILY...
...AND...
...SOMEHOW... I BECAME CONVINCED THAT THE CURE TO ALL MY PROBLEMS...
...WOULD BE TO GET A FAMILY.
BUT THERE WAS NO WAY TO GET MY BIRTH PARENTS BACK...
I HAD NO WAY OF FINDING THEM.
IT WAS IMPOSSIBLE TO FILL THAT VOID...

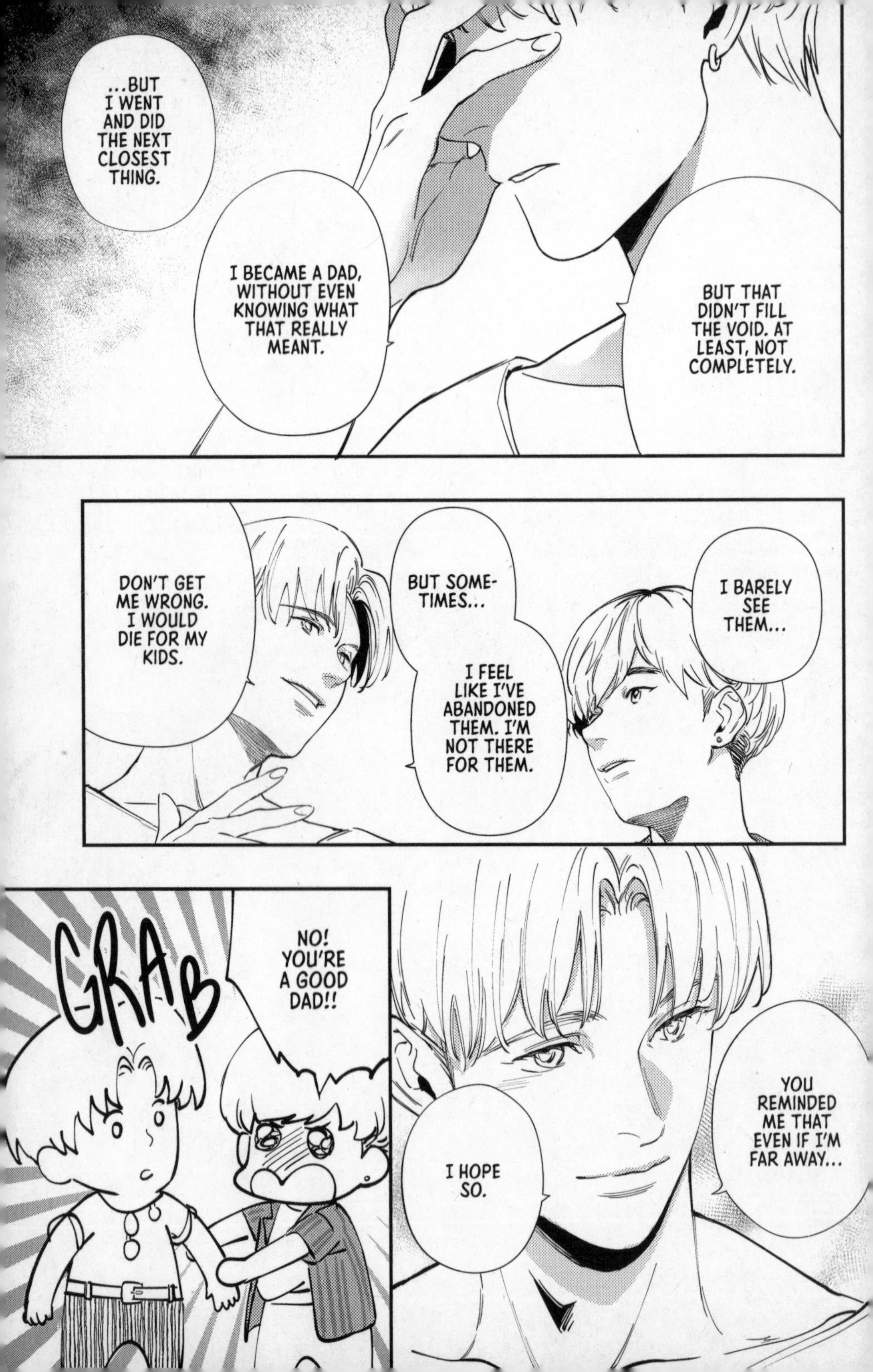
...BUT I WENT AND DID THE NEXT CLOSEST THING.
I BECAME A DAD, WITHOUT EVEN KNOWING WHAT THAT REALLY MEANT.
BUT THAT DIDN'T FILL THE VOID. AT LEAST, NOT COMPLETELY.
DON'T GET ME WRONG. I WOULD DIE FOR MY KIDS.
BUT SOME-TIMES...
I FEEL LIKE I'VE ABANDONED THEM. I'M NOT THERE FOR THEM.
I BARELY SEE THEM...
GRAB
NO! YOU'RE A GOOD DAD!!
I HOPE SO.
YOU REMINDED ME THAT EVEN IF I'M FAR AWAY...

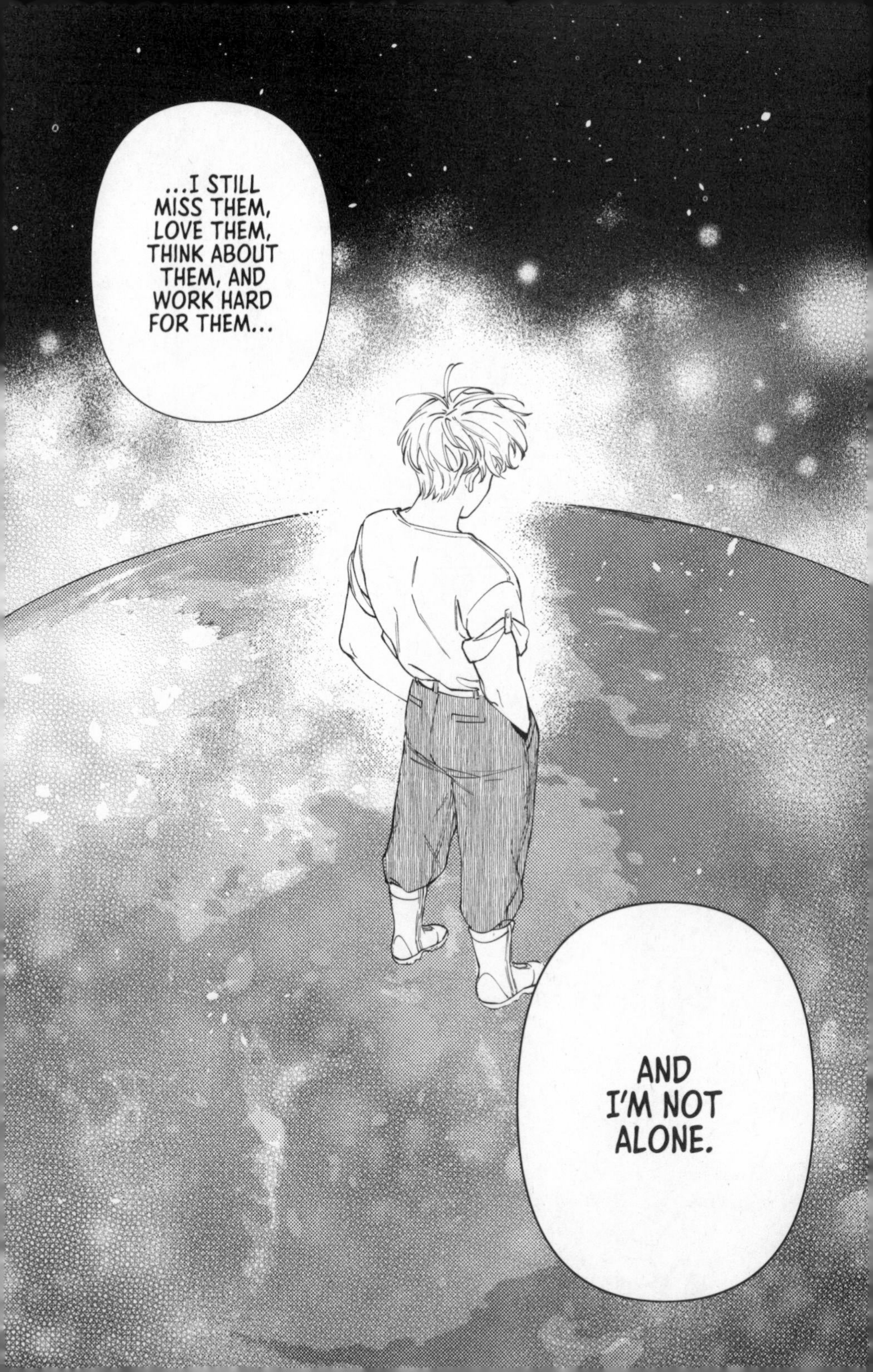
...I STILL MISS THEM, LOVE THEM, THINK ABOUT THEM, AND WORK HARD FOR THEM...
AND I'M NOT ALONE.

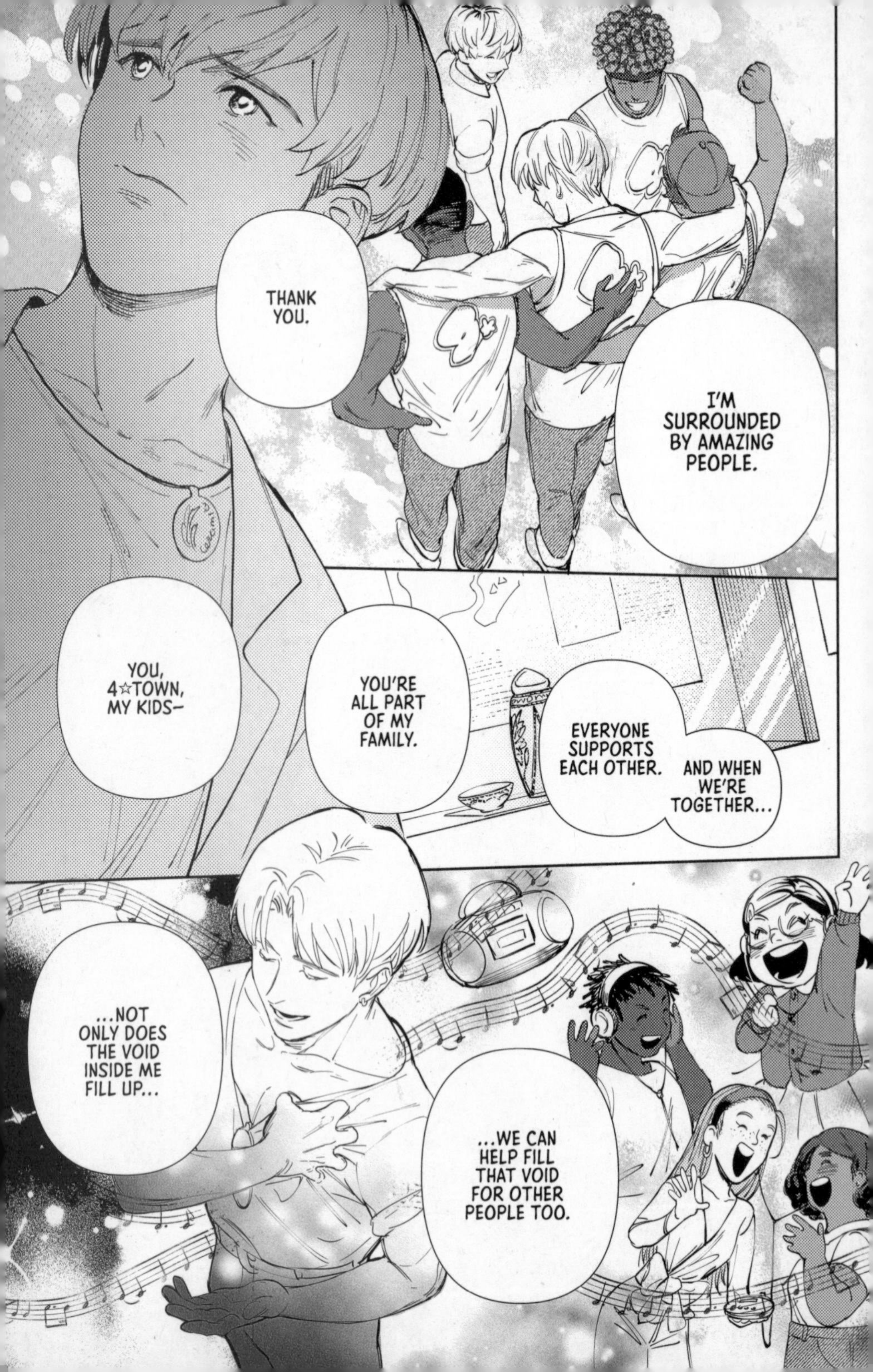

THANK YOU.
I'M SURROUNDED BY AMAZING PEOPLE.
YOU, 4☆TOWN, MY KIDS–
YOU'RE ALL PART OF MY FAMILY.
EVERYONE SUPPORTS EACH OTHER.
AND WHEN WE'RE TOGETHER...
...NOT ONLY DOES THE VOID INSIDE ME FILL UP...
...WE CAN HELP FILL THAT VOID FOR OTHER PEOPLE TOO.

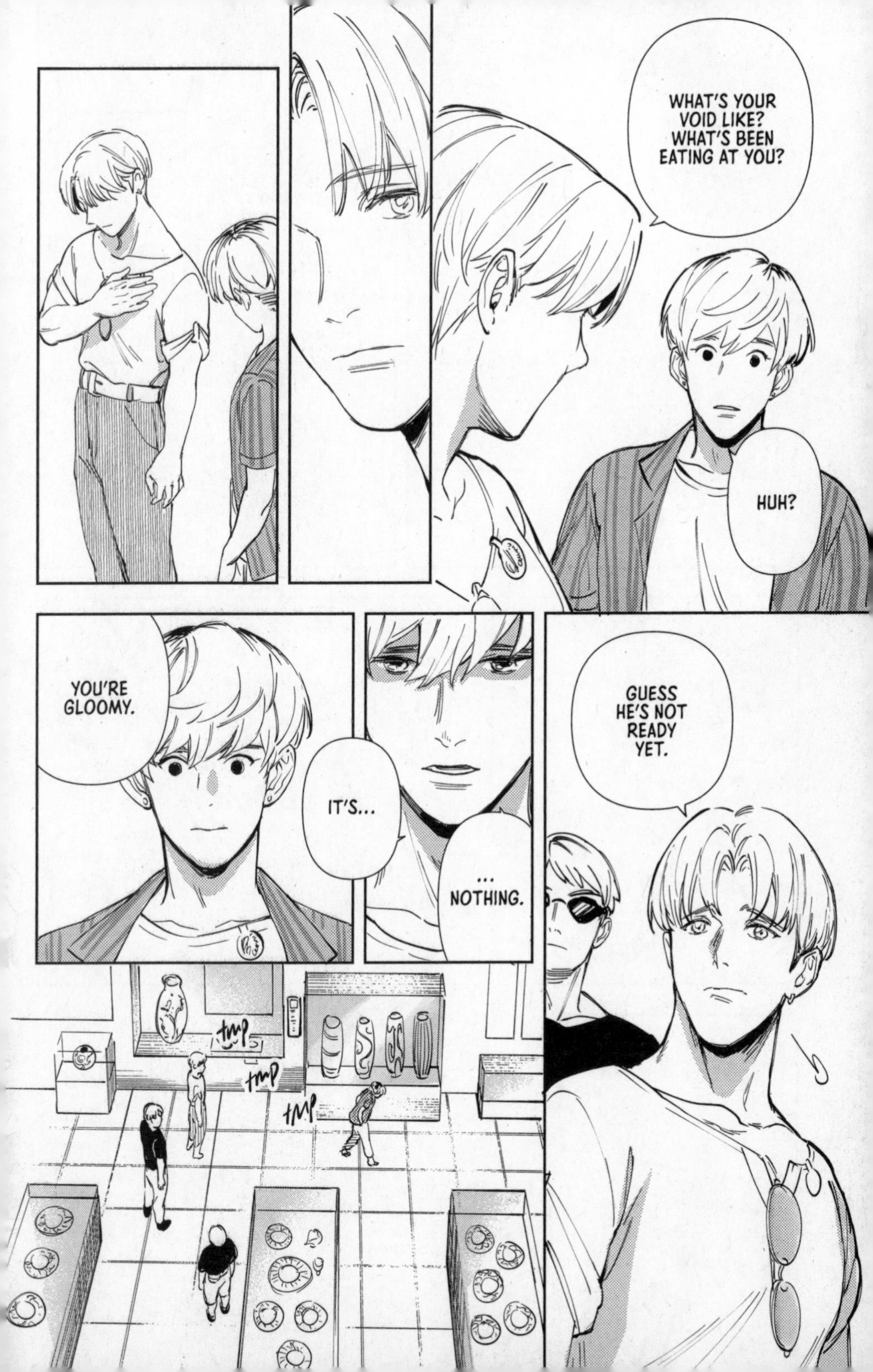
WHAT'S YOUR VOID LIKE? WHAT'S BEEN EATING AT YOU?
HUH?
YOU'RE GLOOMY.
IT'S...
... NOTHING.
TMP
TMP
TMP
GUESS HE'S NOT READY YET.

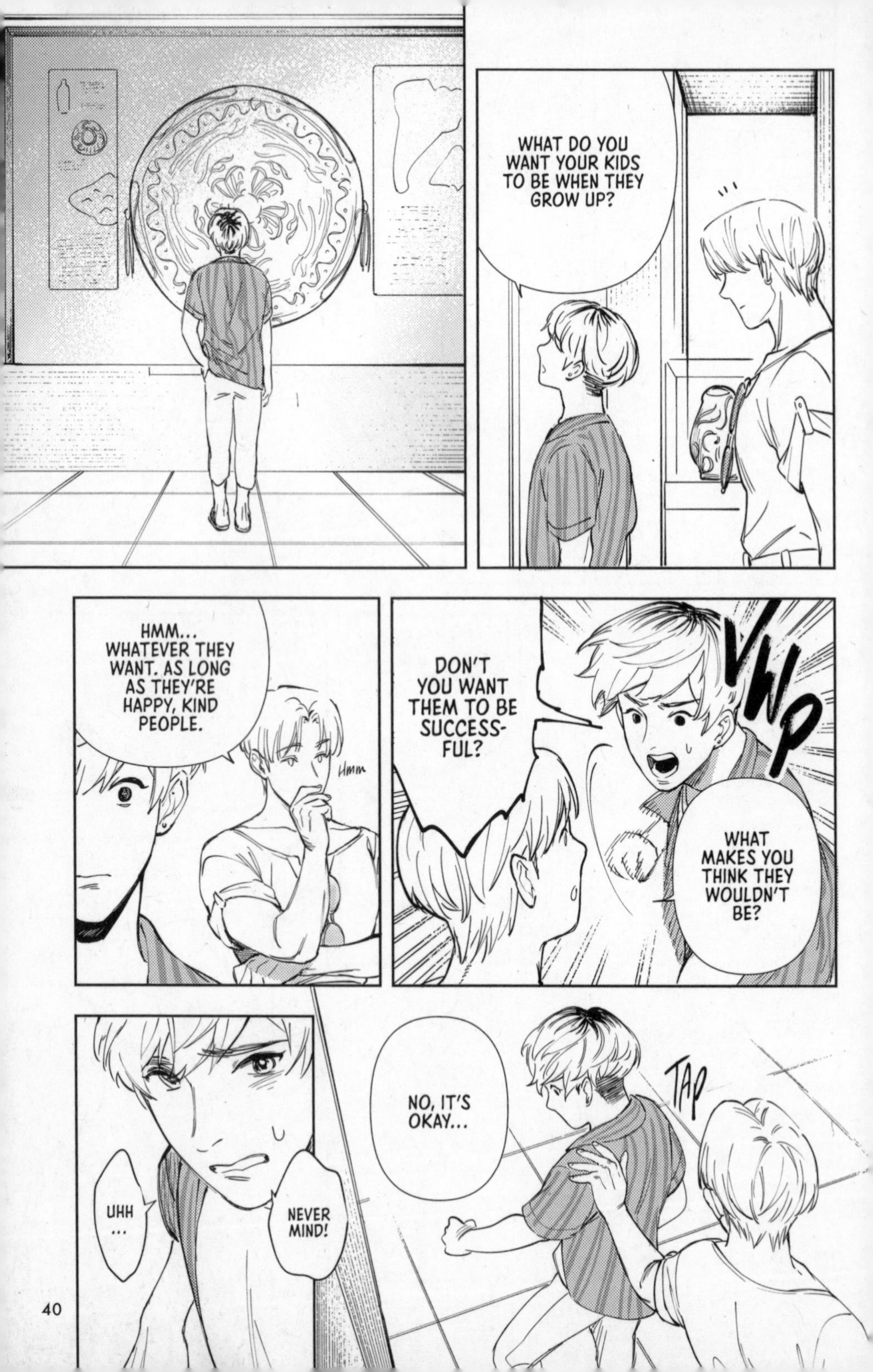
WHAT DO YOU WANT YOUR KIDS TO BE WHEN THEY GROW UP?
HMM... WHATEVER THEY WANT. AS LONG AS THEY'RE HAPPY, KIND PEOPLE.
Hmm
DON'T YOU WANT THEM TO BE SUCCESS-FUL?
VWP
WHAT MAKES YOU THINK THEY WOULDN'T BE?
UHH ...
NEVER MIND!
NO, IT'S OKAY...
TAP

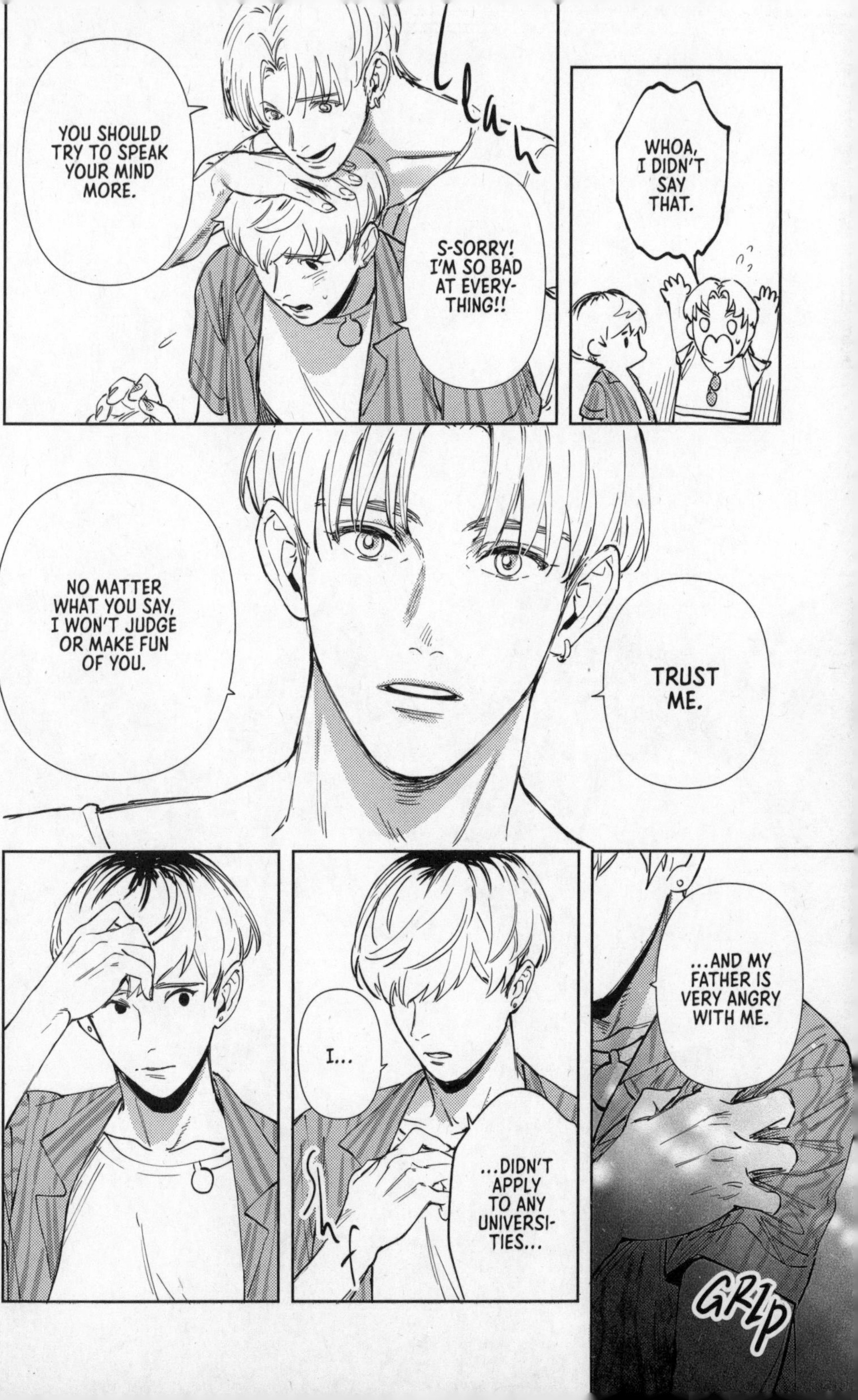
YOU SHOULD TRY TO SPEAK YOUR MIND MORE.
S-SORRY! I'M SO BAD AT EVERY-THING!!
WHOA, I DIDN'T SAY THAT.
NO MATTER WHAT YOU SAY, I WON'T JUDGE OR MAKE FUN OF YOU.
TRUST ME.
I...
...DIDN'T APPLY TO ANY UNIVERSI-TIES...
...AND MY FATHER IS VERY ANGRY WITH ME.
GRIP

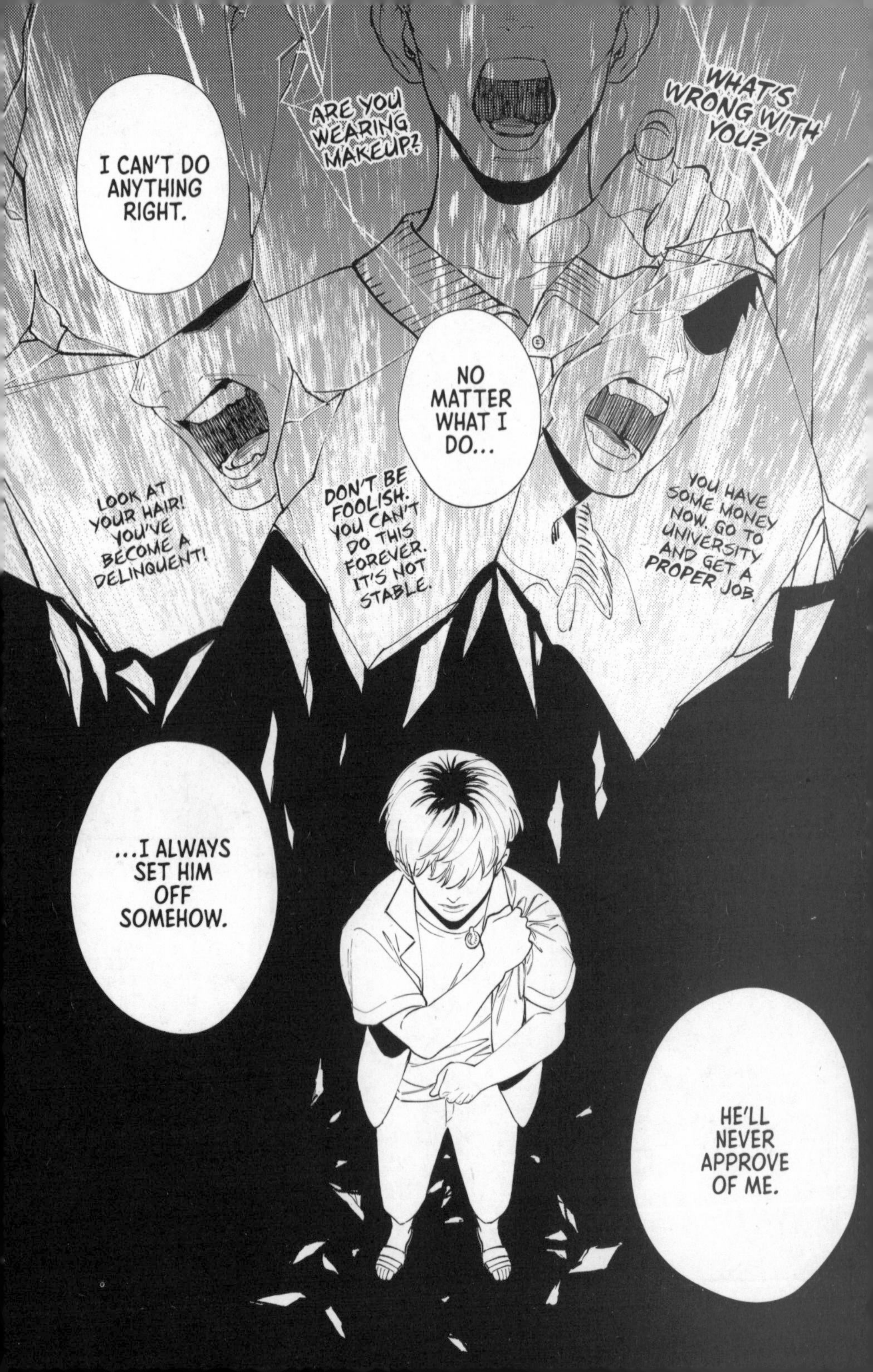
I CAN'T DO ANYTHING RIGHT.
ARE YOU WEARING MAKEUP?
WHAT'S WRONG WITH YOU?
LOOK AT YOUR HAIR! YOU'VE BECOME A DELINQUENT!
DON'T BE FOOLISH. YOU CAN'T DO THIS FOREVER. IT'S NOT STABLE.
NO MATTER WHAT I DO...
YOU HAVE SOME MONEY NOW. GO TO UNIVERSITY AND GET A PROPER JOB.
...I ALWAYS SET HIM OFF SOMEHOW.
HE'LL NEVER APPROVE OF ME.

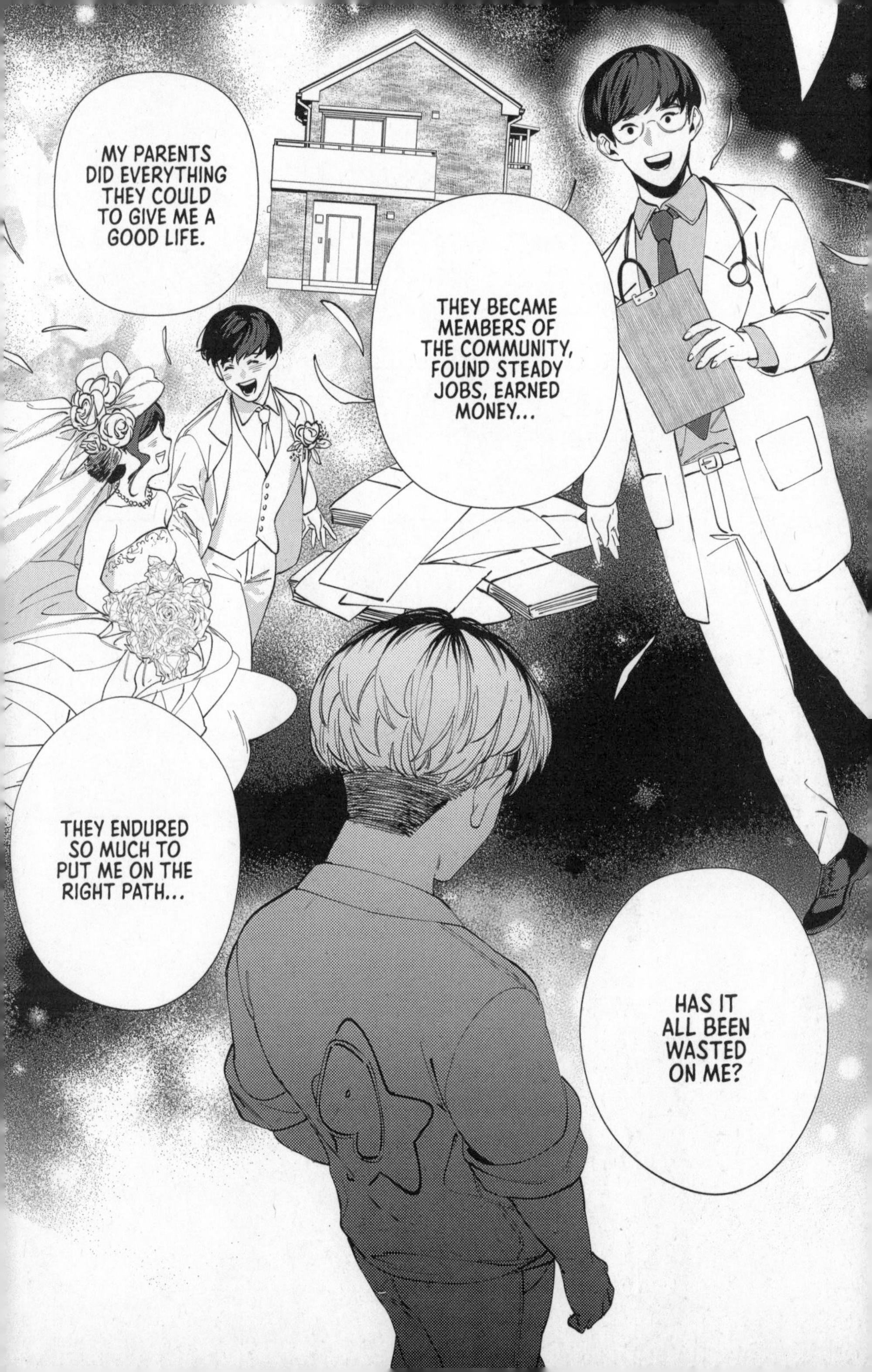
MY PARENTS DID EVERYTHING THEY COULD TO GIVE ME A GOOD LIFE.
THEY BECAME MEMBERS OF THE COMMUNITY, FOUND STEADY JOBS, EARNED MONEY...
THEY ENDURED SO MUCH TO PUT ME ON THE RIGHT PATH...
HAS IT ALL BEEN WASTED ON ME?

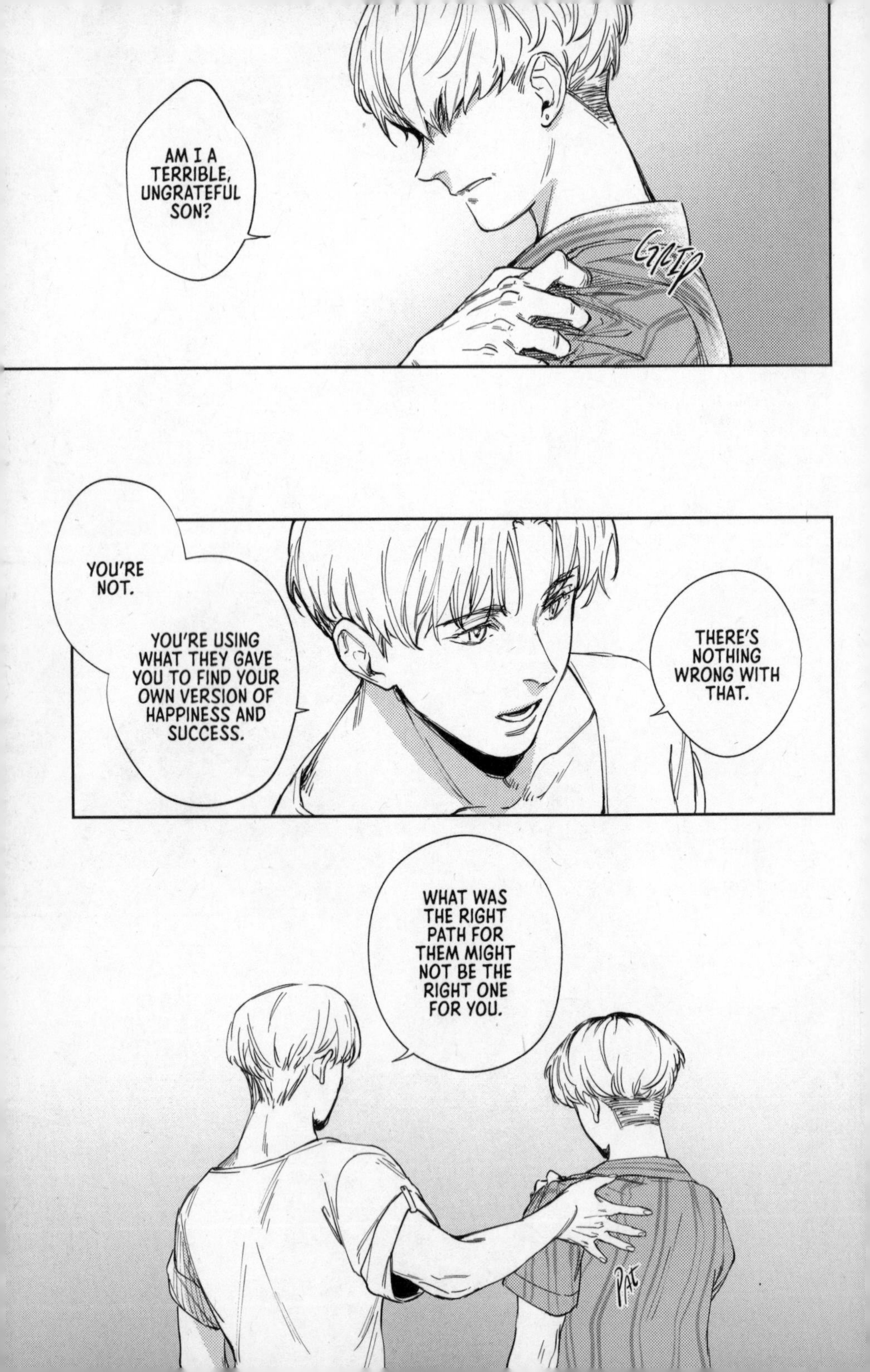

AM I A TERRIBLE, UNGRATEFUL SON?
GRIP
YOU'RE NOT.
YOU'RE USING WHAT THEY GAVE YOU TO FIND YOUR OWN VERSION OF HAPPINESS AND SUCCESS.
THERE'S NOTHING WRONG WITH THAT.
WHAT WAS THE RIGHT PATH FOR THEM MIGHT NOT BE THE RIGHT ONE FOR YOU.
PAT

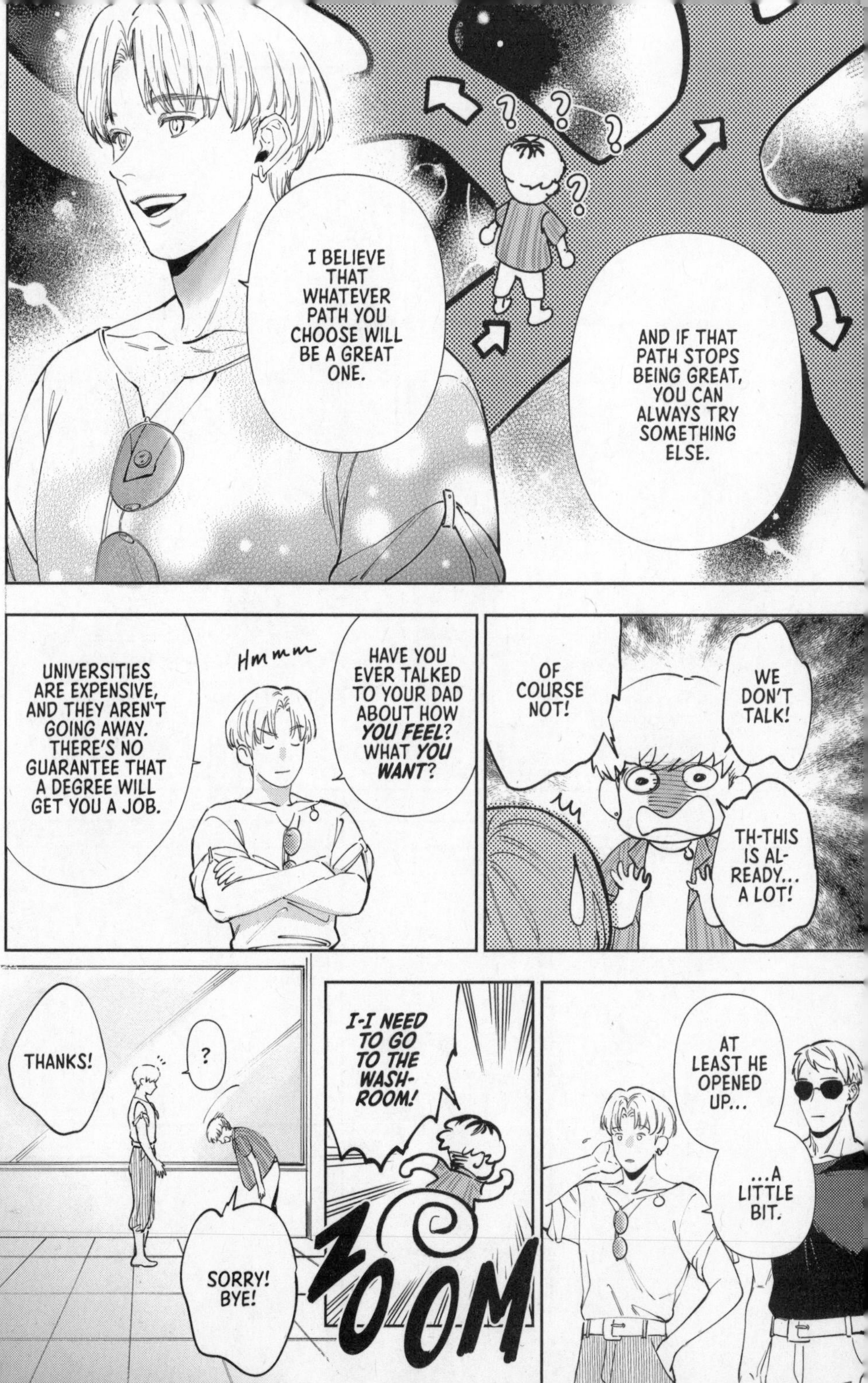
I BELIEVE THAT WHATEVER PATH YOU CHOOSE WILL BE A GREAT ONE.
AND IF THAT PATH STOPS BEING GREAT, YOU CAN ALWAYS TRY SOMETHING ELSE.
UNIVERSITIES ARE EXPENSIVE, AND THEY AREN'T GOING AWAY. THERE'S NO GUARANTEE THAT A DEGREE WILL GET YOU A JOB.
Hmmm
HAVE YOU EVER TALKED TO YOUR DAD ABOUT HOW *YOU FEEL*? WHAT *YOU WANT*?
OF COURSE NOT!
WE DON'T TALK!
TH-THIS IS AL-READY... A LOT!
THANKS!
?
SORRY! BYE!
I-I NEED TO GO TO THE WASH-ROOM!
ZOOM
AT LEAST HE OPENED UP...
...A LITTLE BIT.

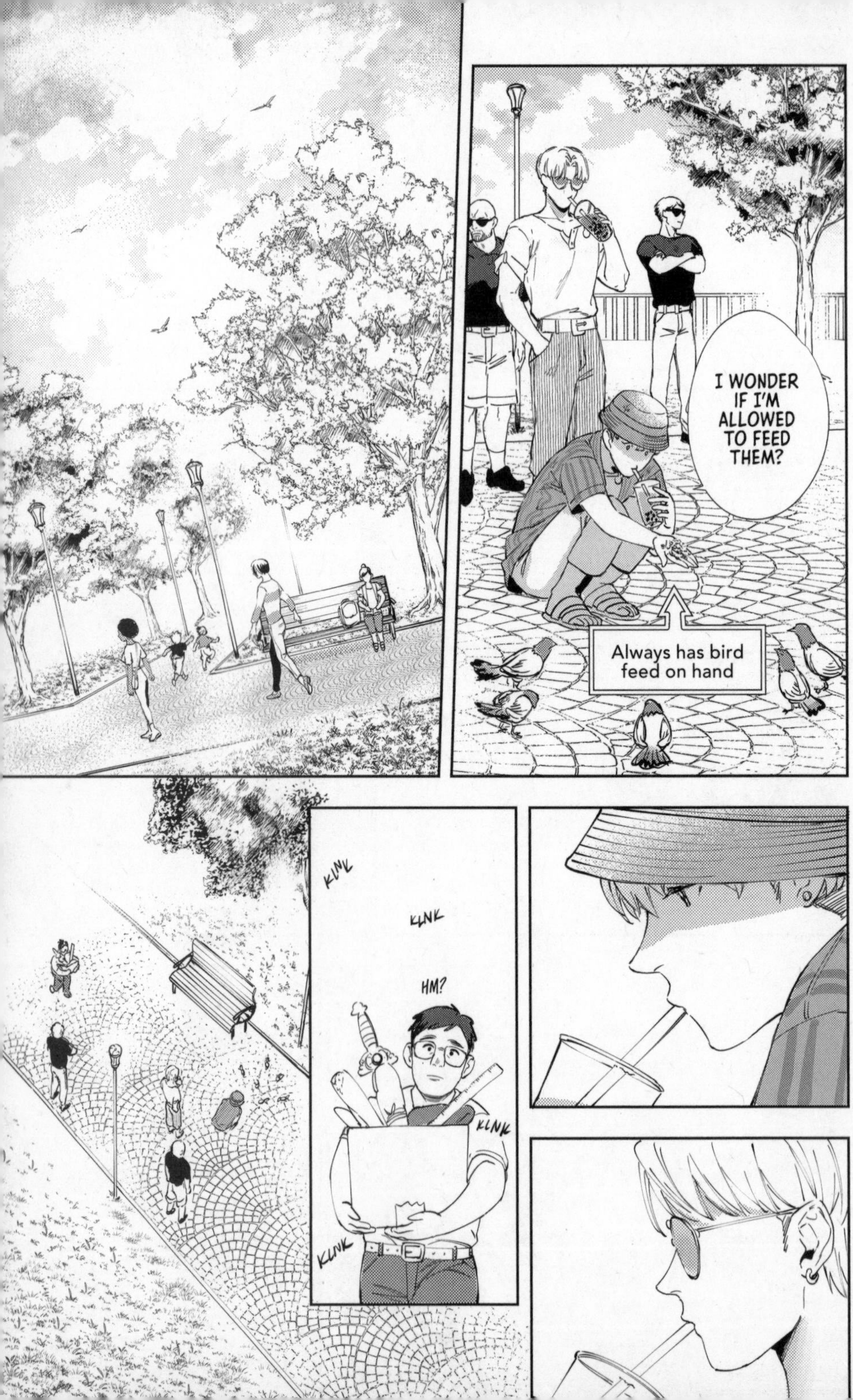
I WONDER IF I'M ALLOWED TO FEED THEM?
Always has bird feed on hand
KLNK
KLNK
HM?
KLNK
KLNK

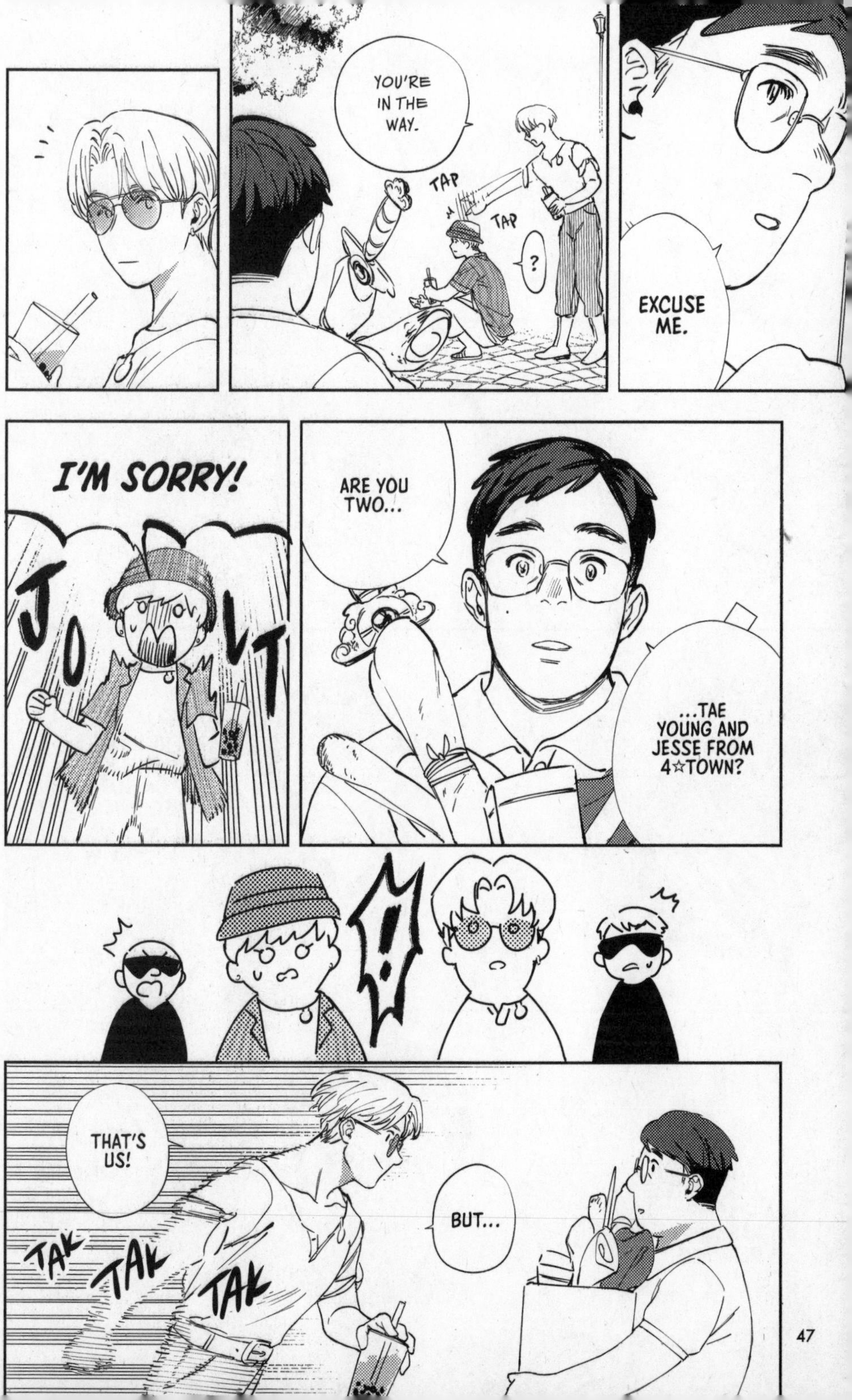
YOU'RE IN THE WAY.
TAP
TAP
?
EXCUSE ME.
I'M SORRY!
JOLT
ARE YOU TWO...
...TAE YOUNG AND JESSE FROM 4☆TOWN?
!
THAT'S US!
TAK
TAK
TAK
BUT...

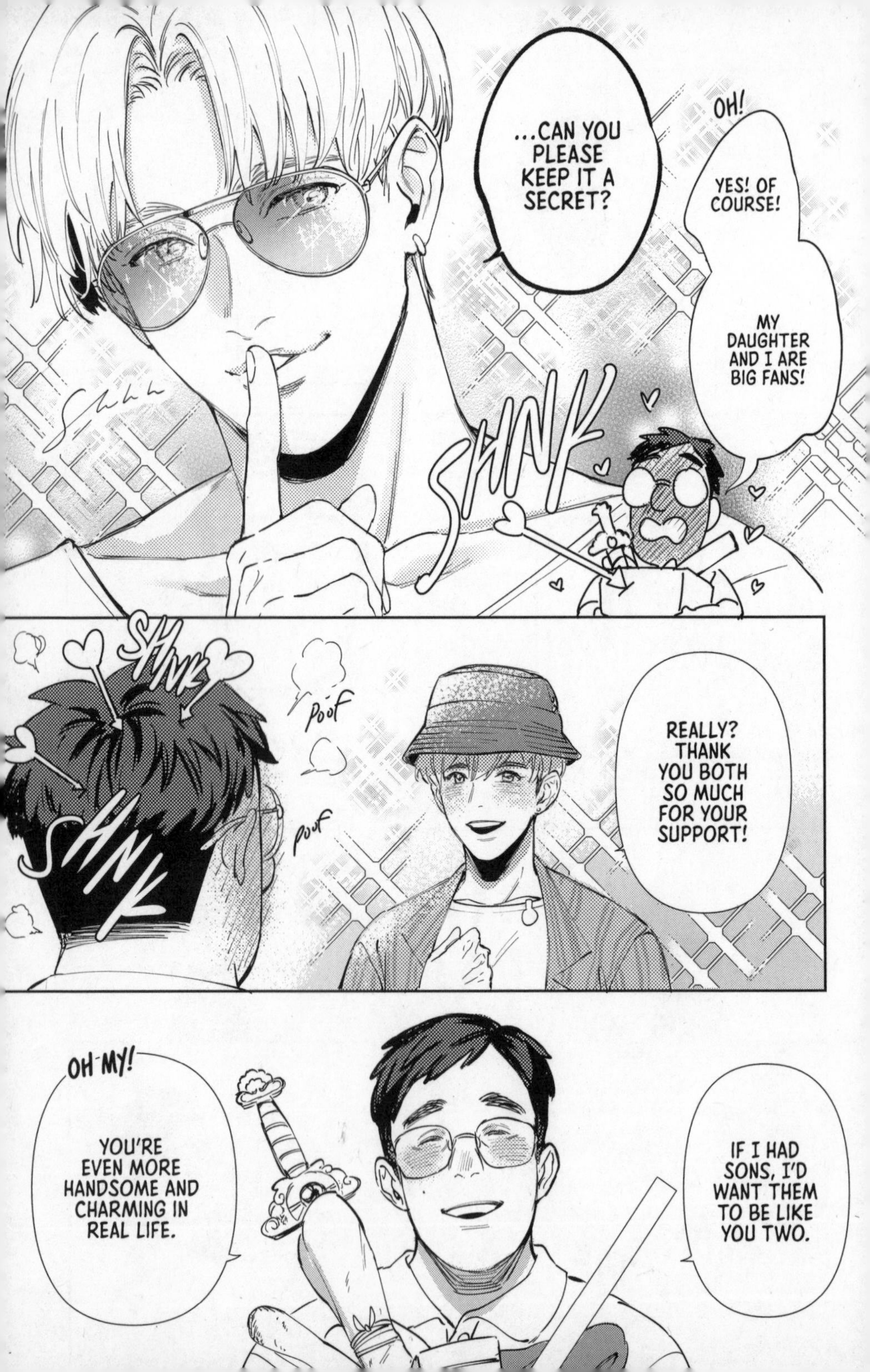
Shhh
SHINK
...CAN YOU PLEASE KEEP IT A SECRET?
OH!
YES! OF COURSE!
MY DAUGHTER AND I ARE BIG FANS!
SHINK
poof
poof
SHINK
REALLY? THANK YOU BOTH SO MUCH FOR YOUR SUPPORT!
OH-MY!
YOU'RE EVEN MORE HANDSOME AND CHARMING IN REAL LIFE.
IF I HAD SONS, I'D WANT THEM TO BE LIKE YOU TWO.

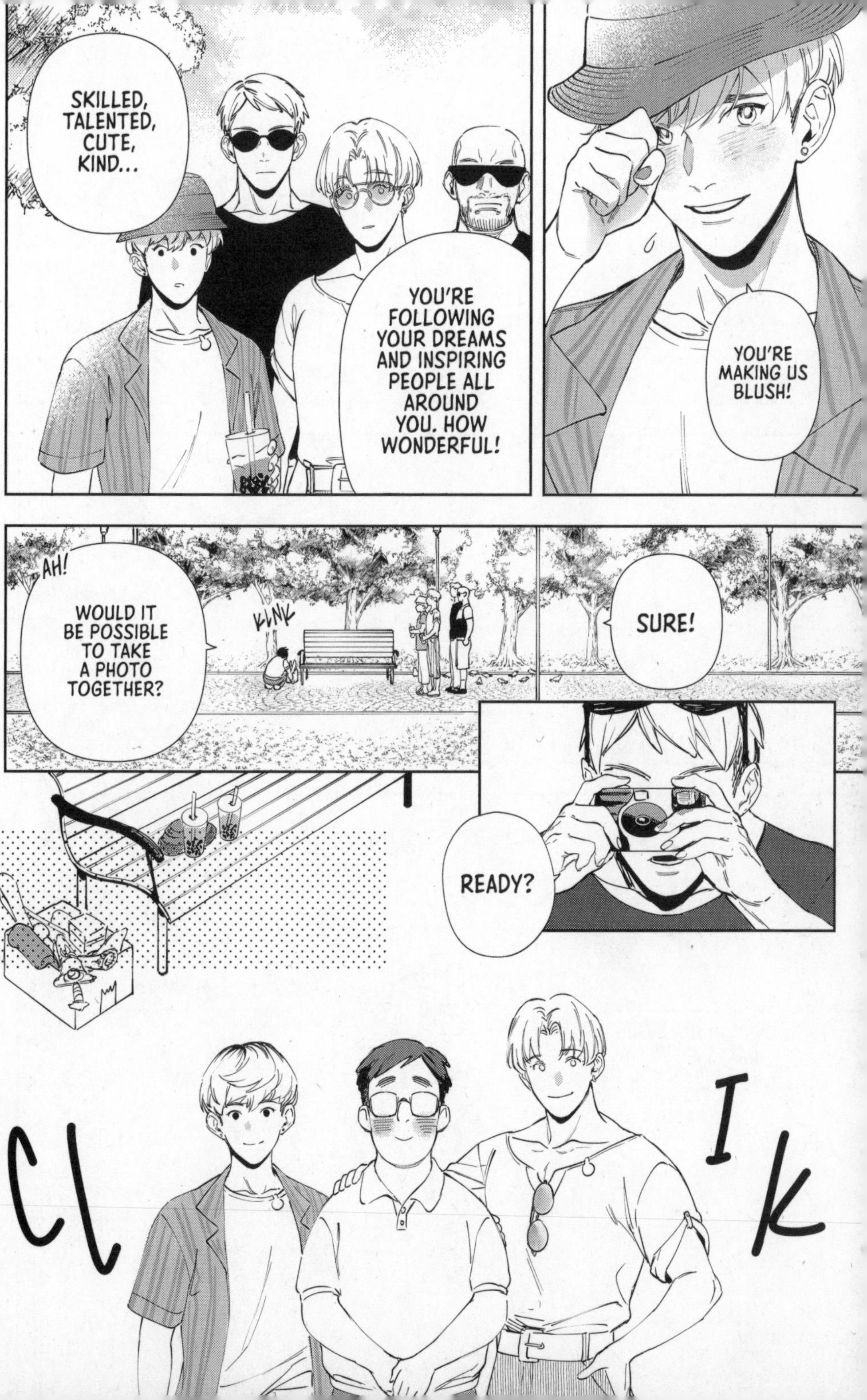
SKILLED, TALENTED, CUTE, KIND...
YOU'RE FOLLOWING YOUR DREAMS AND INSPIRING PEOPLE ALL AROUND YOU. HOW WONDERFUL!
YOU'RE MAKING US BLUSH!
AH!
WOULD IT BE POSSIBLE TO TAKE A PHOTO TOGETHER?
KLINK
SURE!
READY?
CLIK

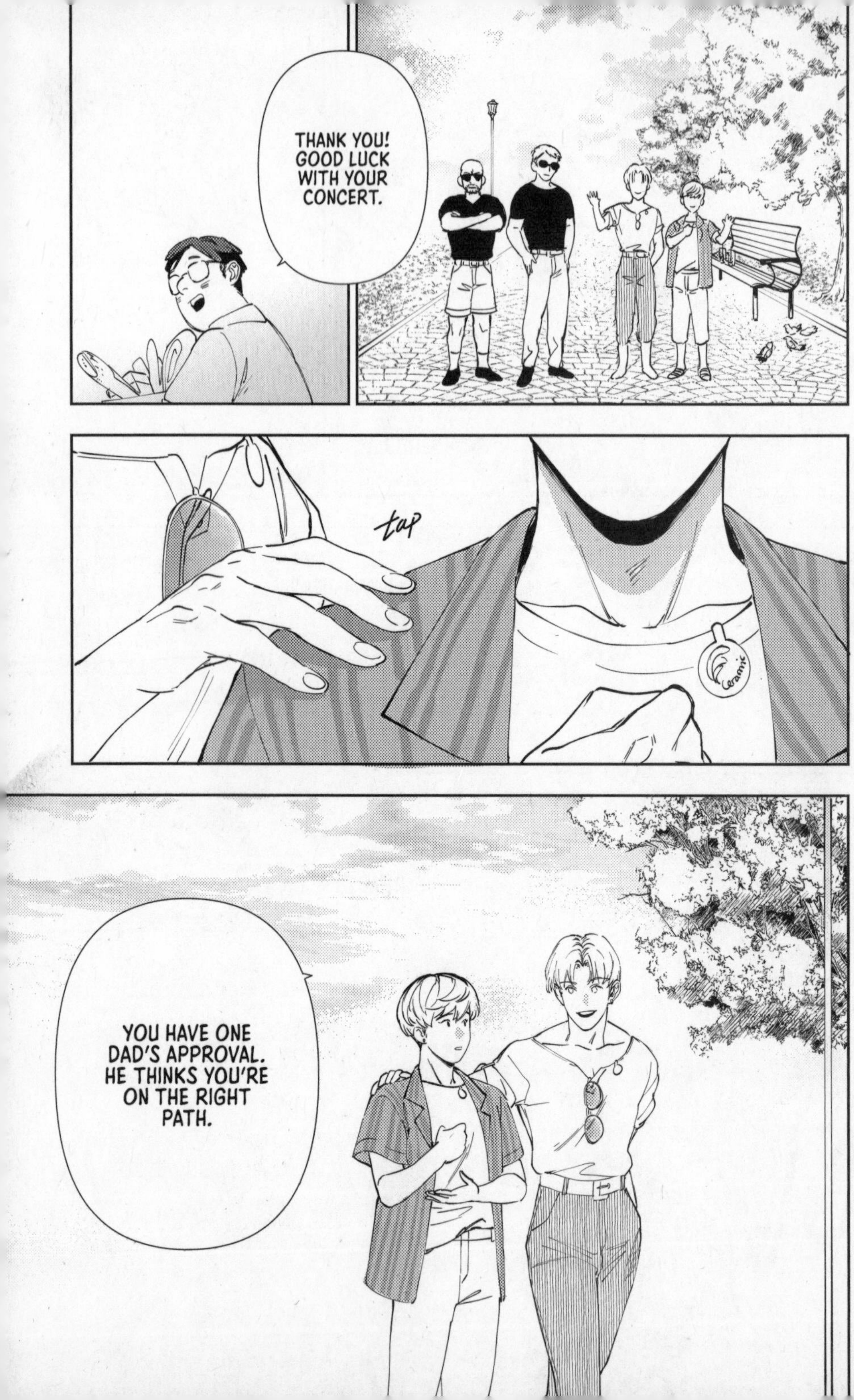
THANK YOU! GOOD LUCK WITH YOUR CONCERT.
tap
YOU HAVE ONE DAD'S APPROVAL. HE THINKS YOU'RE ON THE RIGHT PATH.

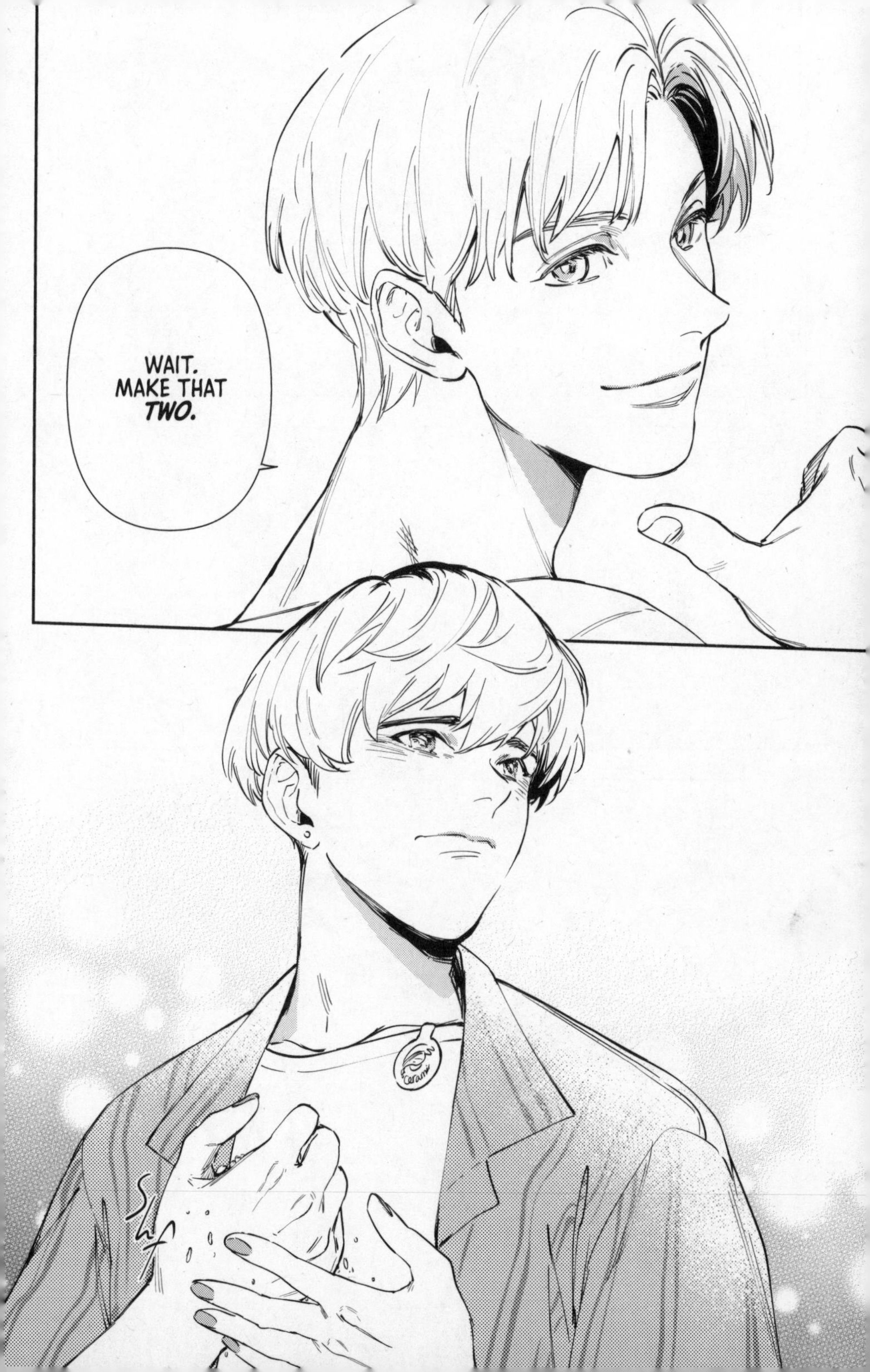
WAIT. MAKE THAT *TWO.*
Shf

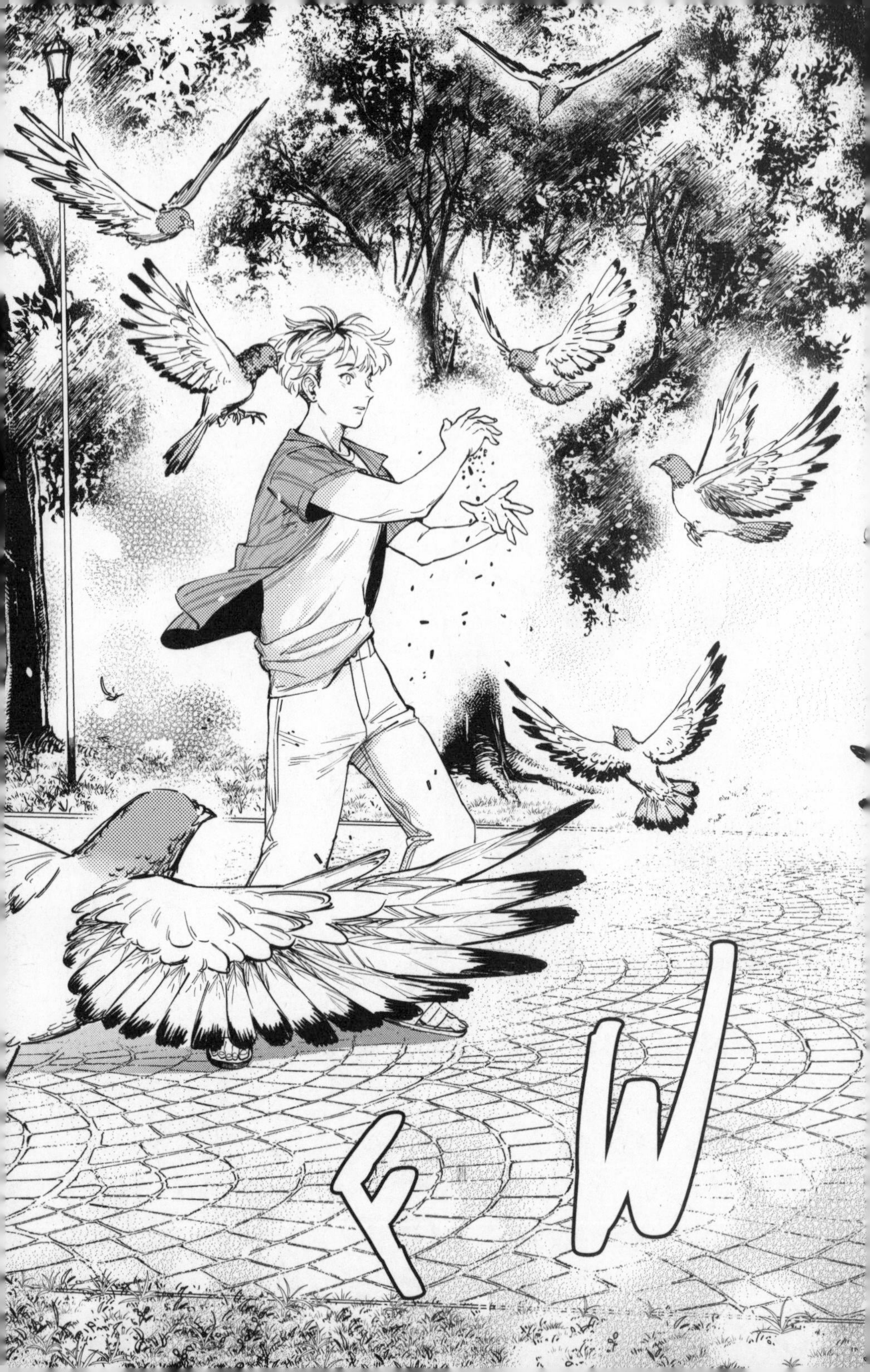
FW

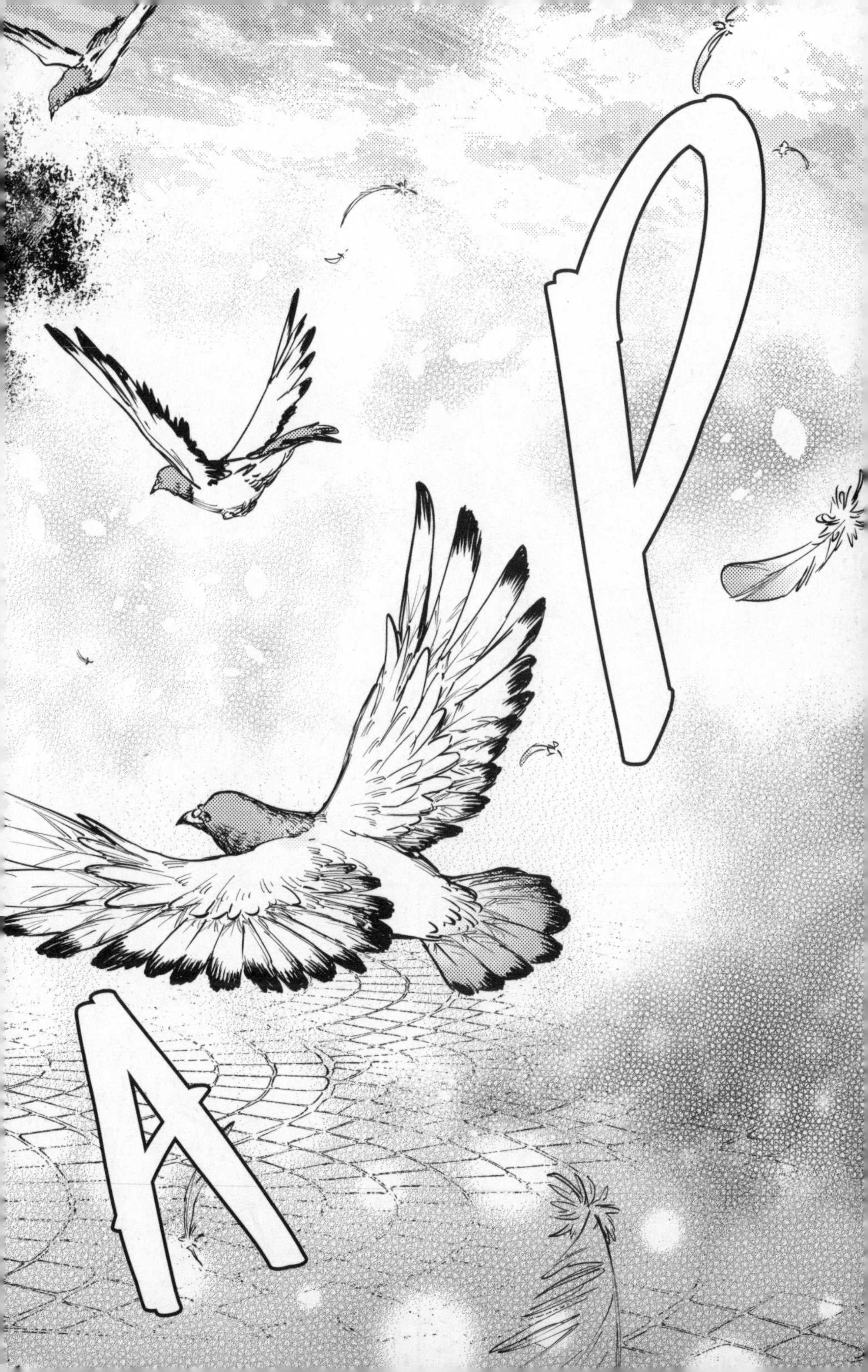
P
A

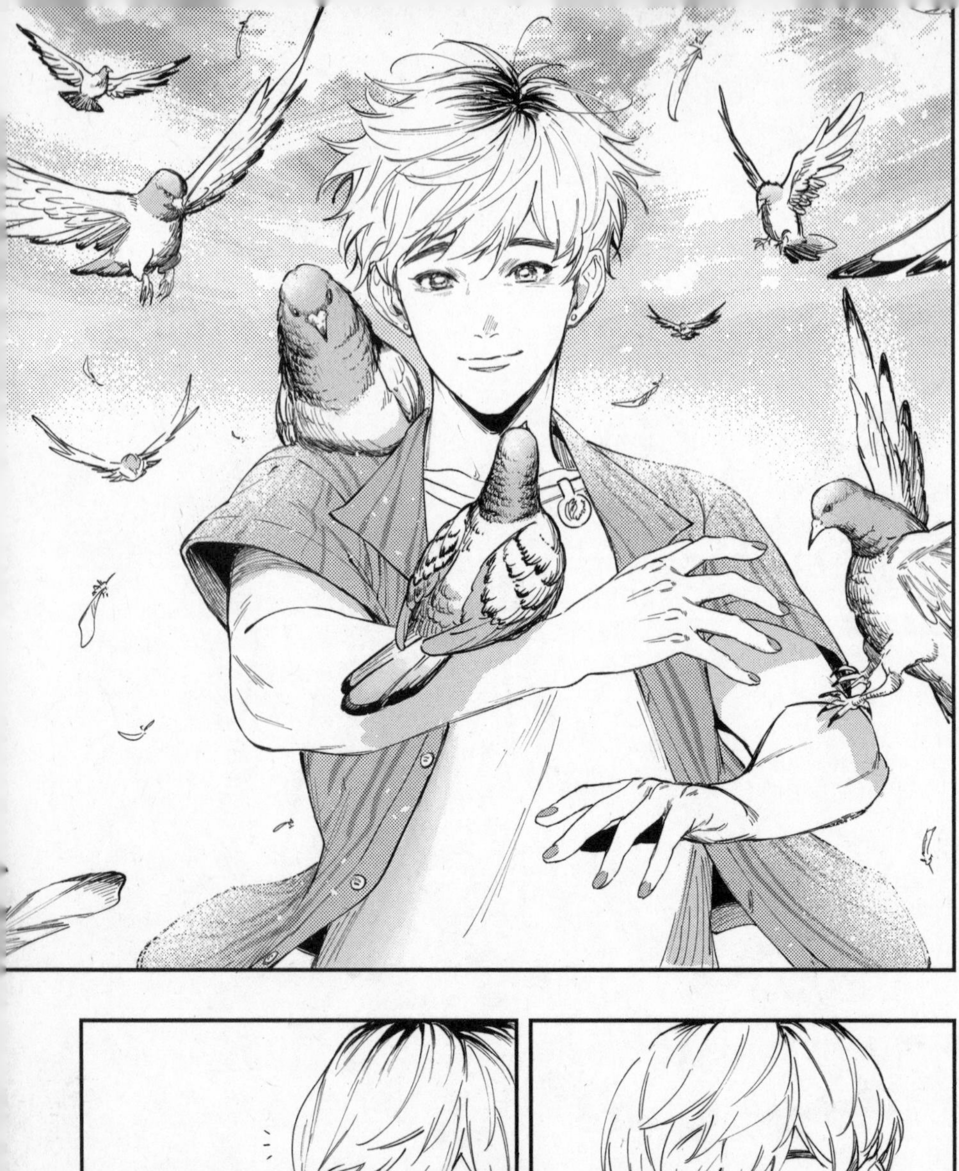
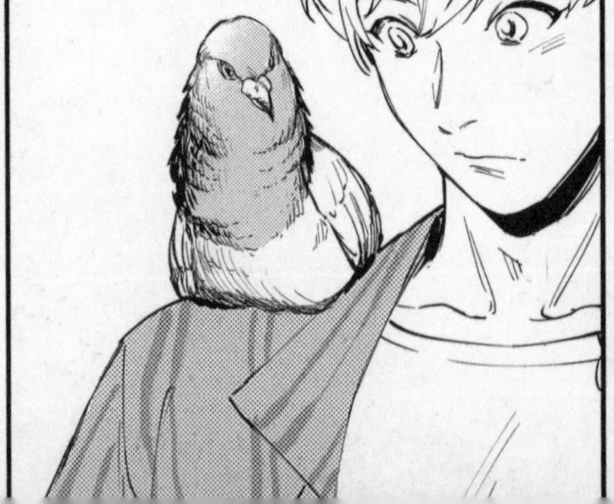
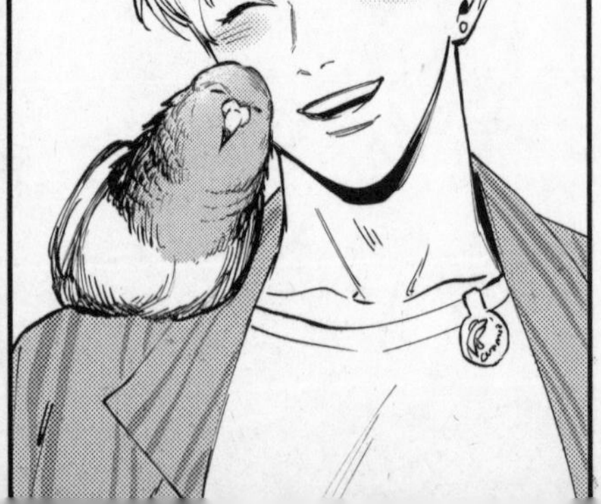

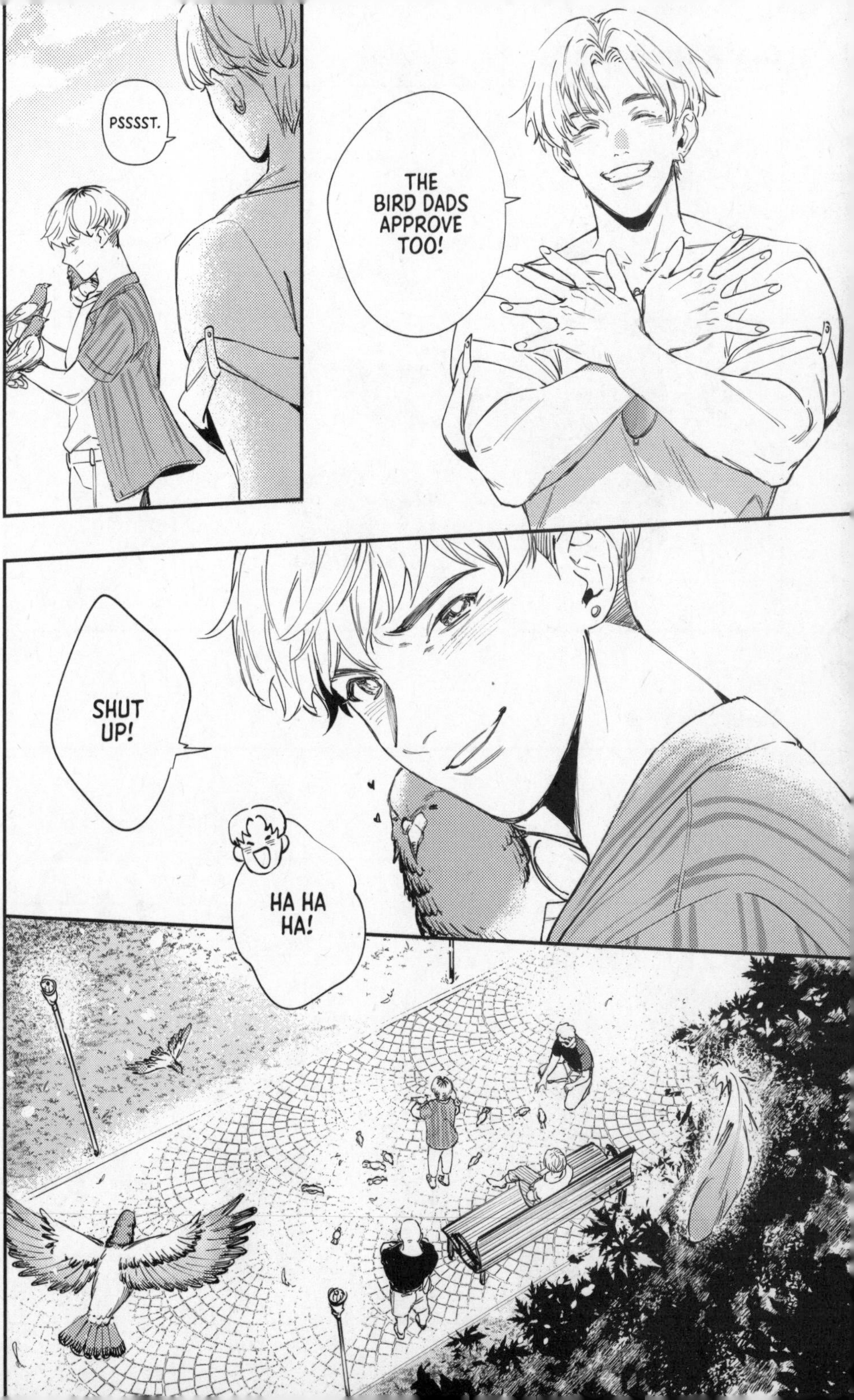
PSSSST.
THE BIRD DADS APPROVE TOO!
SHUT UP!
HA HA HA!

Dad Approval +2

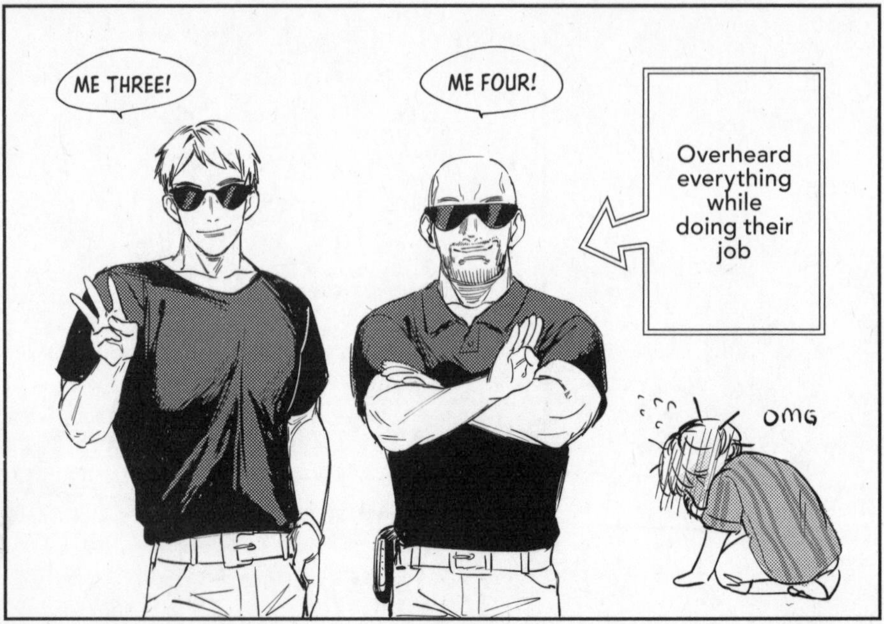
ME THREE!
ME FOUR!
Overheard everything while doing their job
OMG

Dad Club +1

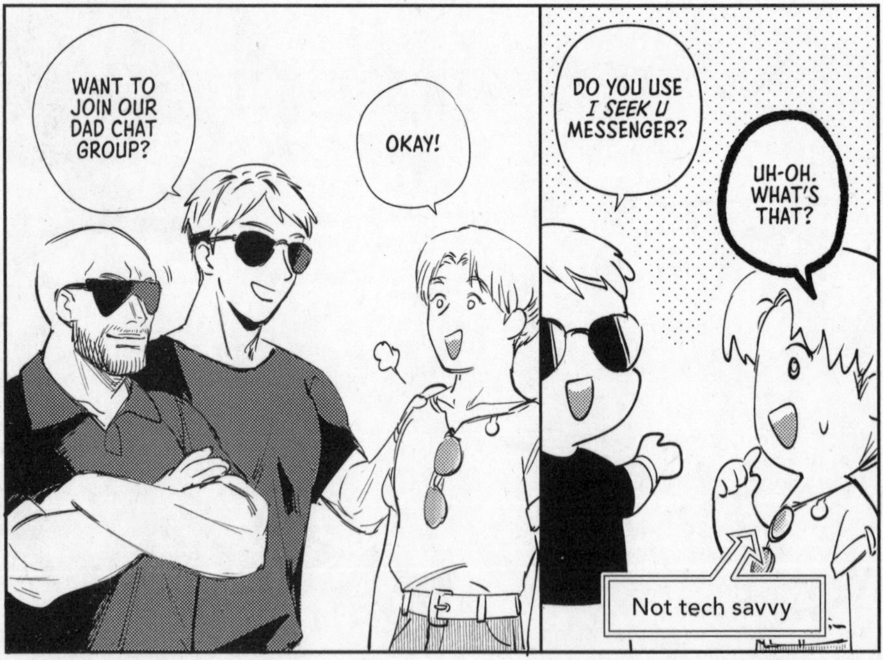
WANT TO JOIN OUR DAD CHAT GROUP?
OKAY!
DO YOU USE *I SEEK U* MESSENGER?
UH-OH. WHAT'S THAT?
Not tech savvy

ATTENTION

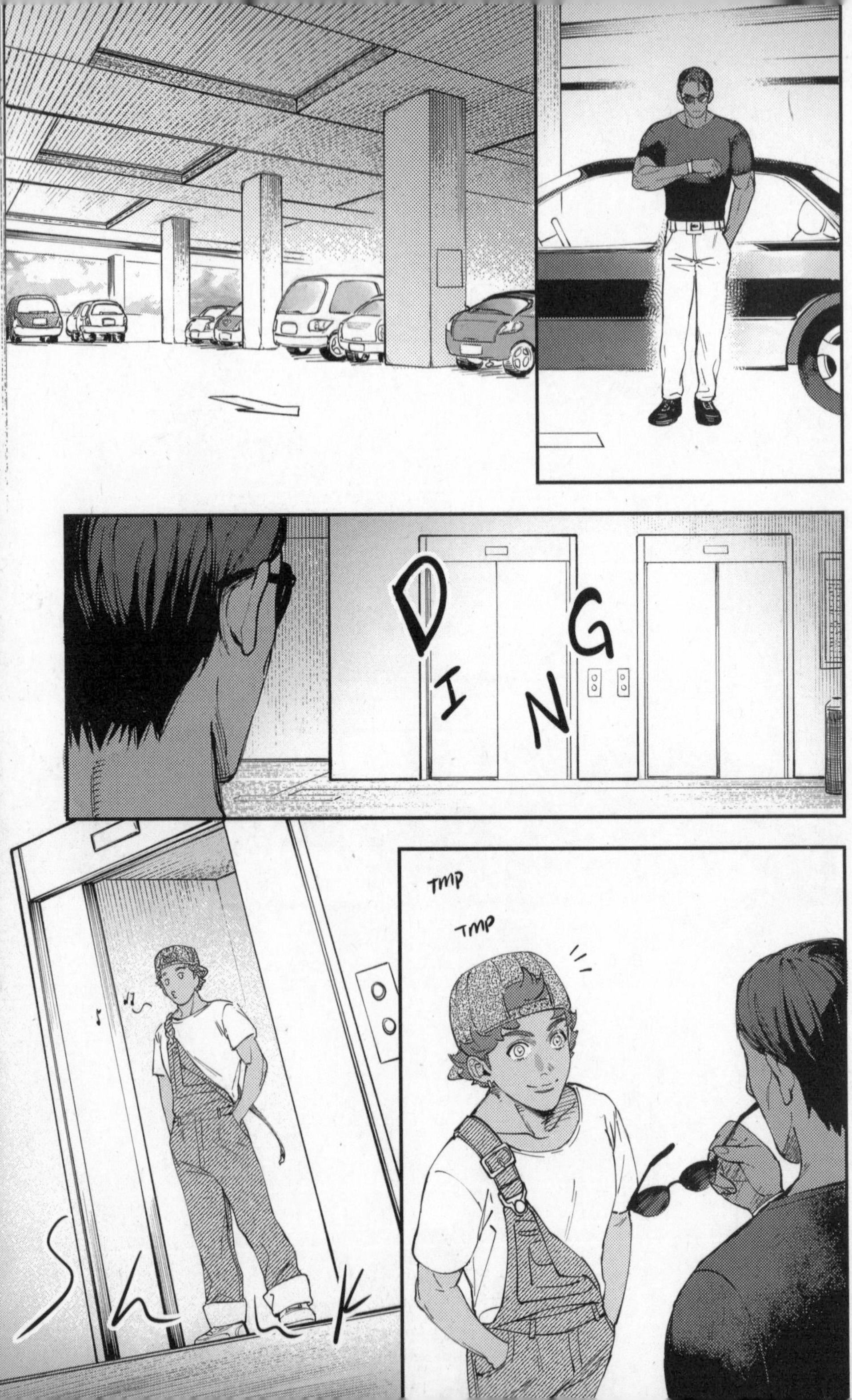
DING
SHLK
TMP
TMP

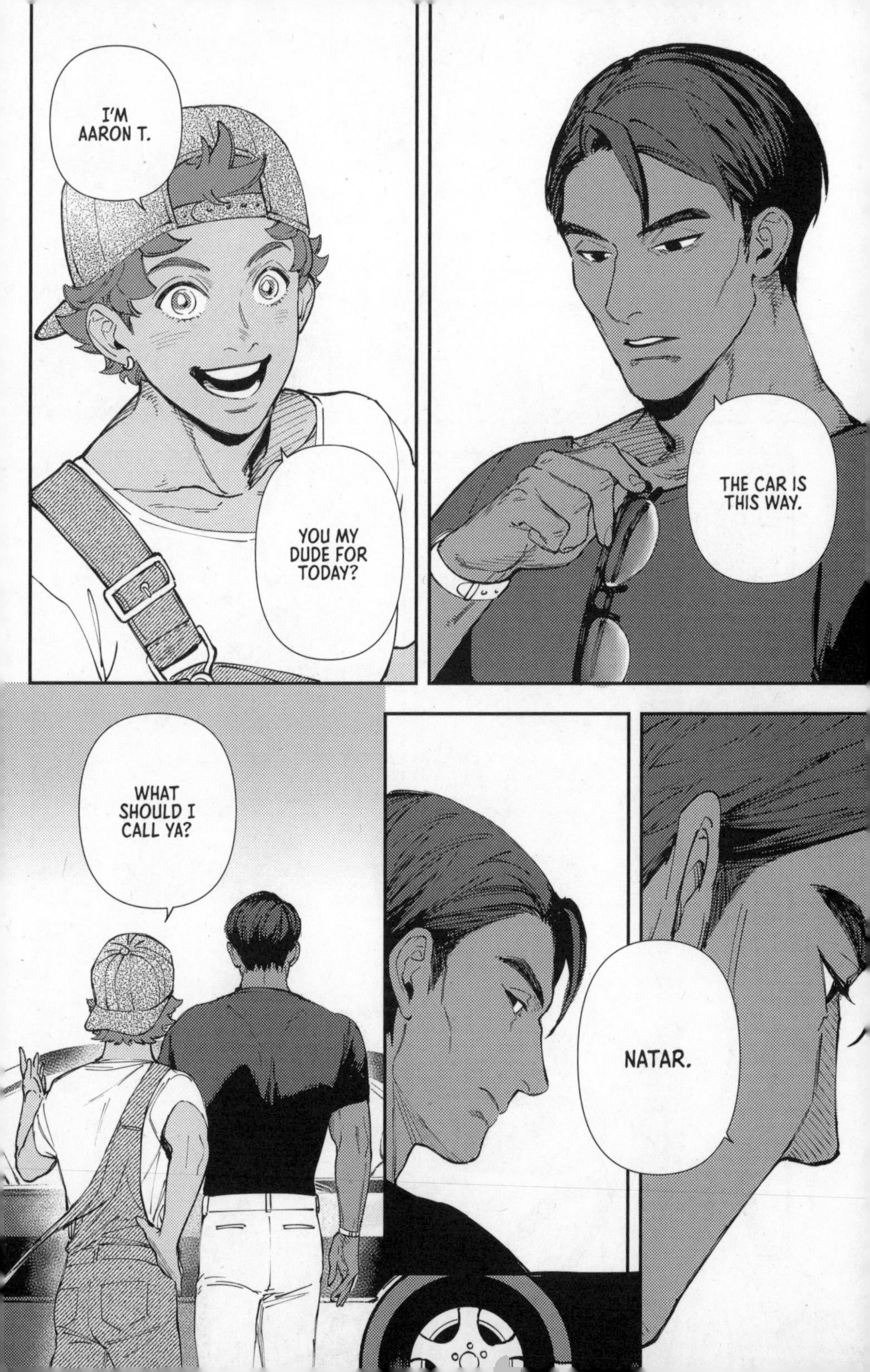
I'M AARON T.
YOU MY DUDE FOR TODAY?
THE CAR IS THIS WAY.
WHAT SHOULD I CALL YA?
NATAR.

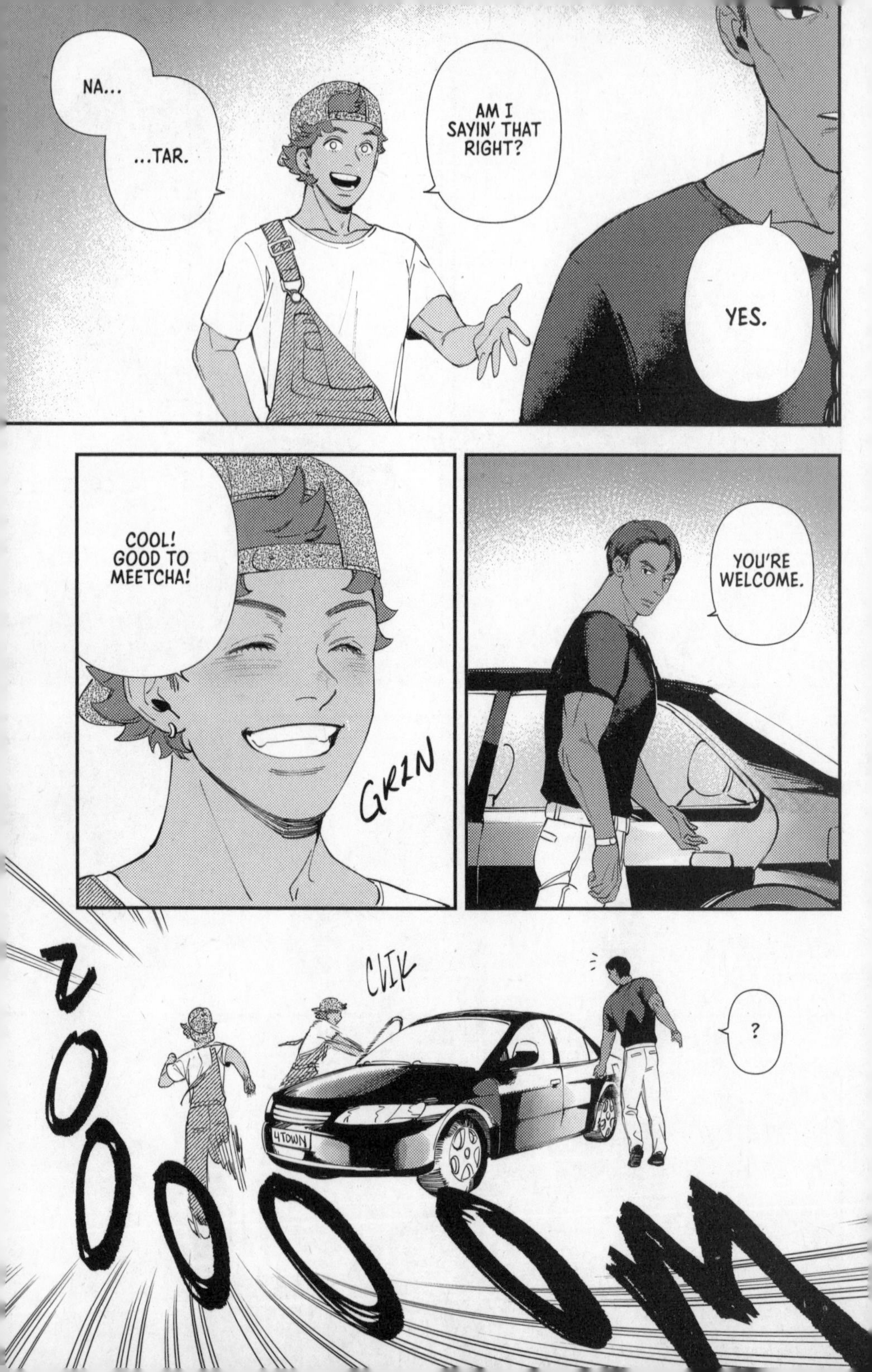
NA...
...TAR.
AM I SAYIN' THAT RIGHT?
YES.
COOL! GOOD TO MEETCHA!
GRIN
YOU'RE WELCOME.
CLIK
?
4TOWN
ZOOOOOM

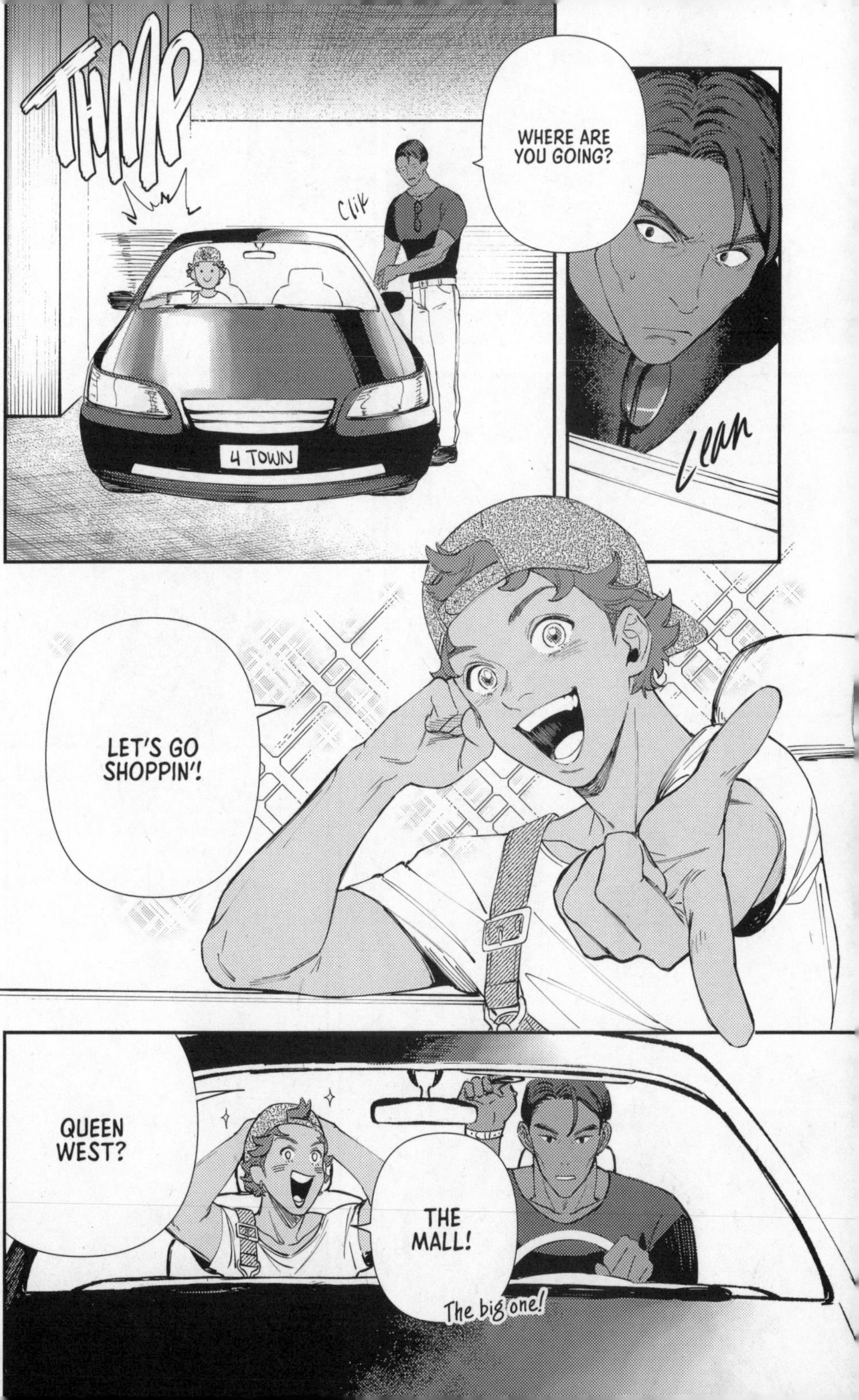
THMP
Clik
WHERE ARE YOU GOING?
Lean
4 TOWN
LET'S GO SHOPPIN'!
QUEEN WEST?
THE MALL!
The big one!

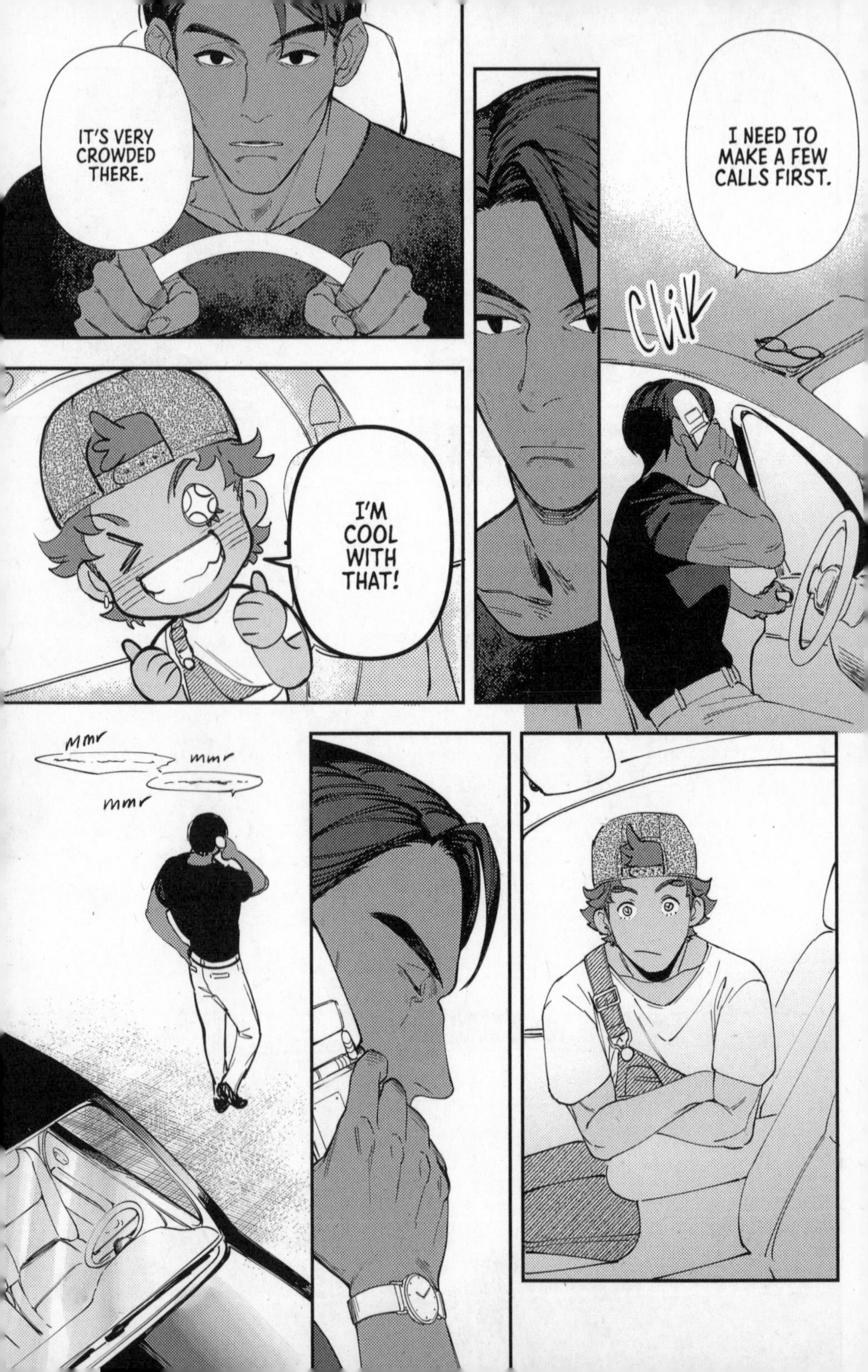
IT'S VERY CROWDED THERE.
I'M COOL WITH THAT!
I NEED TO MAKE A FEW CALLS FIRST.
CLIK
mmr
mmr
mmr

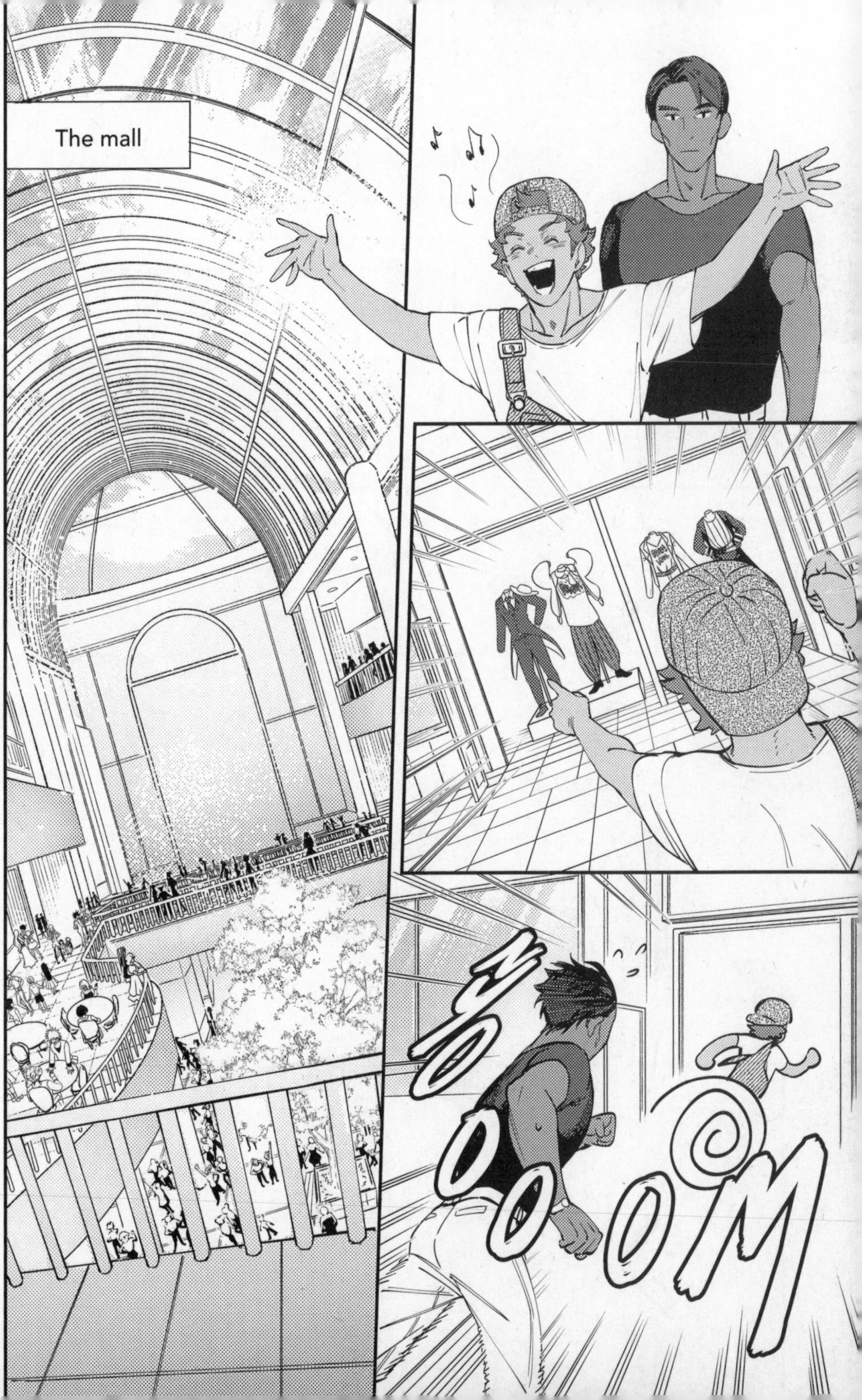
The mall

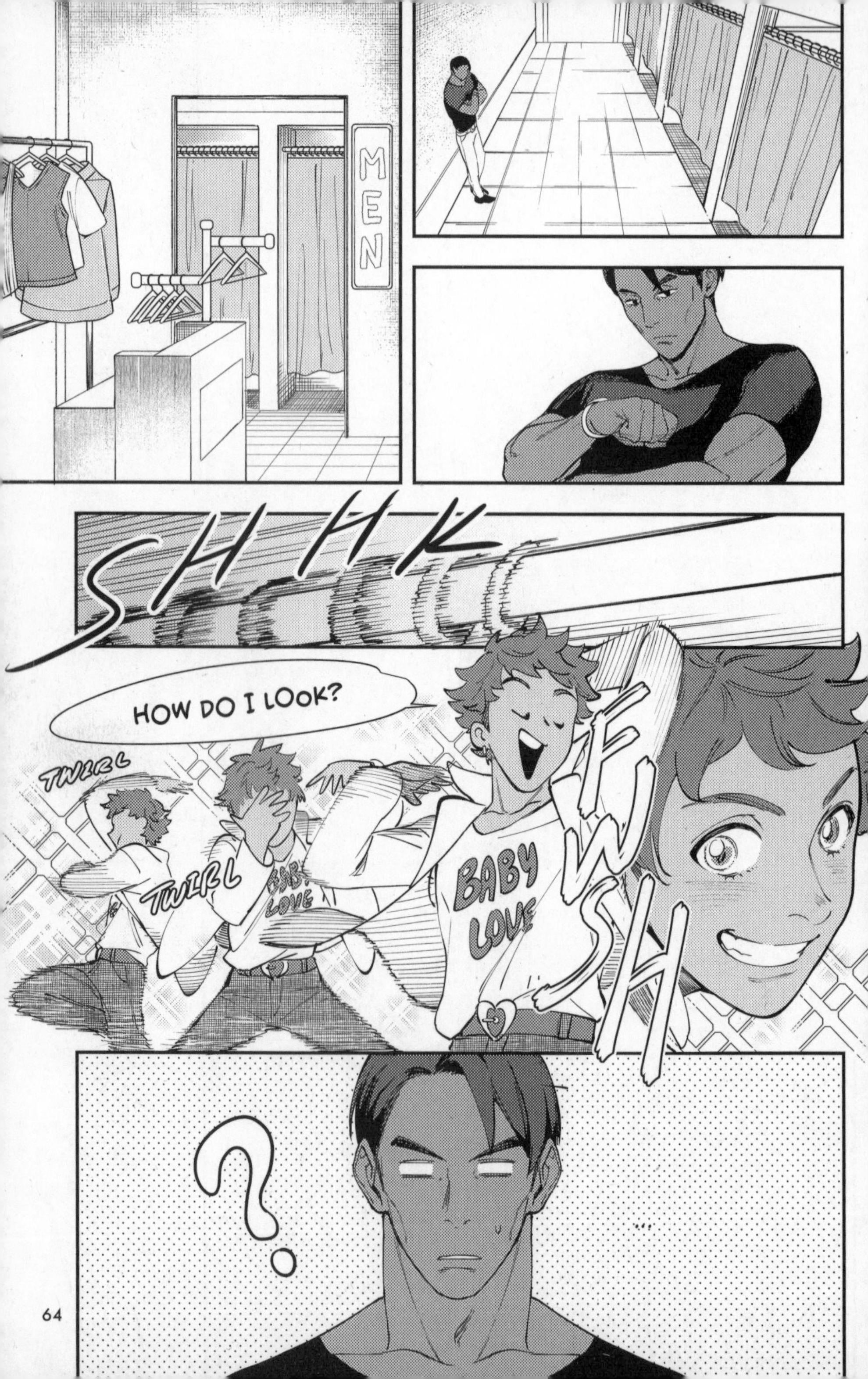
MEN
SHHK
HOW DO I LOOK?
TWIRL
TWIRL
BABY LOVE
BABY LOVE
FWSH
...

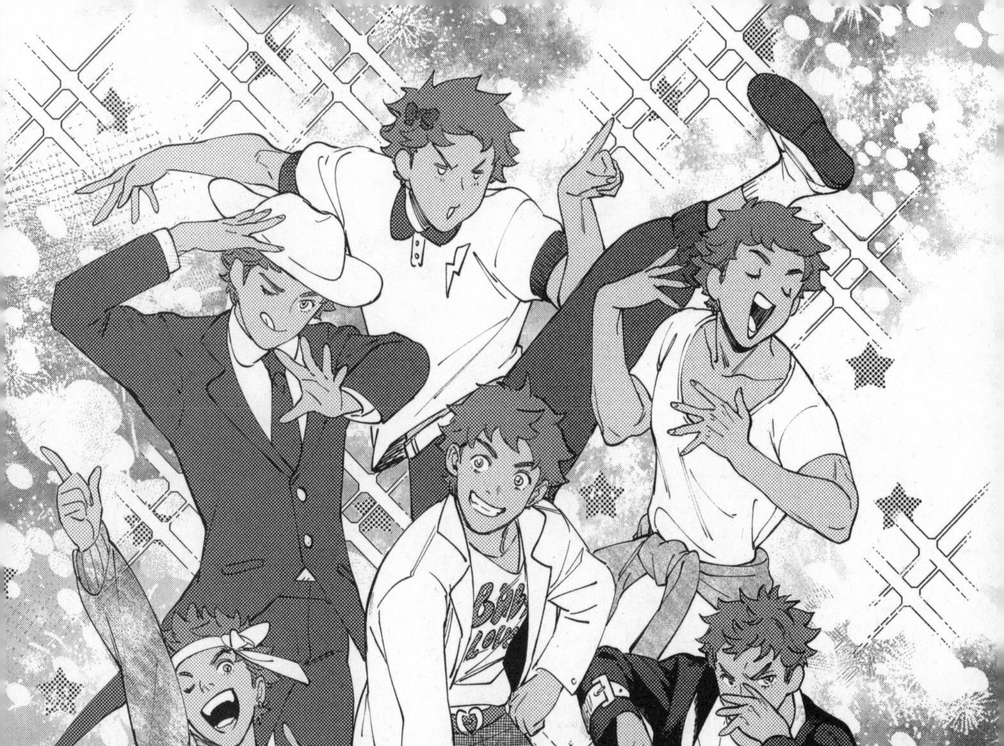

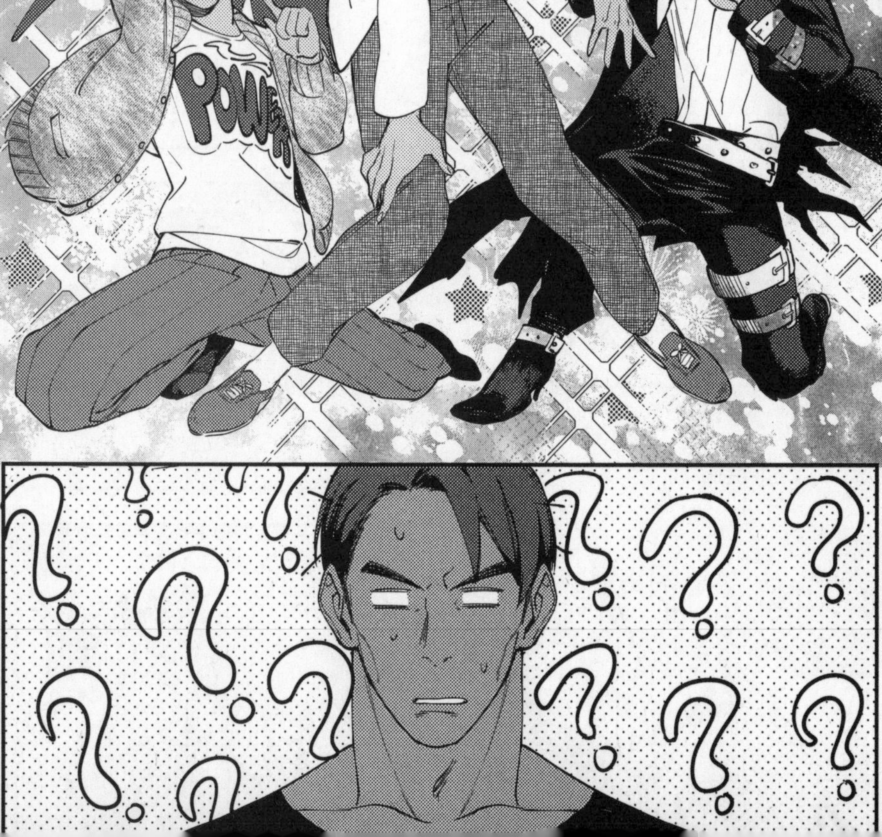

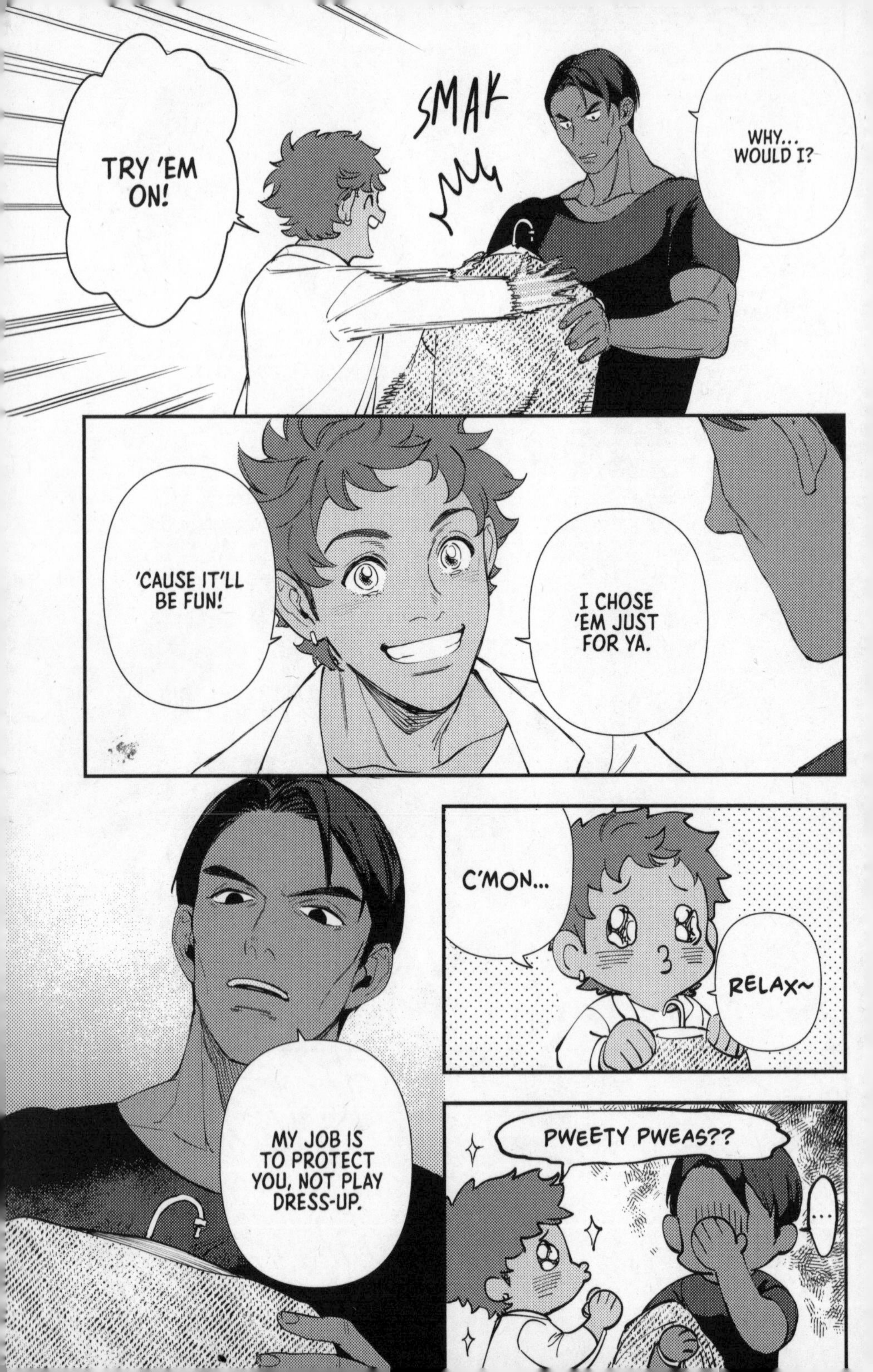
TRY 'EM ON!
SMAK
WHY... WOULD I?
'CAUSE IT'LL BE FUN!
I CHOSE 'EM JUST FOR YA.
MY JOB IS TO PROTECT YOU, NOT PLAY DRESS-UP.
C'MON...
RELAX~
PWEETY PWEAS??
...

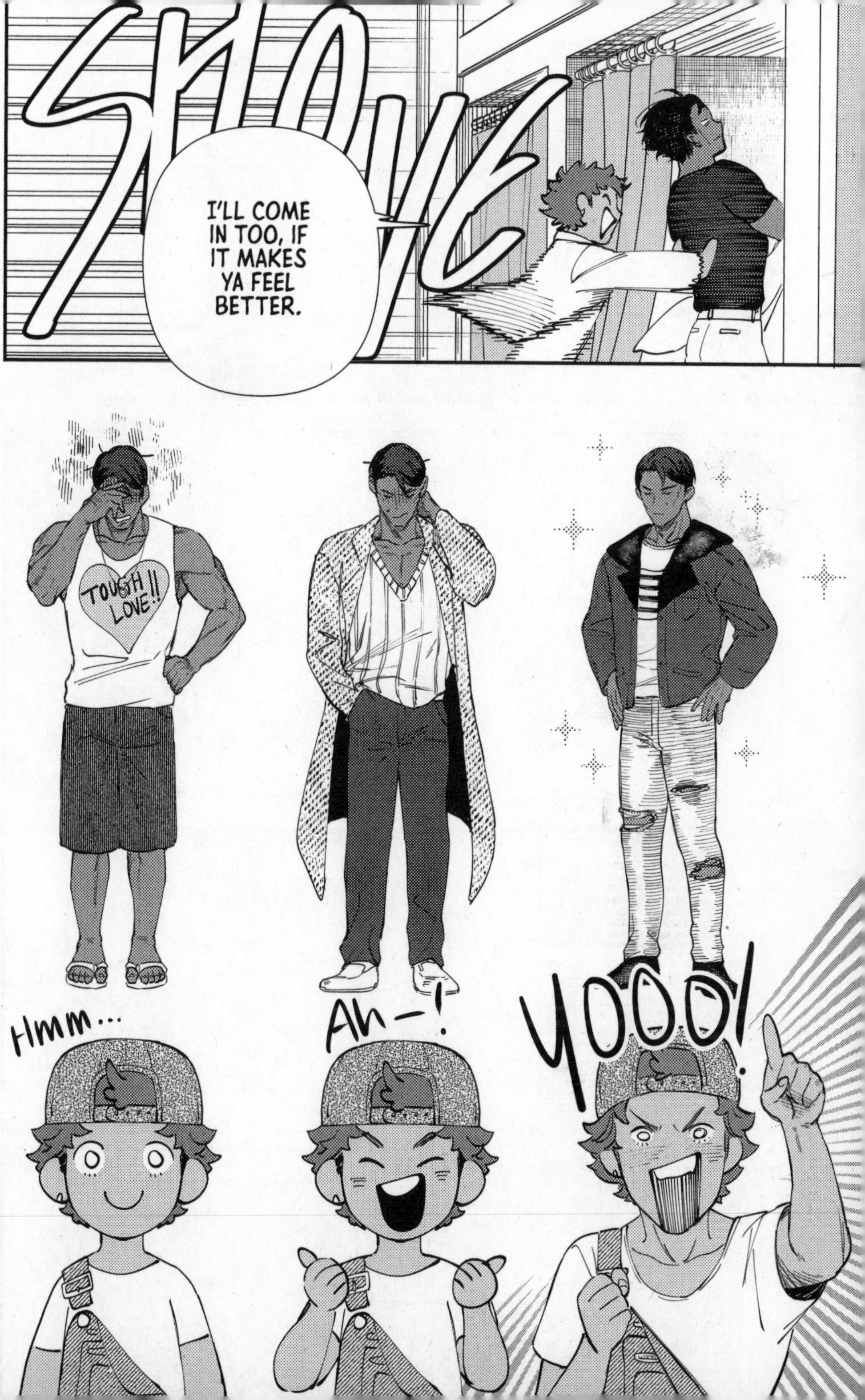
SHOVE
I'LL COME IN TOO, IF IT MAKES YA FEEL BETTER.
TOUGH LOVE!!
Hmm...
Ah—!
YOOO!

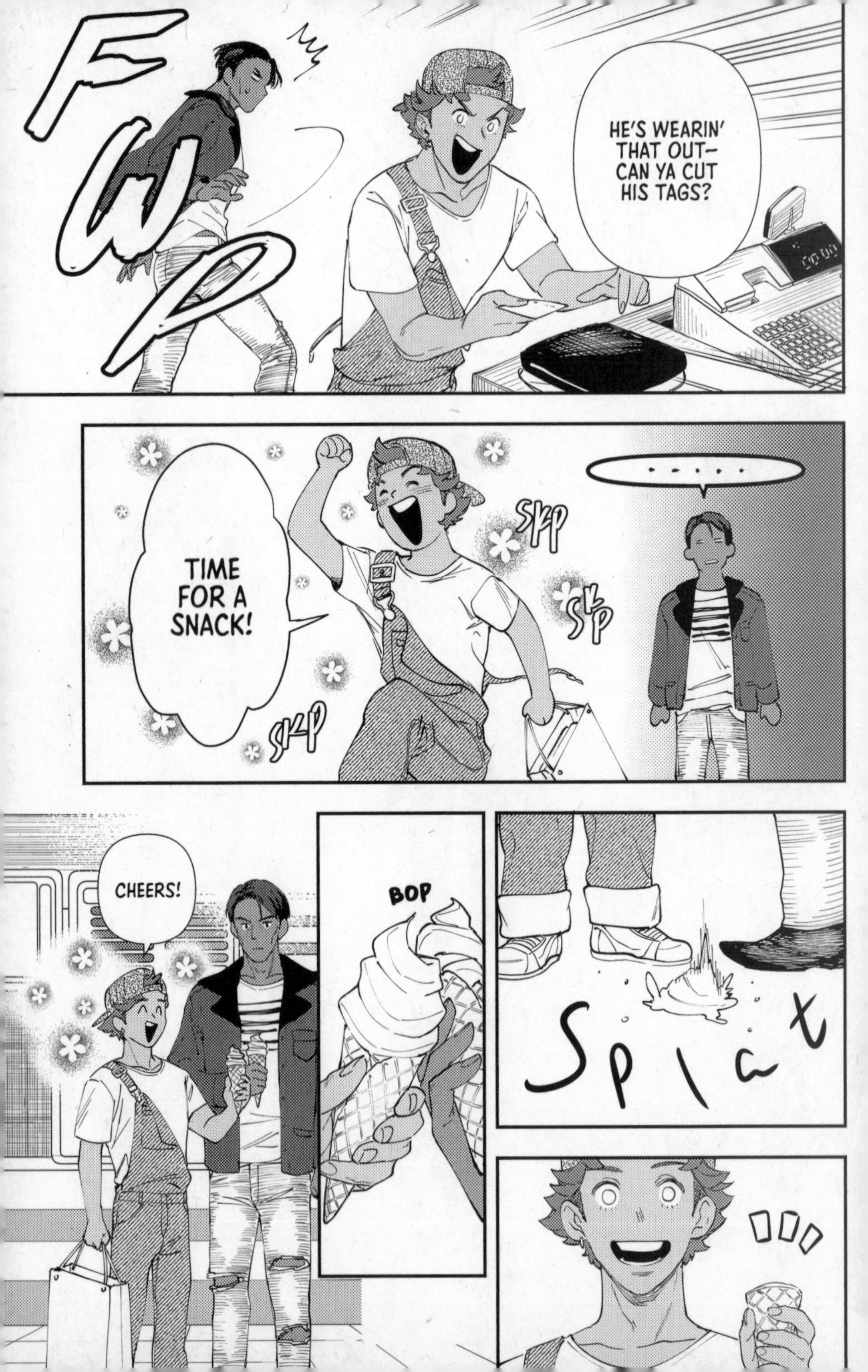
FWP
HE'S WEARIN' THAT OUT— CAN YA CUT HIS TAGS?
.....
SKP
SKP
TIME FOR A SNACK!
SKP
BOP
CHEERS!
Splat

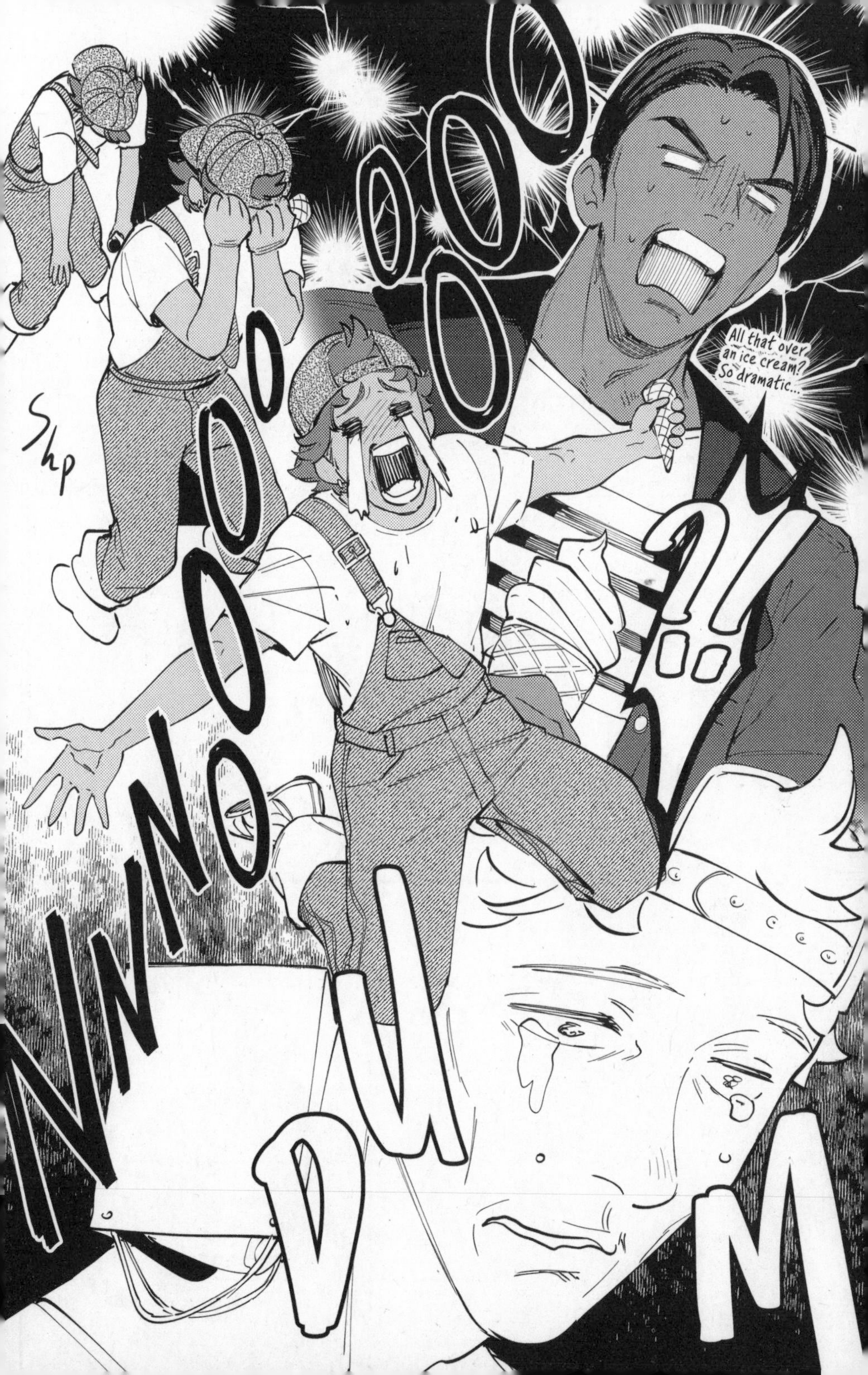
Shp
NNNNOOOOOOOOOOOOO
?!!
All that over an ice cream? So dramatic...
DUM

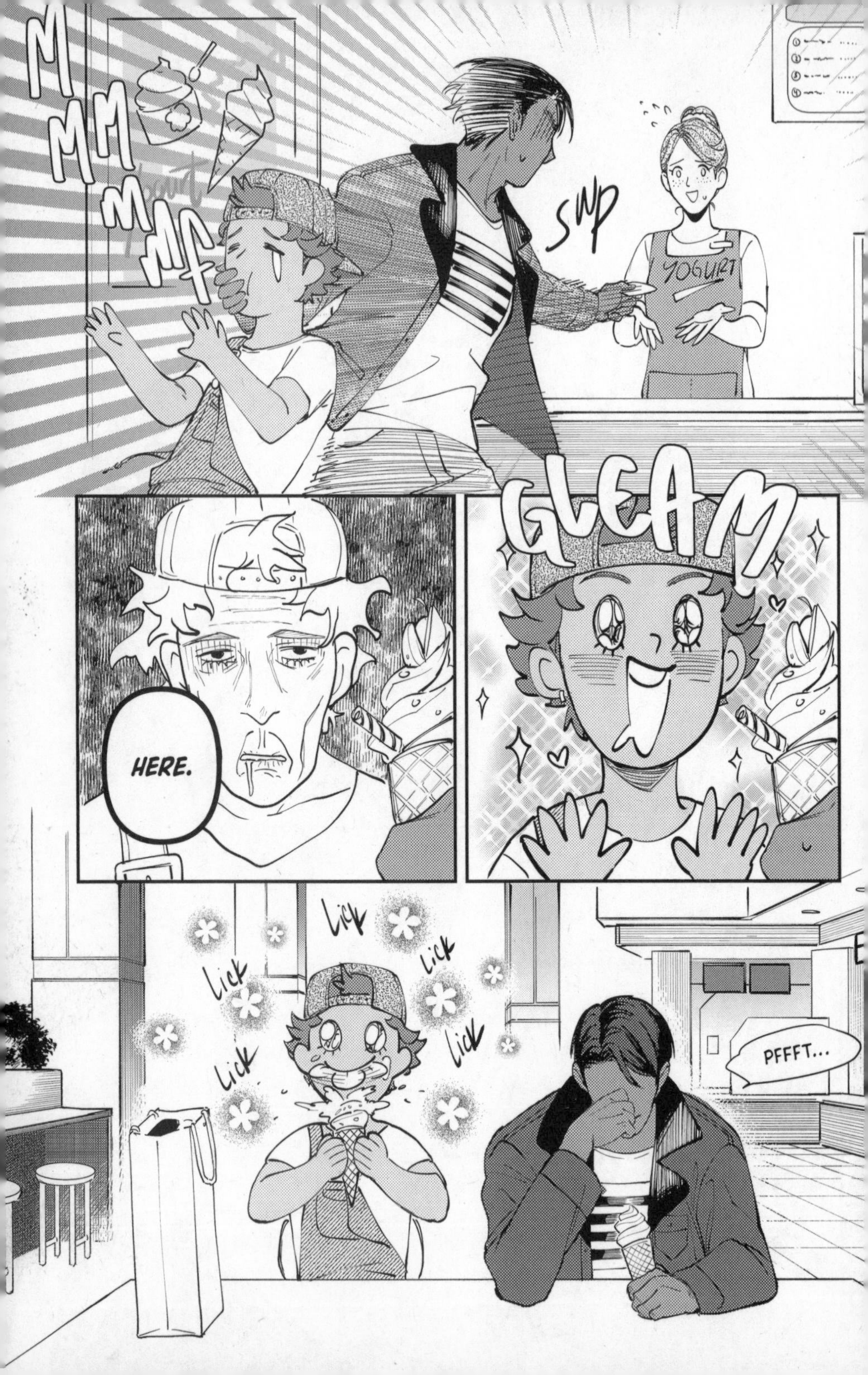
MMMMMF
SWP
YOGURT
HERE.
GLEAM
LICK
LICK
LICK
LICK
LICK
PFFFT...

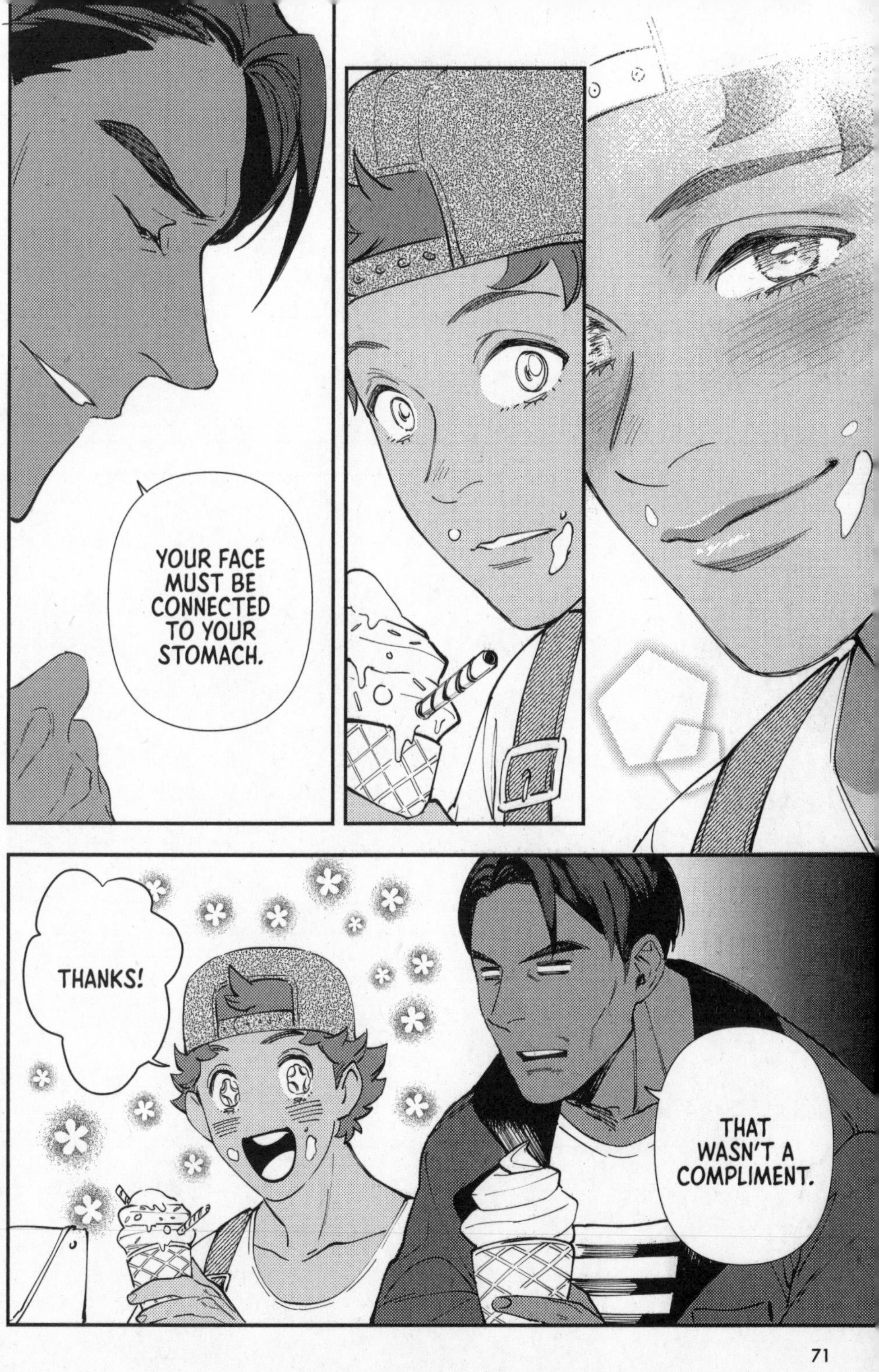
YOUR FACE MUST BE CONNECTED TO YOUR STOMACH.
THANKS!
THAT WASN'T A COMPLIMENT.

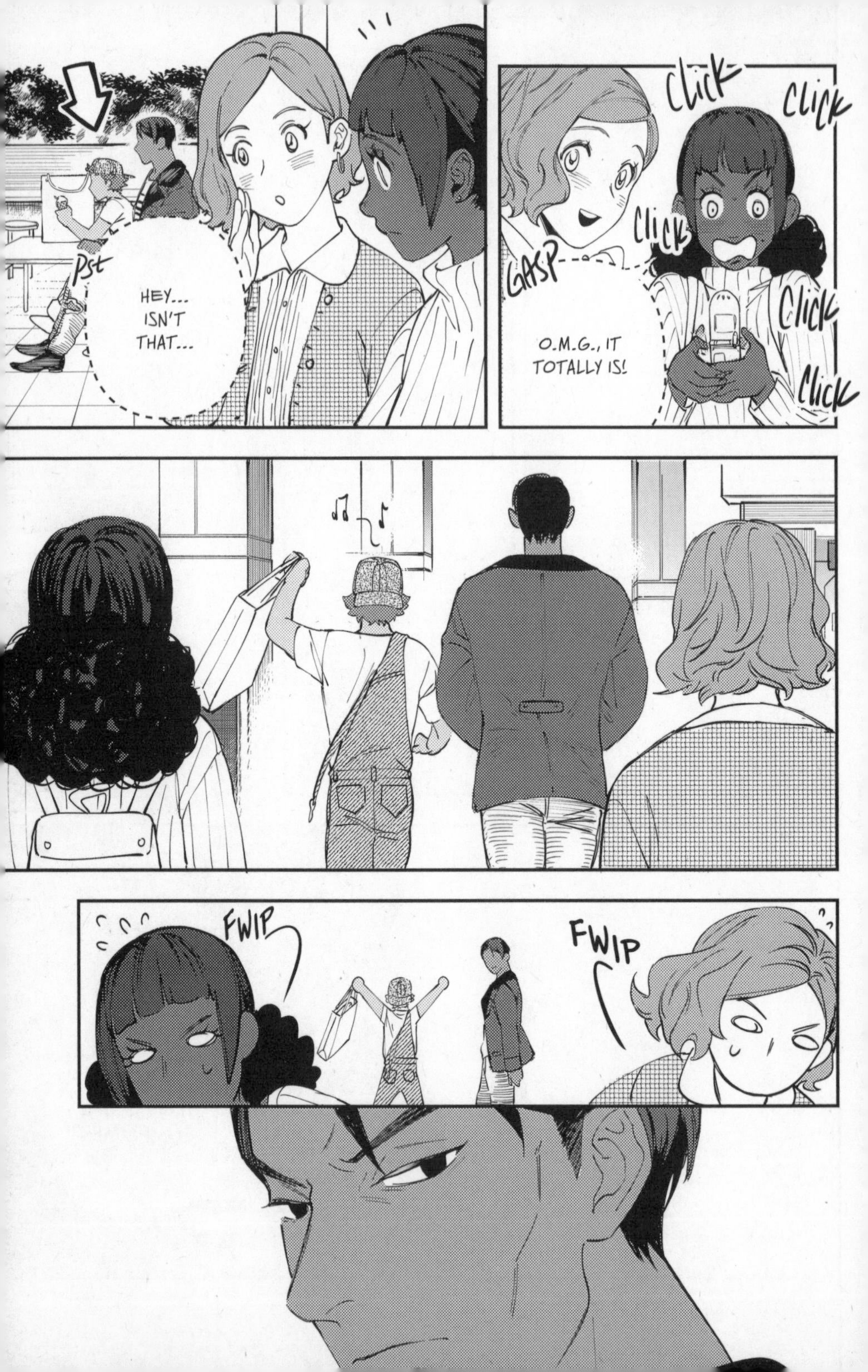
PST
HEY... ISN'T THAT...
CLICK
CLICK
CLICK
GASP
O.M.G., IT TOTALLY IS!
CLICK
CLICK
FWIP
FWIP

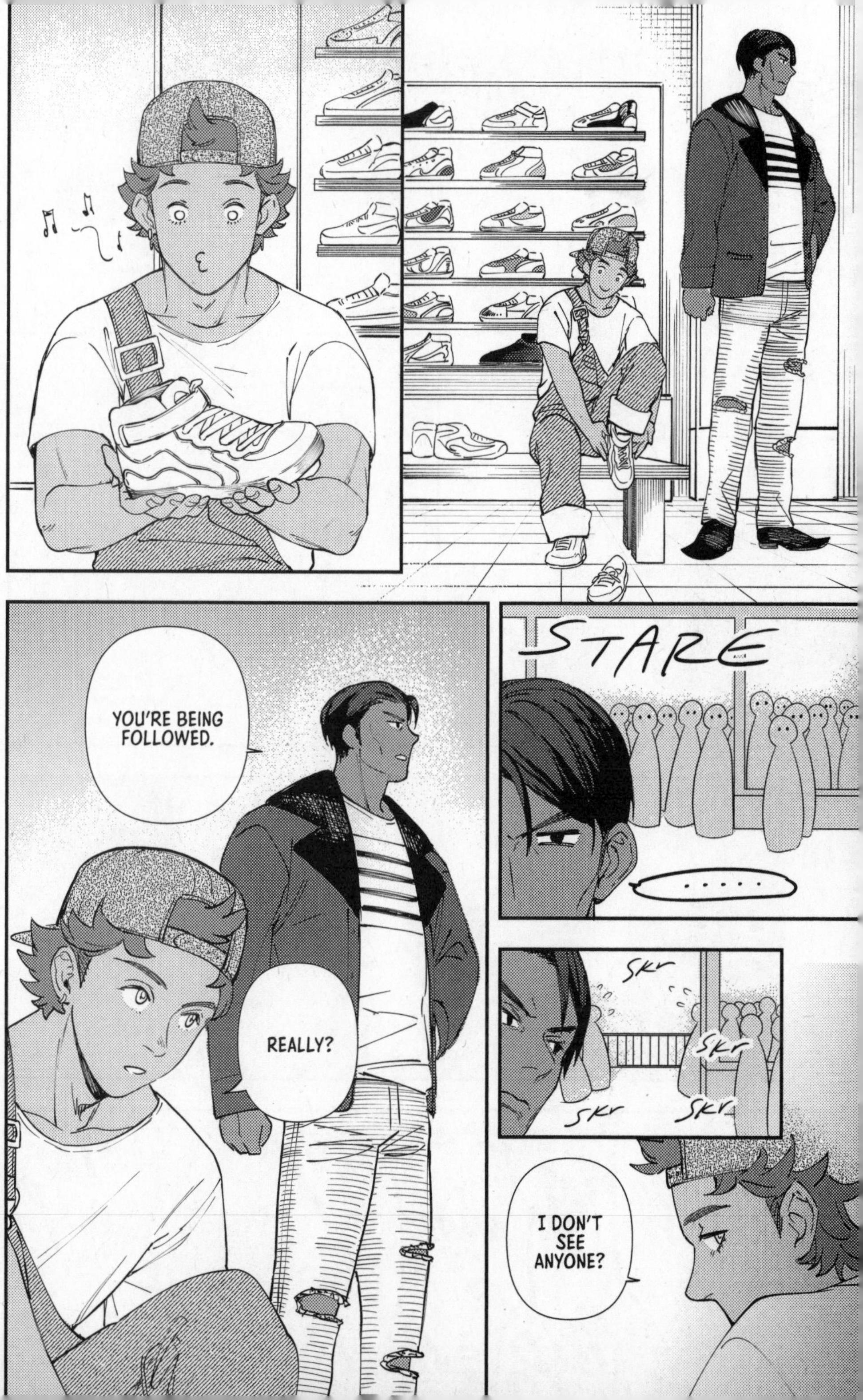
YOU'RE BEING FOLLOWED.
REALLY?
STARE
.....
SKR
SKR
SKR
SKR
I DON'T SEE ANYONE?

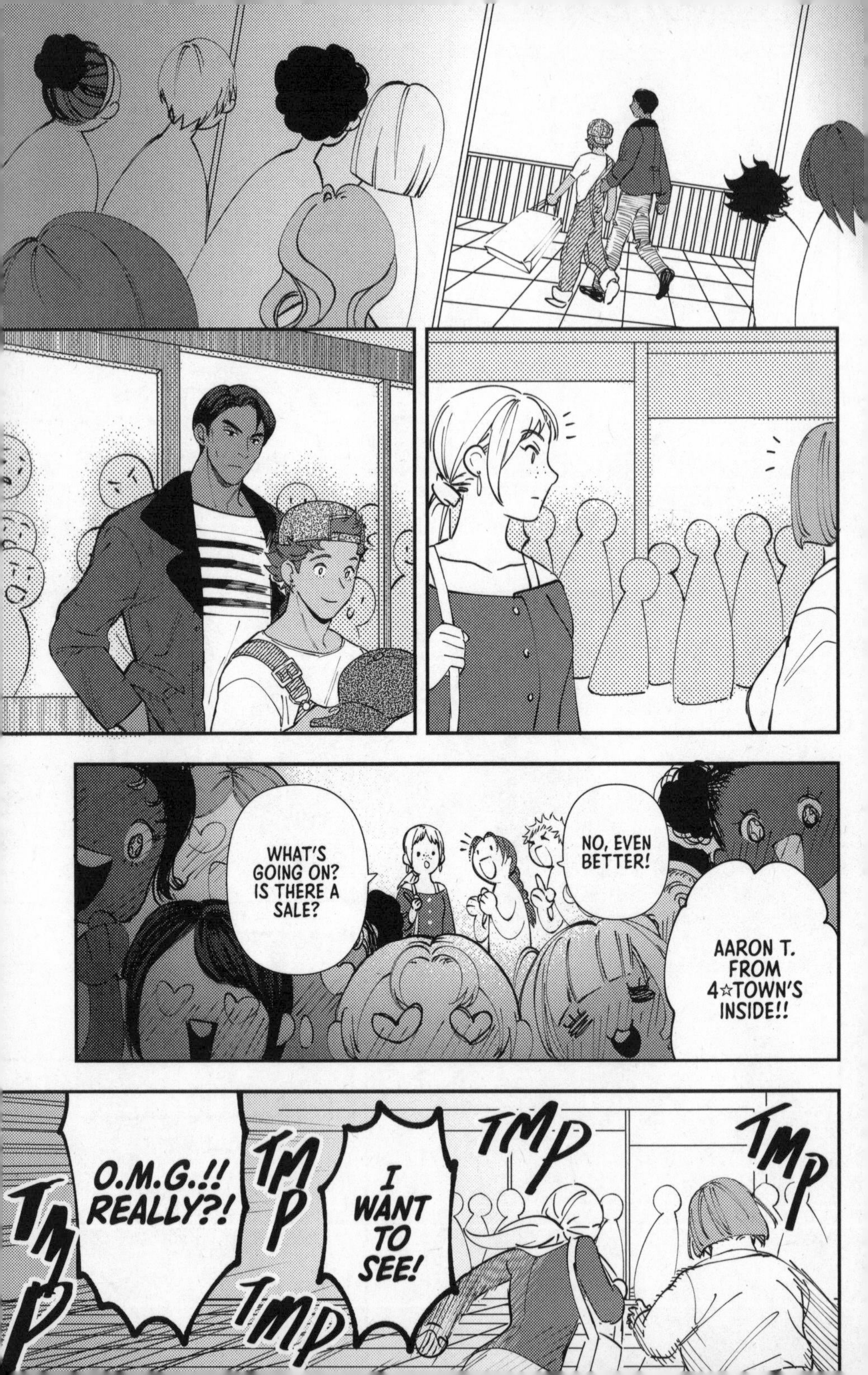
WHAT'S GOING ON? IS THERE A SALE?
NO, EVEN BETTER!
AARON T. FROM 4☆TOWN'S INSIDE!!
TMP
O.M.G.!! REALLY?!
TMP
I WANT TO SEE!
TMP
TMP
TMP

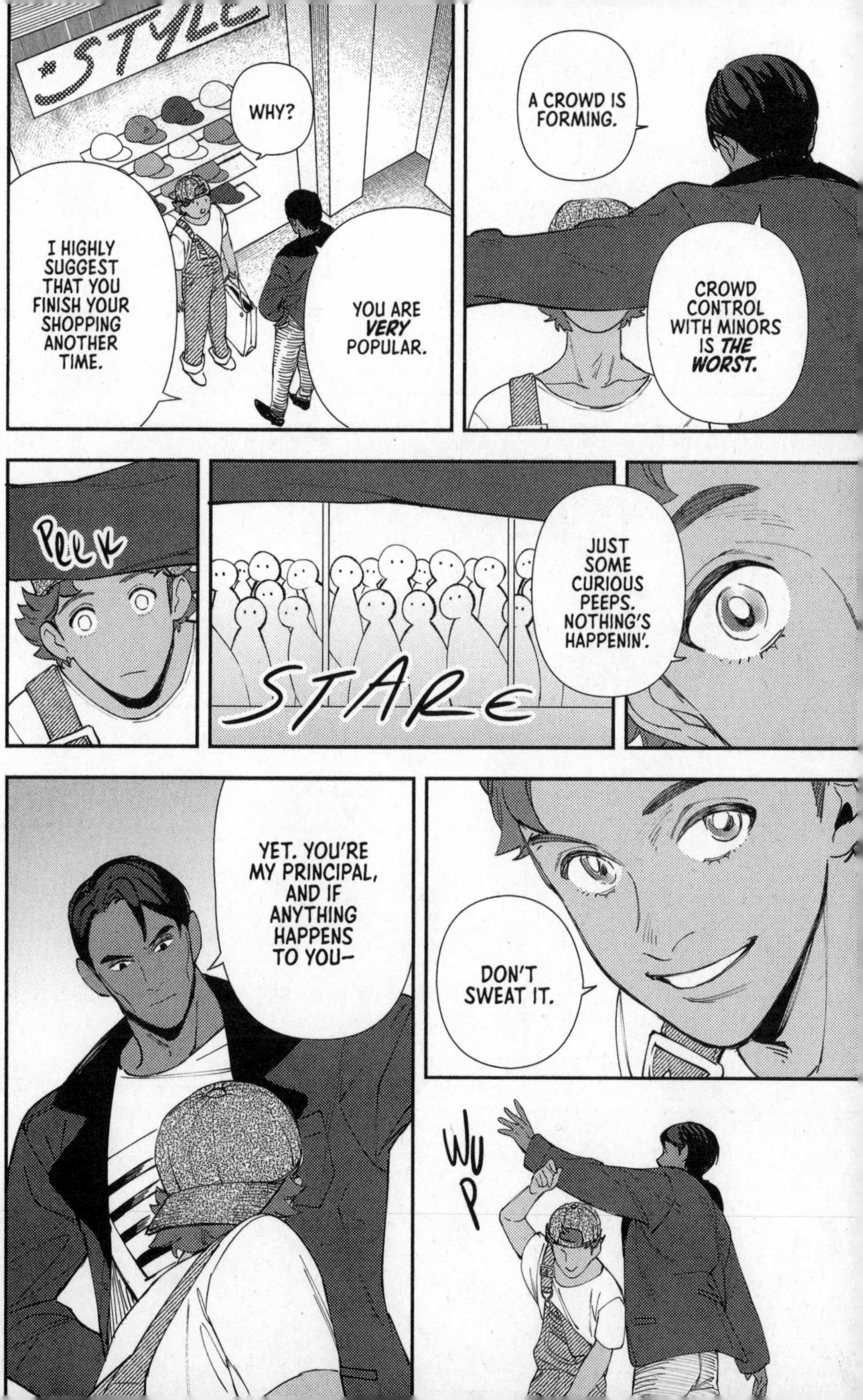
STYLE
WHY?
I HIGHLY SUGGEST THAT YOU FINISH YOUR SHOPPING ANOTHER TIME.
YOU ARE *VERY* POPULAR.
A CROWD IS FORMING.
CROWD CONTROL WITH MINORS IS ***THE WORST.***
PEEK
STARE
JUST SOME CURIOUS PEEPS. NOTHING'S HAPPENIN'.
YET. YOU'RE MY PRINCIPAL, AND IF ANYTHING HAPPENS TO YOU–
DON'T SWEAT IT.
WUP

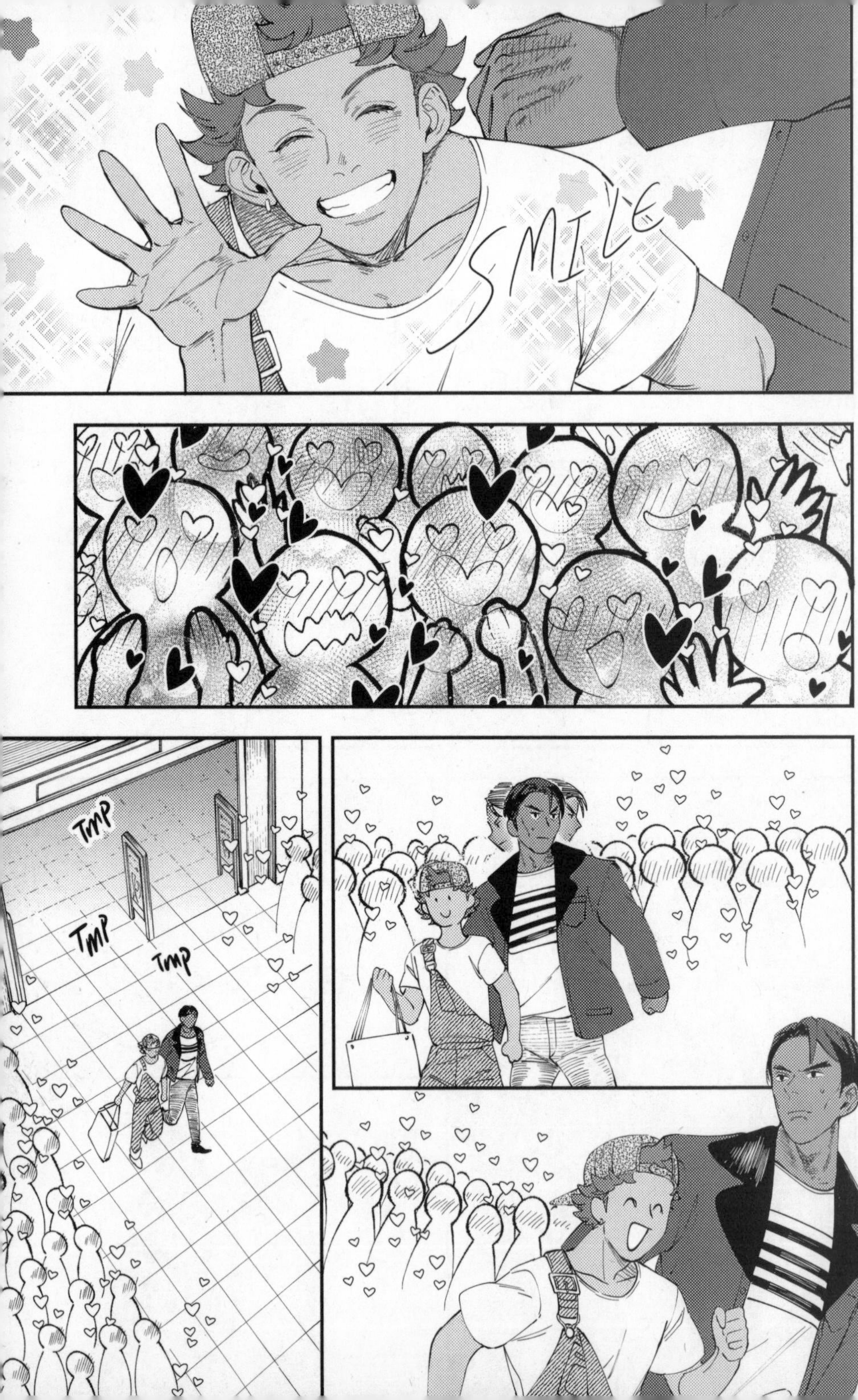
SMILE
TMP
TMP
TMP

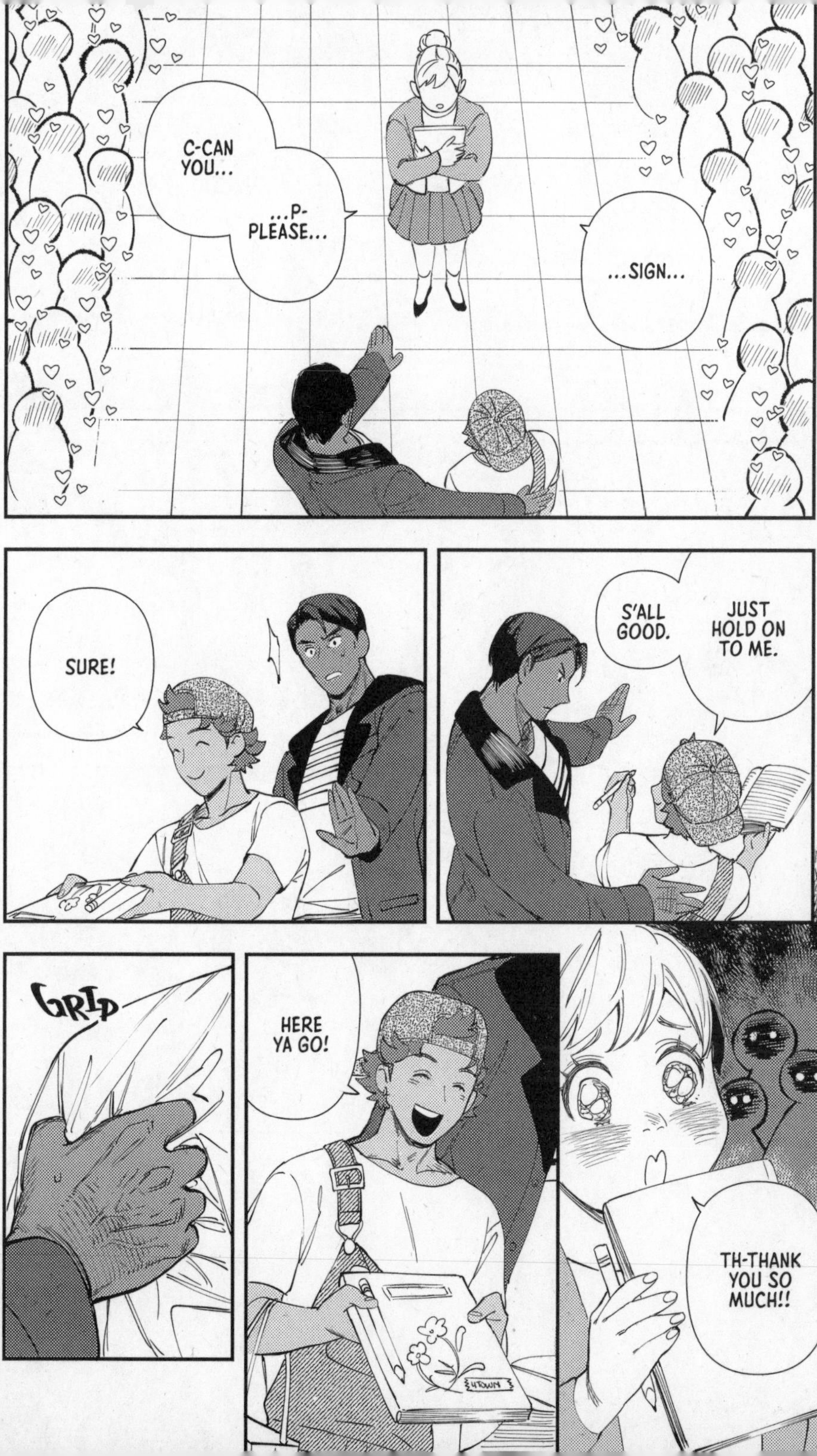
C-CAN YOU...
...P-PLEASE...
...SIGN...
SURE!
S'ALL GOOD.
JUST HOLD ON TO ME.
GRIP
HERE YA GO!
4TOWN
TH-THANK YOU SO MUCH!!

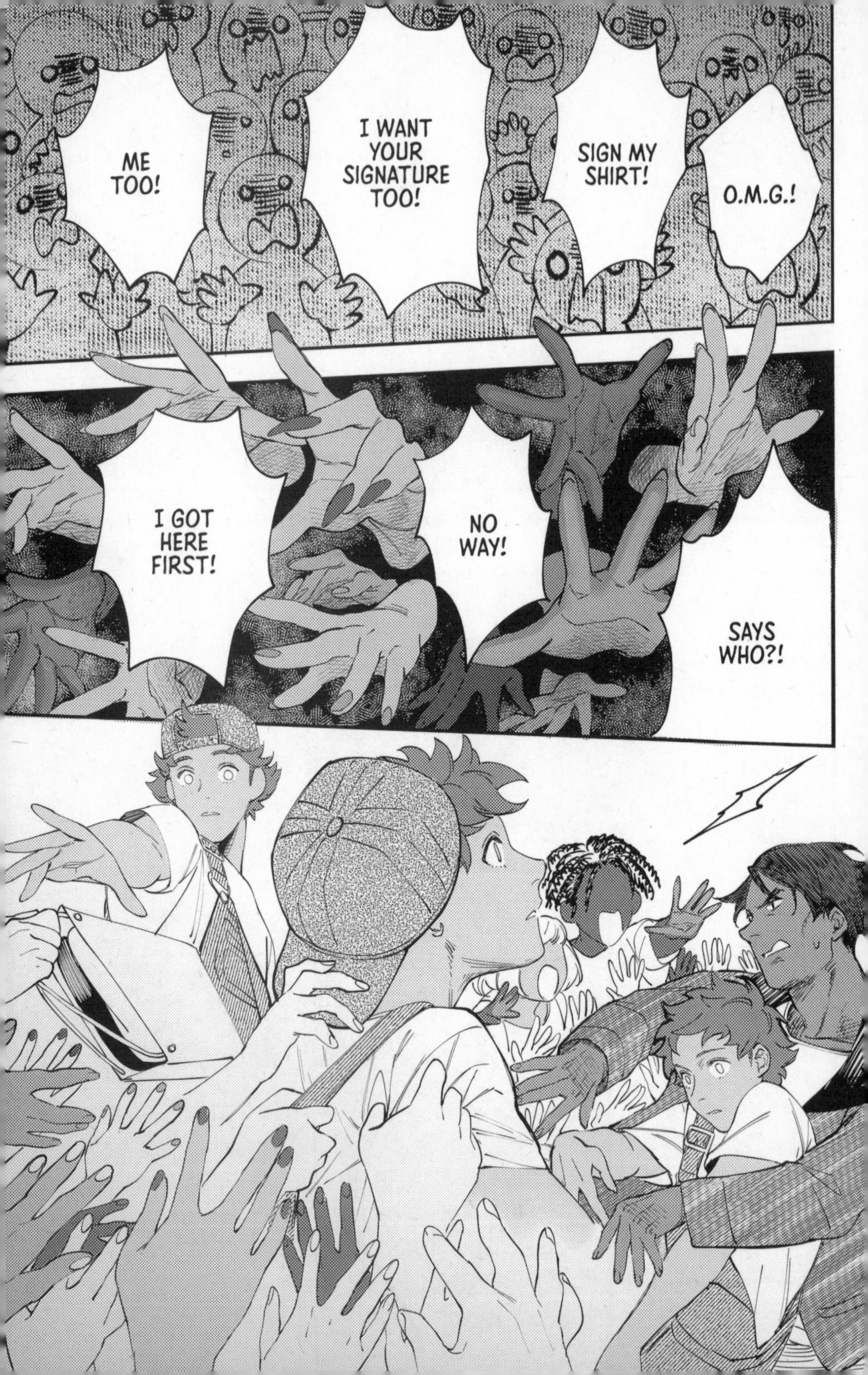
ME TOO!
I WANT YOUR SIGNATURE TOO!
SIGN MY SHIRT!
O.M.G.!
I GOT HERE FIRST!
NO WAY!
SAYS WHO?!

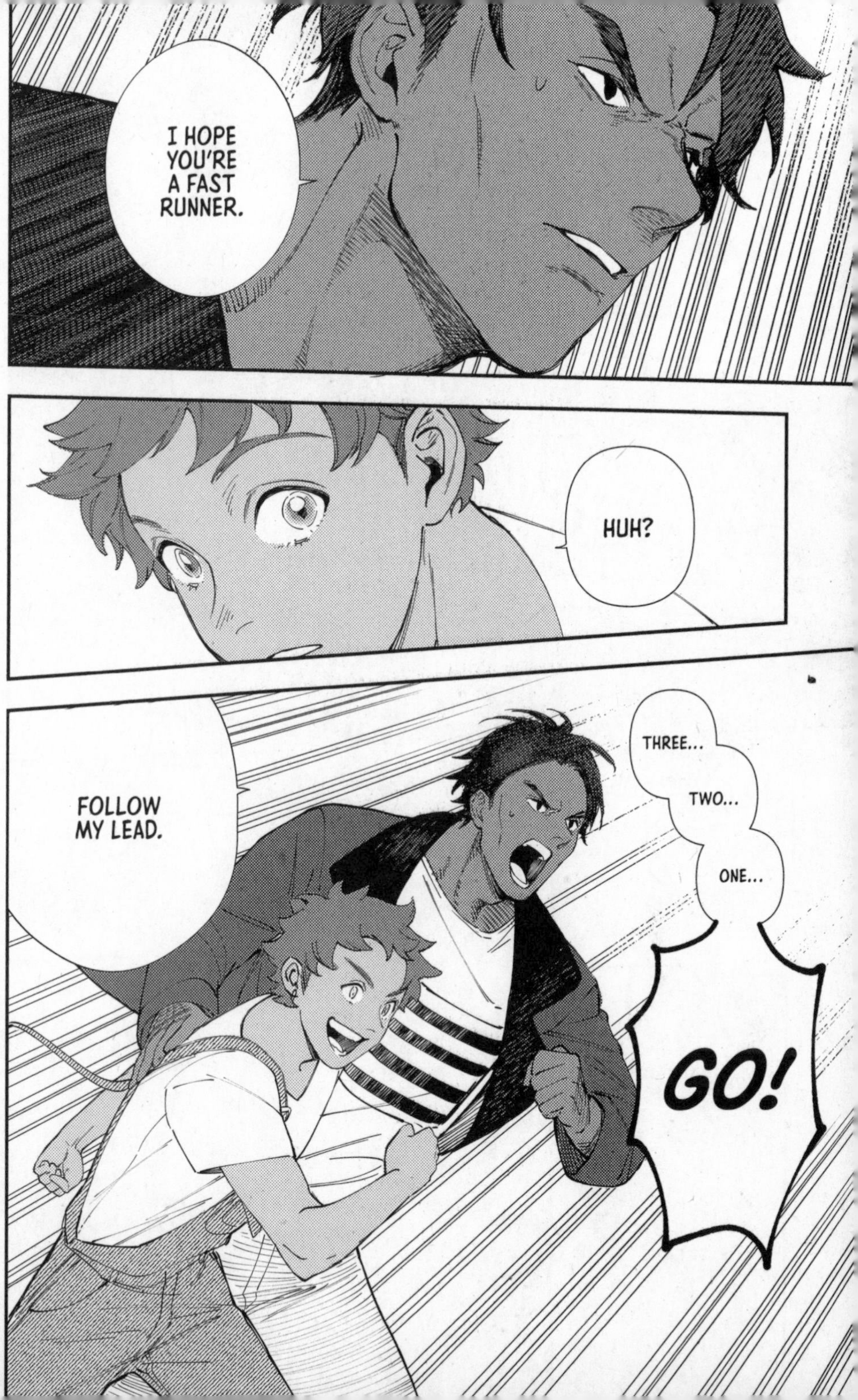
I HOPE YOU'RE A FAST RUNNER.
HUH?
FOLLOW MY LEAD.
THREE...
TWO...
ONE...
GO!

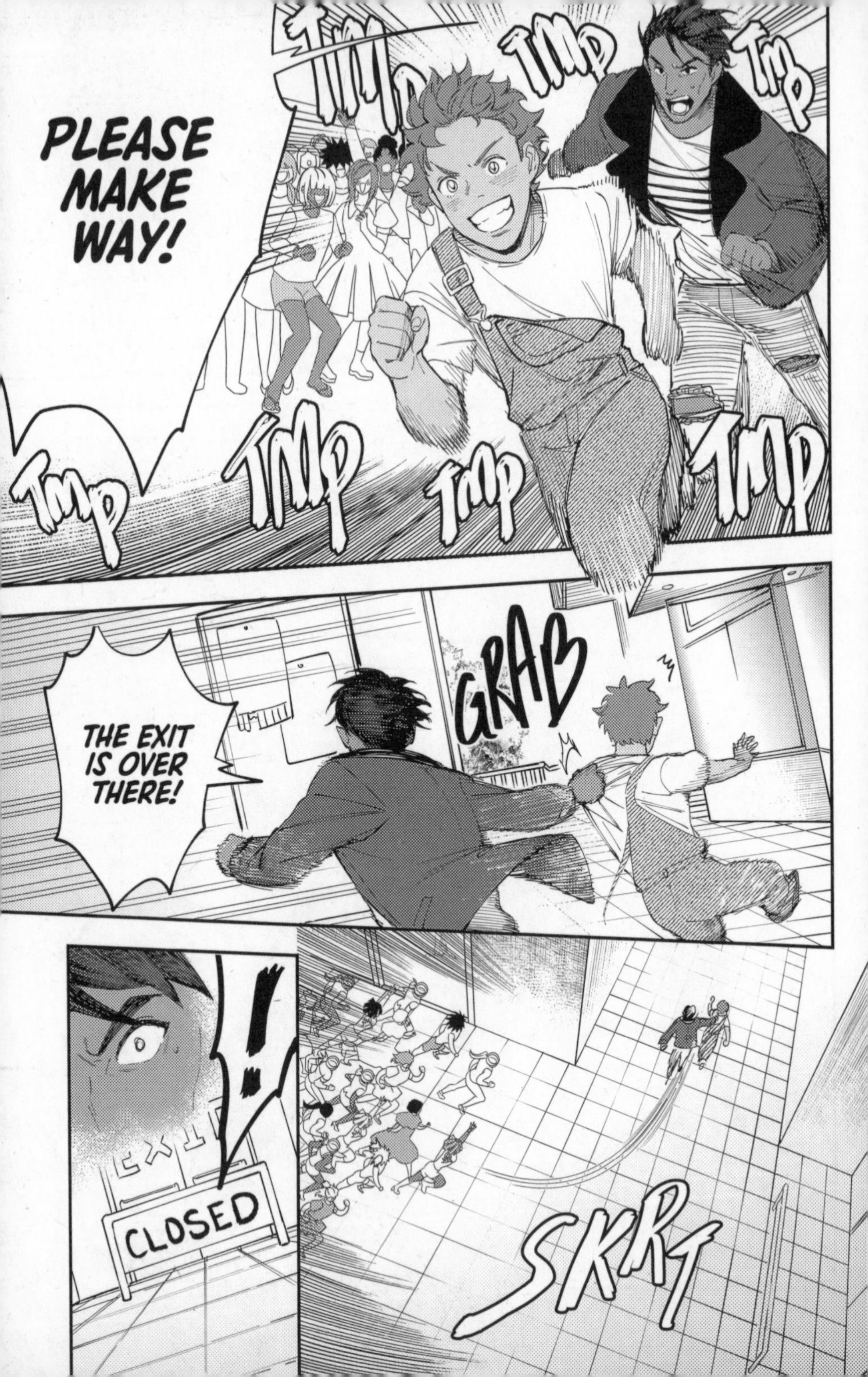
TMP
PLEASE MAKE WAY!
TMP
TMP
TMP
TMP
TMP
TMP
TMP
THE EXIT IS OVER THERE!
GRAB
!!
EXIT
CLOSED
SKRT

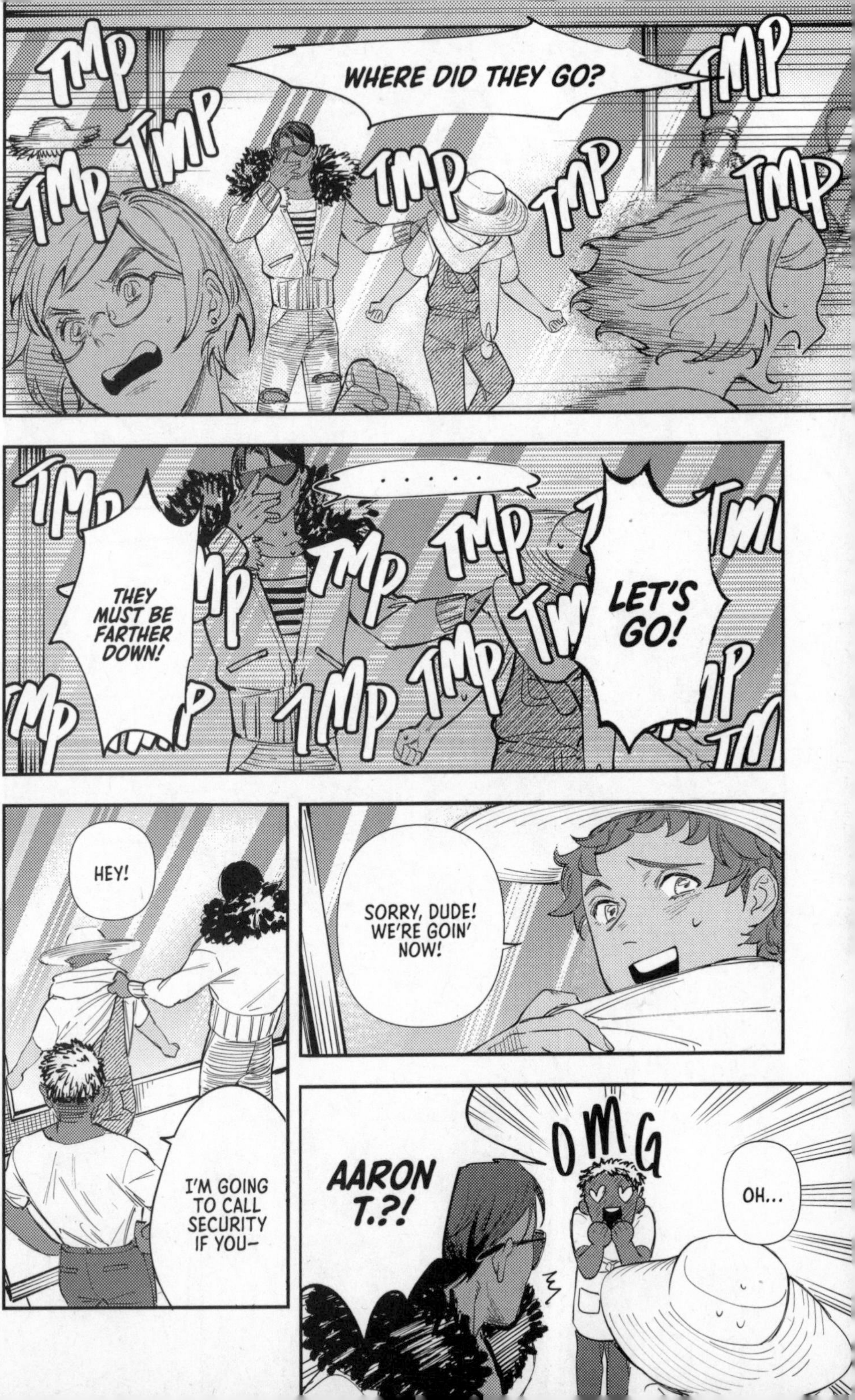
TMP TMP TMP TMP
WHERE DID THEY GO?
TMP TMP TMP TMP
THEY MUST BE FARTHER DOWN!
. . . . .
TMP TMP TMP TMP
LET'S GO!
HEY!
I'M GOING TO CALL SECURITY IF YOU–
SORRY, DUDE! WE'RE GOIN' NOW!
AARON T.?!
OMG
OH...

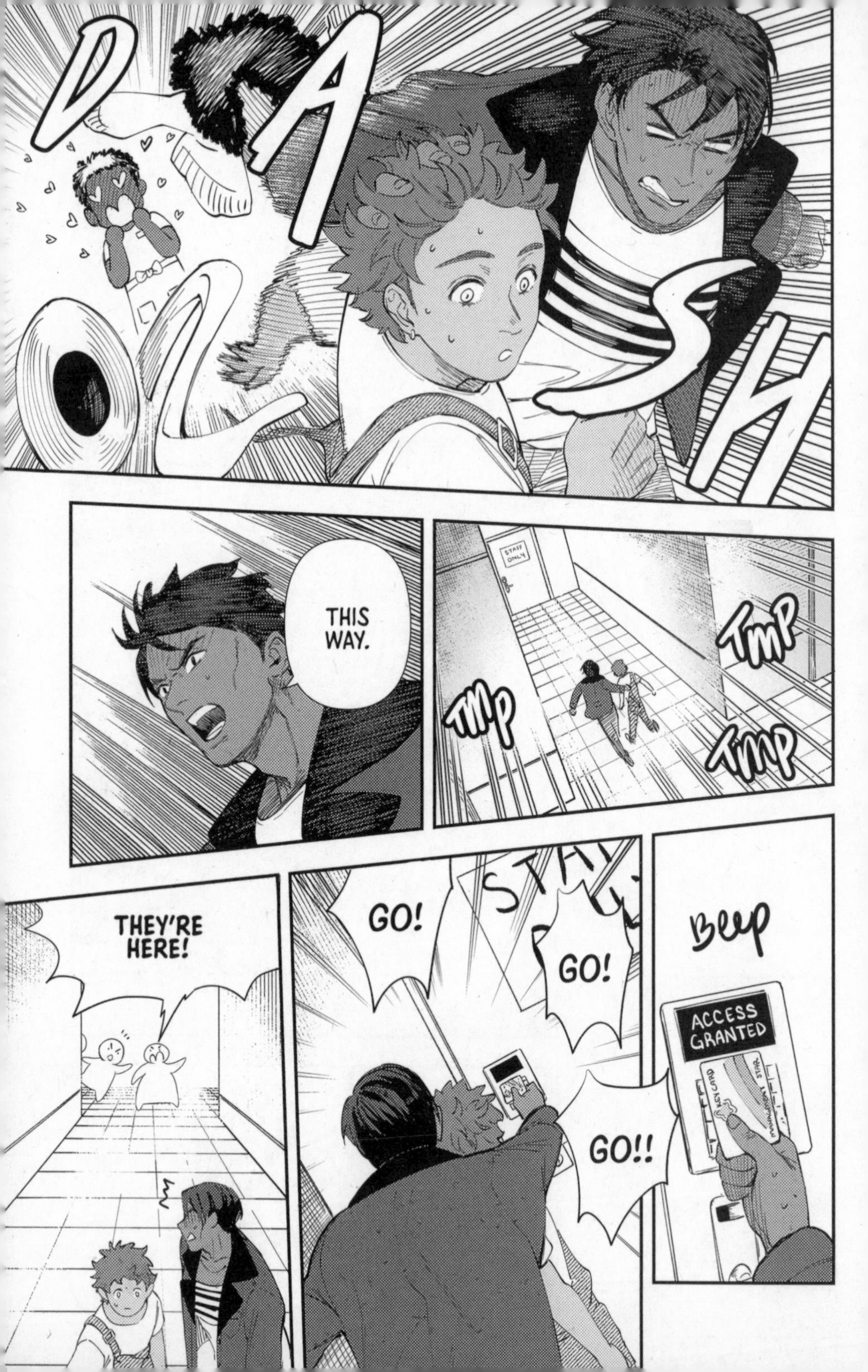
DASH
THIS WAY.
STAFF ONLY
TMP
TMP
TMP
THEY'RE HERE!
GO!
GO!
GO!!
Beep
ACCESS GRANTED

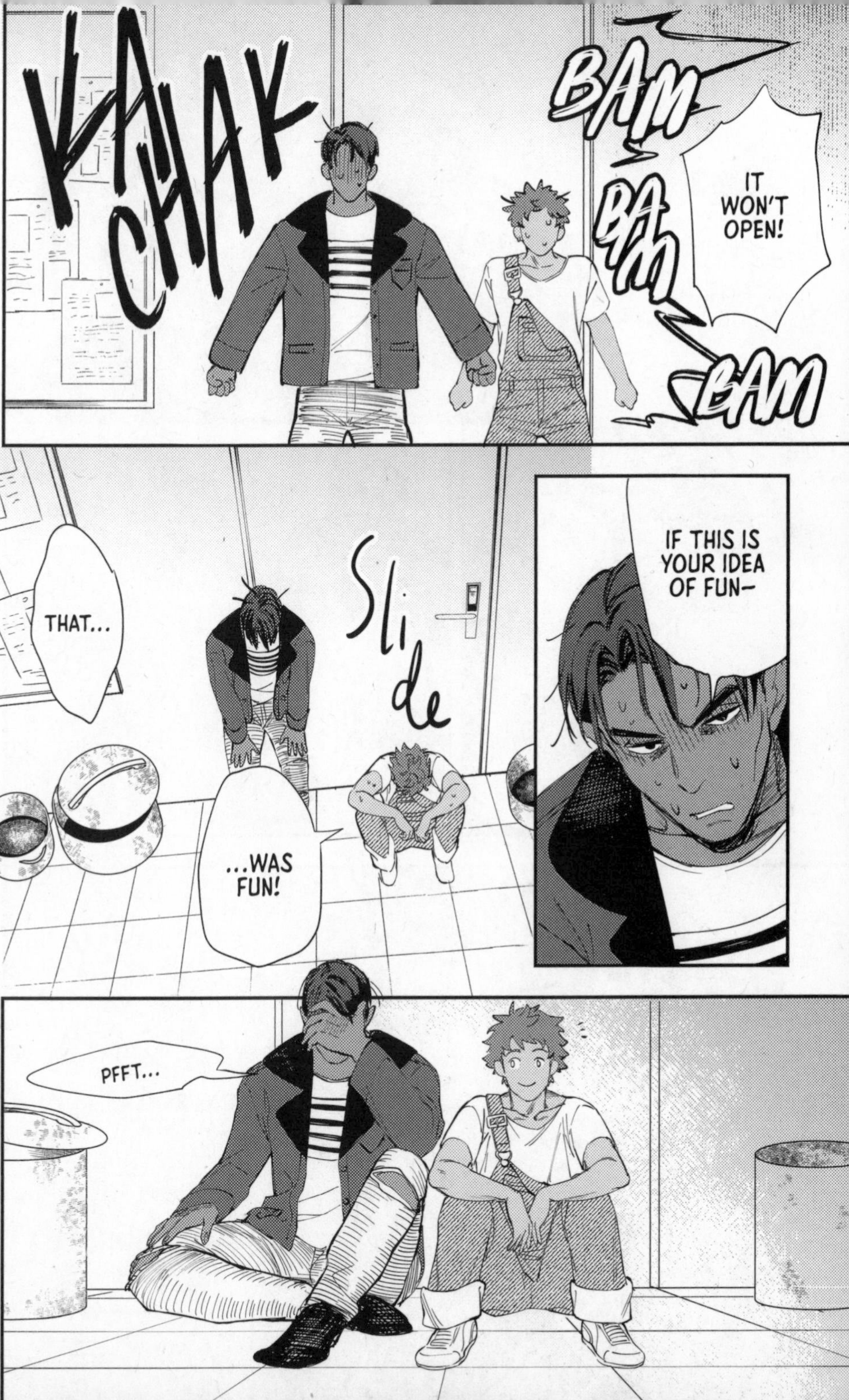
KA CHAK
BAM
BAM
IT WON'T OPEN!
BAM
THAT...
Slide
...WAS FUN!
IF THIS IS YOUR IDEA OF FUN—
PFFT...

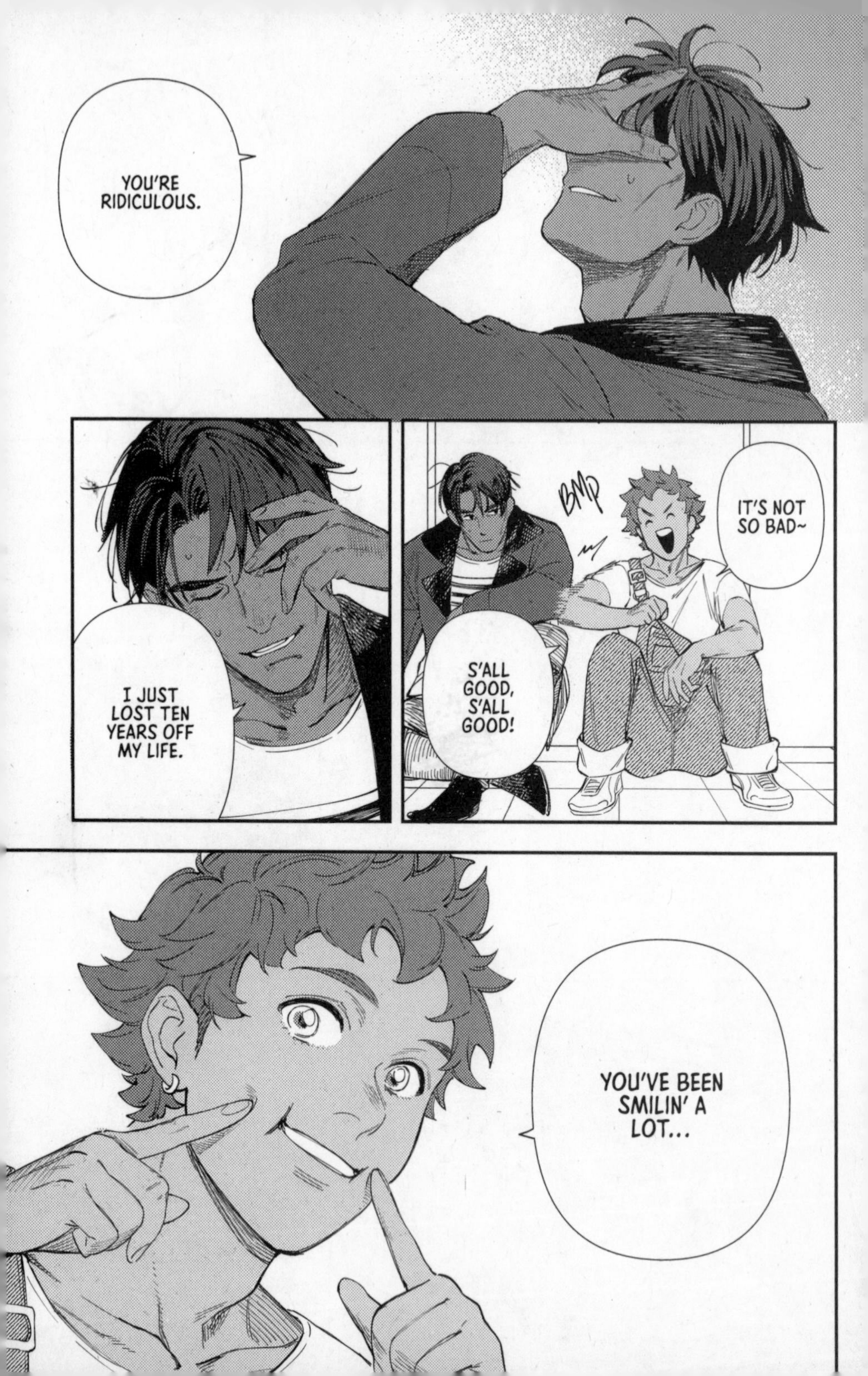
YOU'RE RIDICULOUS.
I JUST LOST TEN YEARS OFF MY LIFE.
BMP
IT'S NOT SO BAD~
S'ALL GOOD, S'ALL GOOD!
YOU'VE BEEN SMILIN' A LOT...

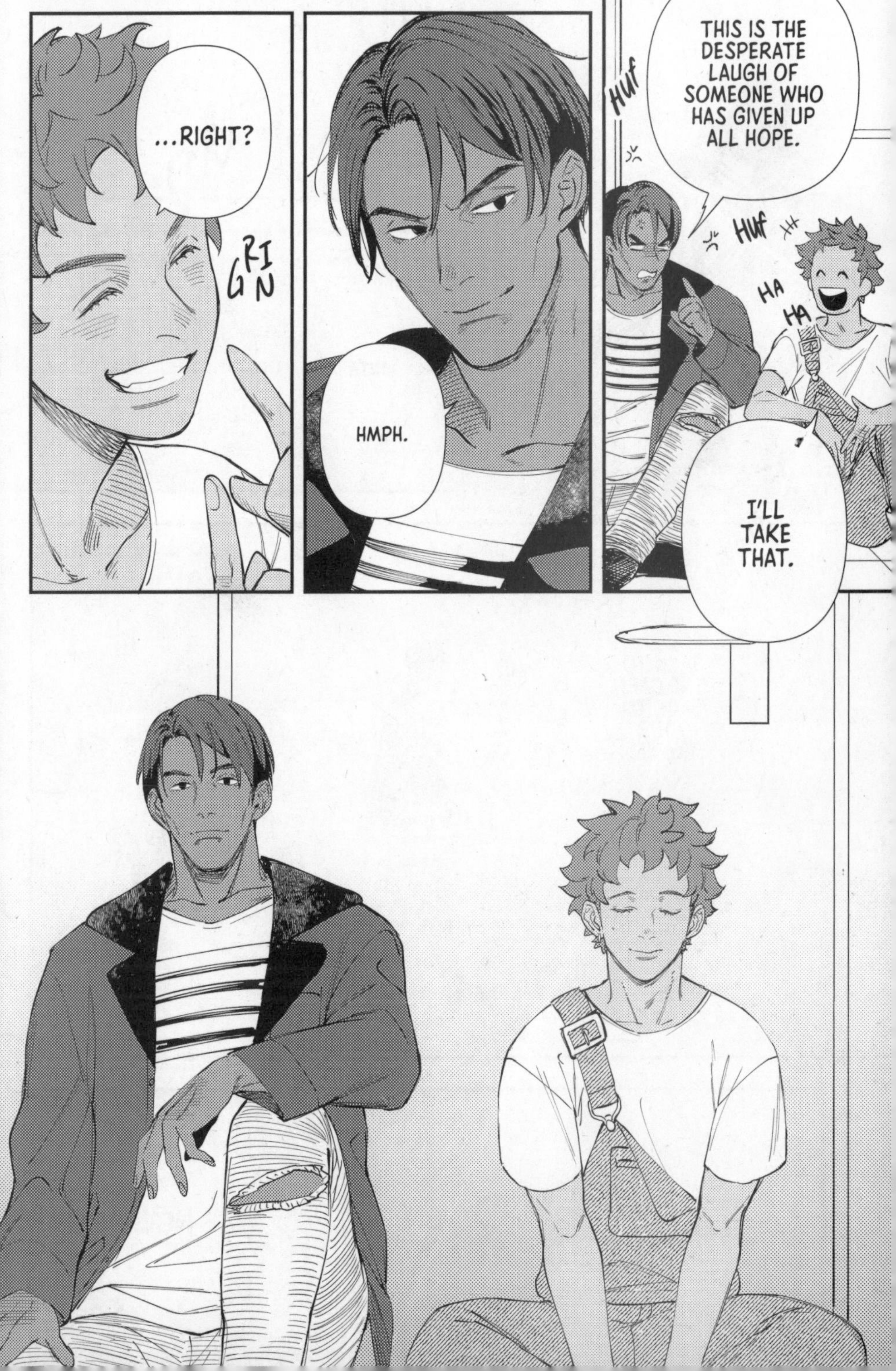
...RIGHT?
GRIN
HMPH.
HUF
THIS IS THE DESPERATE LAUGH OF SOMEONE WHO HAS GIVEN UP ALL HOPE.
HUF
HA HA
I'LL TAKE THAT.

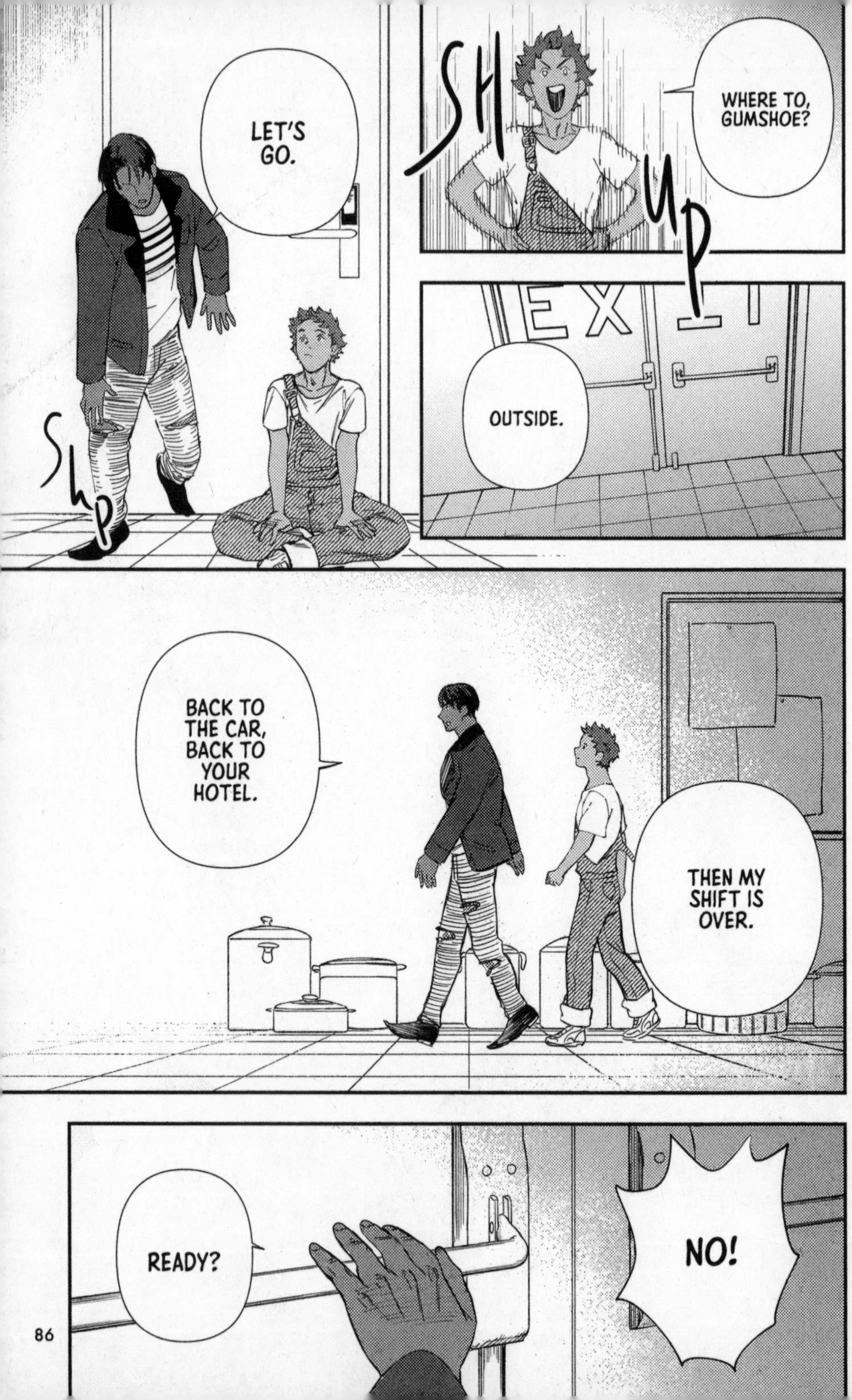
WHERE TO, GUMSHOE?
SHUP
LET'S GO.
SHP
OUTSIDE.
EXI
BACK TO THE CAR, BACK TO YOUR HOTEL.
THEN MY SHIFT IS OVER.
READY?
NO!

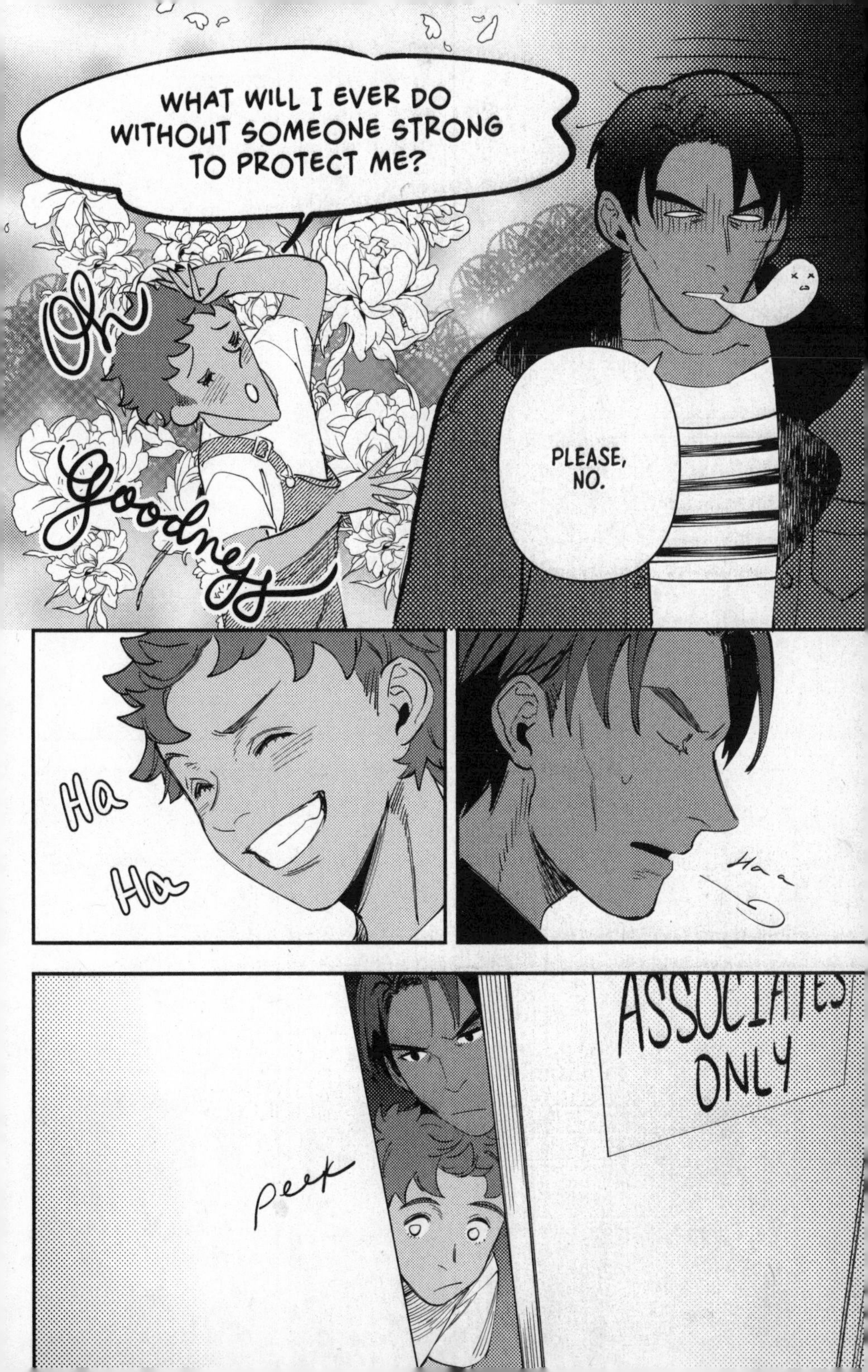
WHAT WILL I EVER DO WITHOUT SOMEONE STRONG TO PROTECT ME?
Oh
Goodness
PLEASE, NO.
Ha
Ha
Haa
ASSOCIATES ONLY
peek

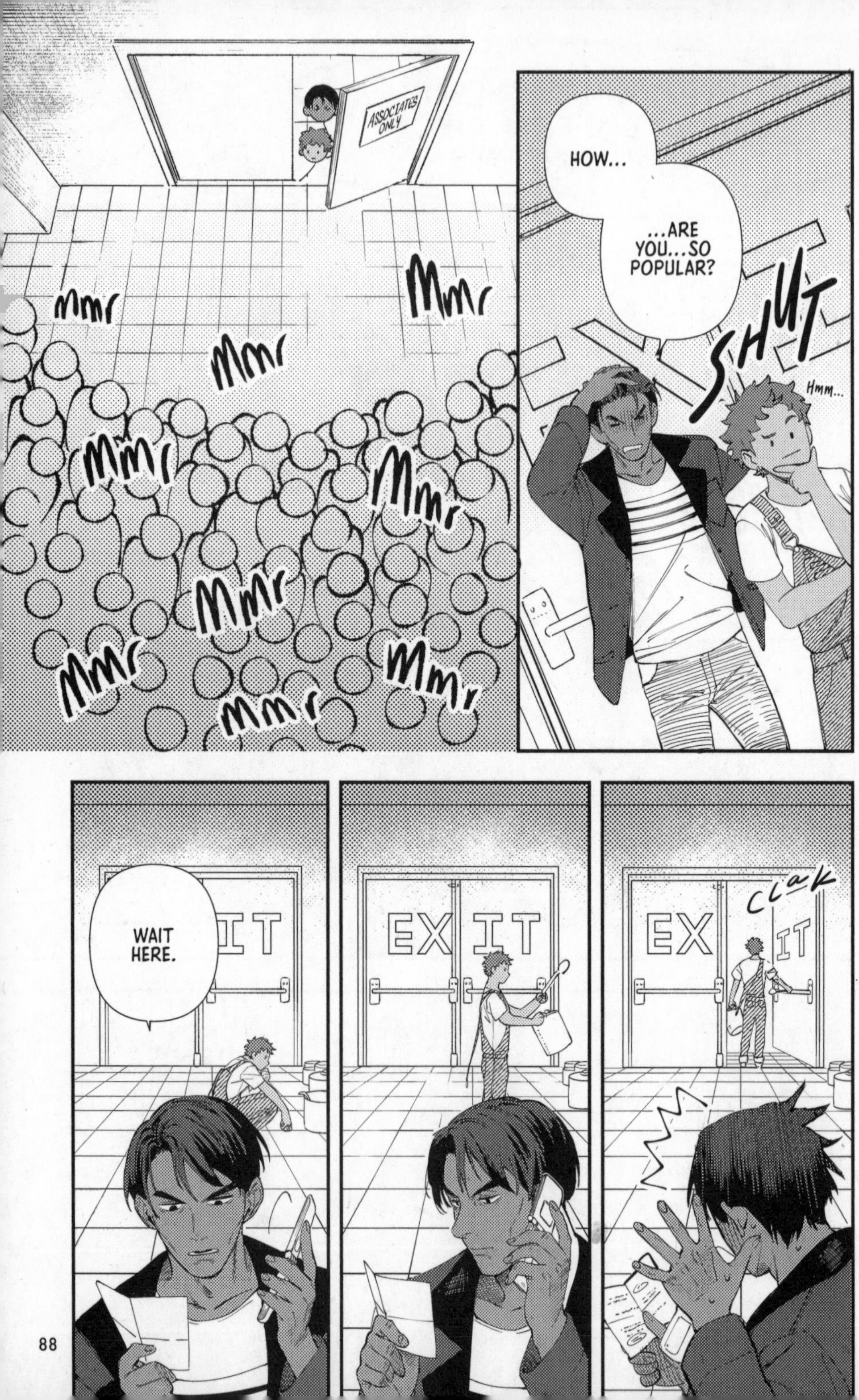
ASSOCIATES ONLY
Mmr
Mmr
Mmr
Mmr
Mmr
Mmr
Mmr
Mmr
Mmr
HOW...
...ARE YOU...SO POPULAR?
SHUT
Hmm...
WAIT HERE.
EXIT
EX IT
CLAK

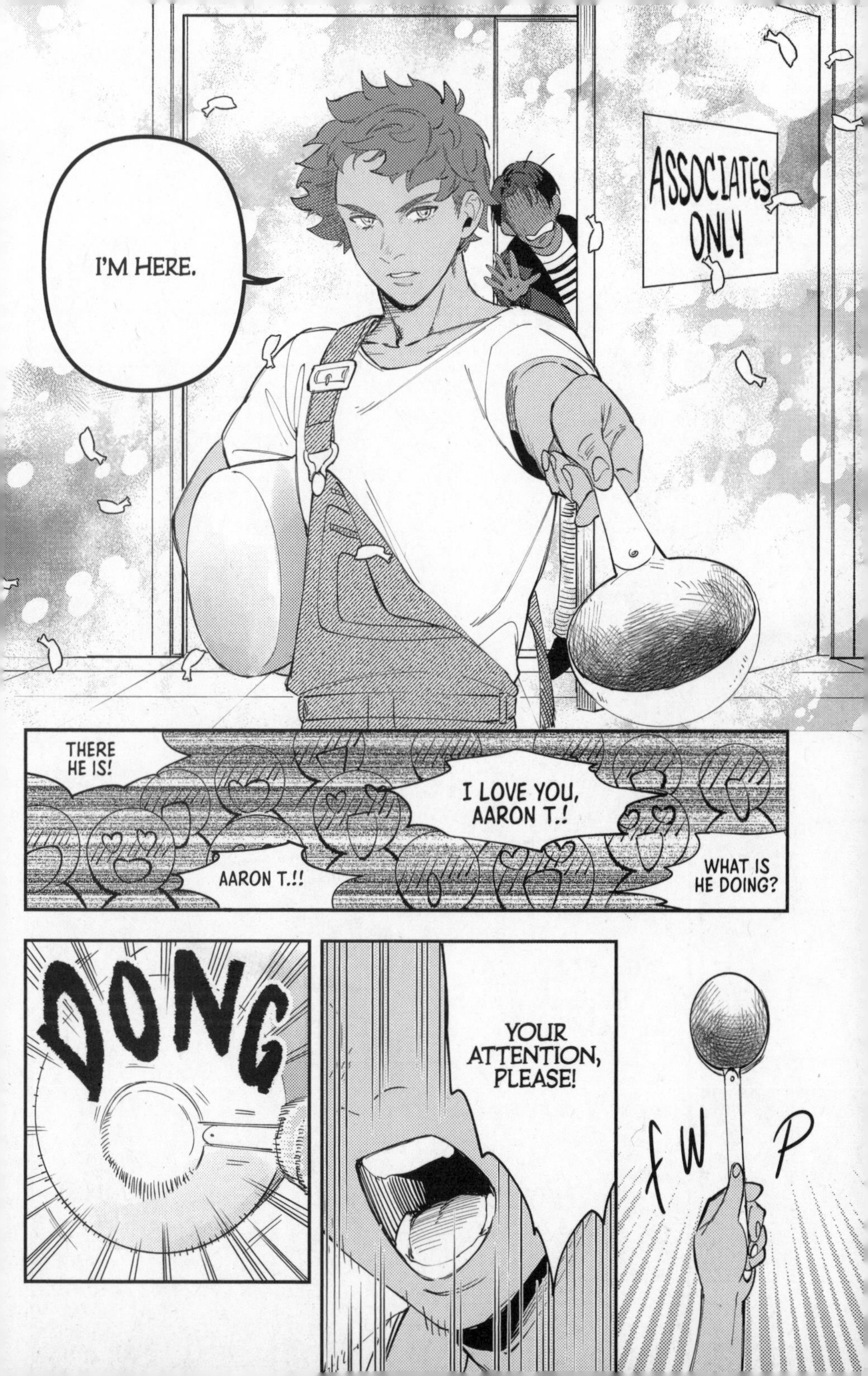
I'M HERE.
ASSOCIATES ONLY
THERE HE IS!
I LOVE YOU, AARON T.!
AARON T.!!
WHAT IS HE DOING?
DONG
YOUR ATTENTION, PLEASE!
FWP

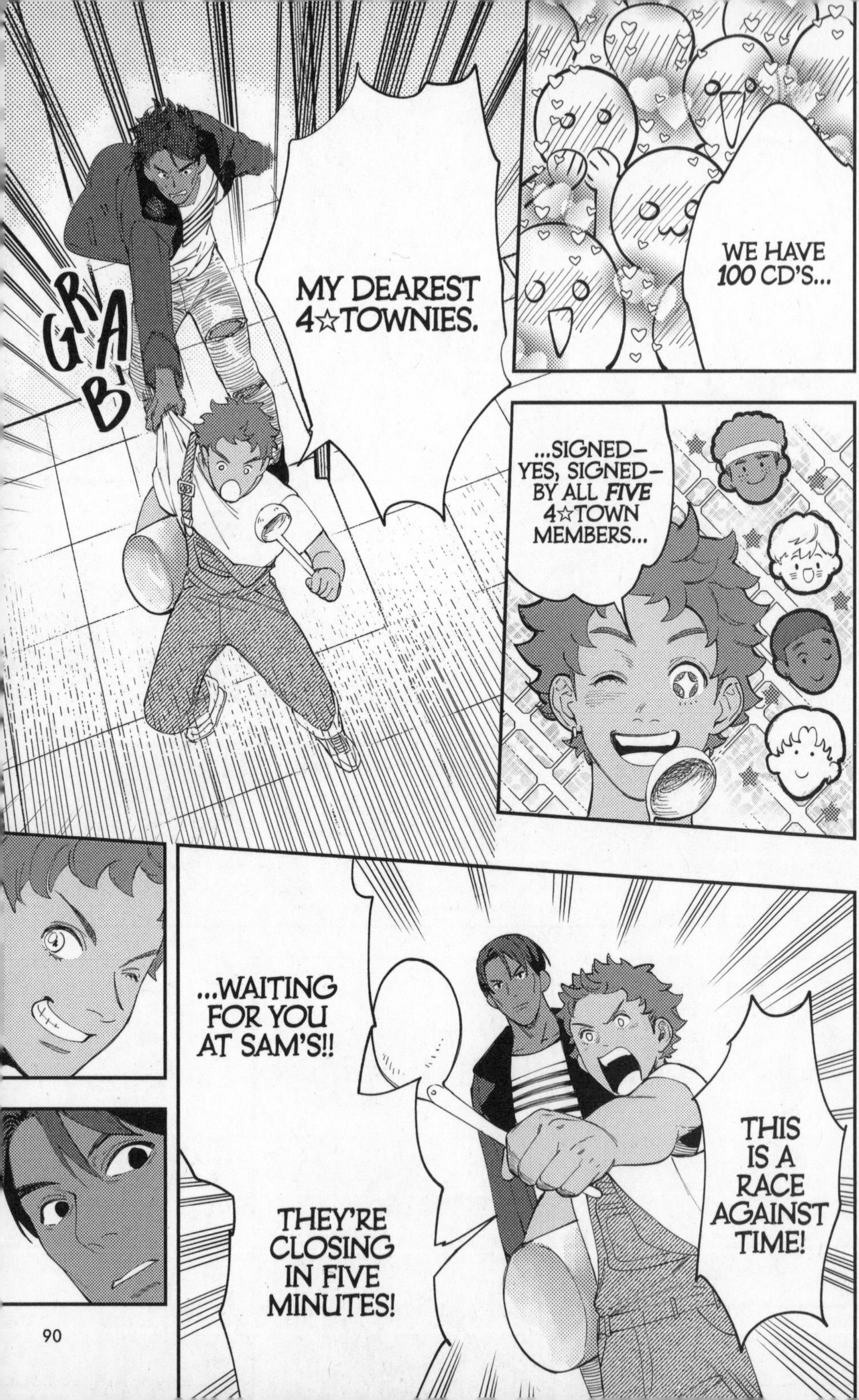
GRAB
MY DEAREST 4☆TOWNIES.
WE HAVE 100 CD'S...
...SIGNED—YES, SIGNED—BY ALL FIVE 4☆TOWN MEMBERS...
...WAITING FOR YOU AT SAM'S!!
THEY'RE CLOSING IN FIVE MINUTES!
THIS IS A RACE AGAINST TIME!

GO FORTH!!

CHAAA-AAAARRR-RRRGE!!

RAAAAA AAA A

Mmr

SIGNED BY ALL OF THEM?

REALLY?

Mmr

O.M.G.!

SKILE

DASH

FIVE MINUTES!!

COAST CLEAR

WHY...

...DIDN'T YOU DO THAT SOONER?

Planned Reunion

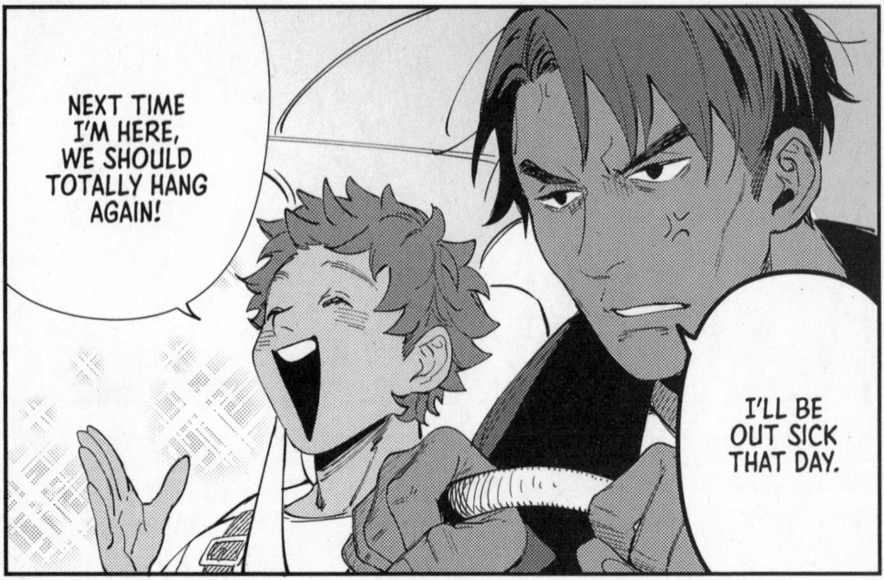
NEXT TIME I'M HERE, WE SHOULD TOTALLY HANG AGAIN!
I'LL BE OUT SICK THAT DAY.

After His Shift

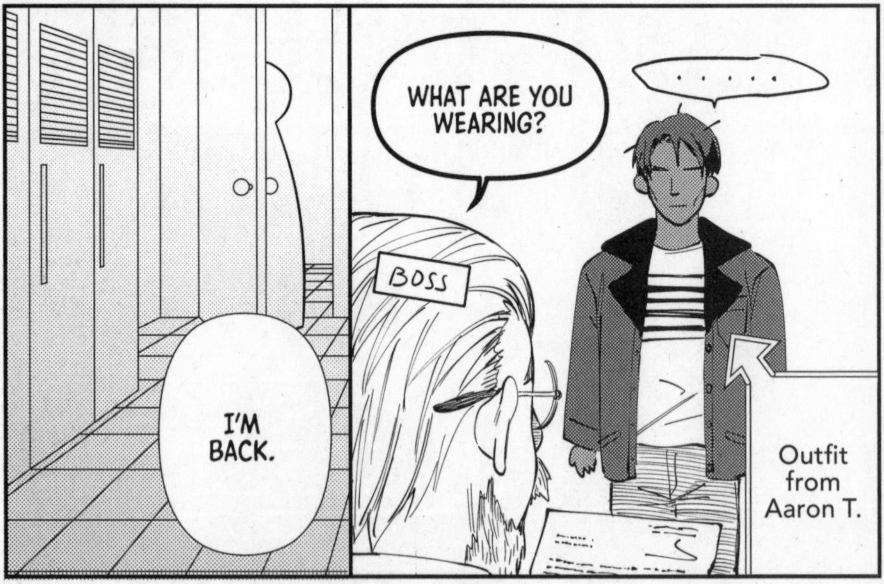
I'M BACK.
WHAT ARE YOU WEARING?
. . . . .
BOSS
Outfit from Aaron T.

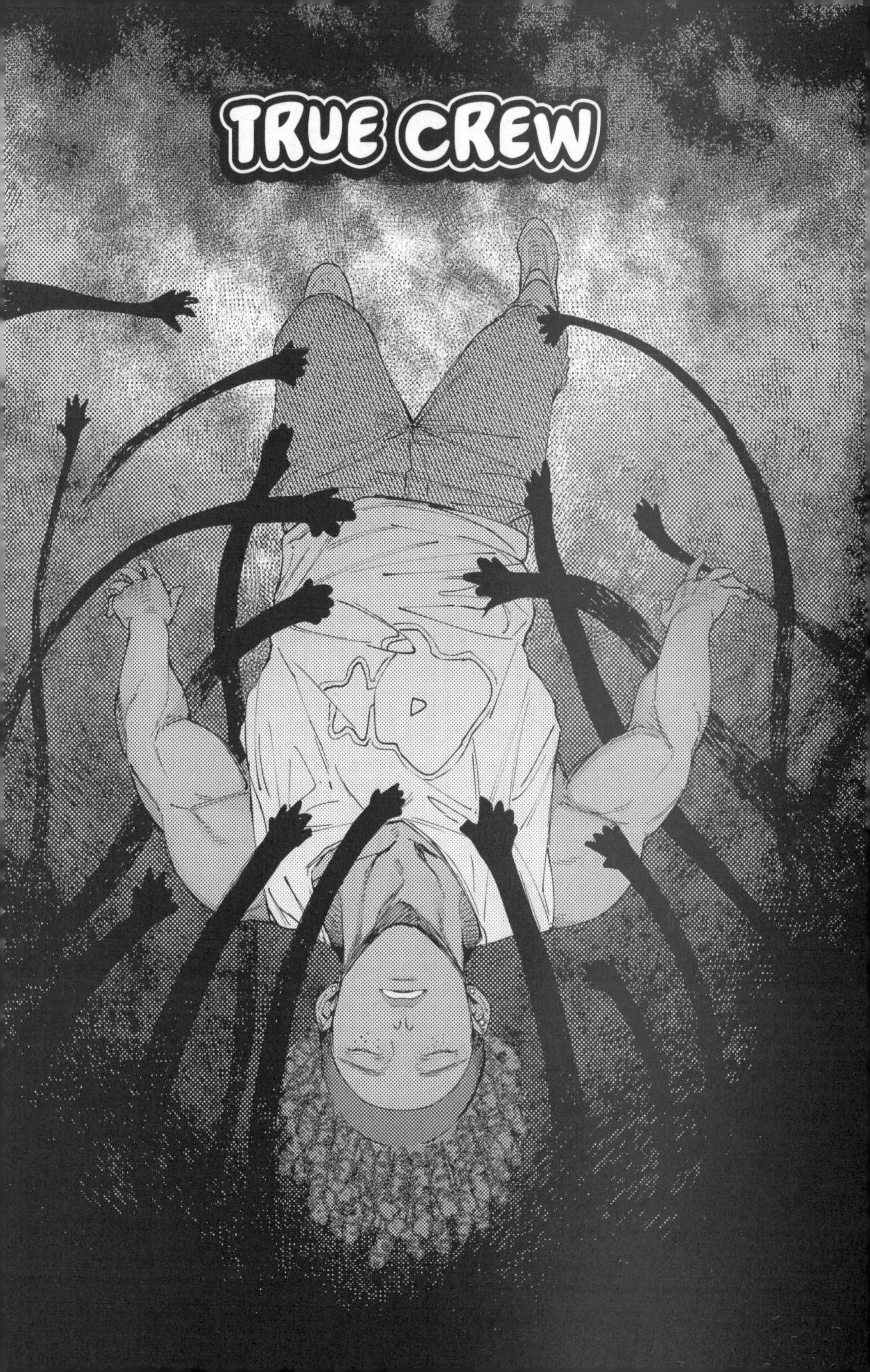
TRUE CREW

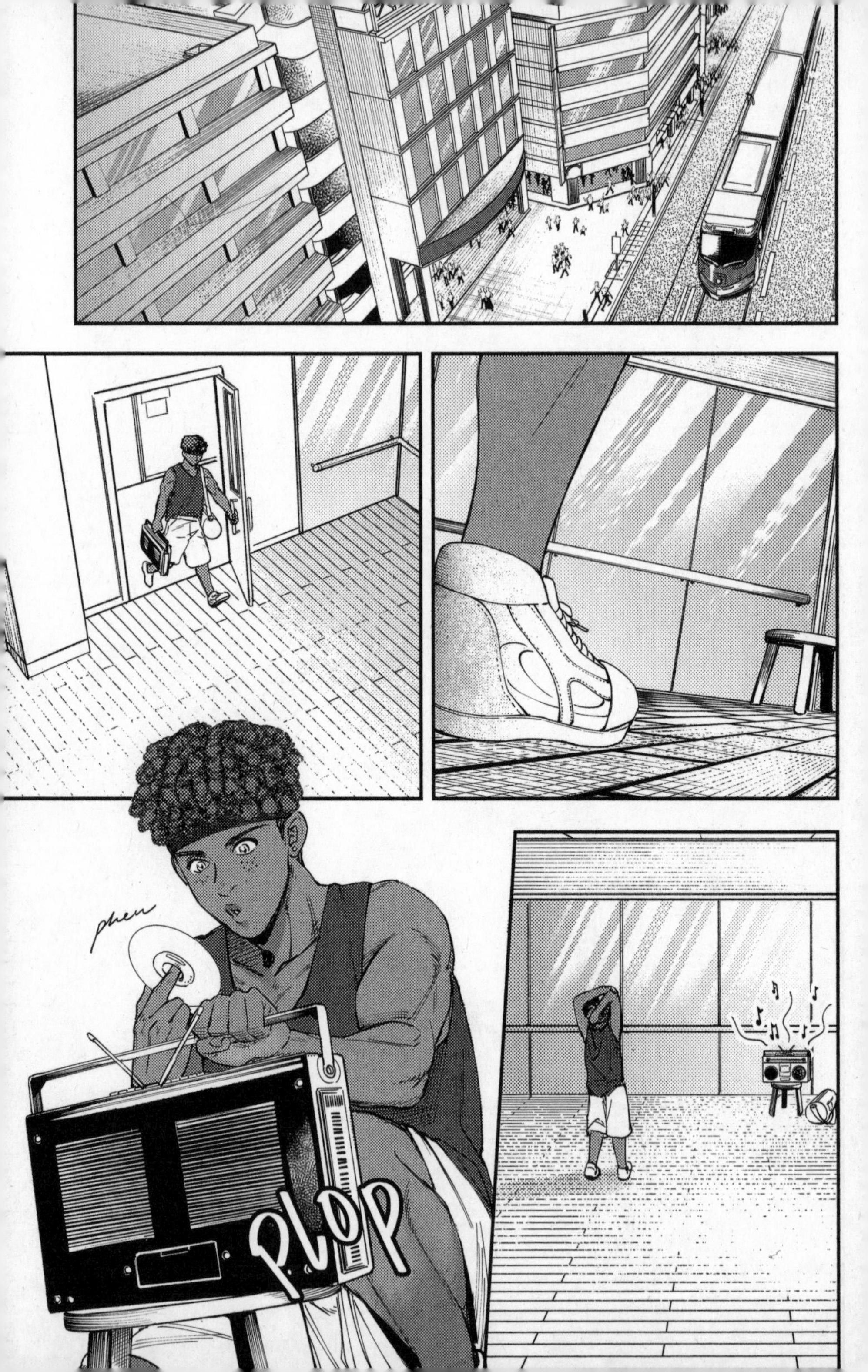
phew
PLOP

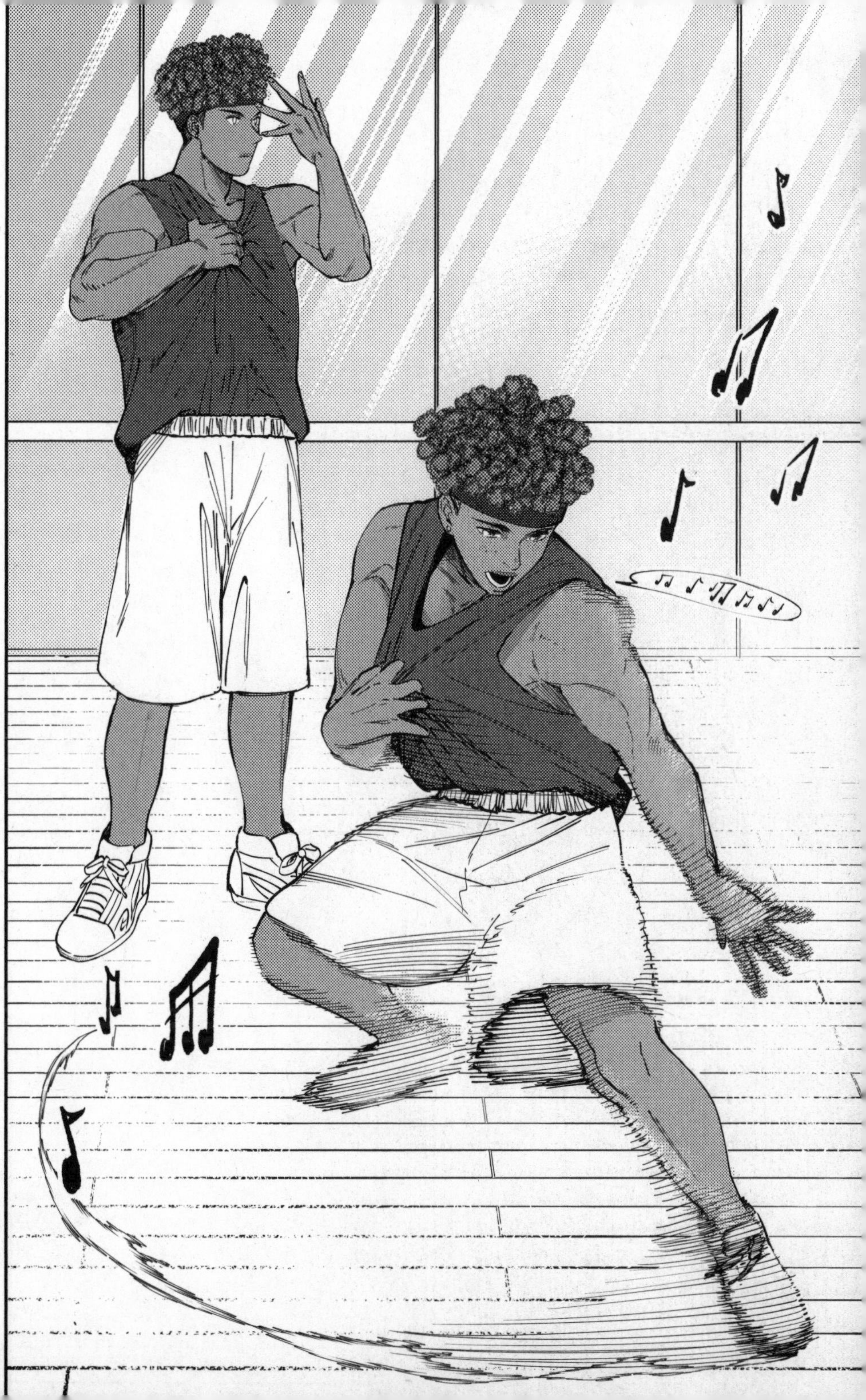

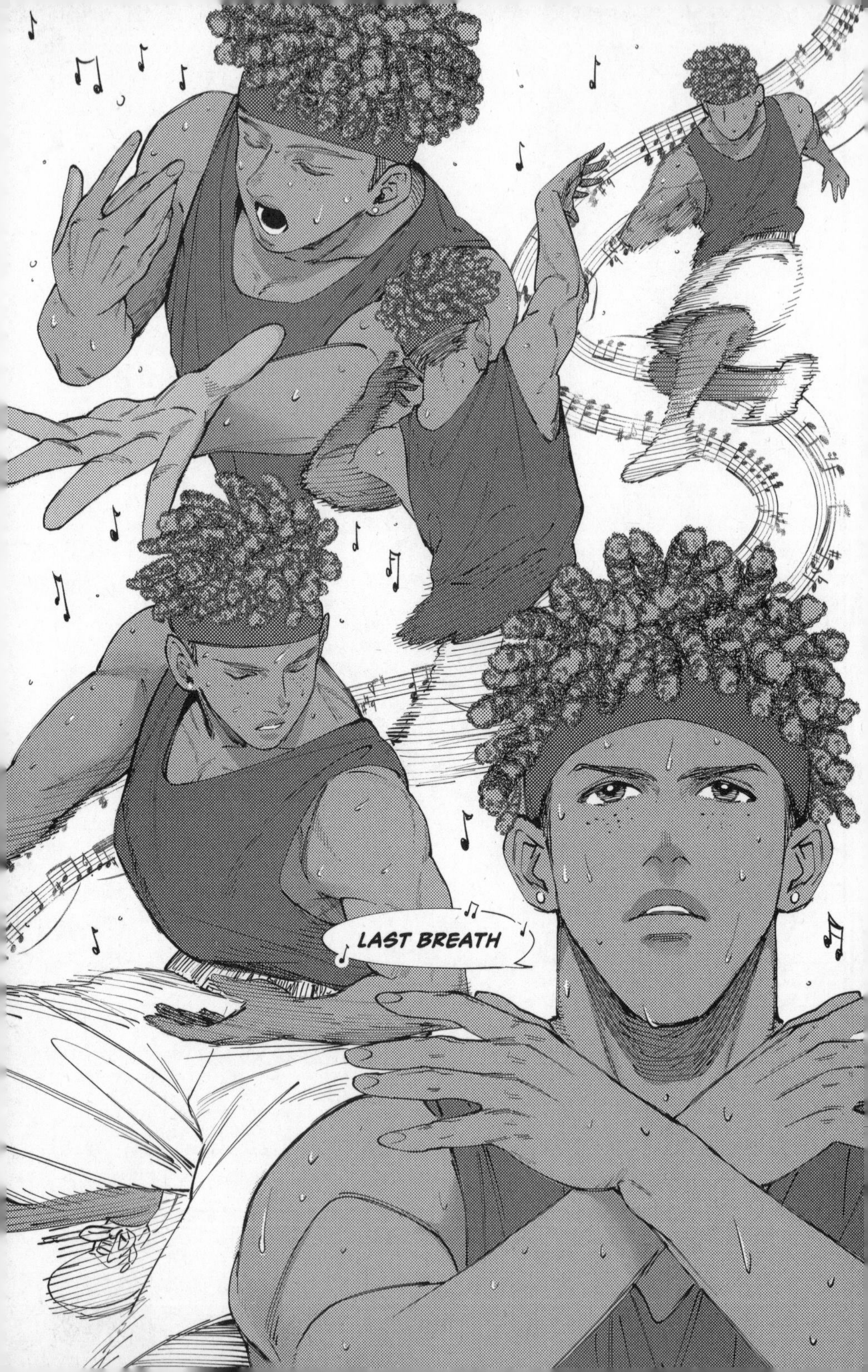
LAST BREATH

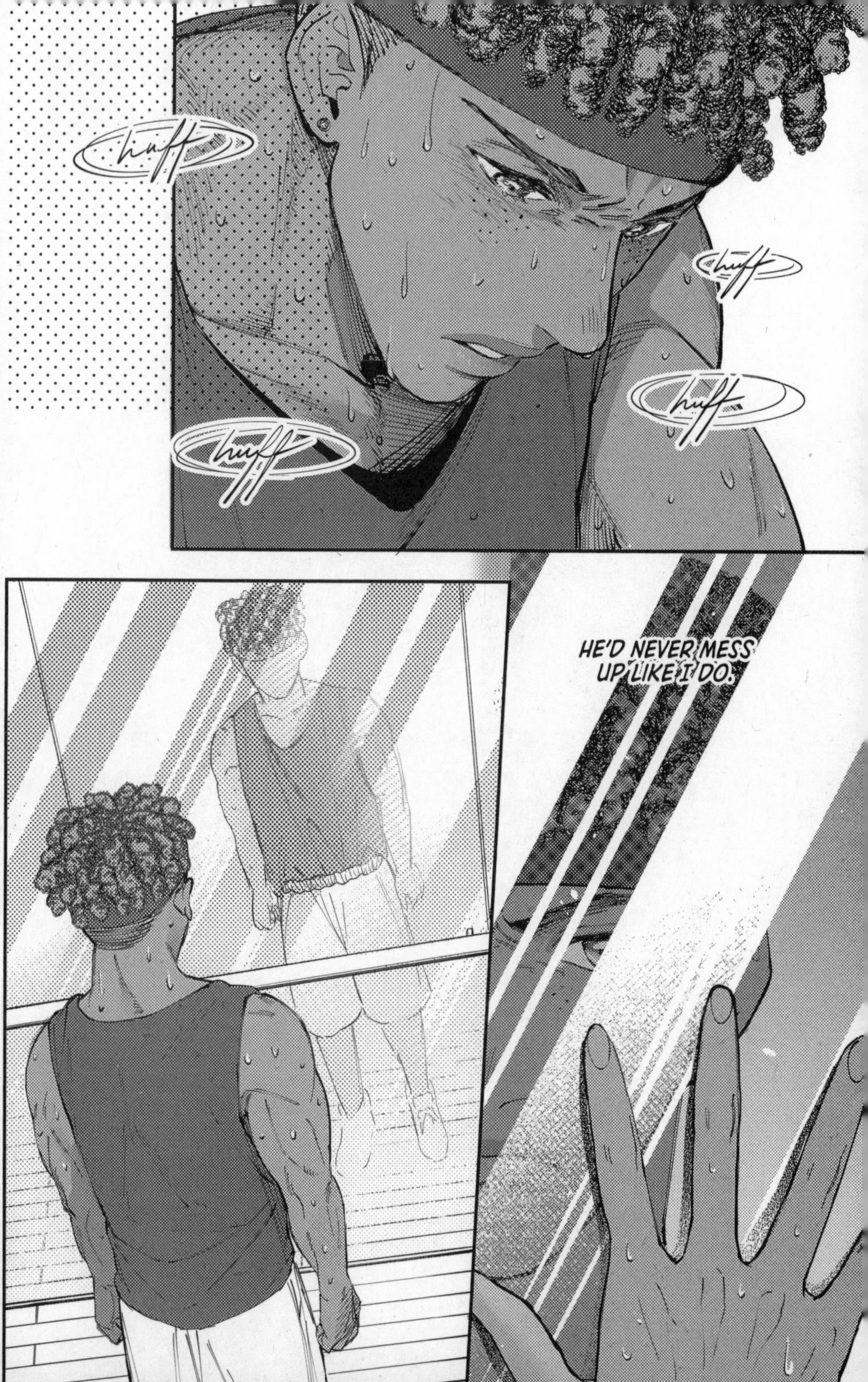
huff
huff
huff
huff
HE'D NEVER MESS UP LIKE I DO.

MR. PERFECT ROBAIRE.

THE FANS SCREAM THE LOUDEST FOR HIM.

THE SINGER-DANCER GENIUS ROBAIRE.

HE'S THE ONE IN THE NEWS.

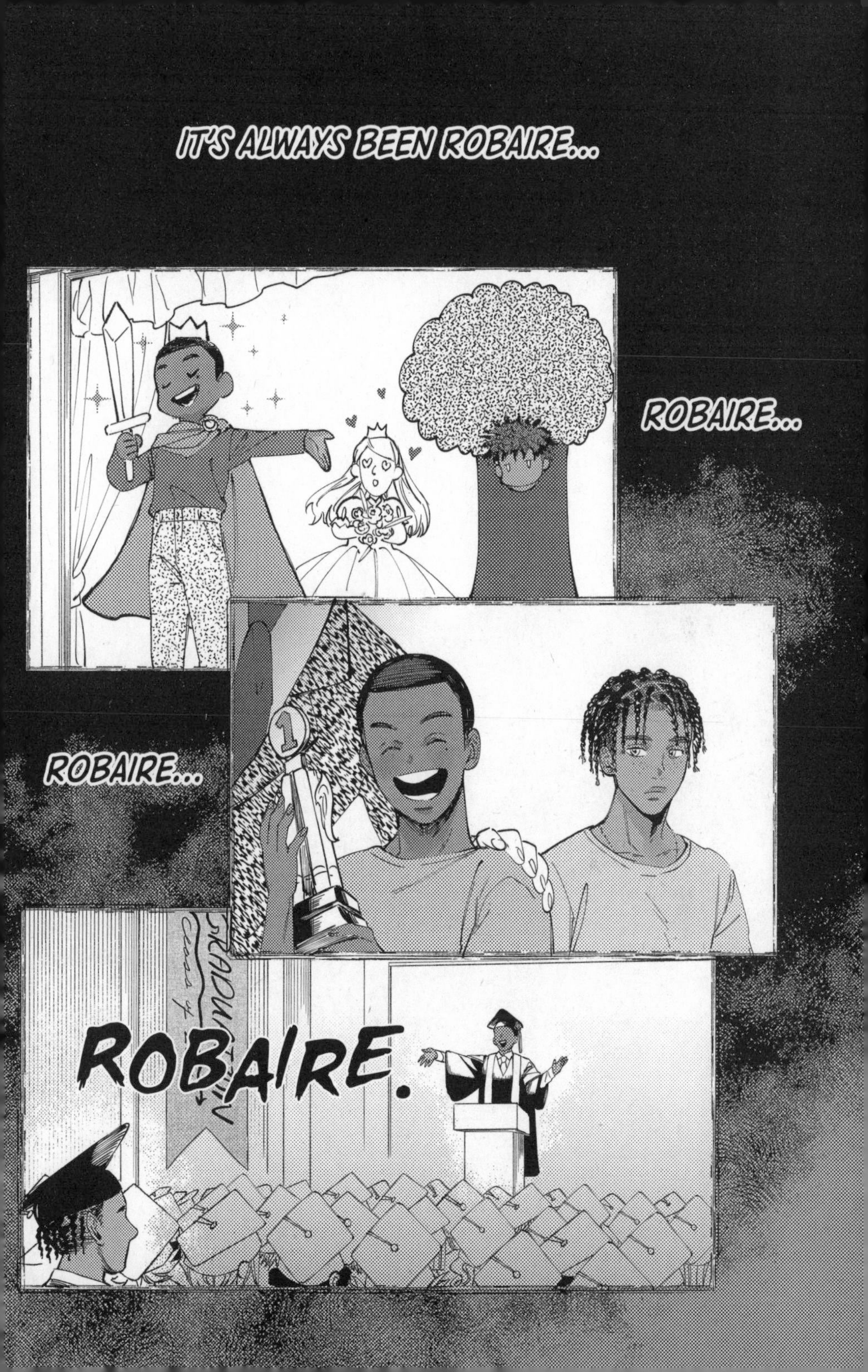
IT'S ALWAYS BEEN ROBAIRE...
ROBAIRE...
ROBAIRE...
ROBAIRE.

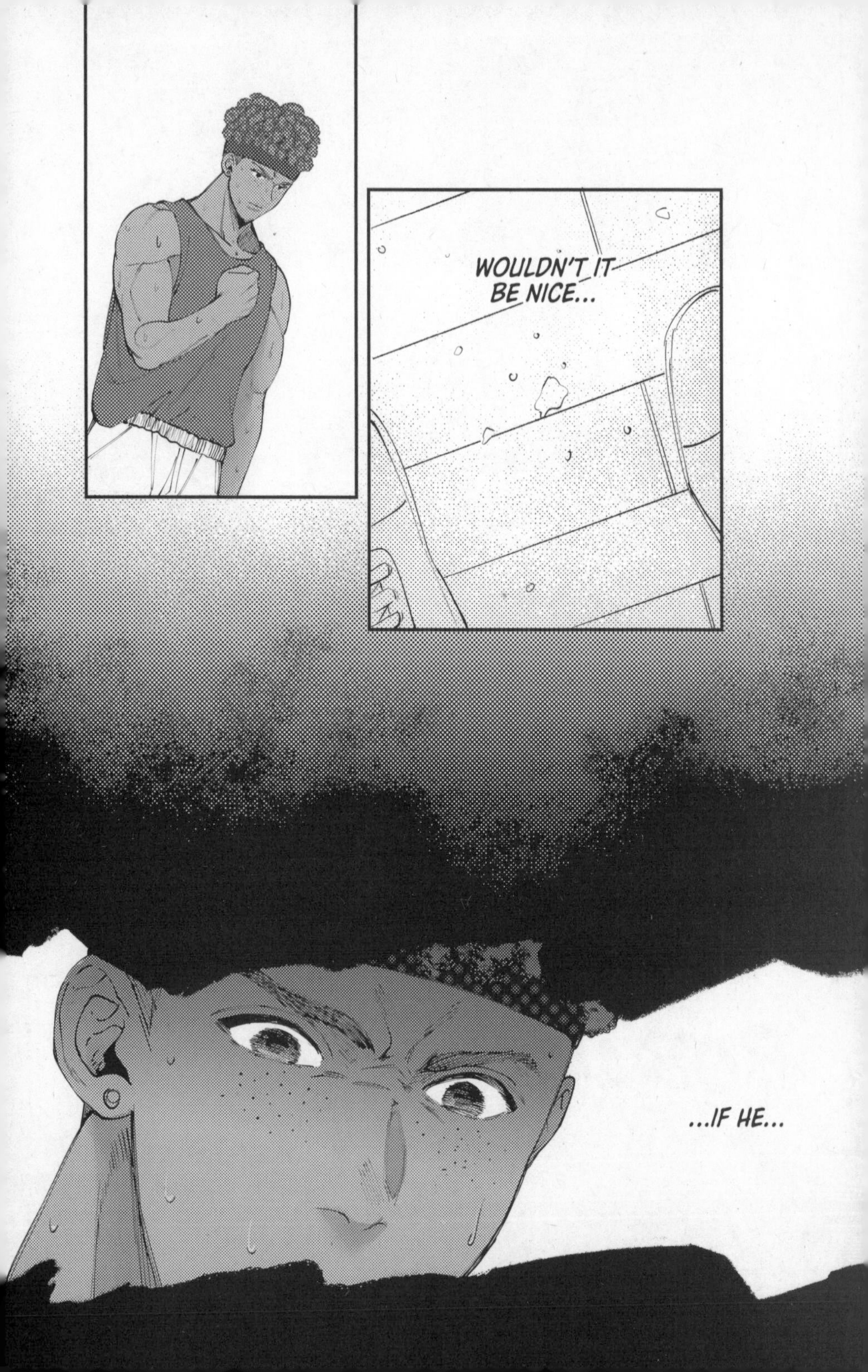
WOULDN'T IT BE NICE...
...IF HE...

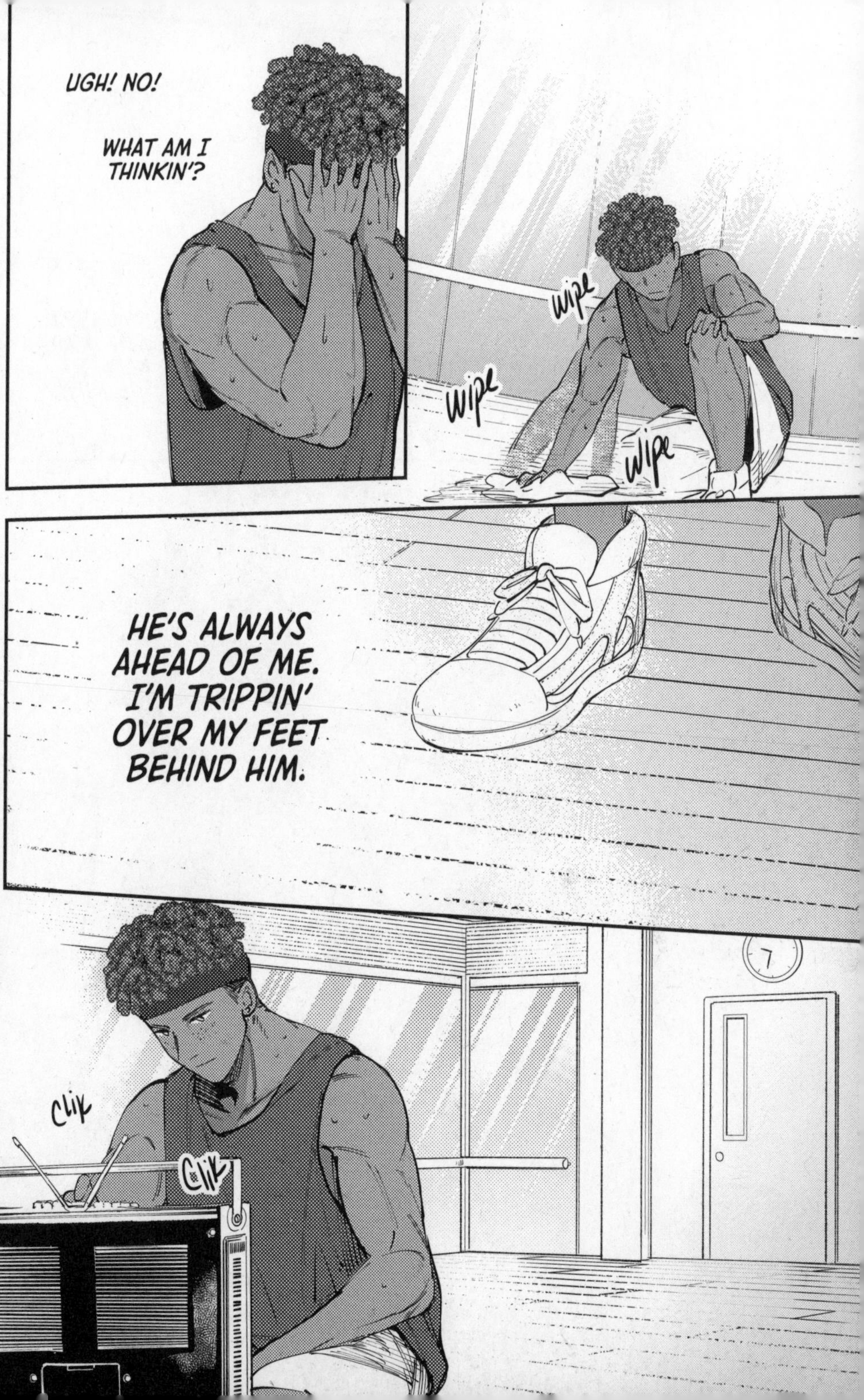
UGH! NO!
WHAT AM I THINKIN'?
wipe
wipe
wipe
HE'S ALWAYS AHEAD OF ME. I'M TRIPPIN' OVER MY FEET BEHIND HIM.
CLIK
CLIK

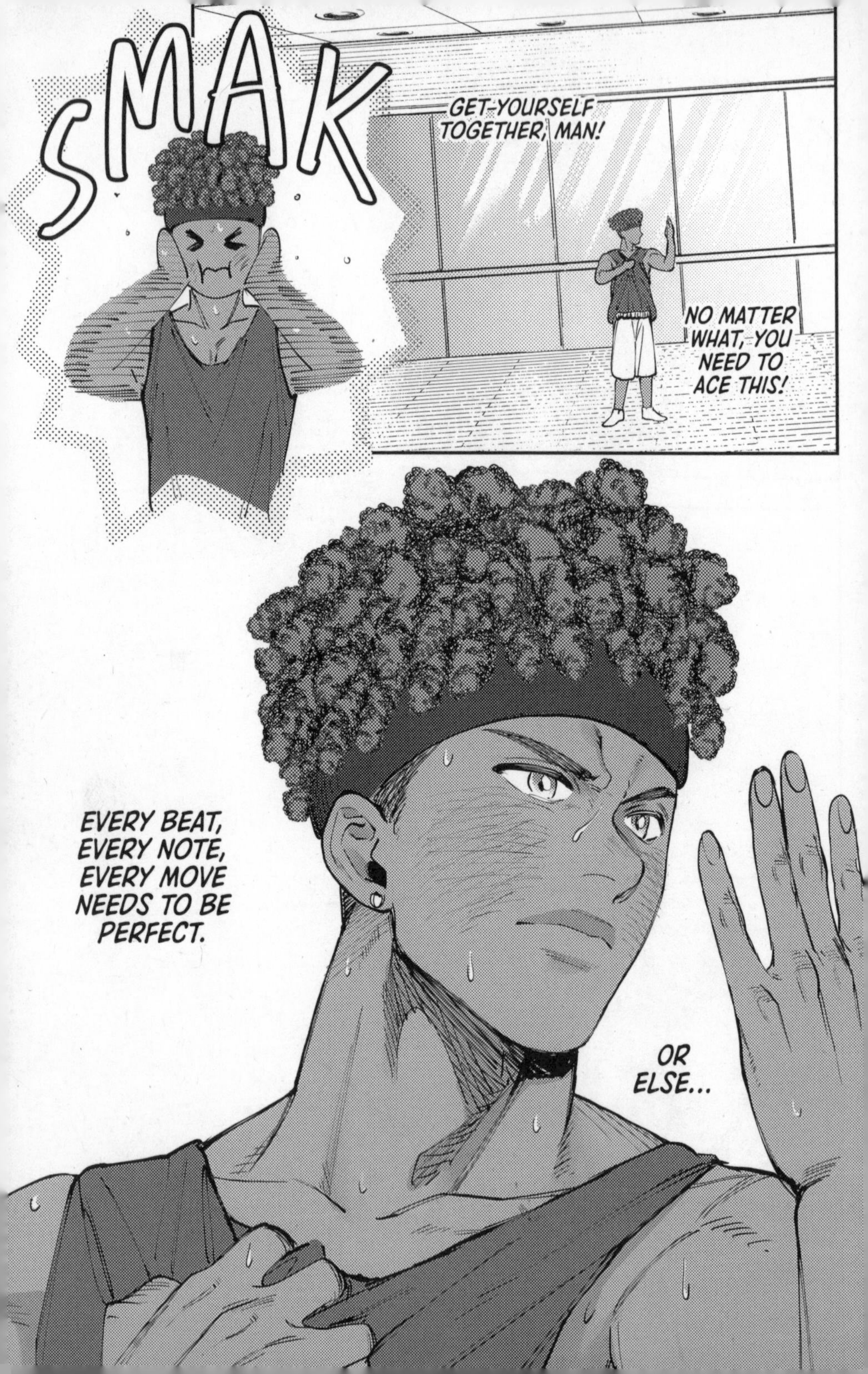
SMAK
GET-YOURSELF TOGETHER, MAN!
NO MATTER WHAT, YOU NEED TO ACE THIS!
EVERY BEAT, EVERY NOTE, EVERY MOVE NEEDS TO BE PERFECT.
OR ELSE...

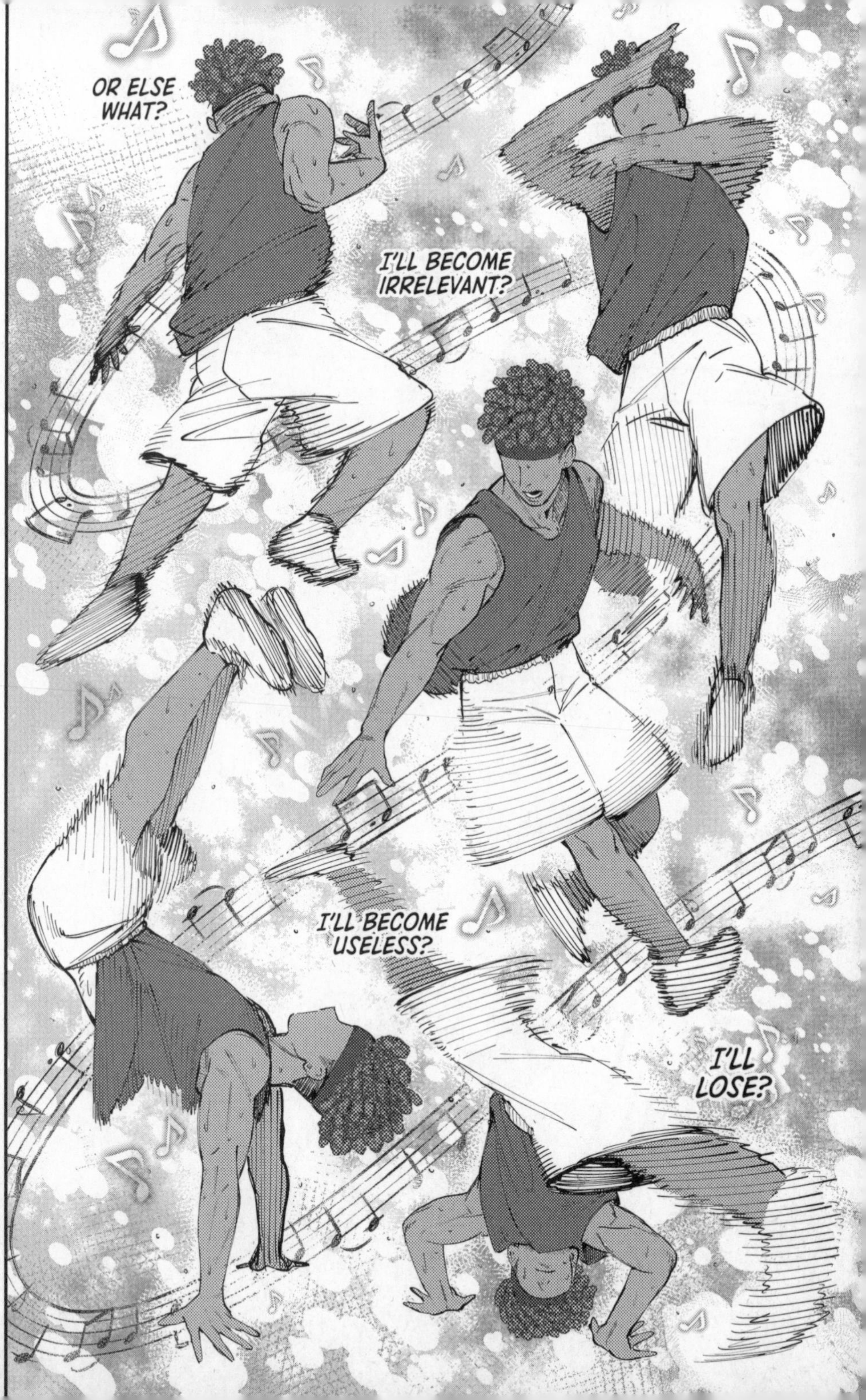
OR ELSE WHAT?
I'LL BECOME IRRELEVANT?
I'LL BECOME USELESS?
I'LL LOSE?

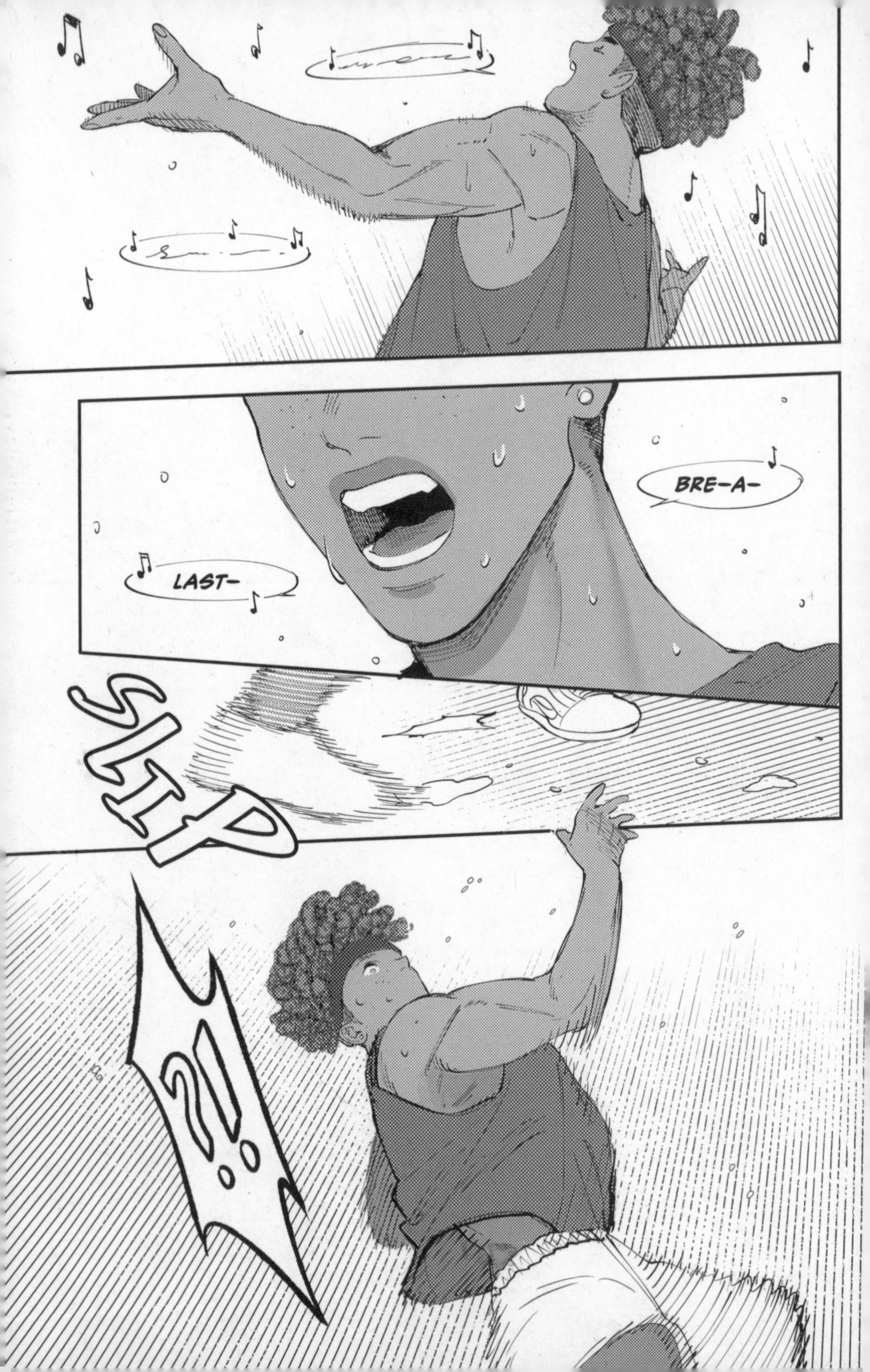
BRE-A-
LAST-
SLIP
?!

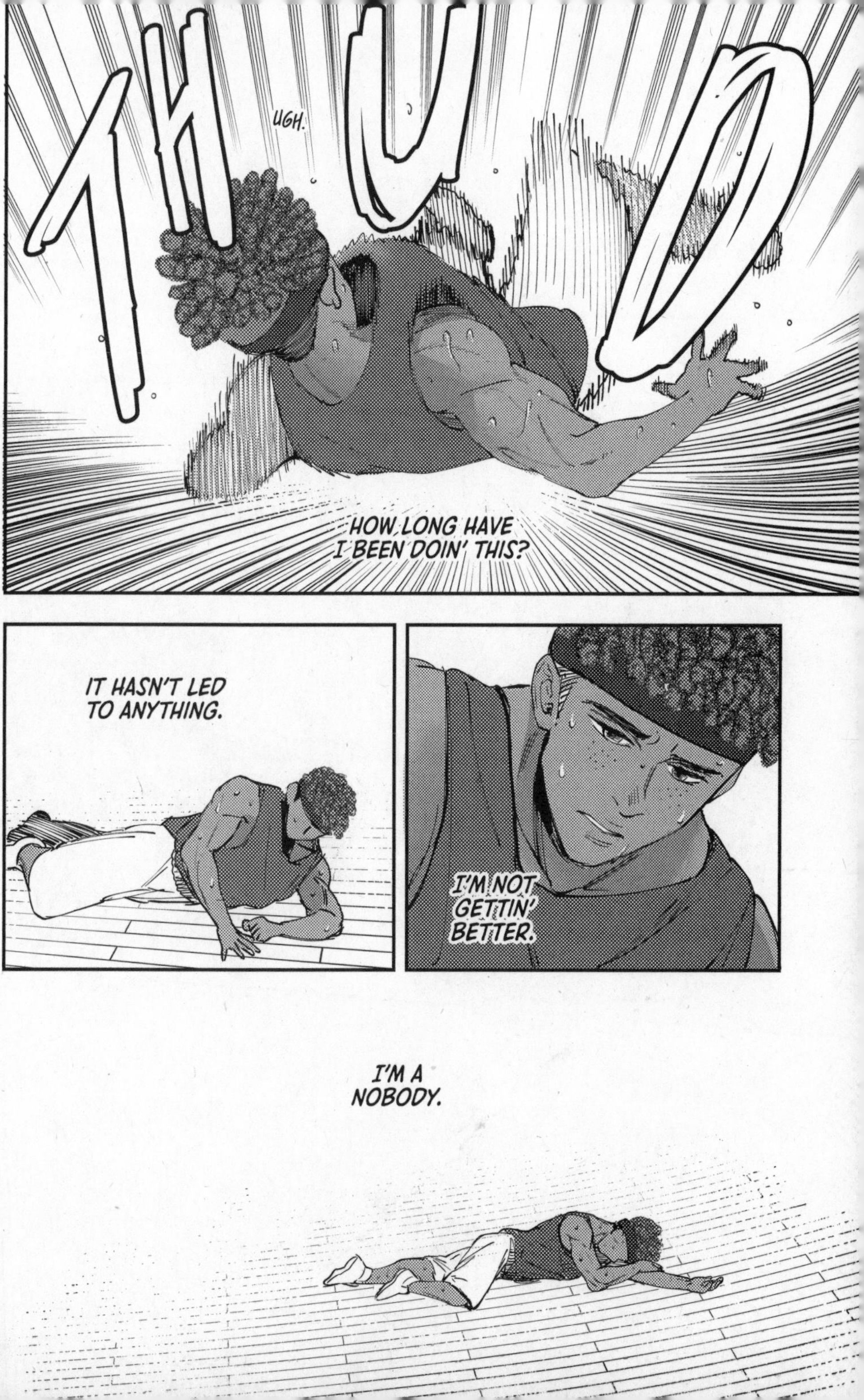
THUD
UGH.
HOW LONG HAVE I BEEN DOIN' THIS?
IT HASN'T LED TO ANYTHING.
I'M NOT GETTIN' BETTER.
I'M A NOBODY.

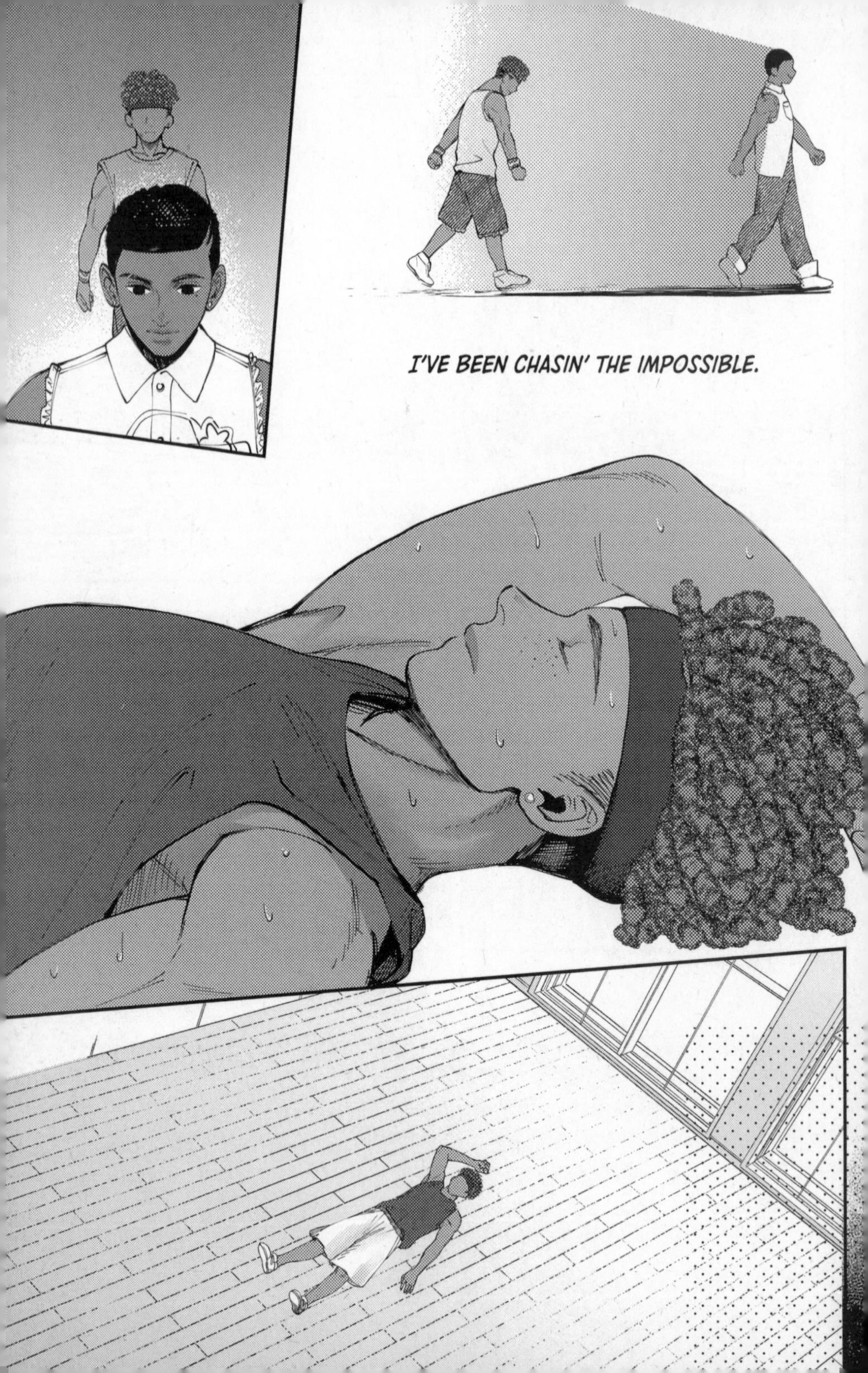
I'VE BEEN CHASIN' THE IMPOSSIBLE.

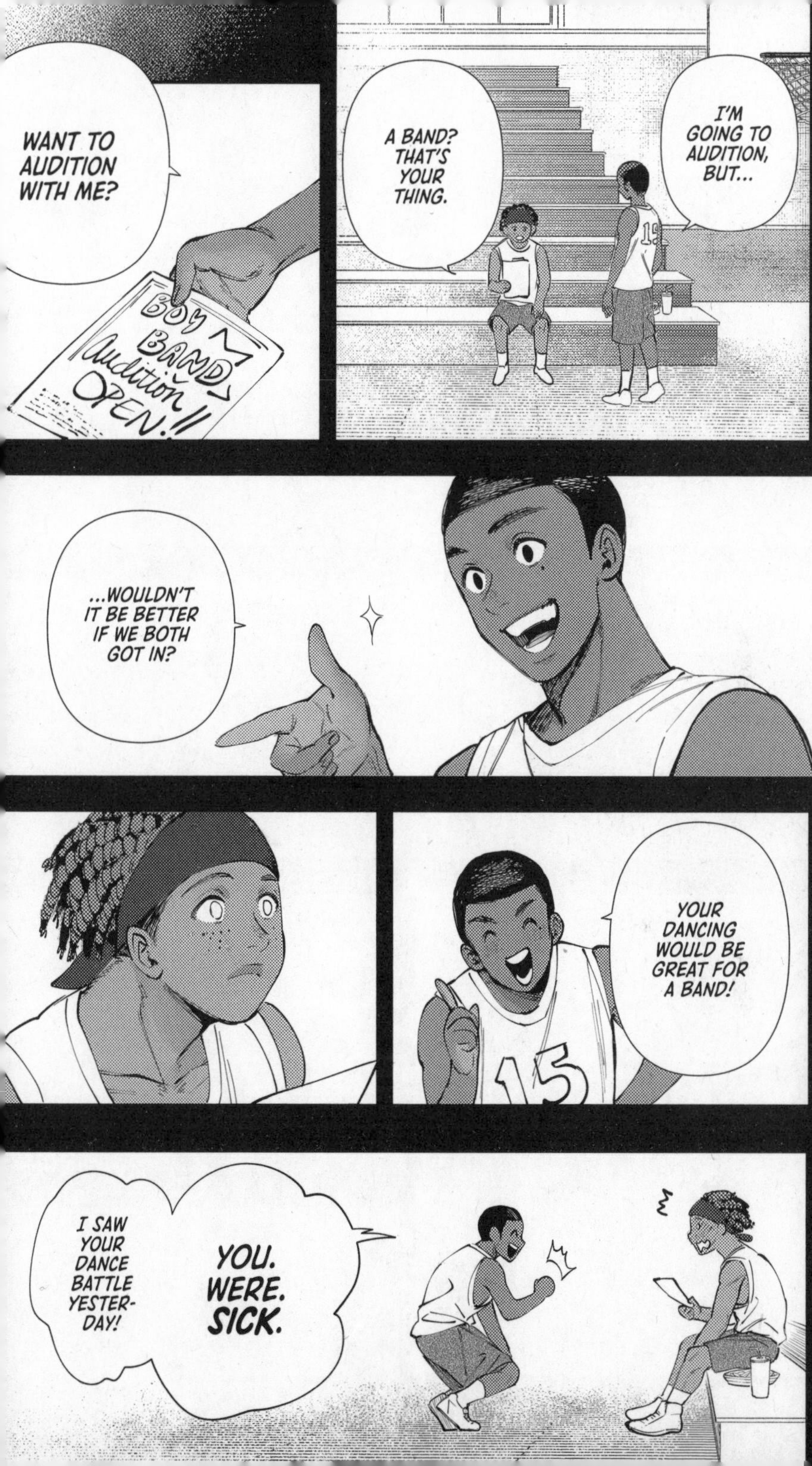
WANT TO AUDITION WITH ME?
BOY BAND Audition OPEN!!
A BAND? THAT'S YOUR THING.
I'M GOING TO AUDITION, BUT...
...WOULDN'T IT BE BETTER IF WE BOTH GOT IN?
YOUR DANCING WOULD BE GREAT FOR A BAND!
I SAW YOUR DANCE BATTLE YESTER-DAY!
YOU. WERE. SICK.

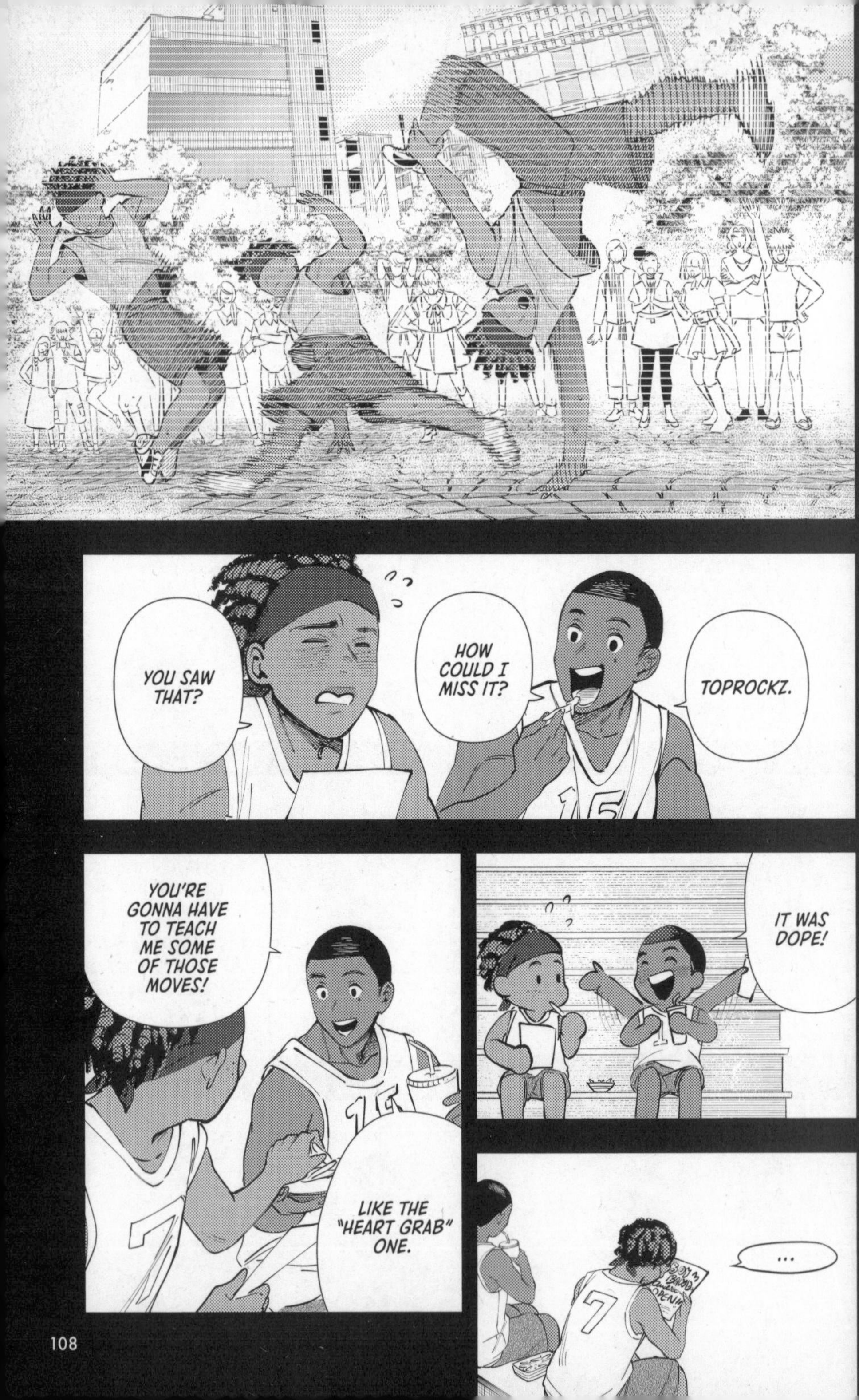
YOU SAW THAT?
HOW COULD I MISS IT?
TOPROCKZ.
YOU'RE GONNA HAVE TO TEACH ME SOME OF THOSE MOVES!
LIKE THE "HEART GRAB" ONE.
IT WAS DOPE!
...

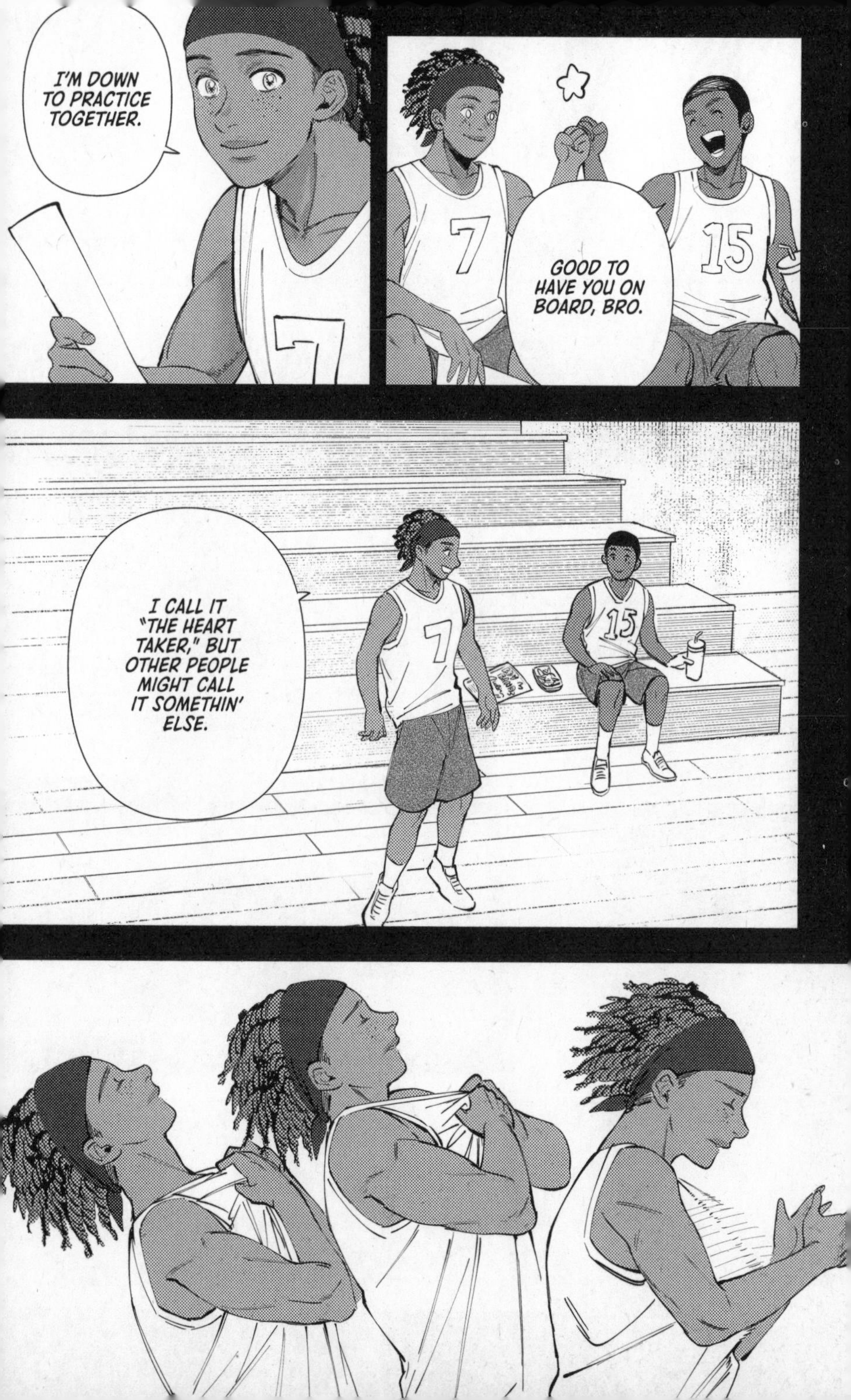
I'M DOWN TO PRACTICE TOGETHER.
GOOD TO HAVE YOU ON BOARD, BRO.
I CALL IT "THE HEART TAKER," BUT OTHER PEOPLE MIGHT CALL IT SOMETHIN' ELSE.

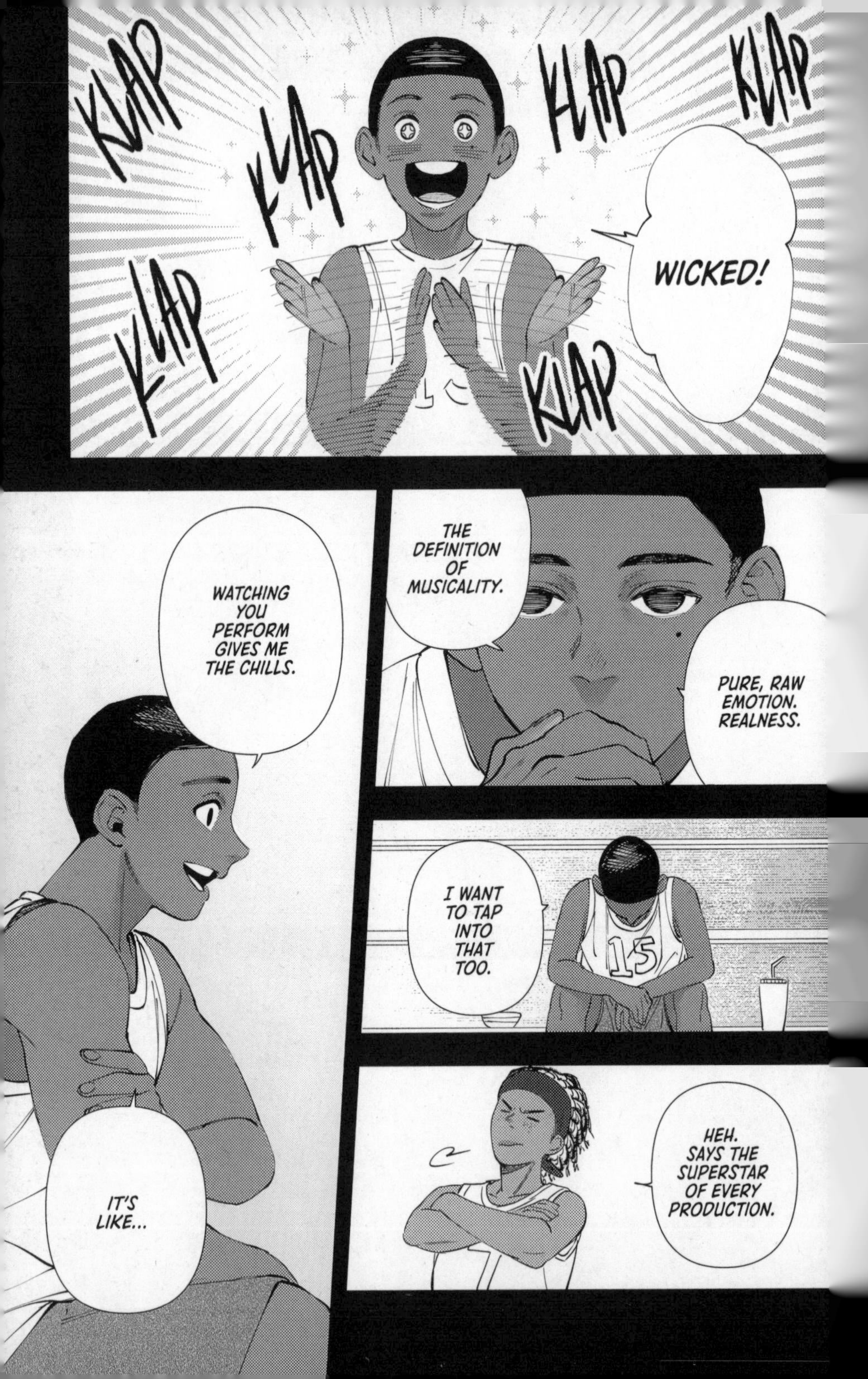
KLAP
KLAP
KLAP
KLAP
KLAP
KLAP
WICKED!
WATCHING YOU PERFORM GIVES ME THE CHILLS.
IT'S LIKE...
THE DEFINITION OF MUSICALITY.
PURE, RAW EMOTION. REALNESS.
I WANT TO TAP INTO THAT TOO.
HEH. SAYS THE SUPERSTAR OF EVERY PRODUCTION.

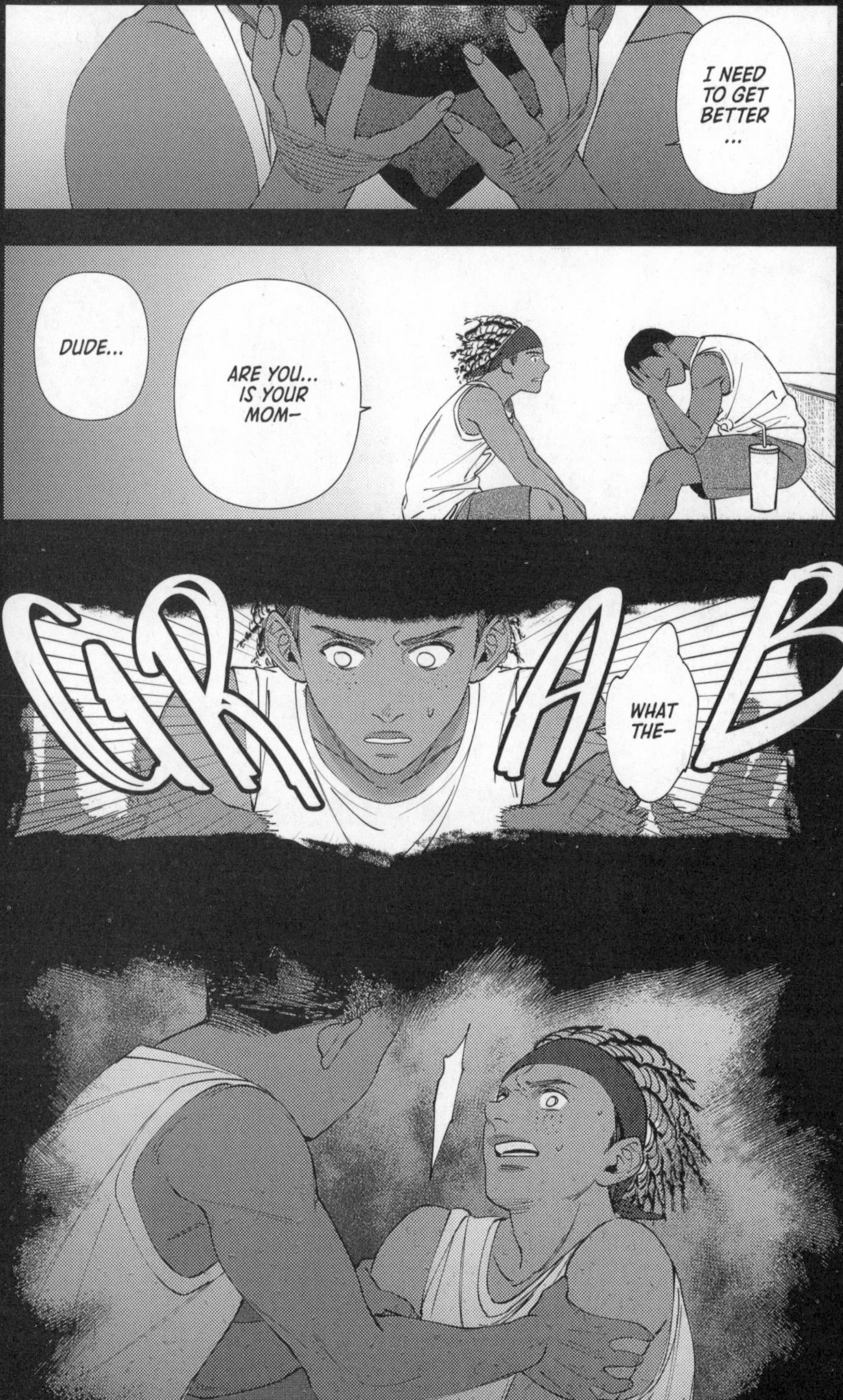
I NEED TO GET BETTER ...
DUDE...
ARE YOU... IS YOUR MOM—
GRAB
WHAT THE—

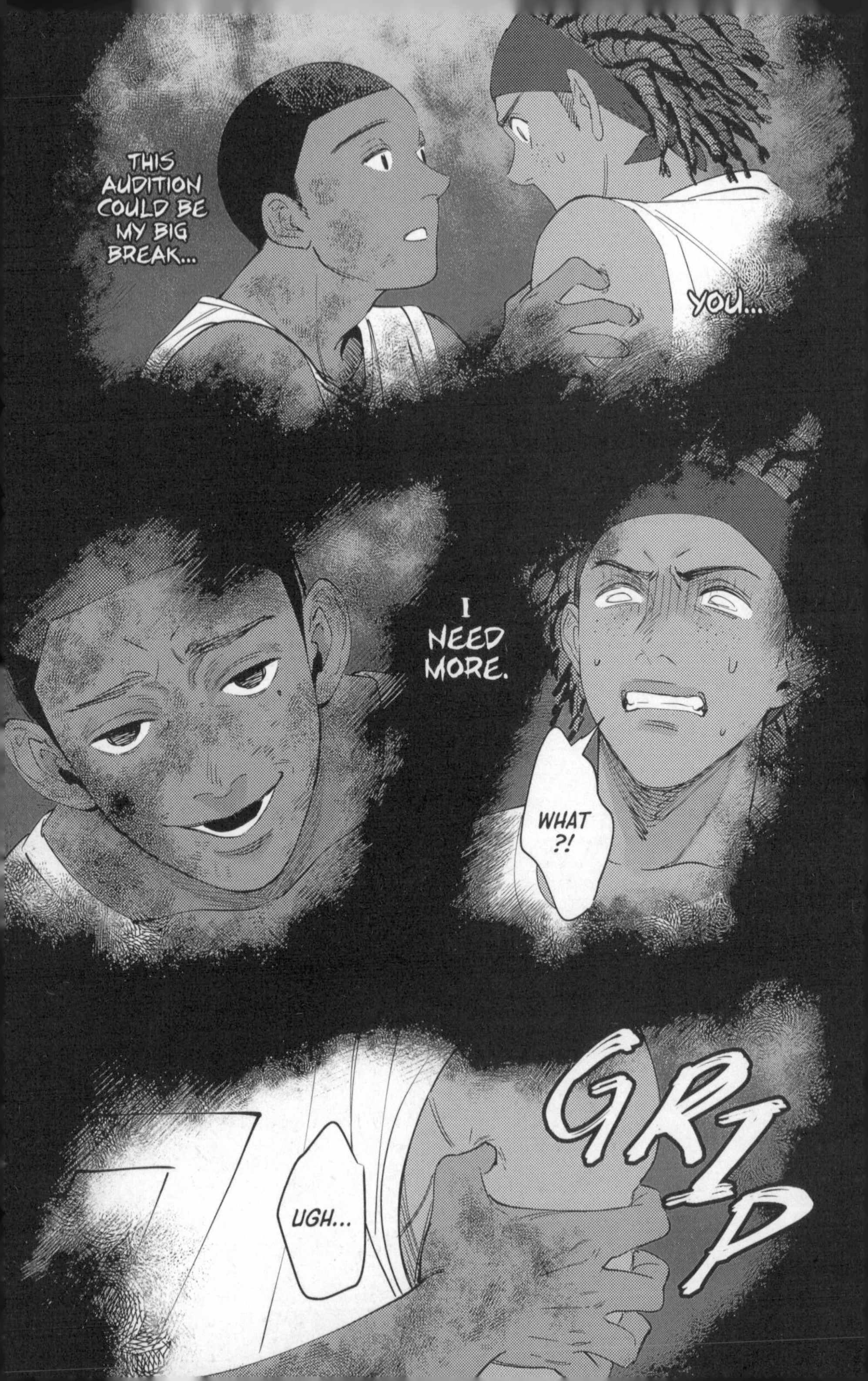
YOU...
THIS AUDITION COULD BE MY BIG BREAK...
WHAT ?!
I NEED MORE.
GRIP
UGH...

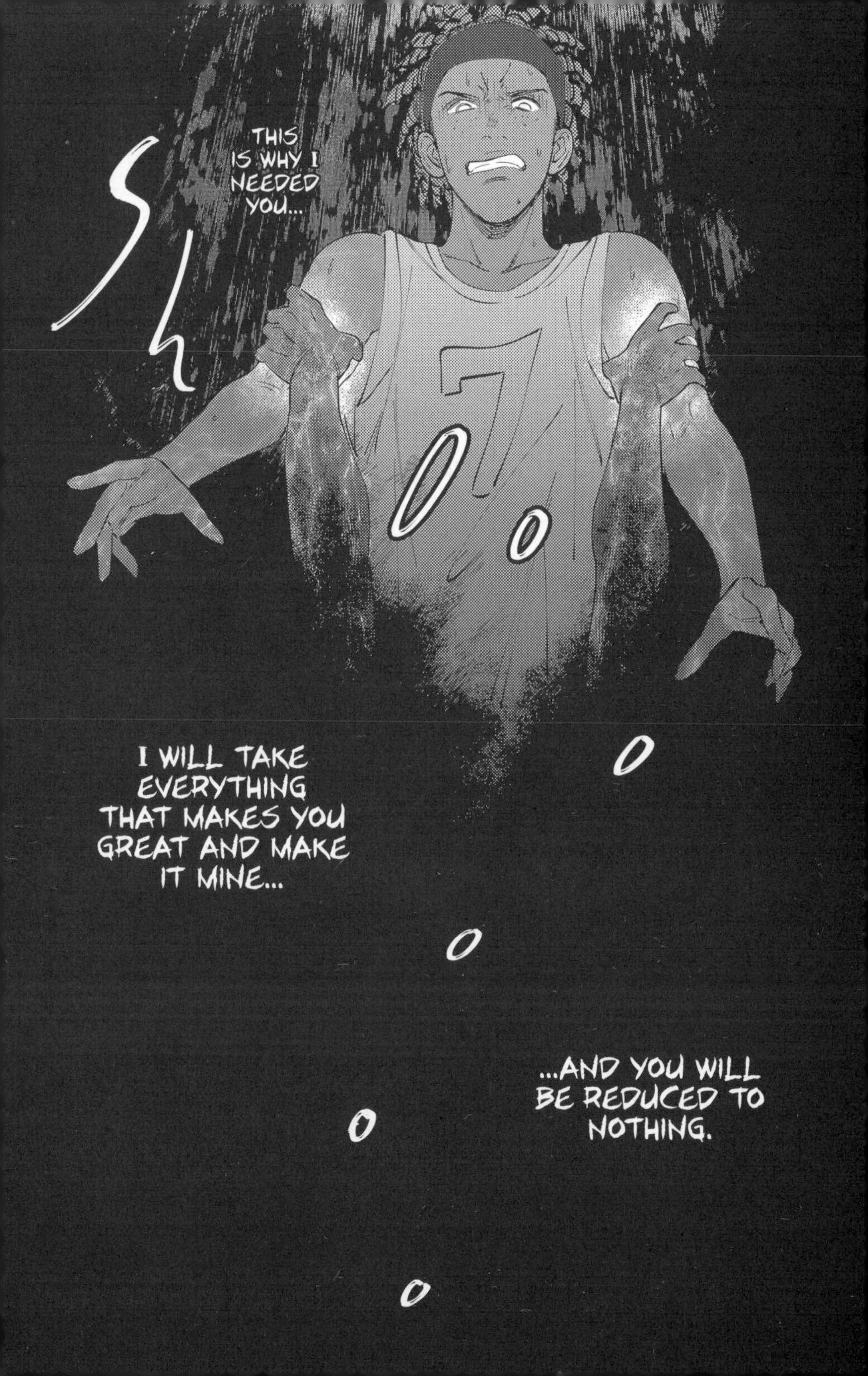
THIS IS WHY I NEEDED YOU...
I WILL TAKE EVERYTHING THAT MAKES YOU GREAT AND MAKE IT MINE...
...AND YOU WILL BE REDUCED TO NOTHING.

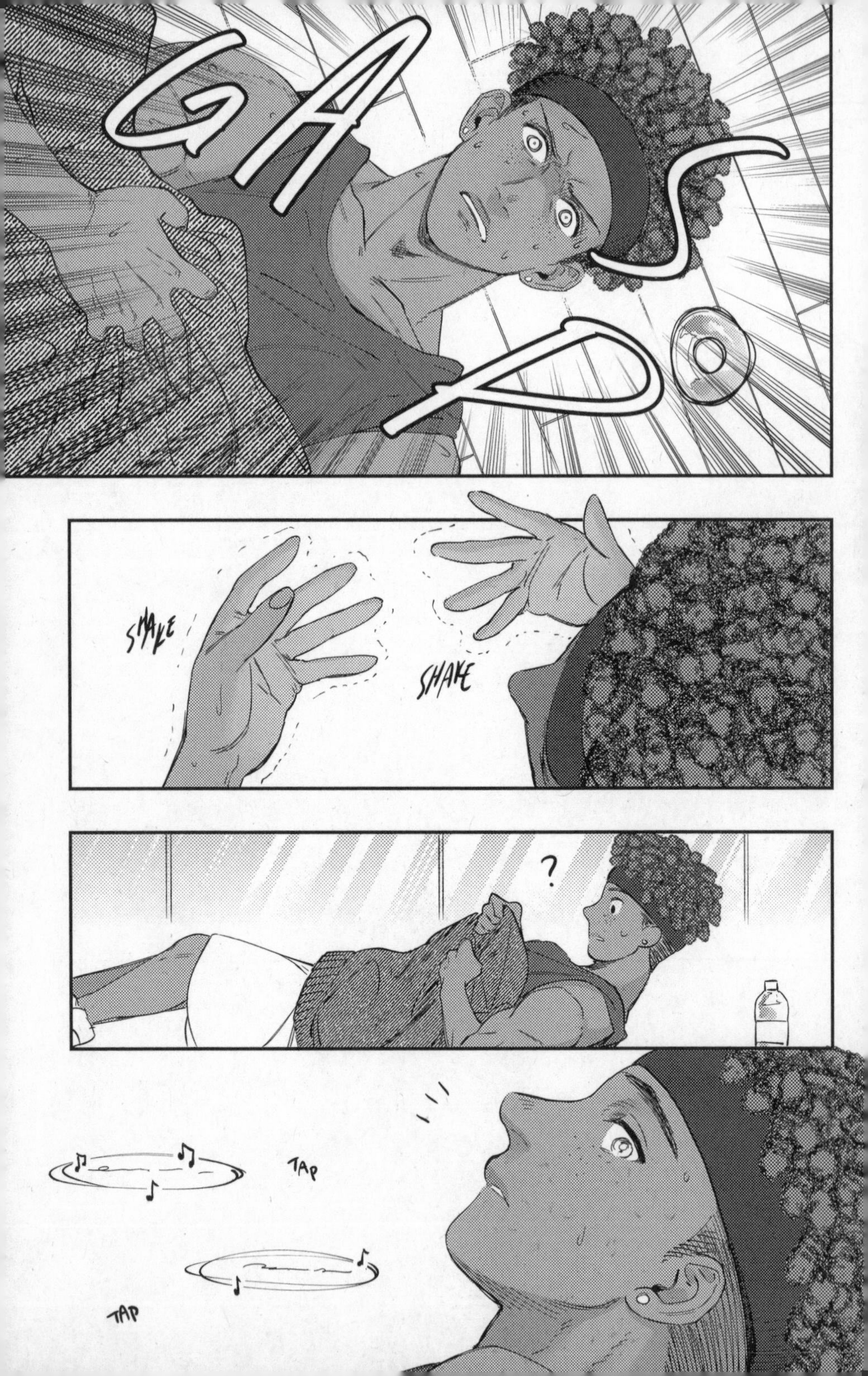
GASP
SHAKE
SHAKE
?
TAP
TAP

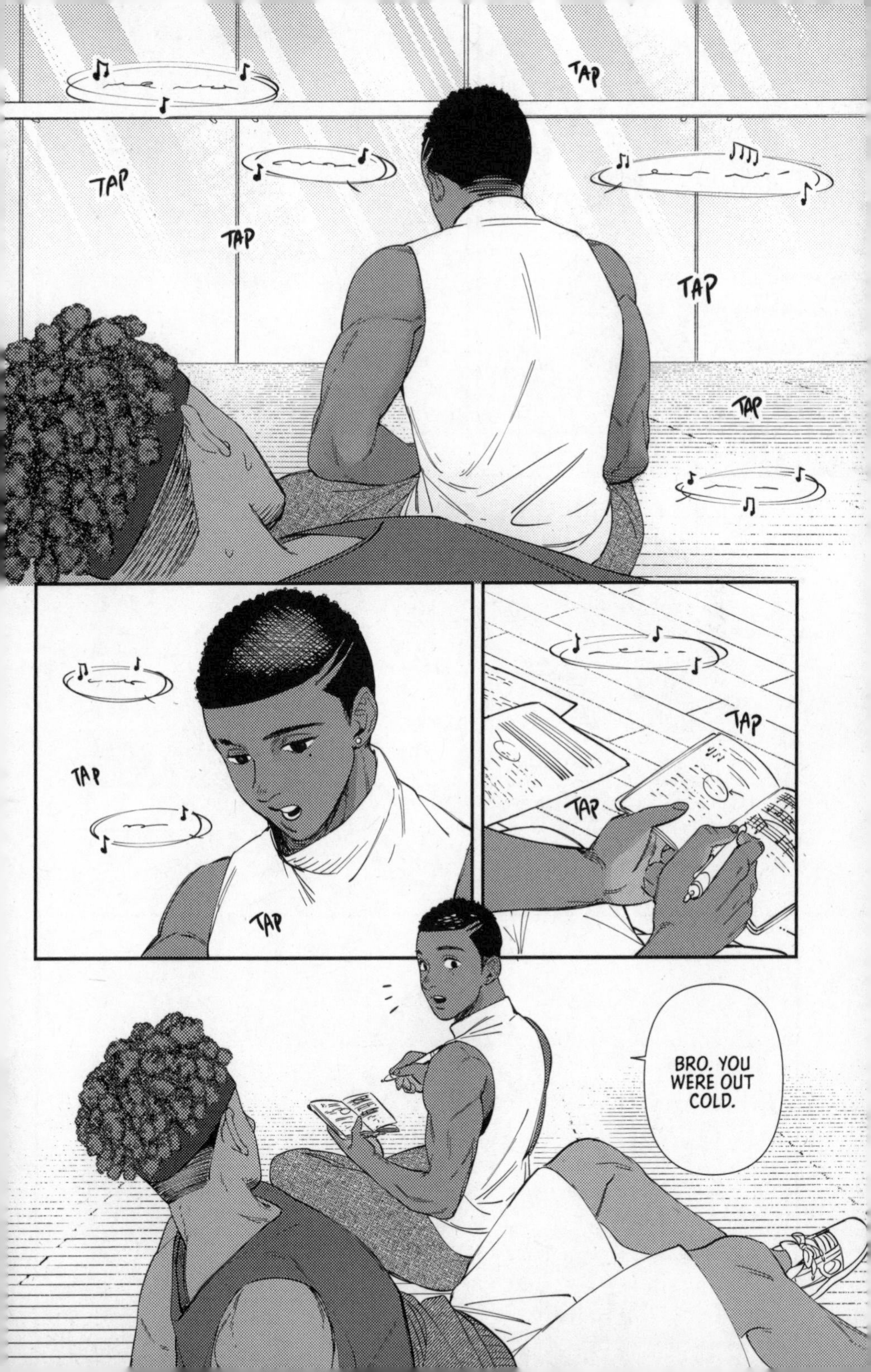
TAP
TAP
TAP
TAP
TAP
TAP
TAP
TAP
TAP
BRO. YOU WERE OUT COLD.

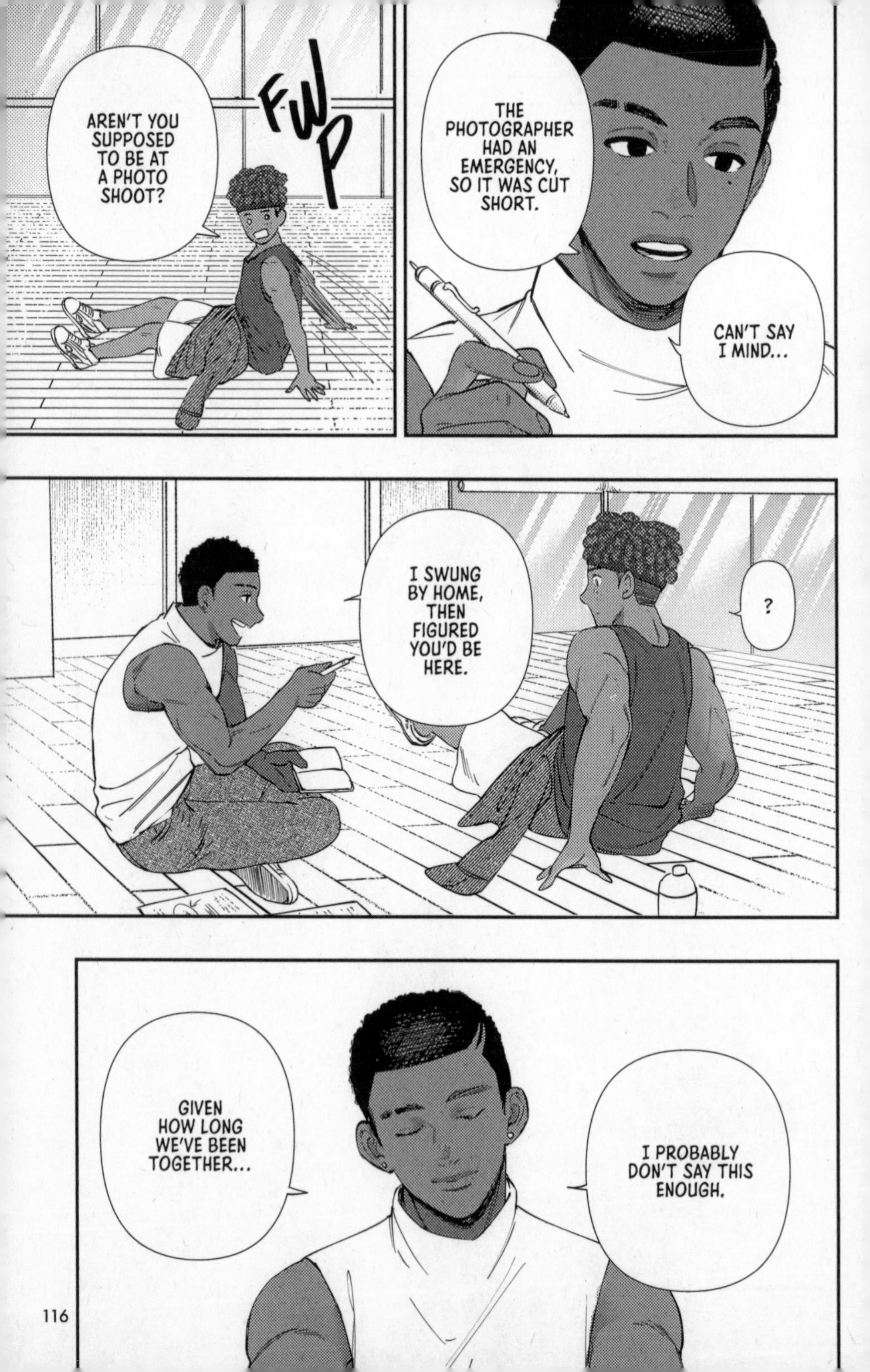
AREN'T YOU SUPPOSED TO BE AT A PHOTO SHOOT?
FWP
THE PHOTOGRAPHER HAD AN EMERGENCY, SO IT WAS CUT SHORT.
CAN'T SAY I MIND...
I SWUNG BY HOME, THEN FIGURED YOU'D BE HERE.
?
GIVEN HOW LONG WE'VE BEEN TOGETHER...
I PROBABLY DON'T SAY THIS ENOUGH.

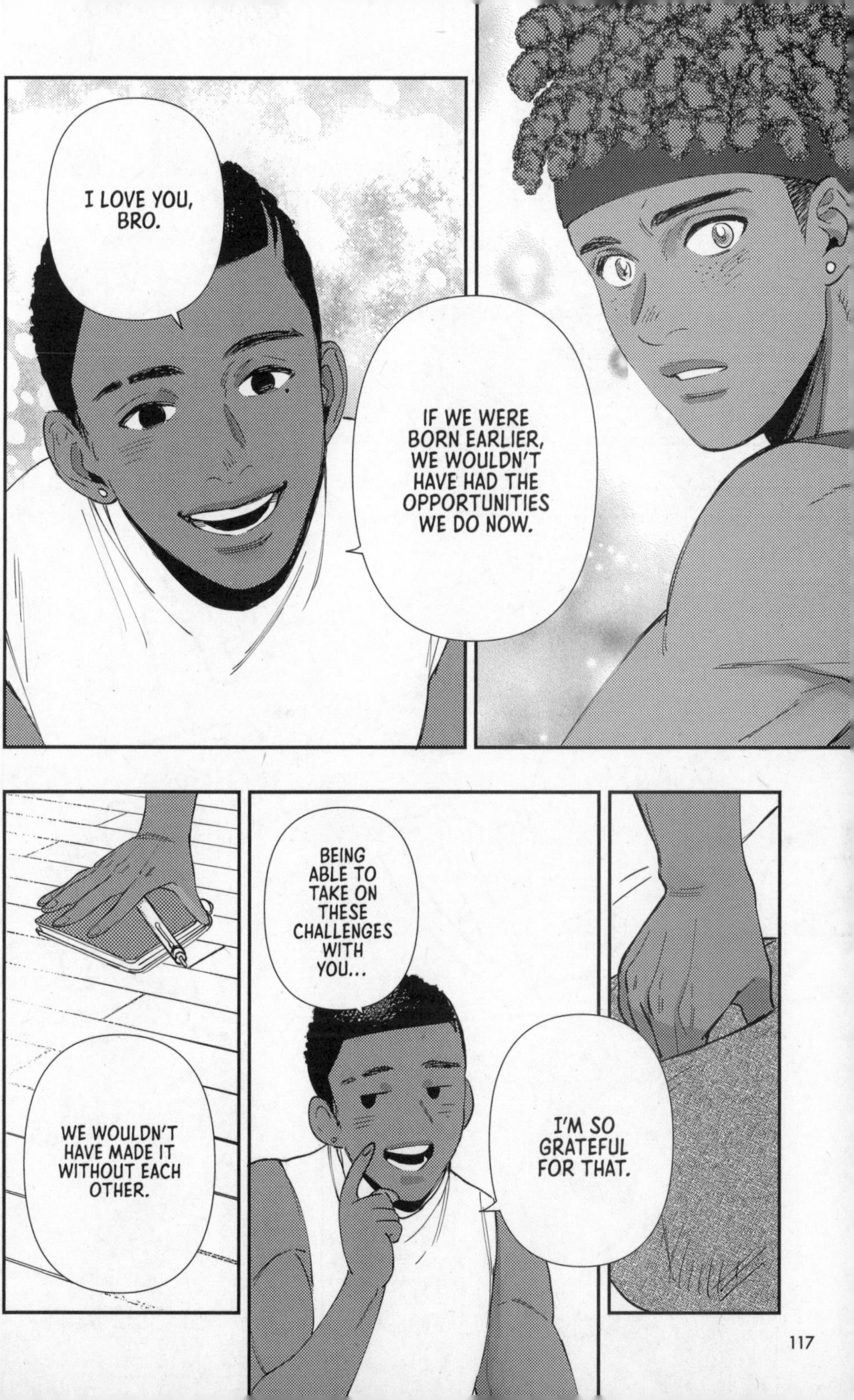
I LOVE YOU, BRO.
IF WE WERE BORN EARLIER, WE WOULDN'T HAVE HAD THE OPPORTUNITIES WE DO NOW.
BEING ABLE TO TAKE ON THESE CHALLENGES WITH YOU...
WE WOULDN'T HAVE MADE IT WITHOUT EACH OTHER.
I'M SO GRATEFUL FOR THAT.

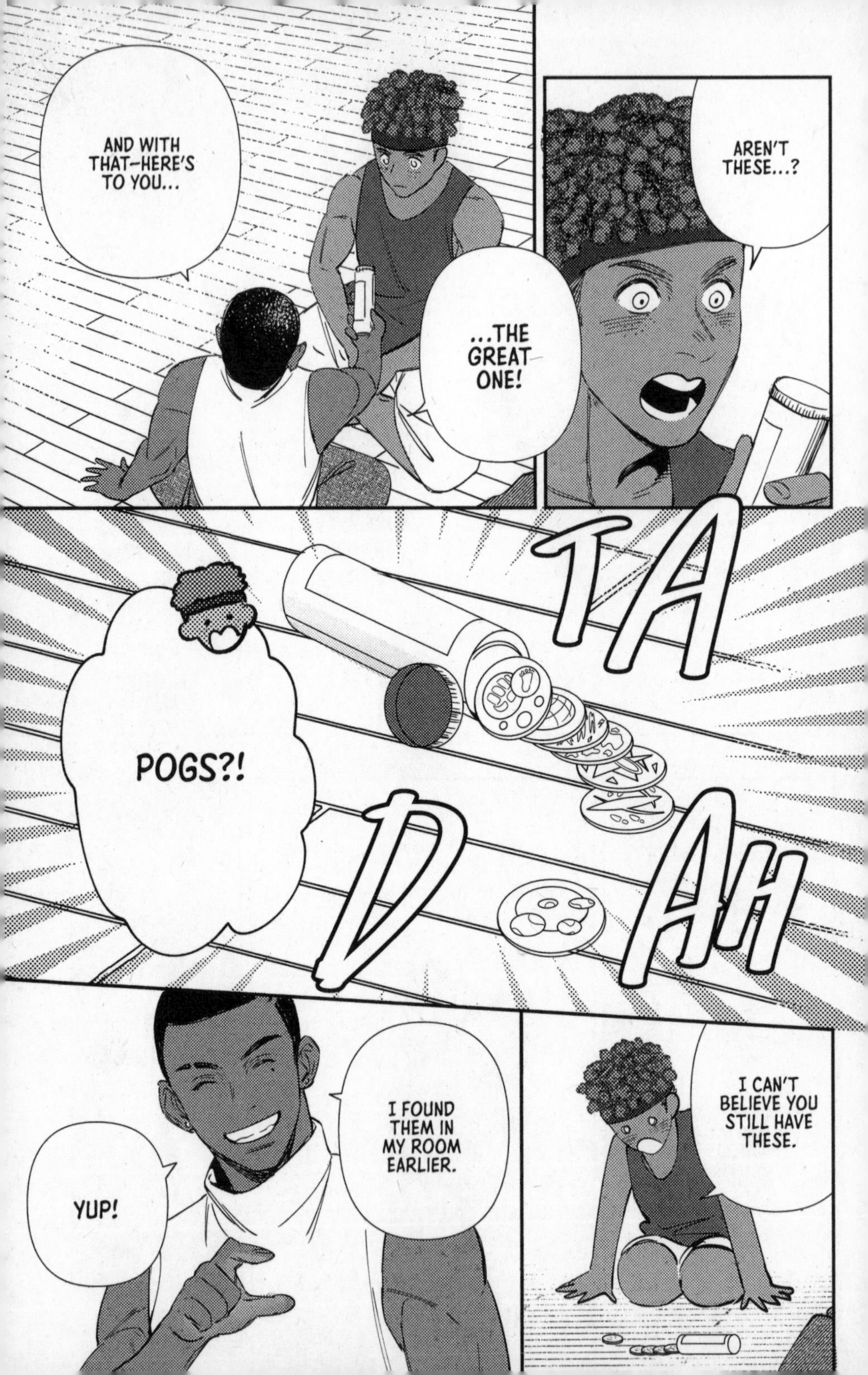
AND WITH THAT—HERE'S TO YOU...
...THE GREAT ONE!
AREN'T THESE...?
POGS?!
TA DAH
YUP!
I FOUND THEM IN MY ROOM EARLIER.
I CAN'T BELIEVE YOU STILL HAVE THESE.

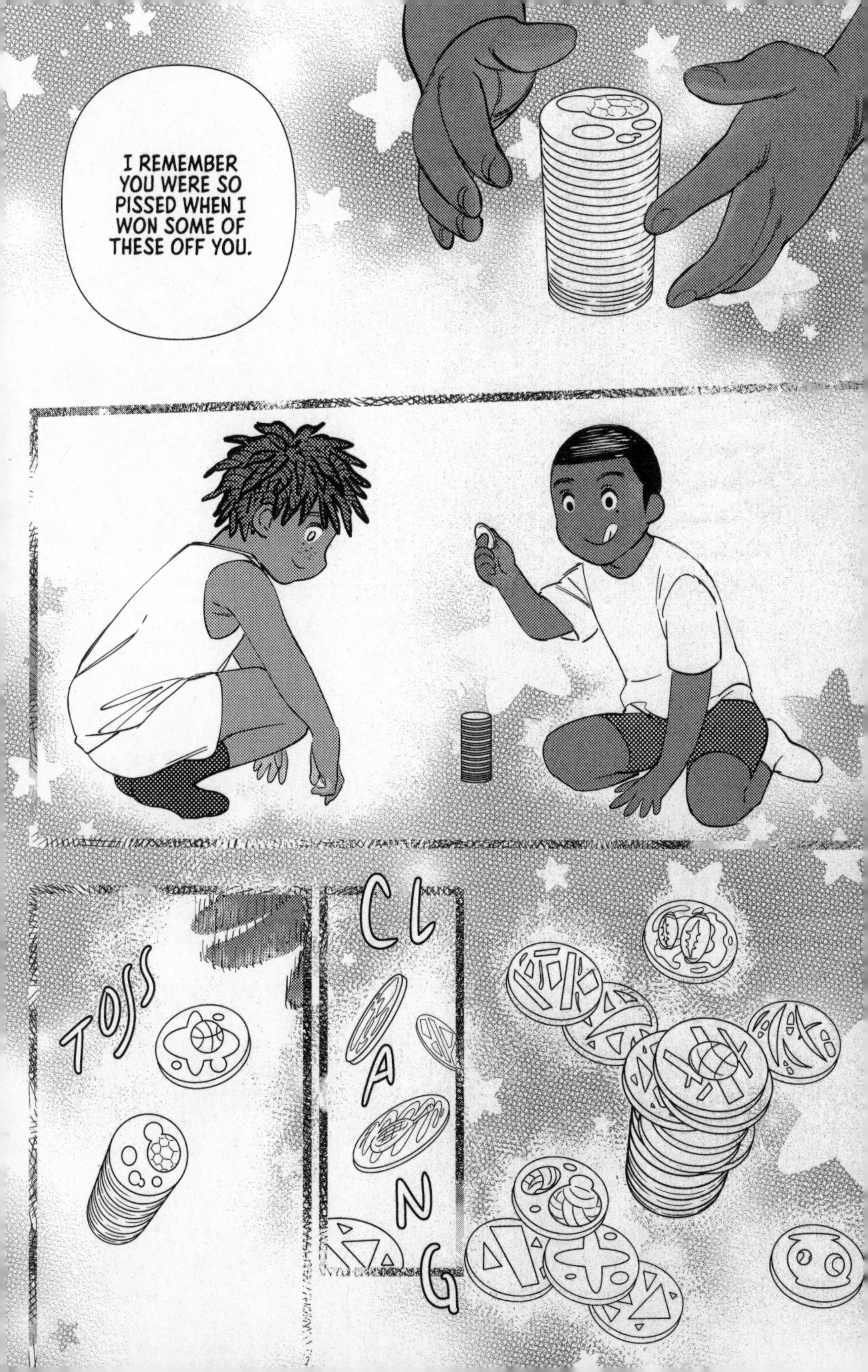

I REMEMBER YOU WERE SO PISSED WHEN I WON SOME OF THESE OFF YOU.
TOSS
CLANG

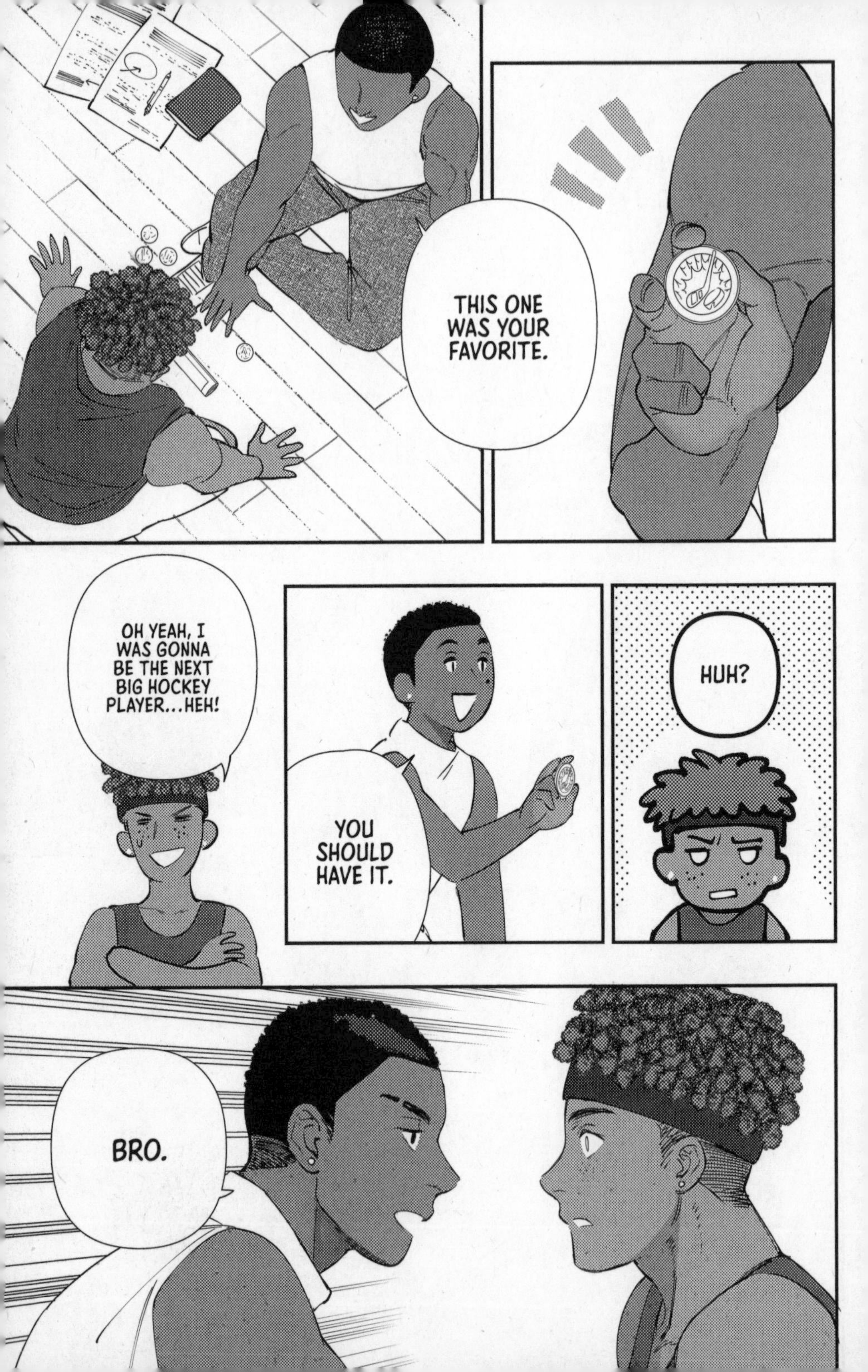
THIS ONE WAS YOUR FAVORITE.
OH YEAH, I WAS GONNA BE THE NEXT BIG HOCKEY PLAYER...HEH!
YOU SHOULD HAVE IT.
HUH?
BRO.

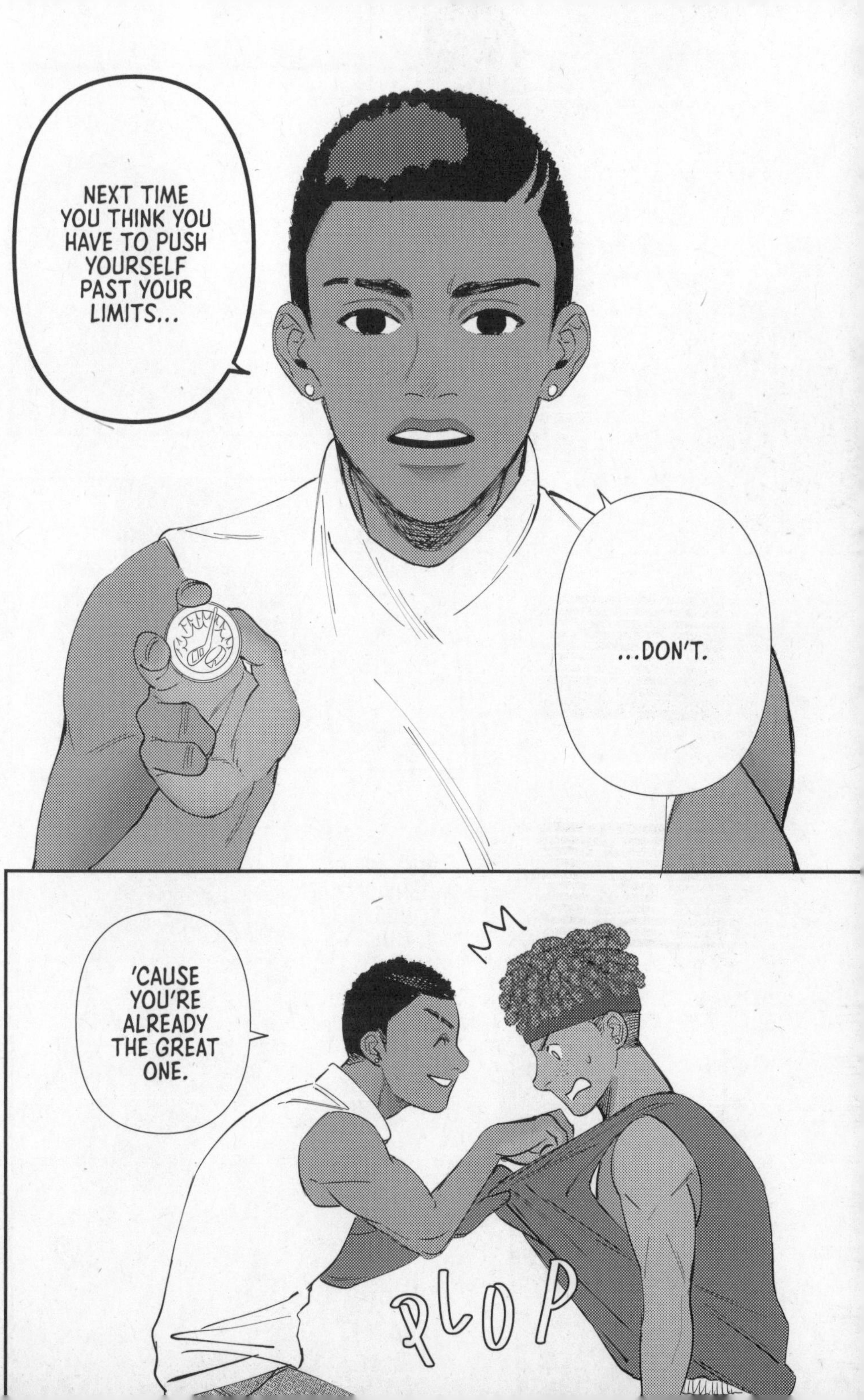
NEXT TIME YOU THINK YOU HAVE TO PUSH YOURSELF PAST YOUR LIMITS...
...DON'T.
'CAUSE YOU'RE ALREADY THE GREAT ONE.
PLOP

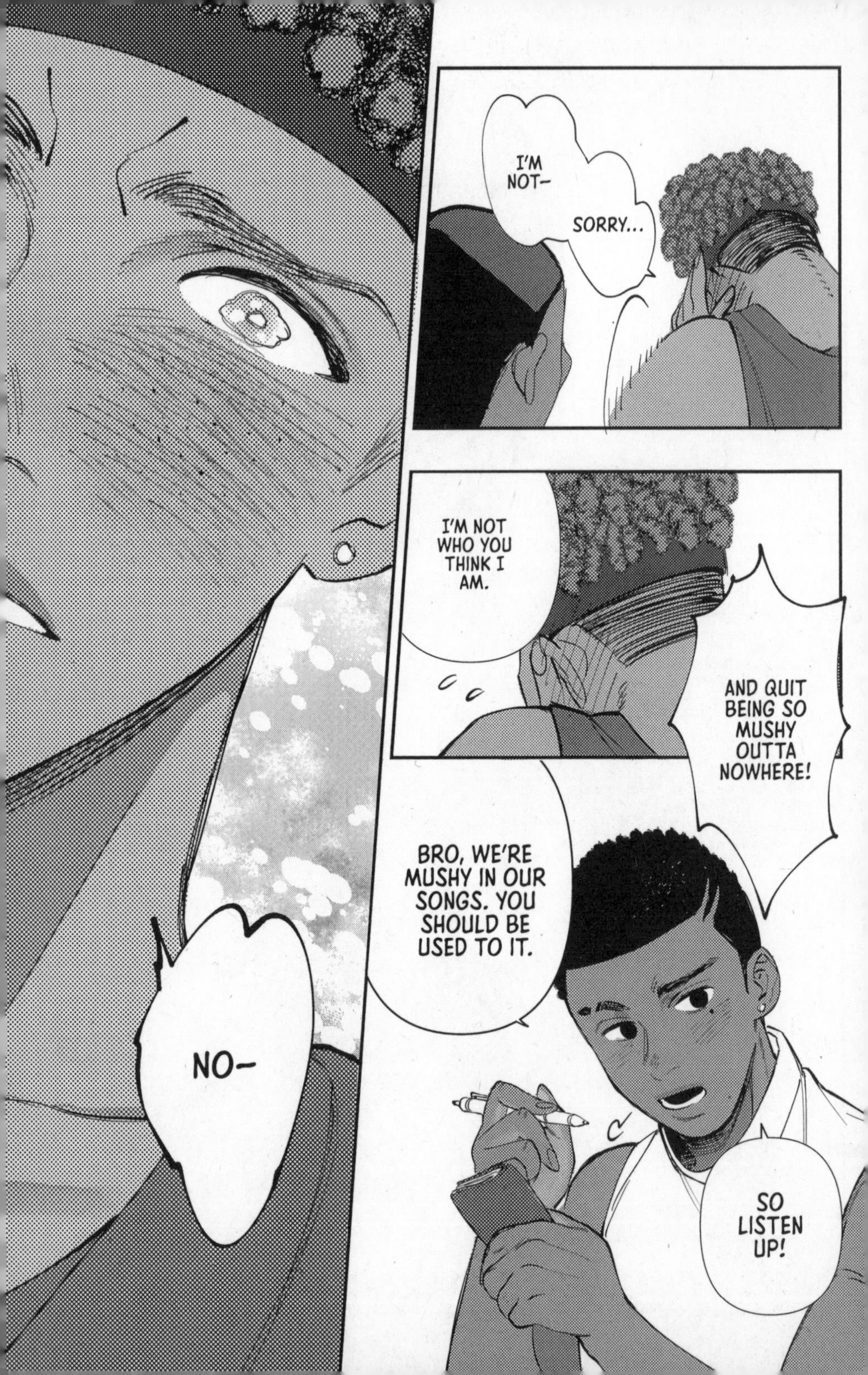
NO-
I'M NOT-
SORRY...
I'M NOT WHO YOU THINK I AM.
AND QUIT BEING SO MUSHY OUTTA NOWHERE!
BRO, WE'RE MUSHY IN OUR SONGS. YOU SHOULD BE USED TO IT.
SO LISTEN UP!

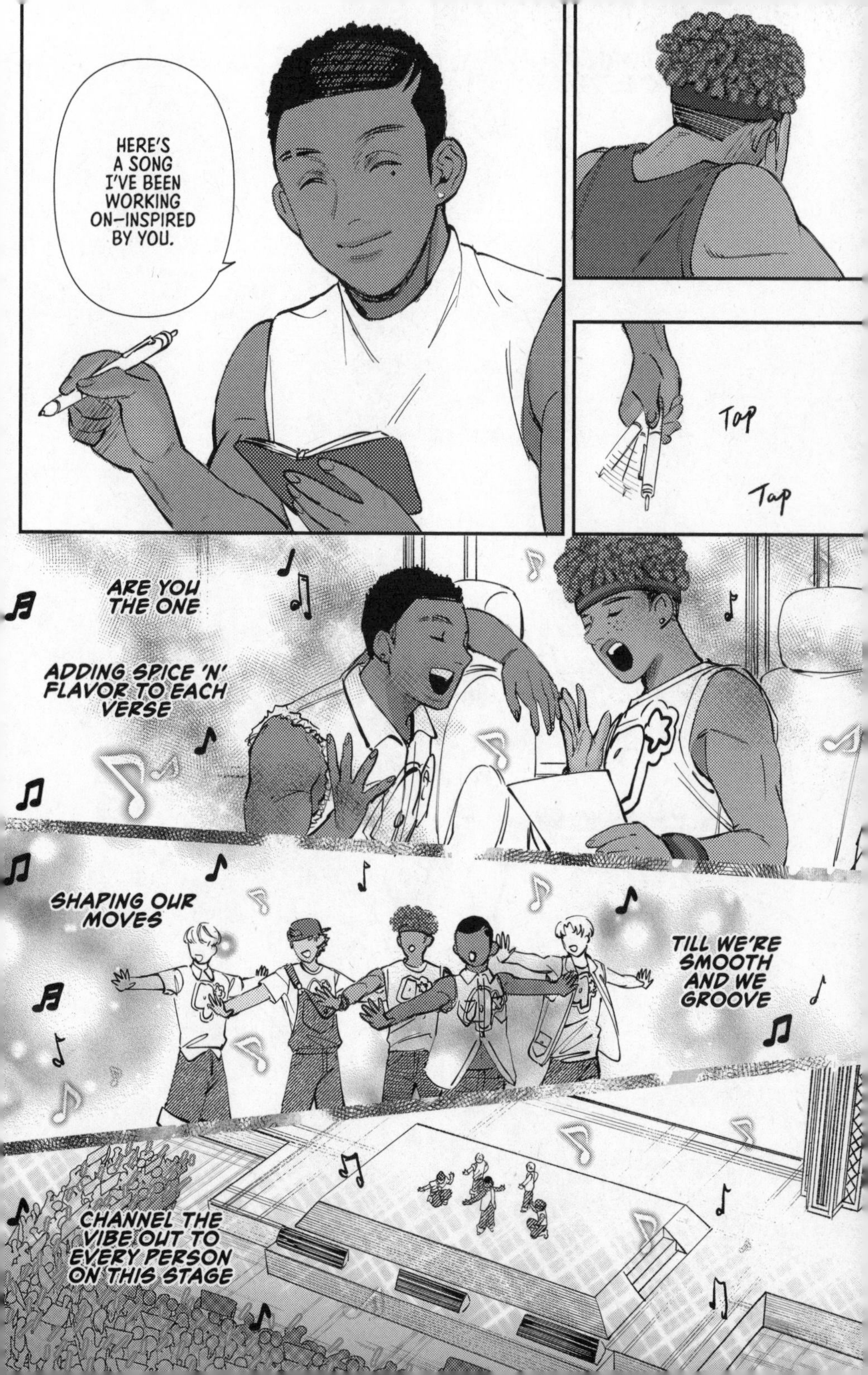
HERE'S A SONG I'VE BEEN WORKING ON—INSPIRED BY YOU.
Tap
Tap
ARE YOU THE ONE
ADDING SPICE 'N' FLAVOR TO EACH VERSE
SHAPING OUR MOVES
TILL WE'RE SMOOTH AND WE GROOVE
CHANNEL THE VIBE OUT TO EVERY PERSON ON THIS STAGE

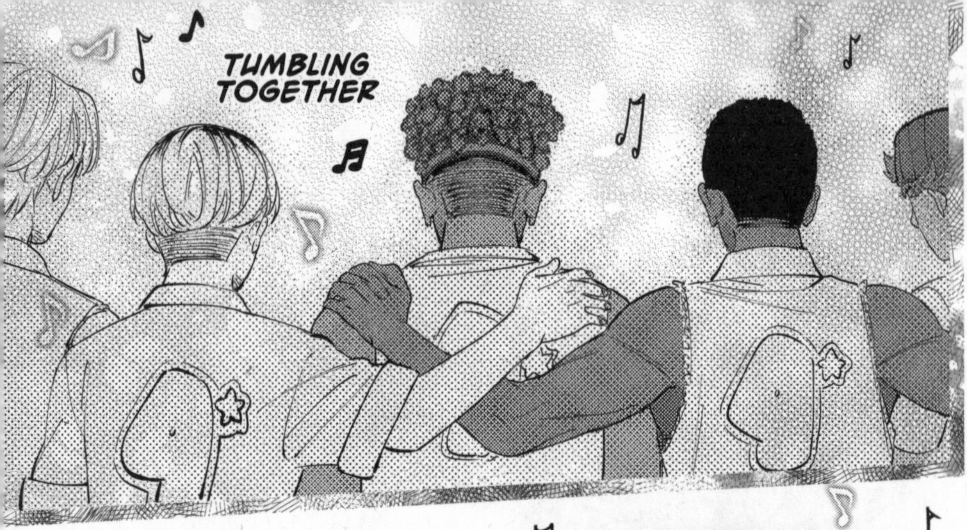
TUMBLING TOGETHER

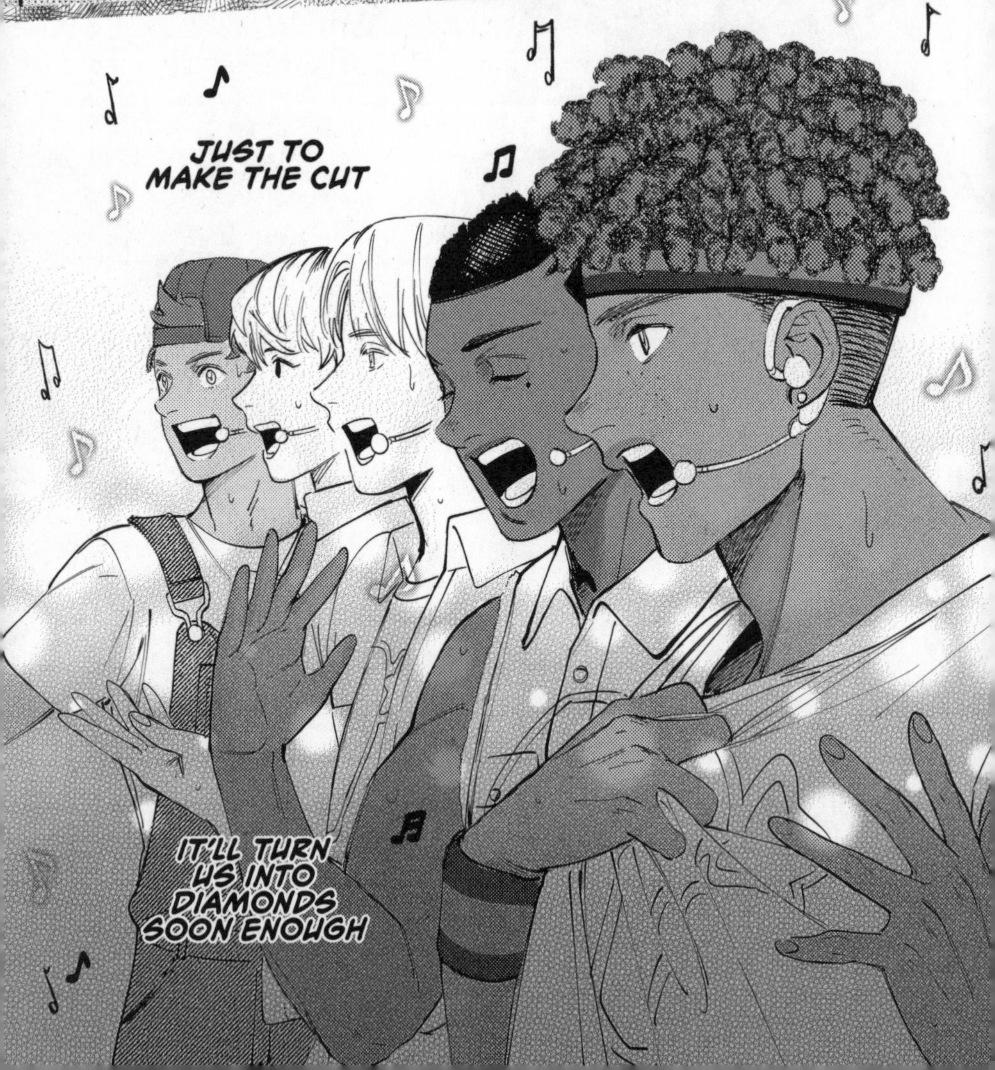
JUST TO MAKE THE CUT
IT'LL TURN US INTO DIAMONDS SOON ENOUGH

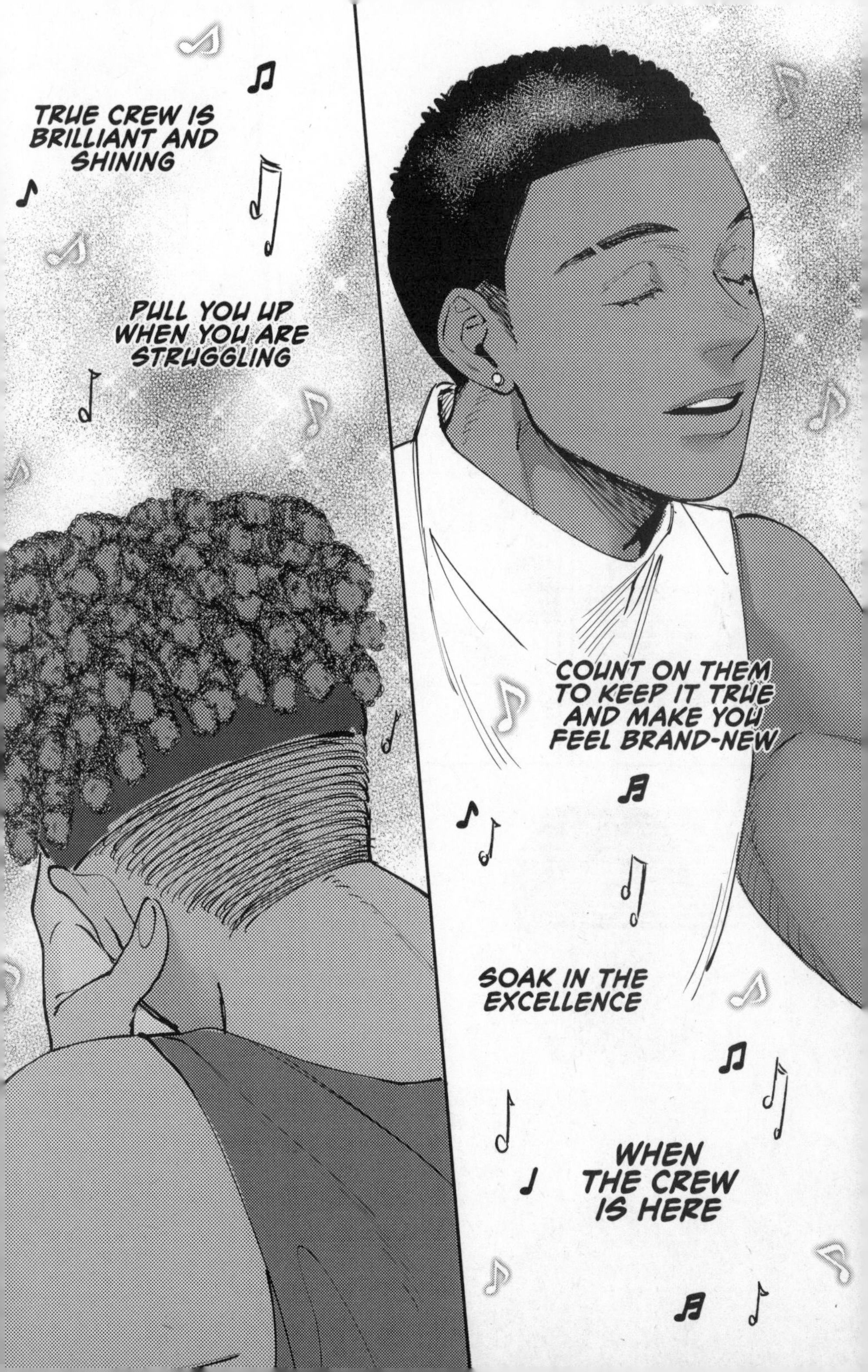
TRUE CREW IS BRILLIANT AND SHINING
PULL YOU UP WHEN YOU ARE STRUGGLING
COUNT ON THEM TO KEEP IT TRUE AND MAKE YOU FEEL BRAND-NEW
SOAK IN THE EXCELLENCE
WHEN THE CREW IS HERE

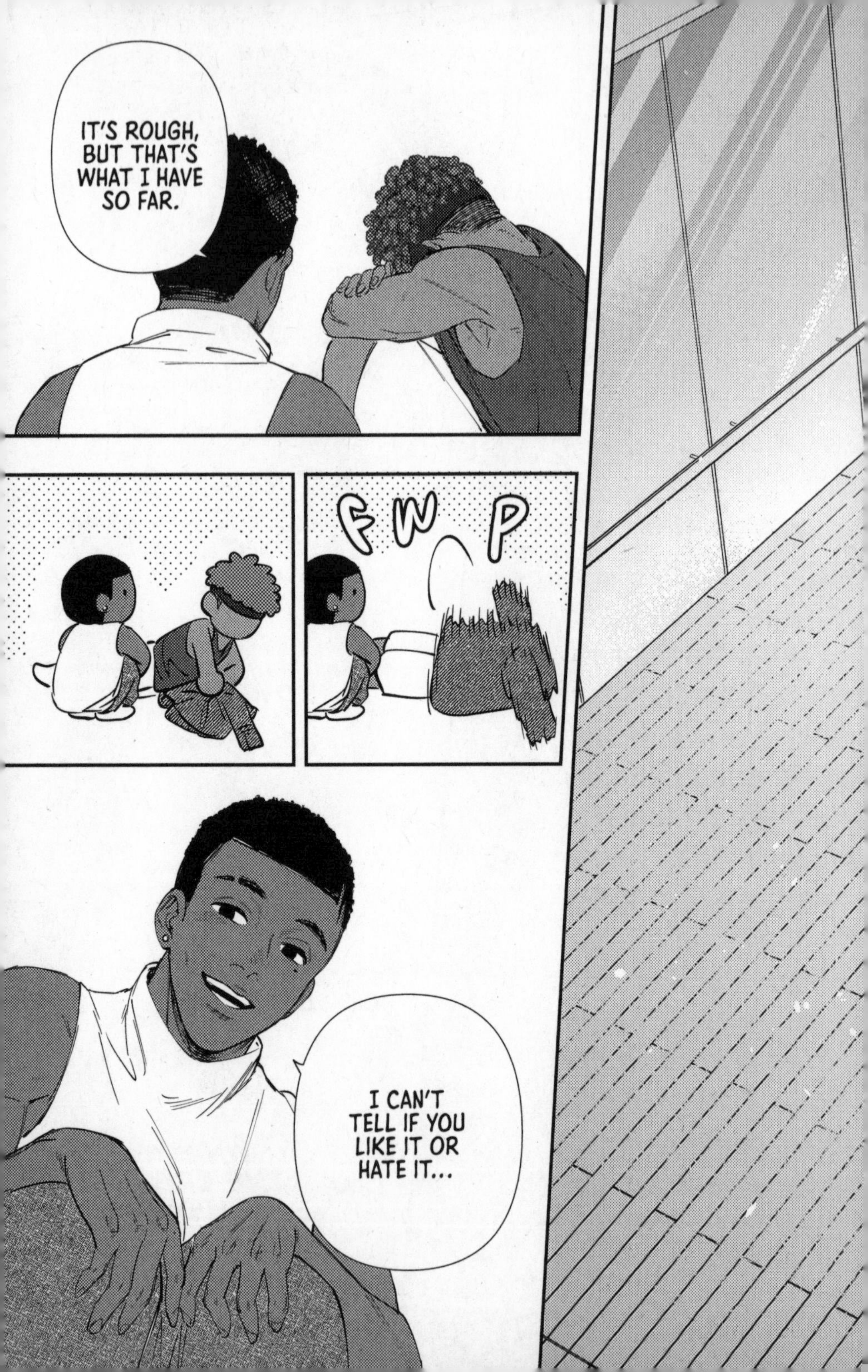
IT'S ROUGH, BUT THAT'S WHAT I HAVE SO FAR.
FWP
I CAN'T TELL IF YOU LIKE IT OR HATE IT...

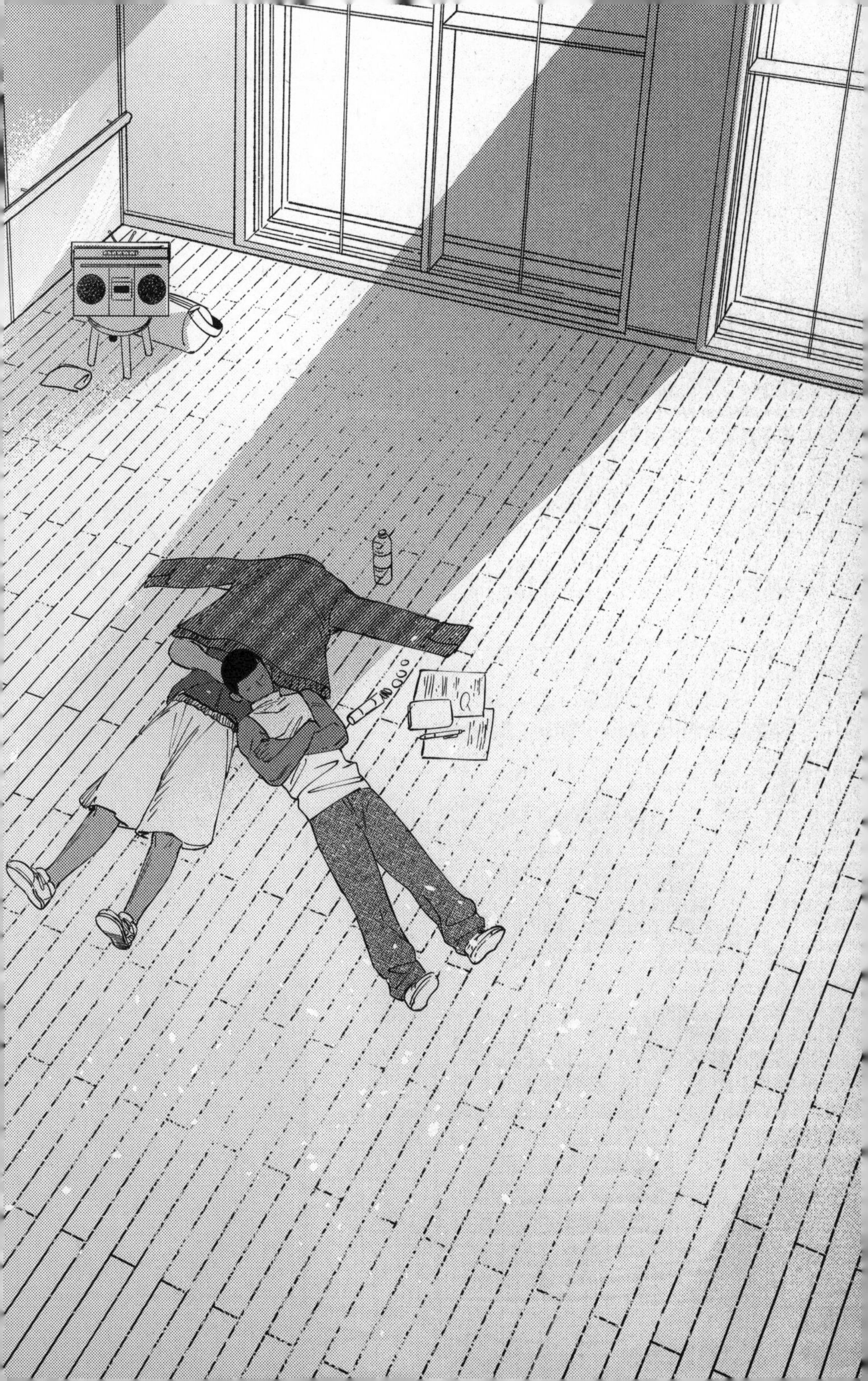

Impossible

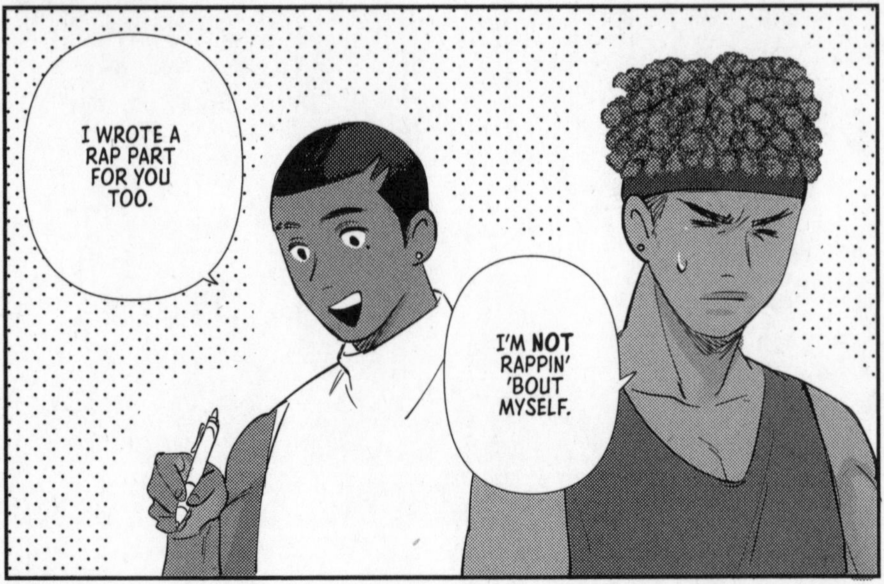
I WROTE A RAP PART FOR YOU TOO.
I'M NOT RAPPIN' 'BOUT MYSELF.

Mush Is a One-Way Street

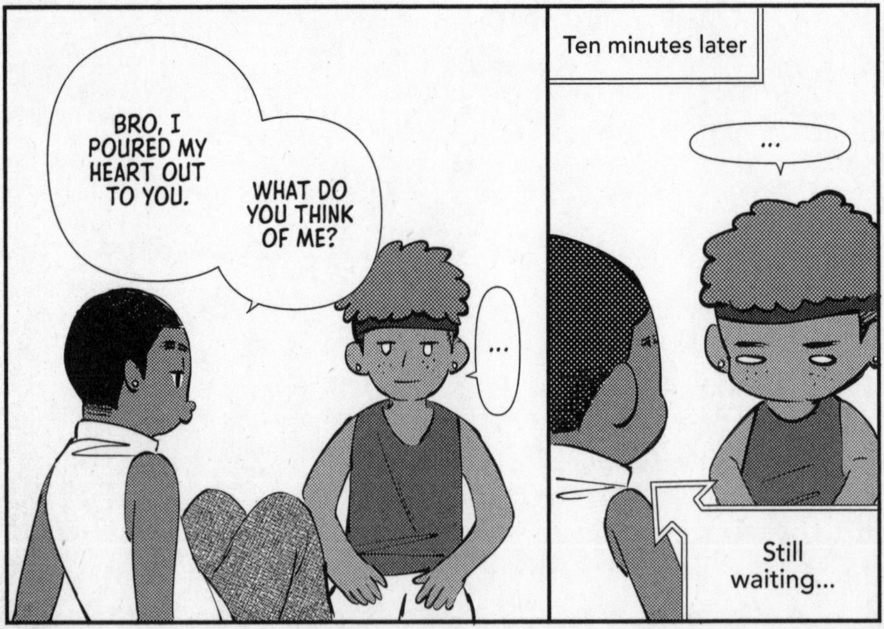
BRO, I POURED MY HEART OUT TO YOU.
WHAT DO YOU THINK OF ME?
...
Ten minutes later
...
Still waiting...

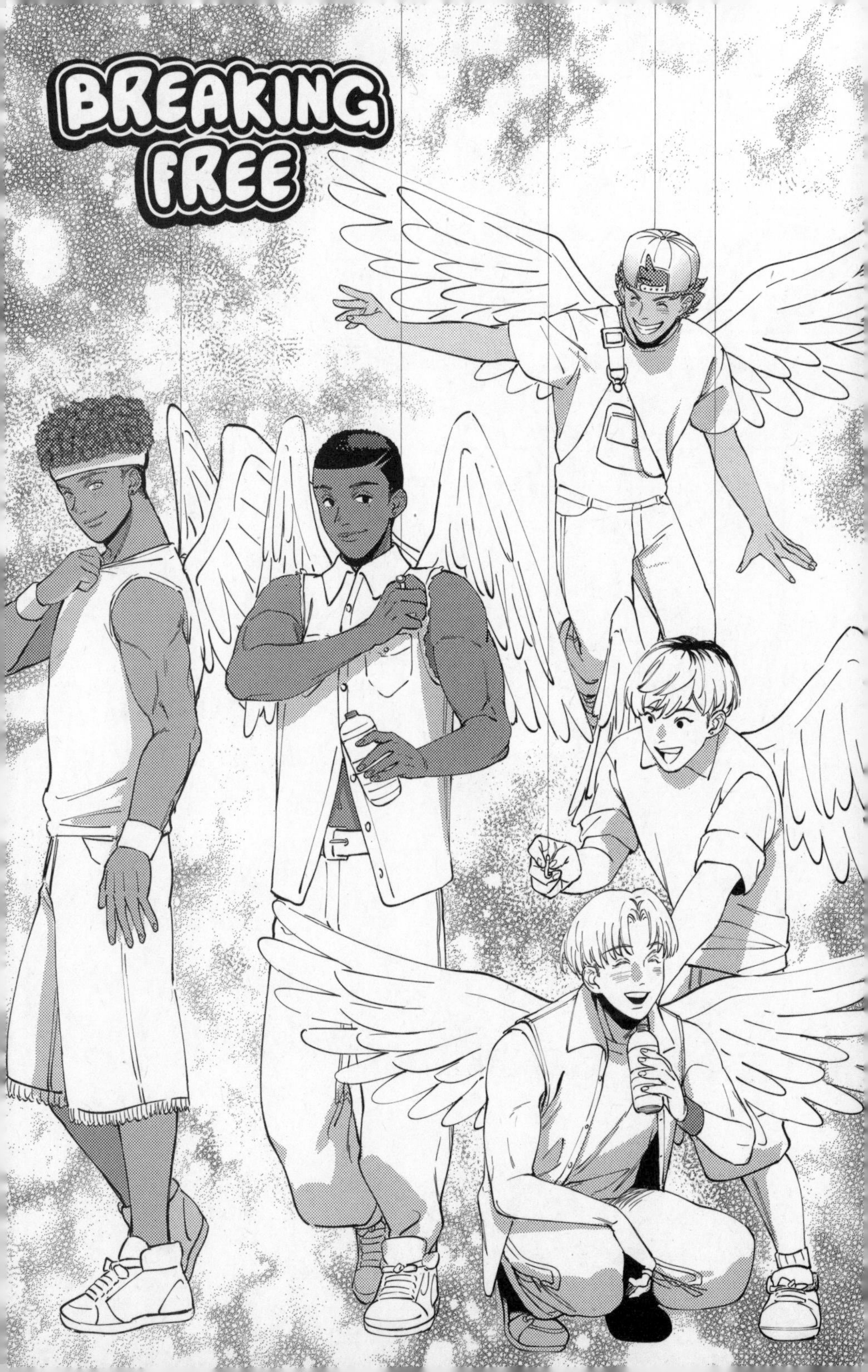
BREAKING
FREE

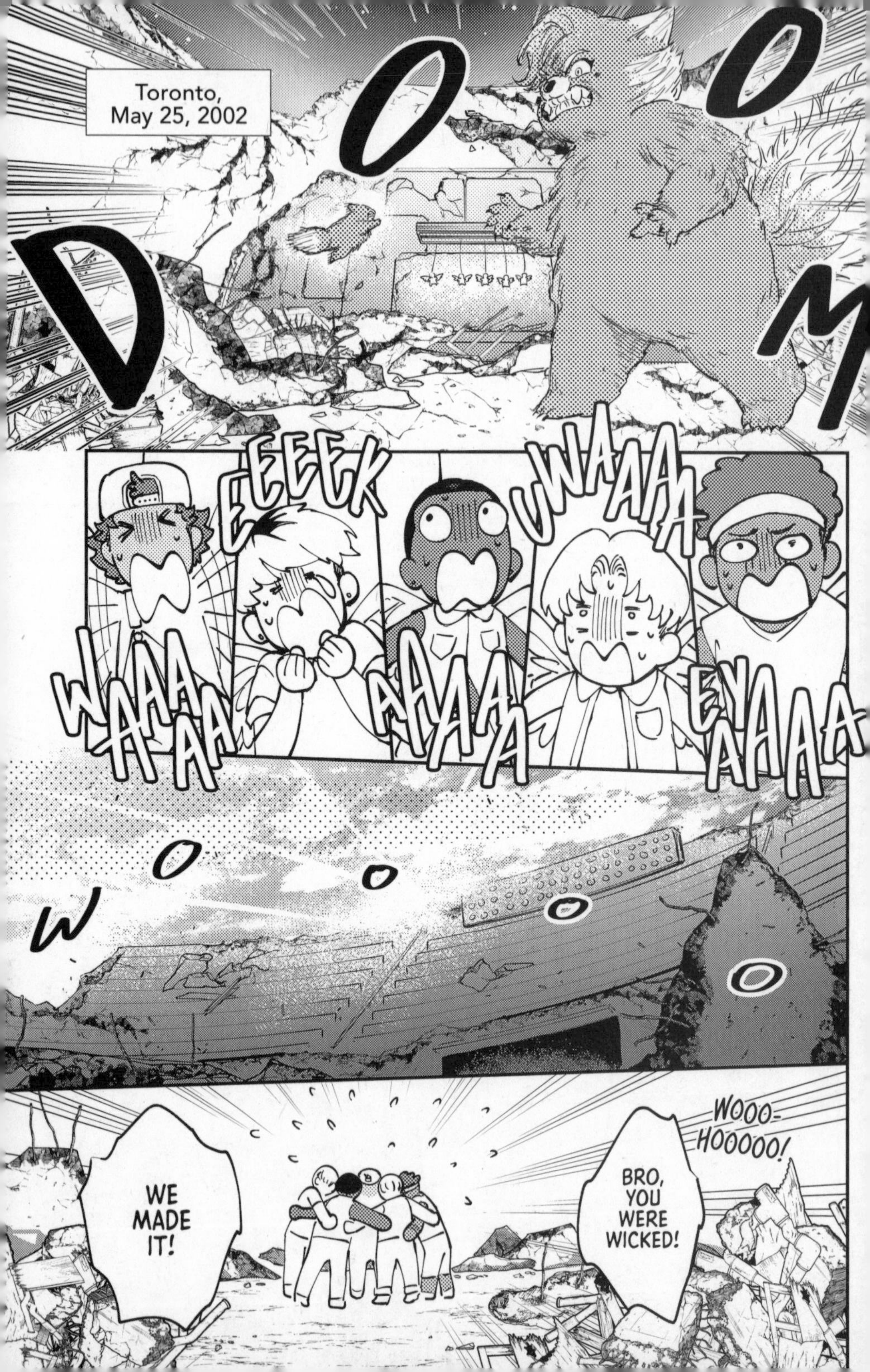
Toronto,
May 25, 2002
DOOOM
WAAAAA
EEEEK
AAAAAA
UWAAAAA
EYAAAAA
WOOOO
WE MADE IT!
WOOO-HOOOOO!
BRO, YOU WERE WICKED!

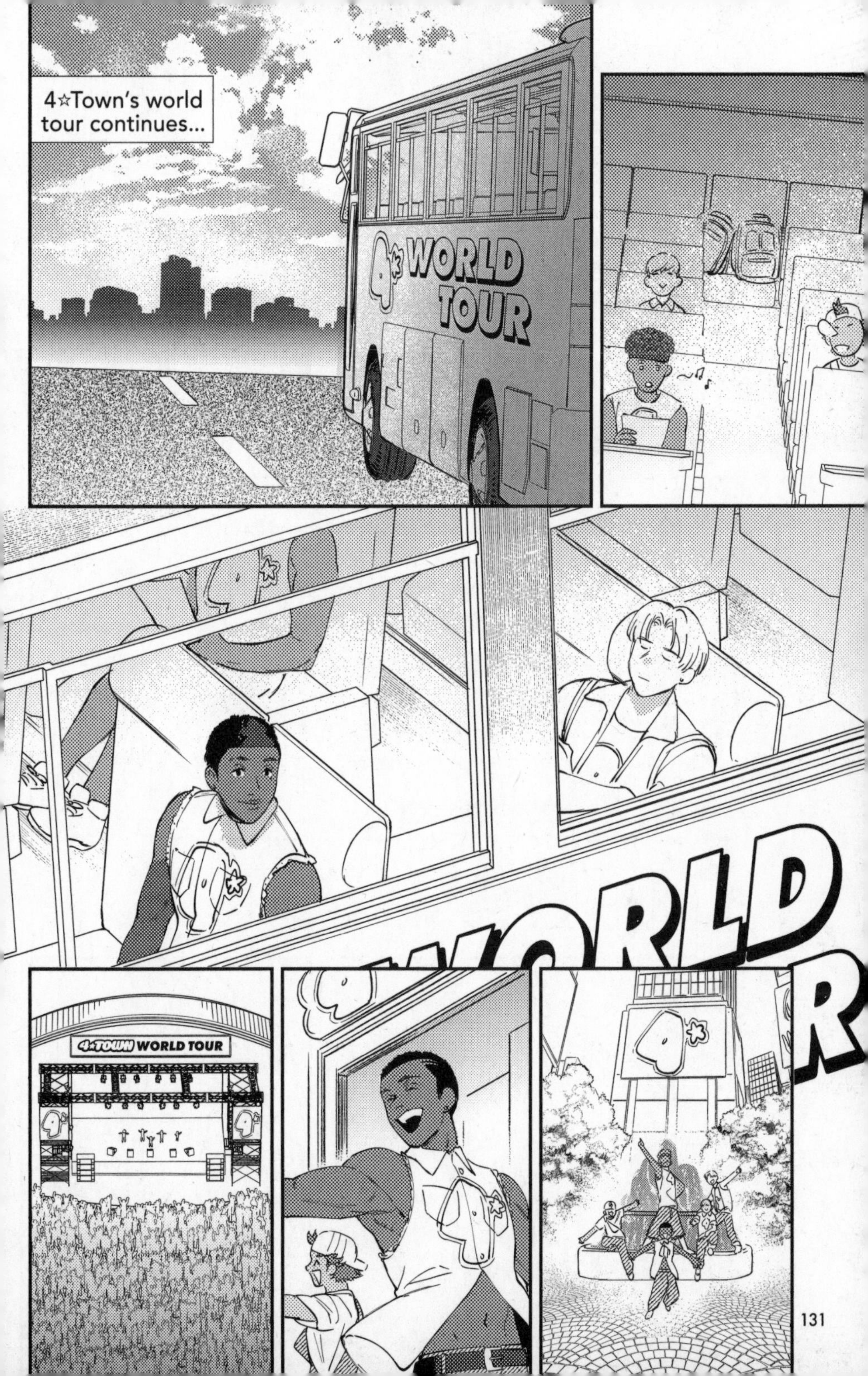
4☆Town's world tour continues...
WORLD TOUR
WORLD
4☆TOWN WORLD TOUR

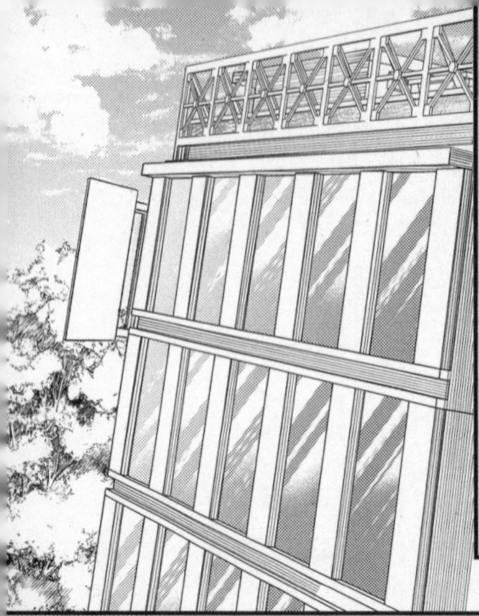

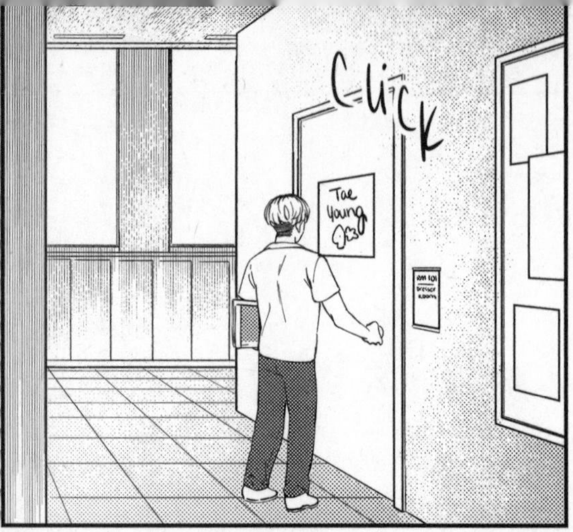
CLICK
Tae Young

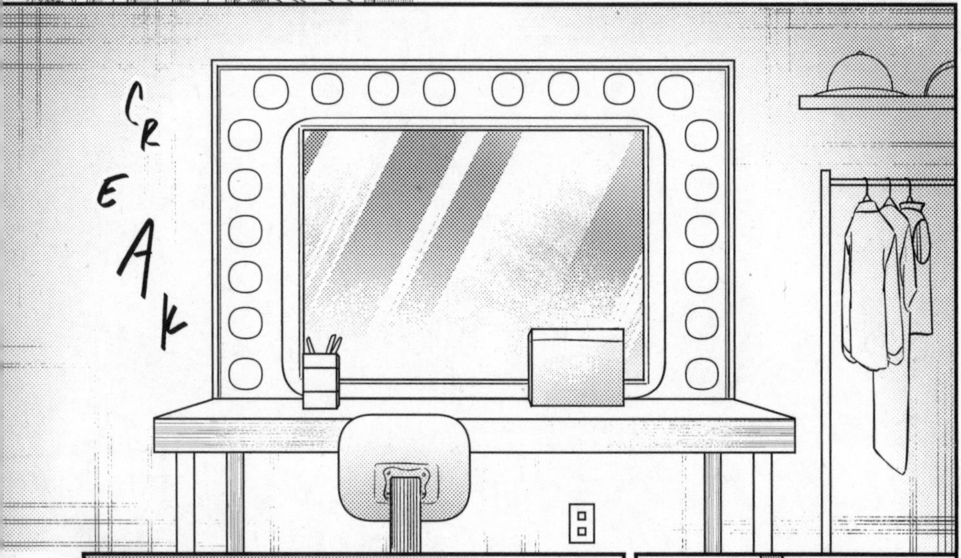
CREAK

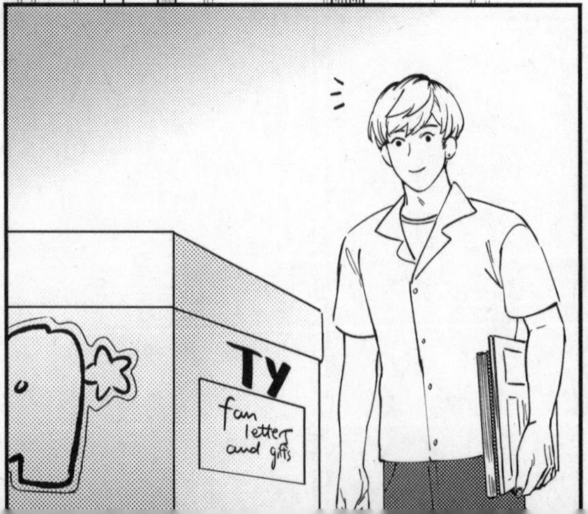
TY
fan letters and gifts

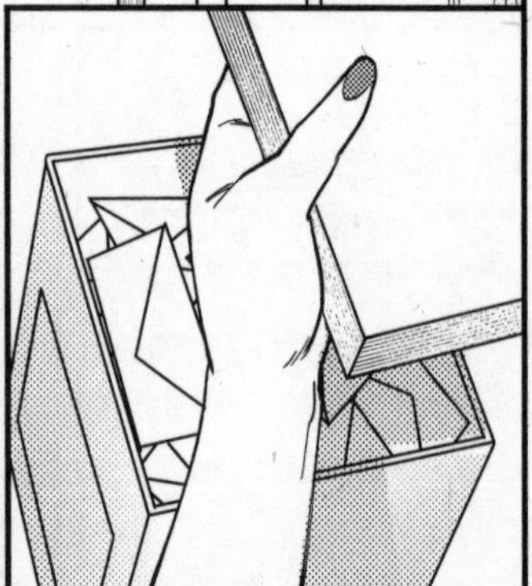

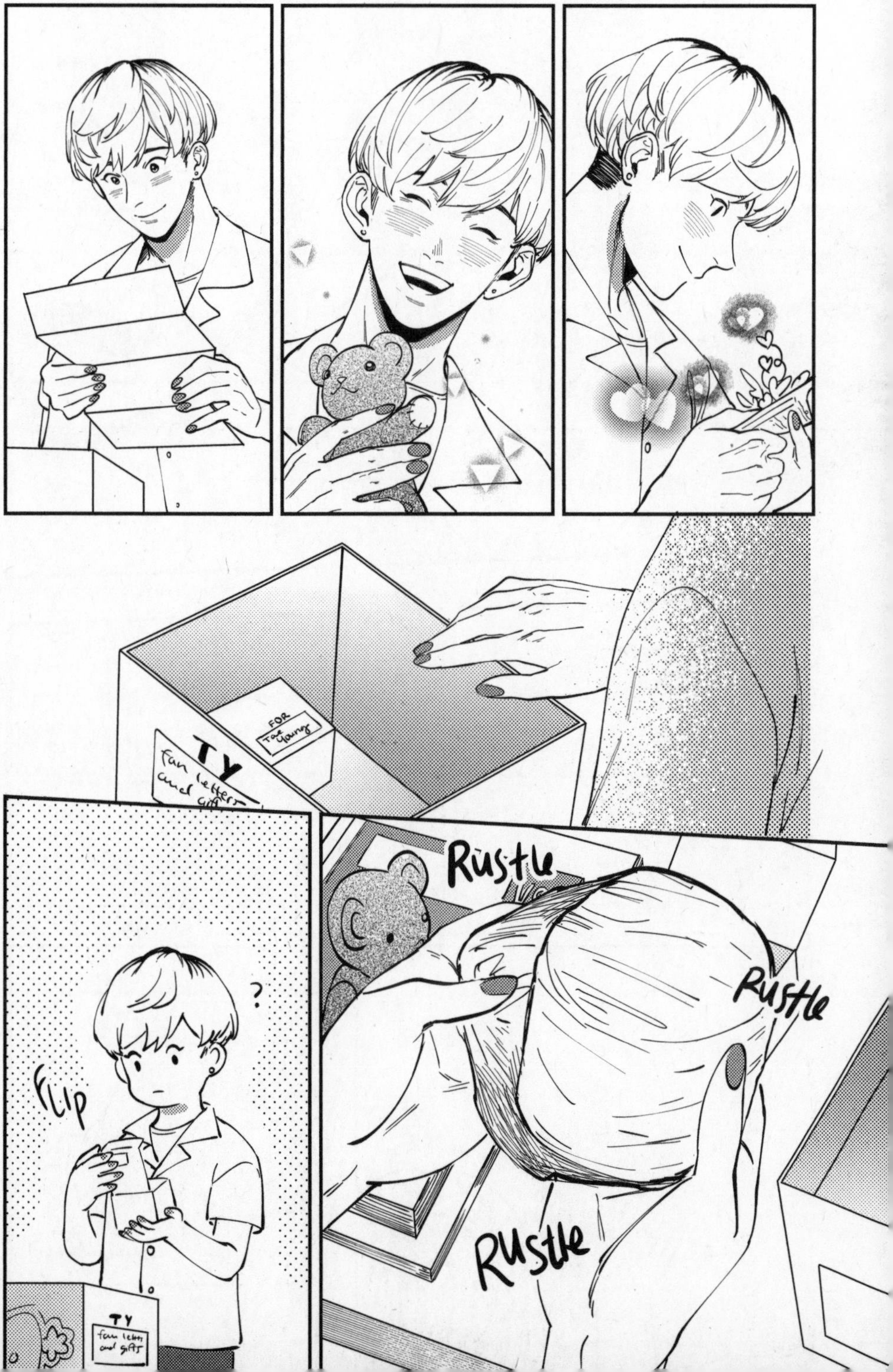

TY
Fan letters and gifts
FOR Tae Young
?
FLIP
TY
fan letters and gifts
Rustle
Rustle
Rustle

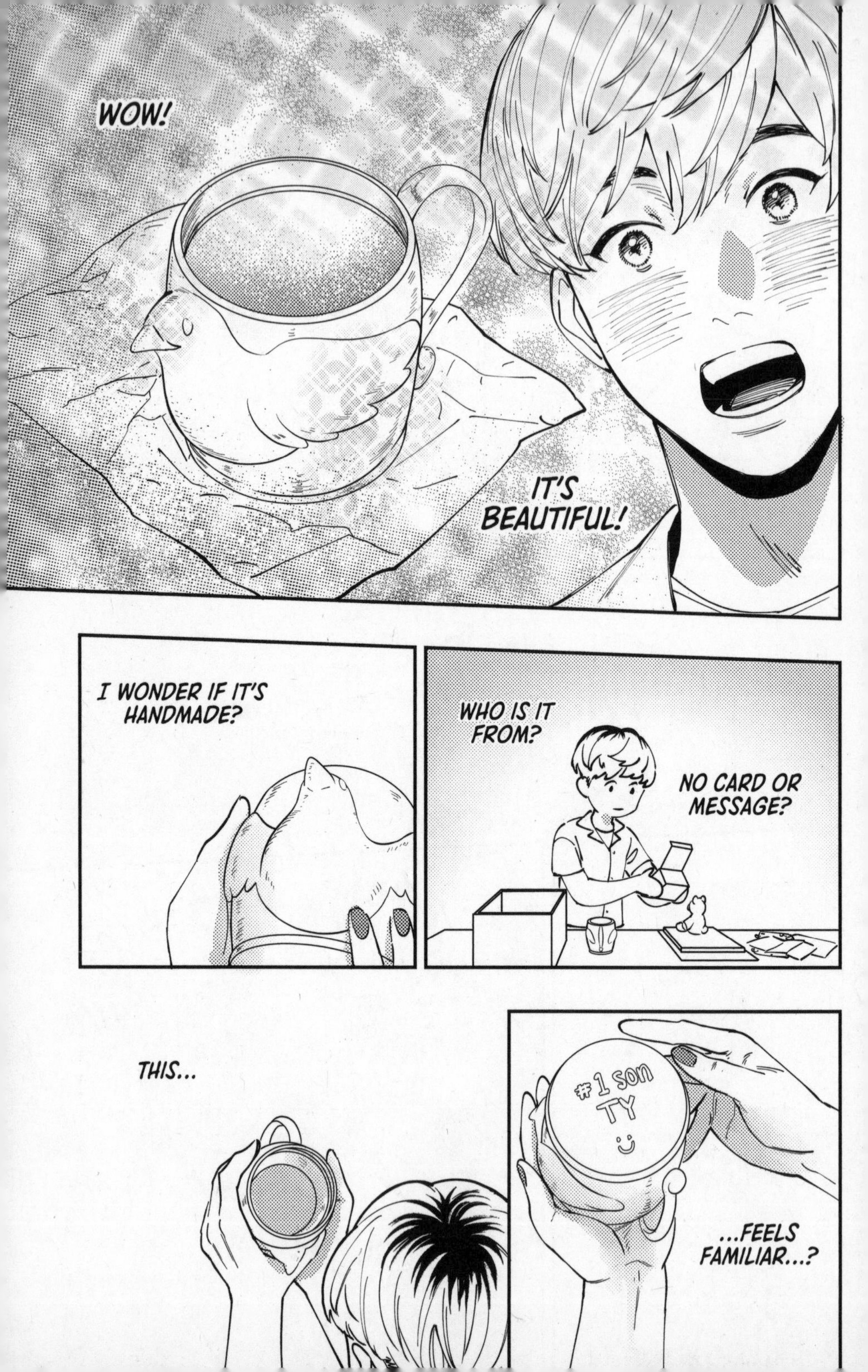
WOW!
IT'S BEAUTIFUL!
I WONDER IF IT'S HANDMADE?
WHO IS IT FROM?
NO CARD OR MESSAGE?
THIS...
#1 son
TY
...FEELS FAMILIAR...?

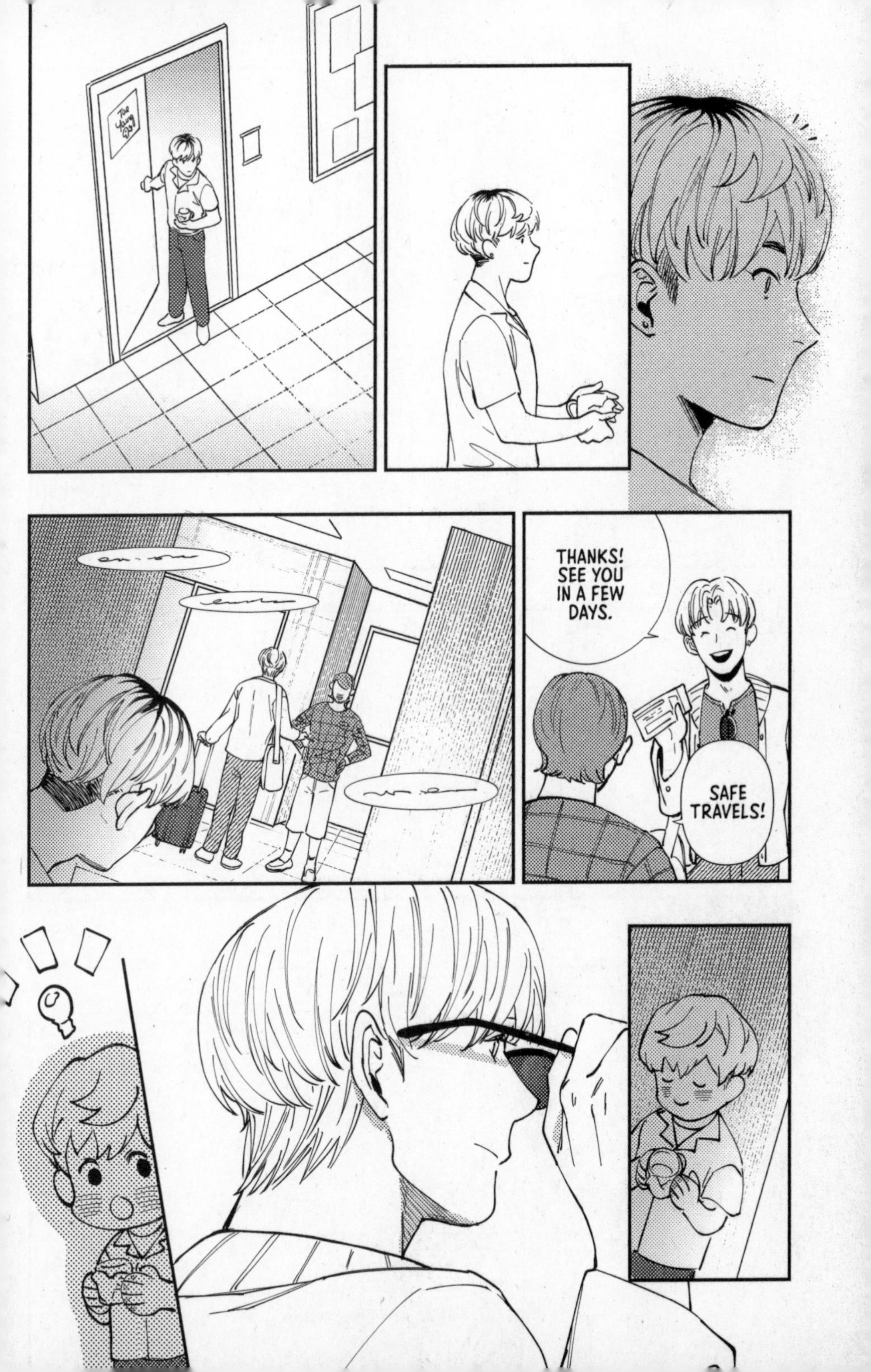
THANKS! SEE YOU IN A FEW DAYS.
SAFE TRAVELS!

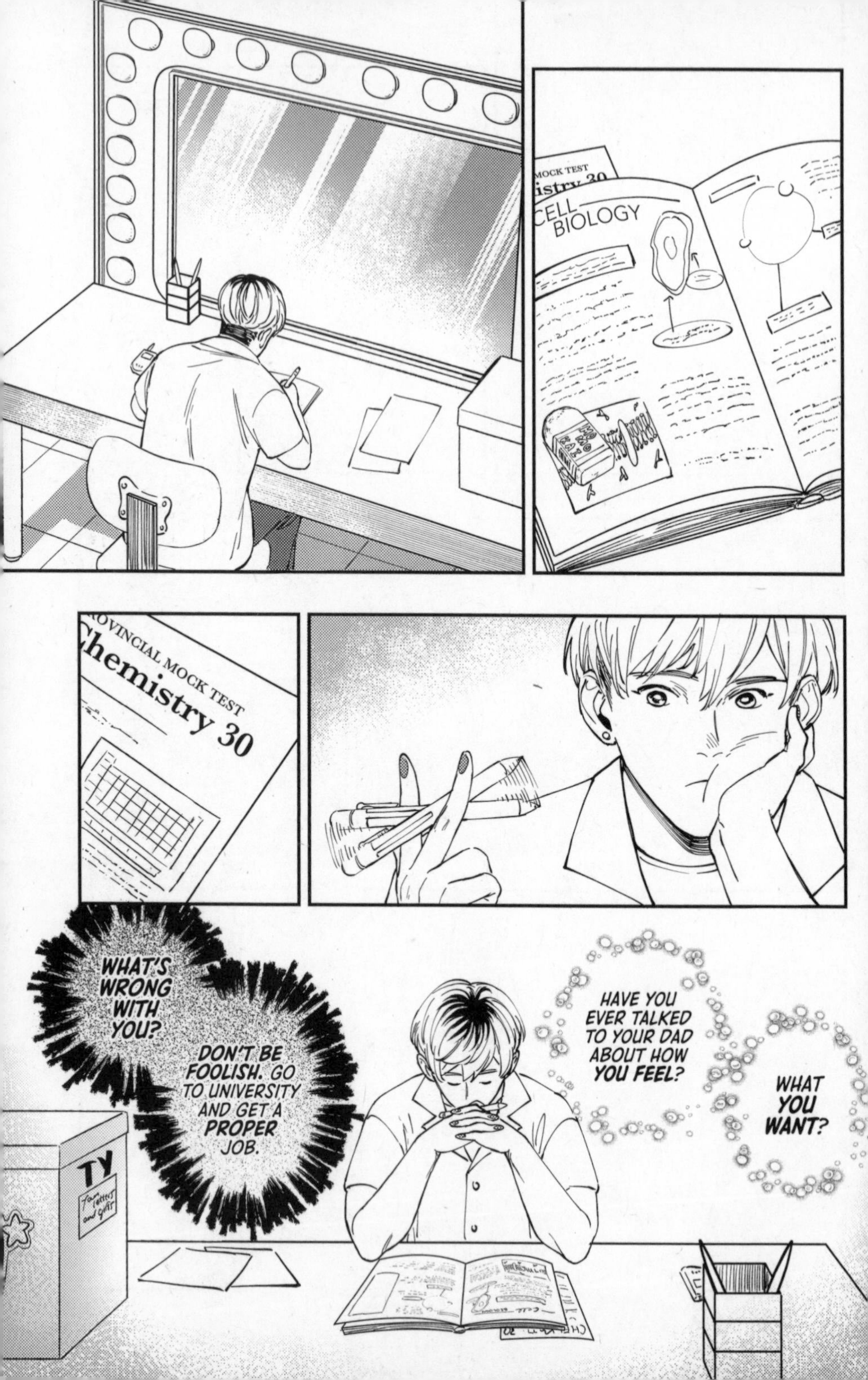
MOCK TEST
istry 30
CELL BIOLOGY
OVINCIAL MOCK TEST
Chemistry 30
WHAT'S WRONG WITH YOU?
DON'T BE FOOLISH. GO TO UNIVERSITY AND GET A PROPER JOB.
TY
Fan letters and gifts
HAVE YOU EVER TALKED TO YOUR DAD ABOUT HOW YOU FEEL?
WHAT YOU WANT?

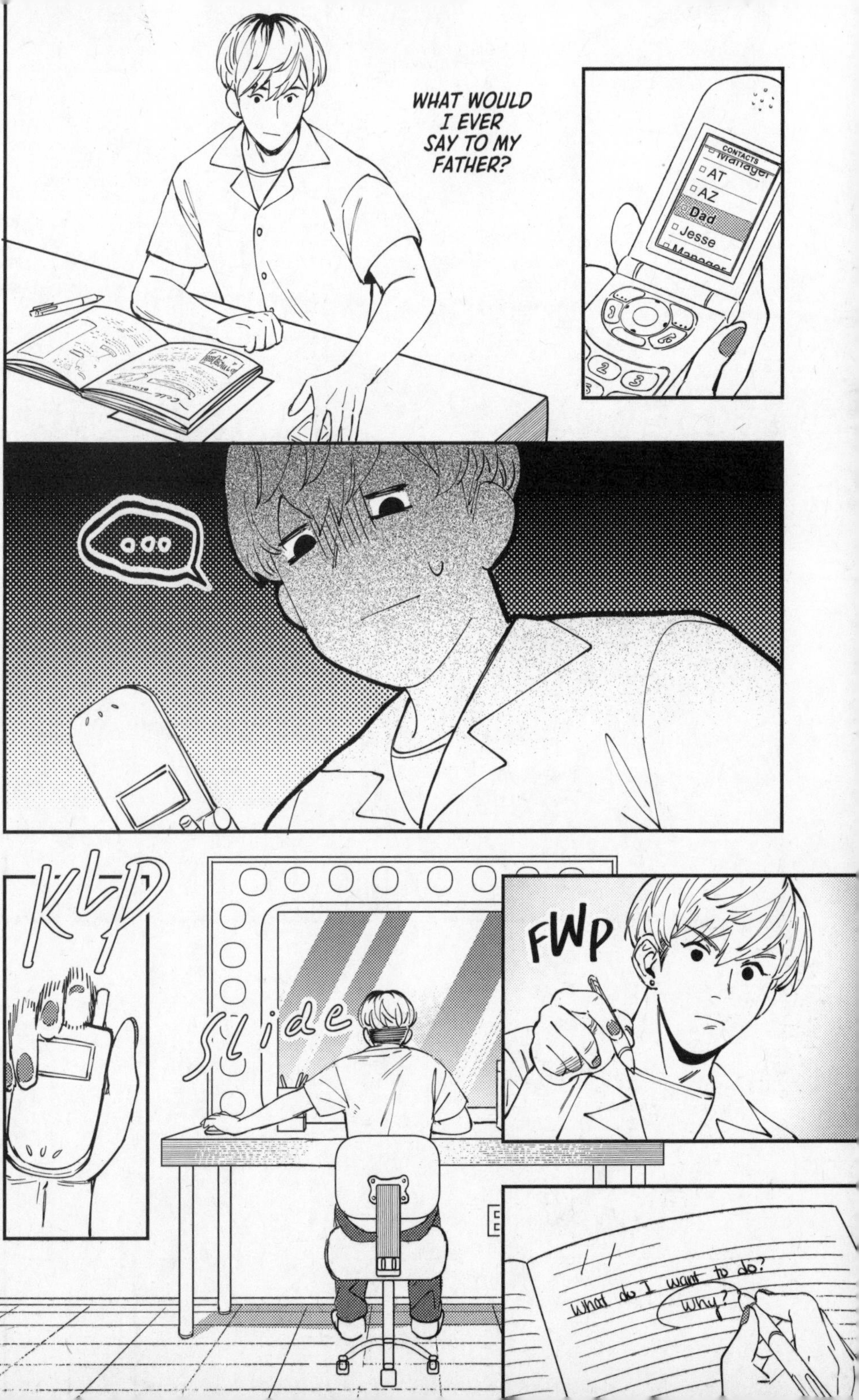
WHAT WOULD I EVER SAY TO MY FATHER?
CONTACTS
AT
AZ
Dad
Jesse
...
KLP
Slide
FWP
What do I want to do?
Why?

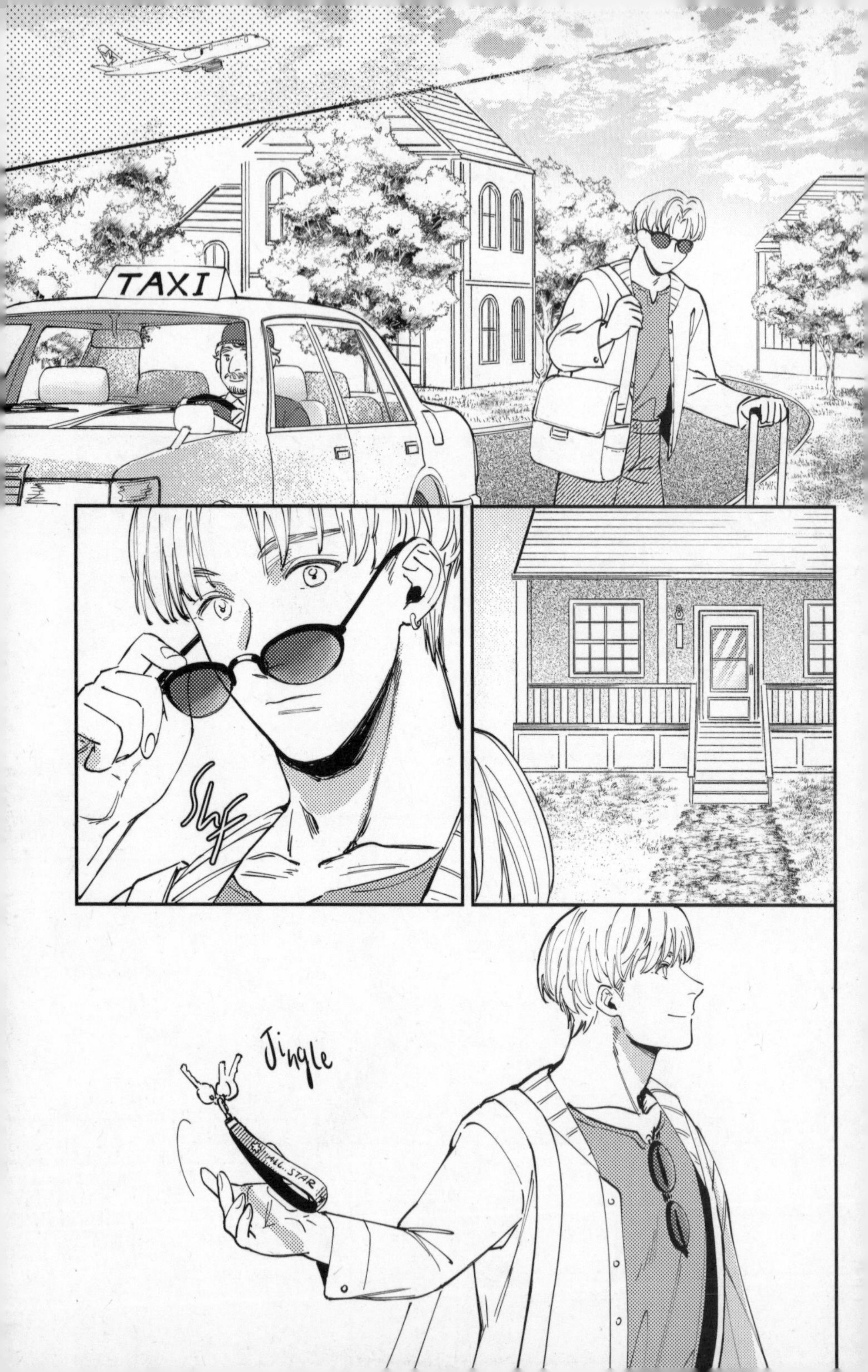
TAXI
Shf
Jingle
ALL..STAR

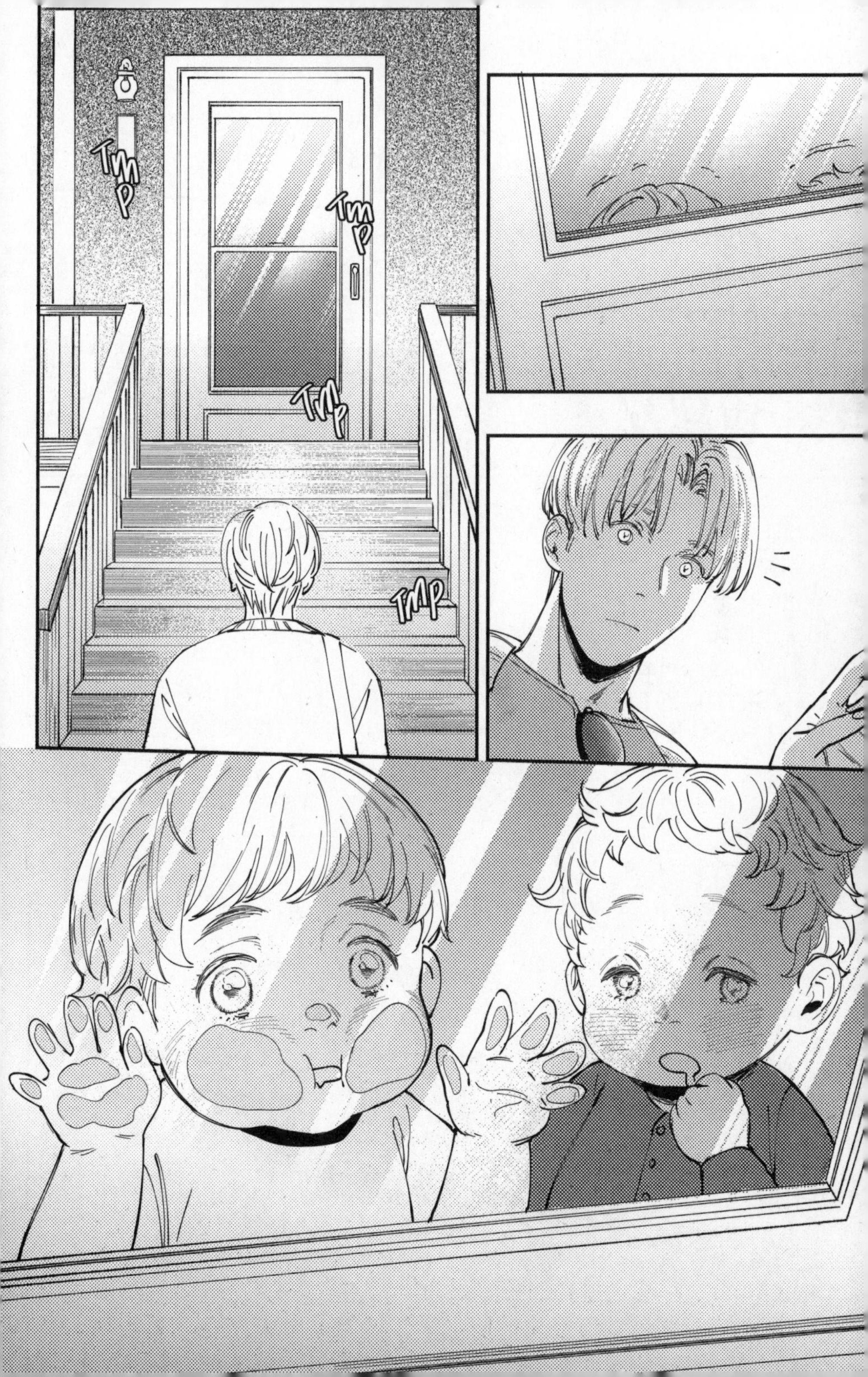
TMP
TMP
TMP
TMP

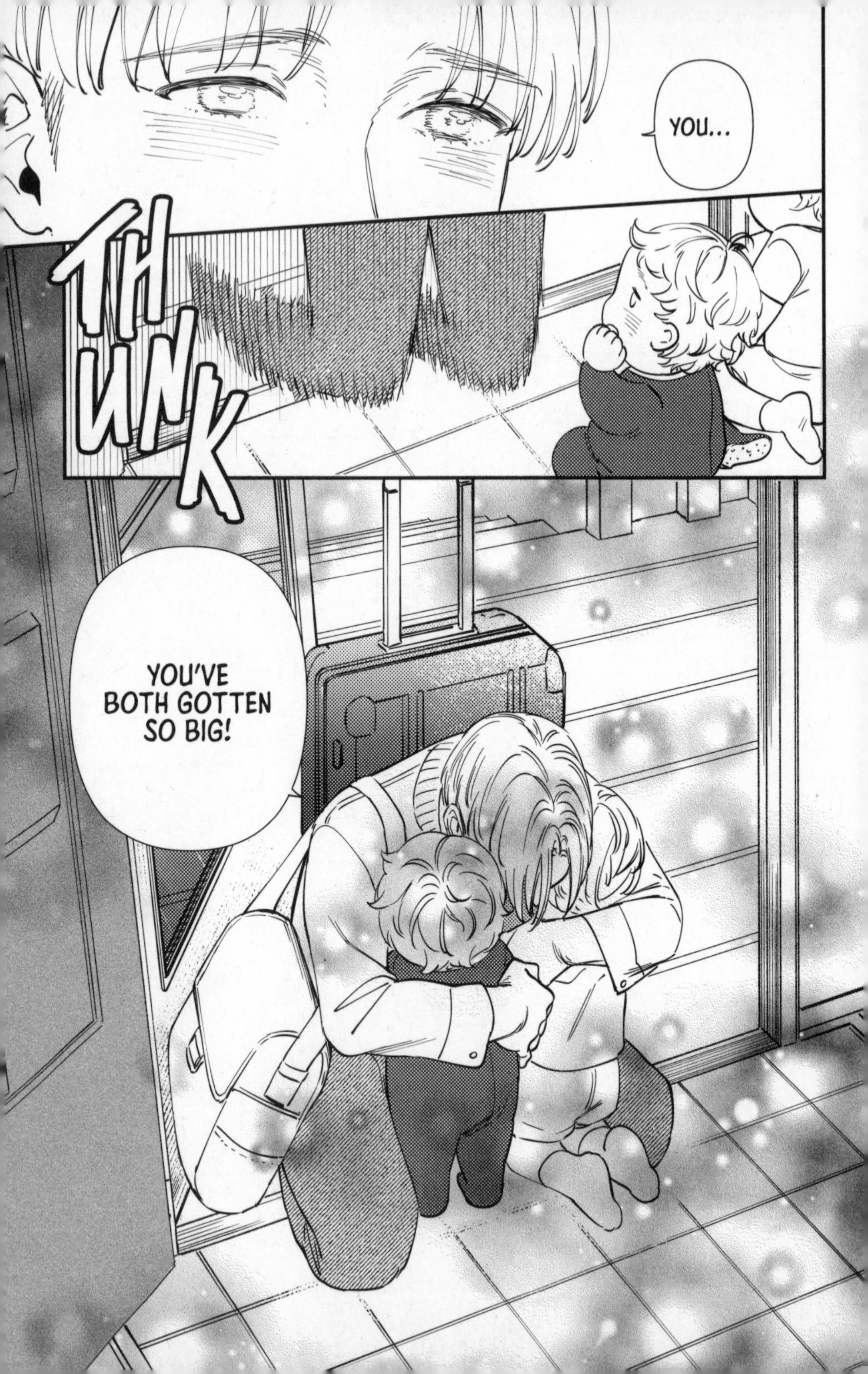
YOU...
THUNK
YOU'VE BOTH GOTTEN SO BIG!

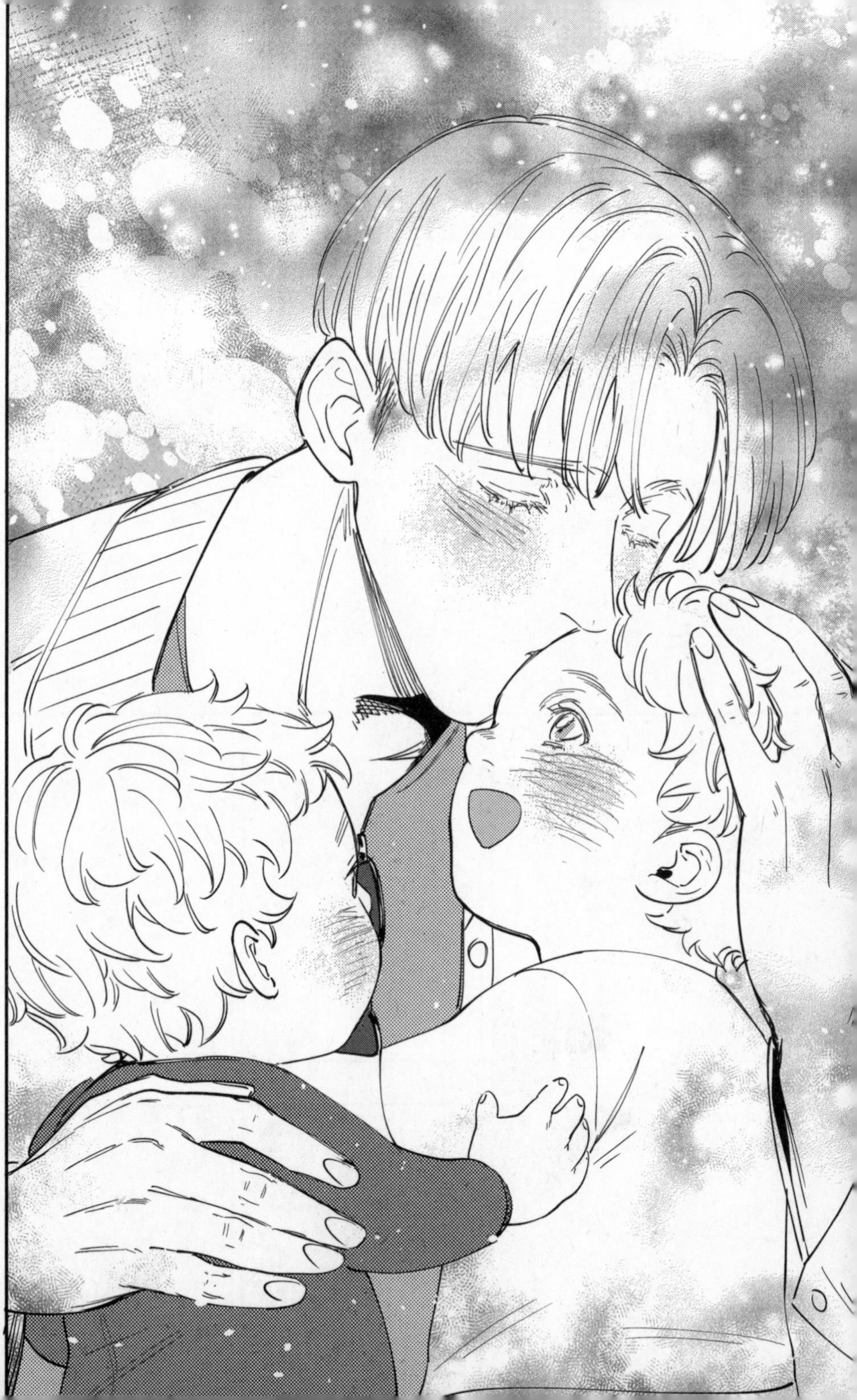

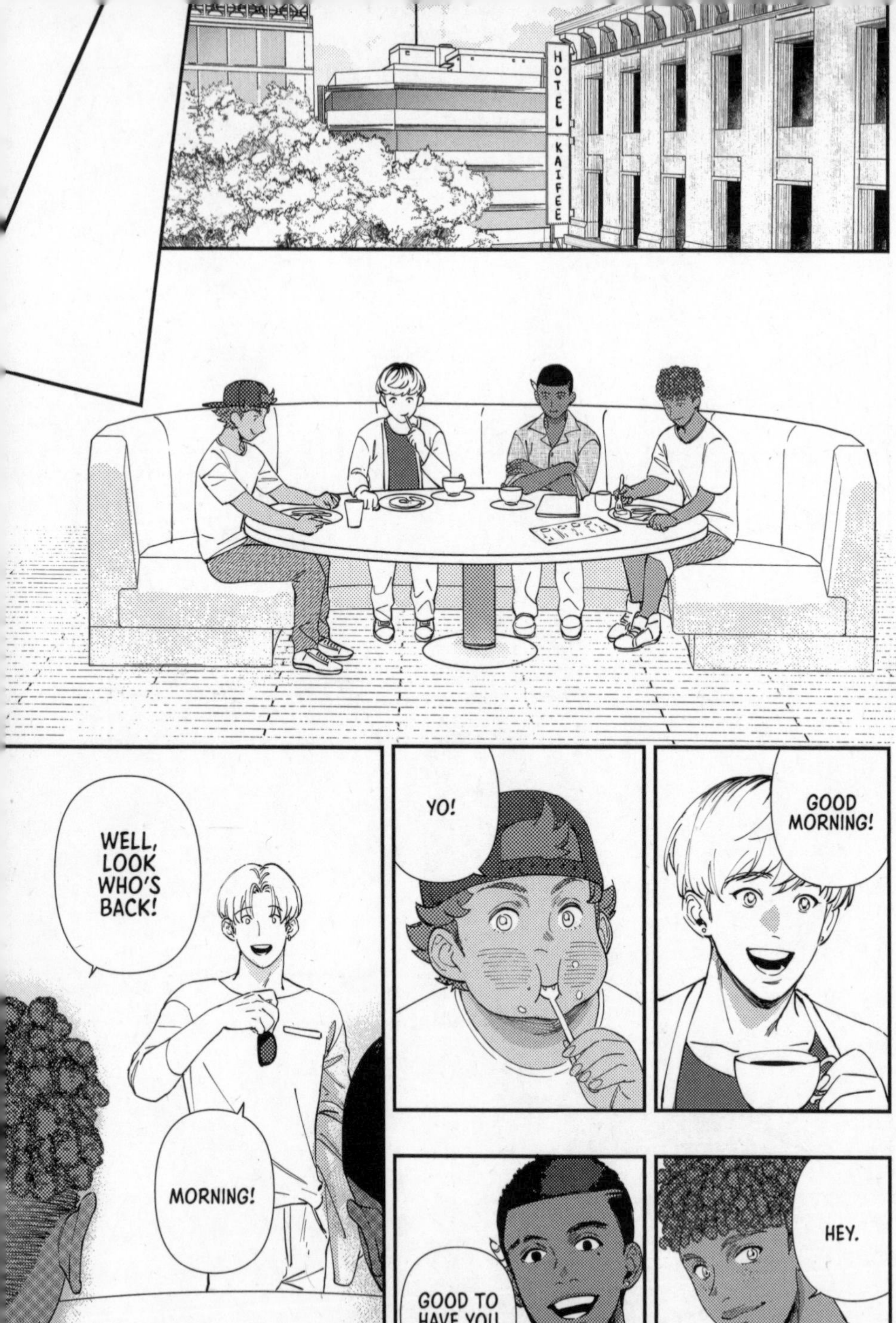
HOTEL KAIFEE
WELL, LOOK WHO'S BACK!
MORNING!
YO!
GOOD MORNING!
GOOD TO HAVE YOU BACK!
HEY.

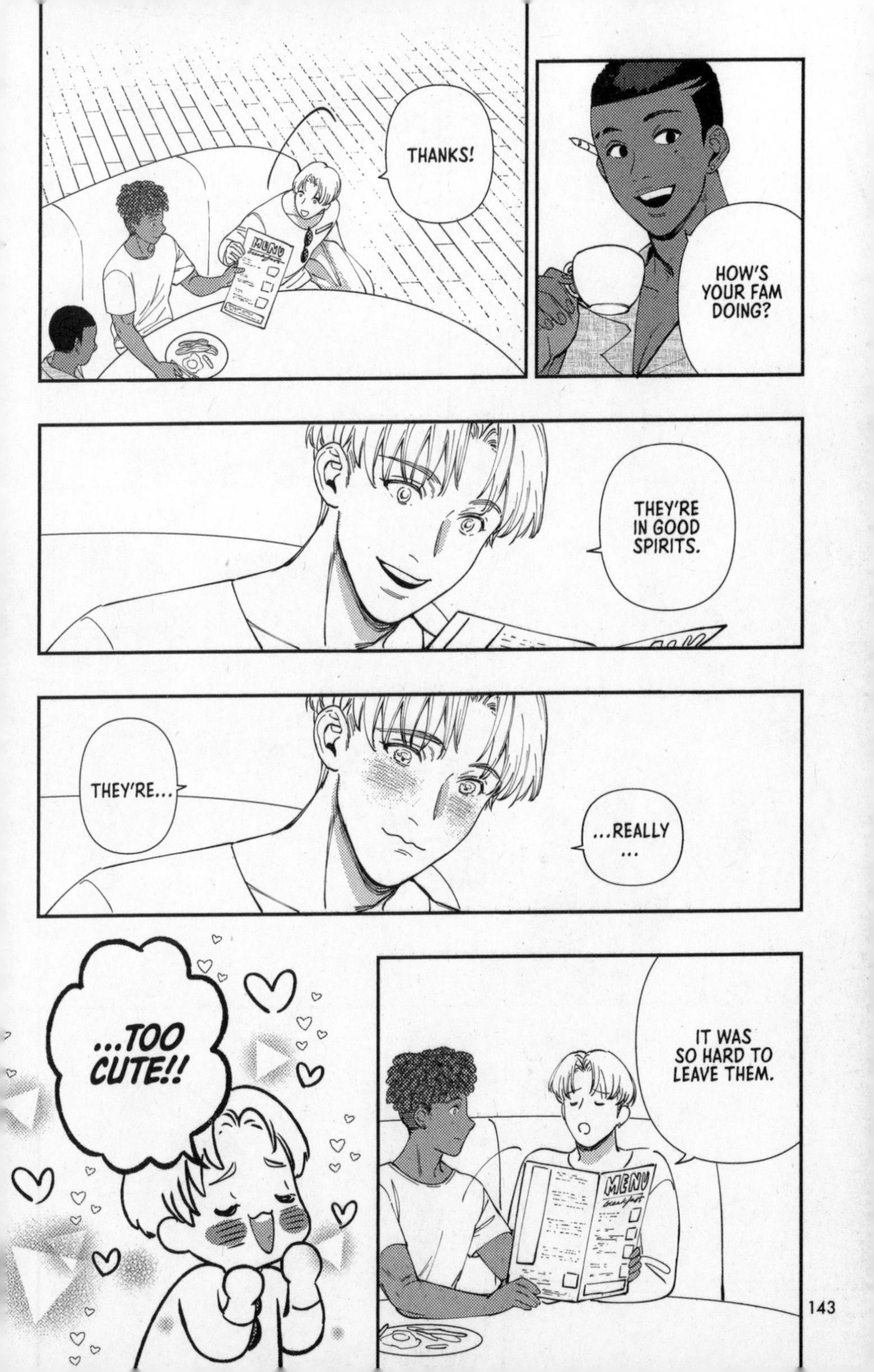
THANKS!
HOW'S YOUR FAM DOING?
THEY'RE IN GOOD SPIRITS.
THEY'RE...
...REALLY ...
...TOO CUTE!!
IT WAS SO HARD TO LEAVE THEM.

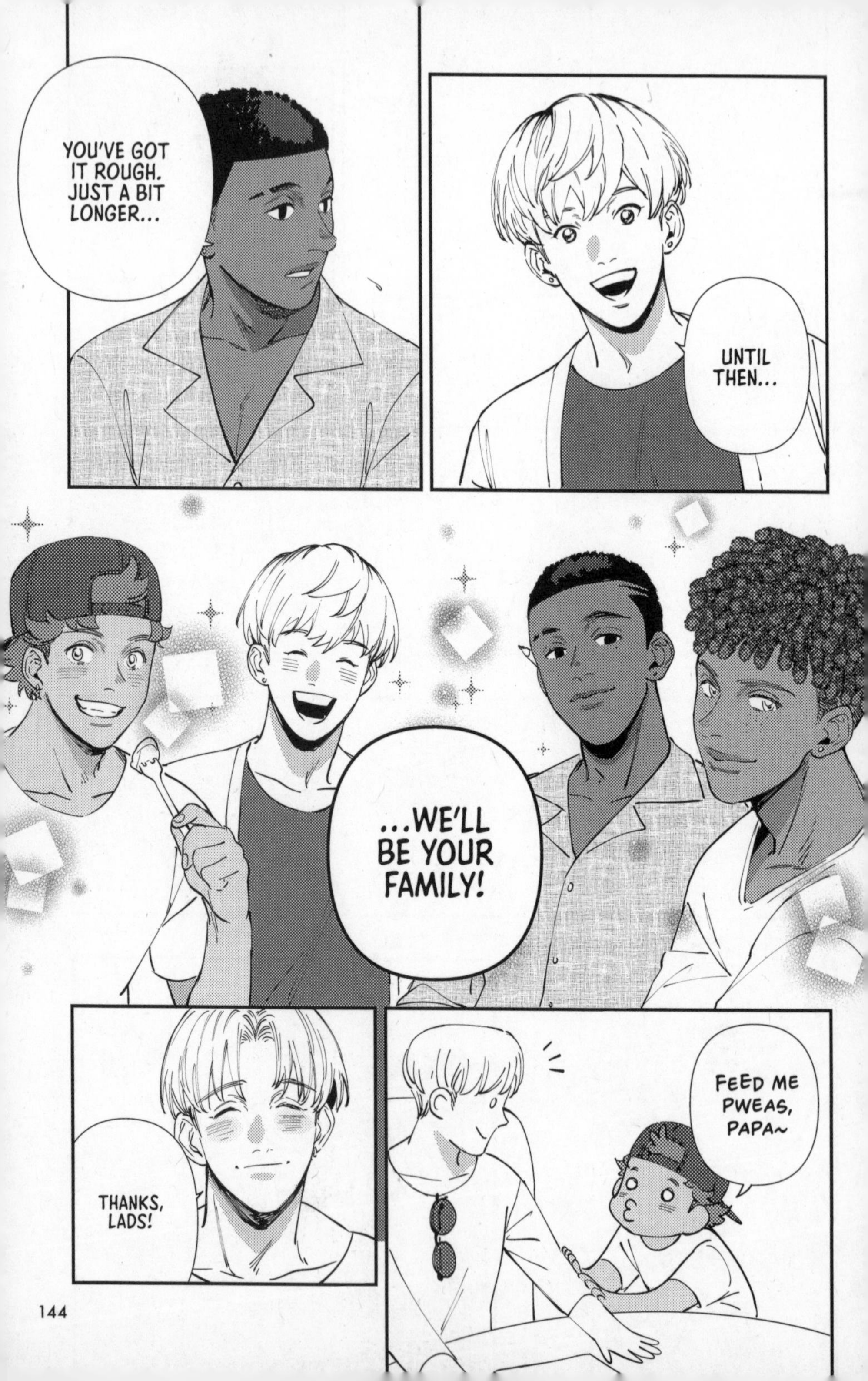
YOU'VE GOT IT ROUGH. JUST A BIT LONGER...
UNTIL THEN...
...WE'LL BE YOUR FAMILY!
THANKS, LADS!
FEED ME PWEAS, PAPA~

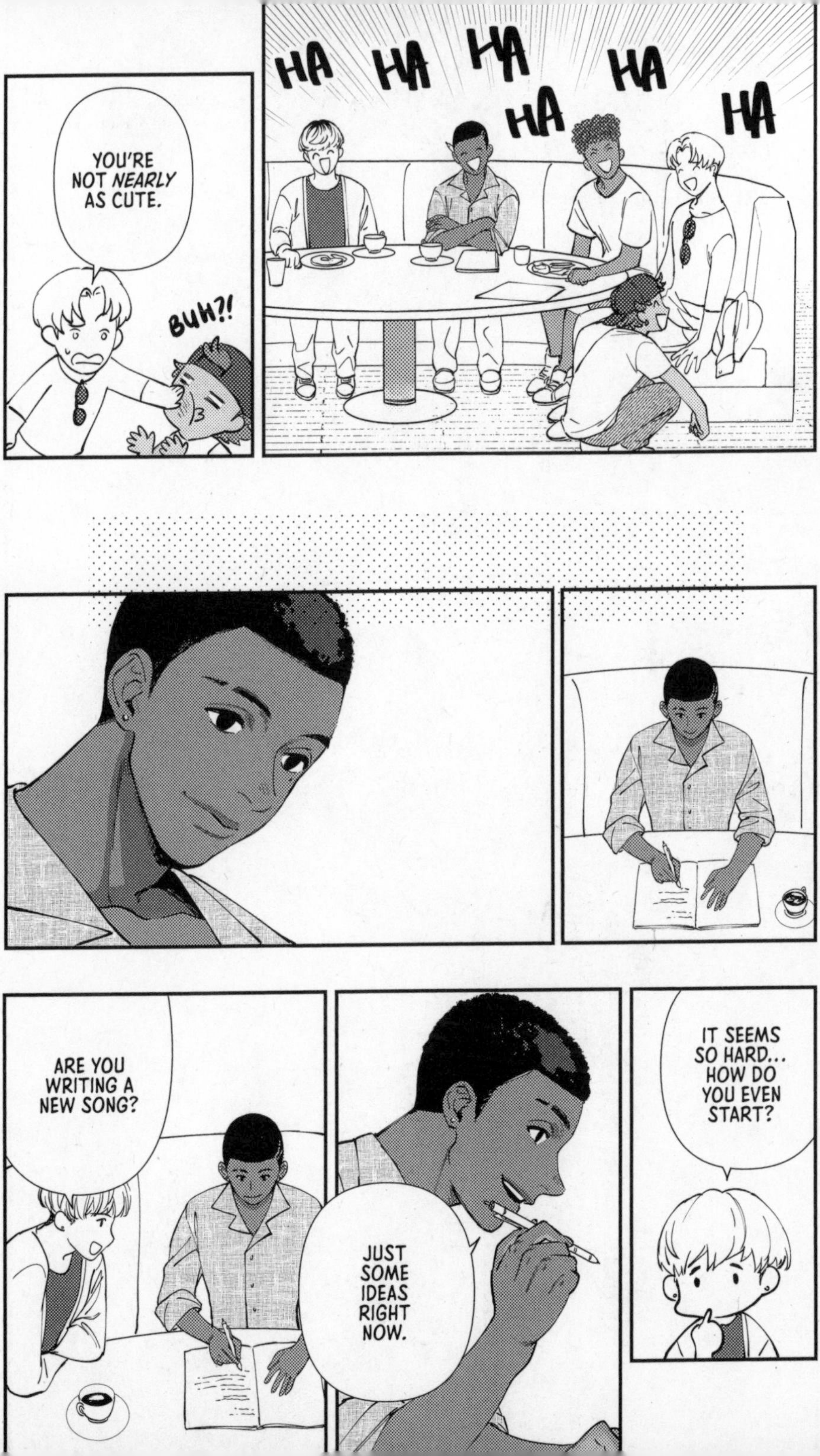
YOU'RE NOT *NEARLY* AS CUTE.
BUH?!
HA HA HA HA HA HA
ARE YOU WRITING A NEW SONG?
JUST SOME IDEAS RIGHT NOW.
IT SEEMS SO HARD... HOW DO YOU EVEN START?

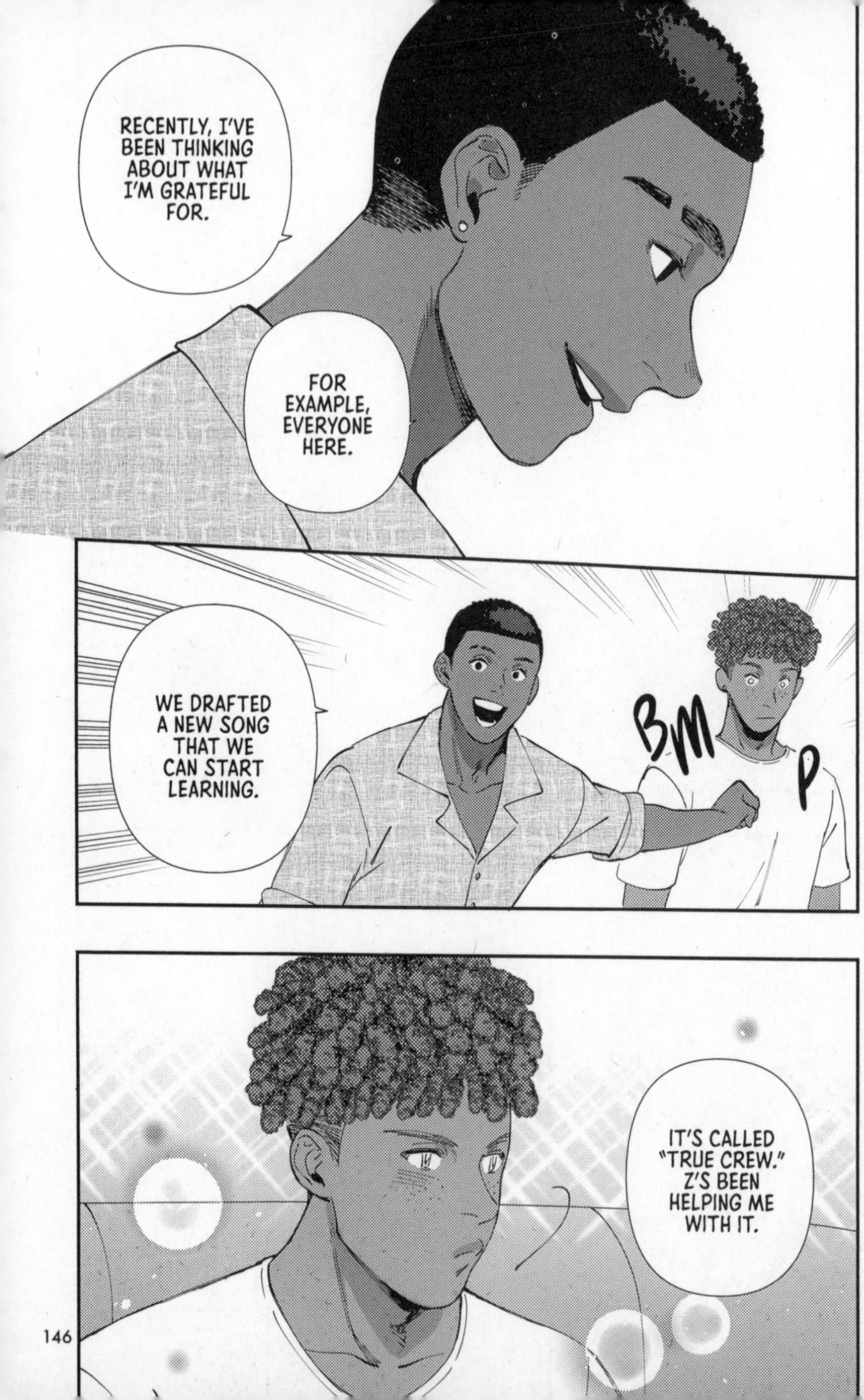
RECENTLY, I'VE BEEN THINKING ABOUT WHAT I'M GRATEFUL FOR.
FOR EXAMPLE, EVERYONE HERE.
WE DRAFTED A NEW SONG THAT WE CAN START LEARNING.
BMP
IT'S CALLED "TRUE CREW." Z'S BEEN HELPING ME WITH IT.

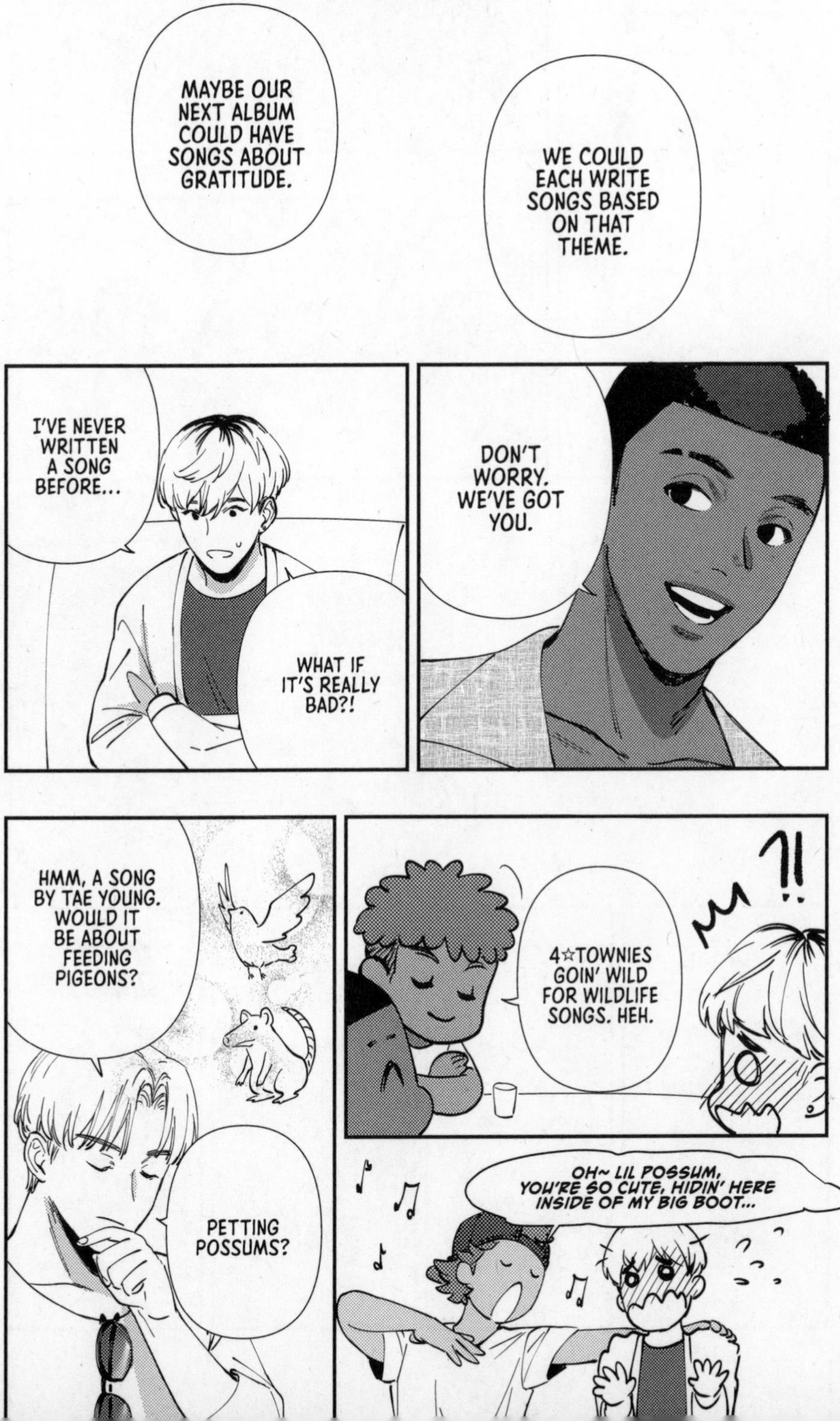
MAYBE OUR NEXT ALBUM COULD HAVE SONGS ABOUT GRATITUDE.
WE COULD EACH WRITE SONGS BASED ON THAT THEME.
I'VE NEVER WRITTEN A SONG BEFORE...
WHAT IF IT'S REALLY BAD?!
DON'T WORRY. WE'VE GOT YOU.
HMM, A SONG BY TAE YOUNG. WOULD IT BE ABOUT FEEDING PIGEONS?
PETTING POSSUMS?
4☆TOWNIES GOIN' WILD FOR WILDLIFE SONGS. HEH.
?!
OH~ LIL POSSUM, YOU'RE SO CUTE, HIDIN' HERE INSIDE OF MY BIG BOOT...

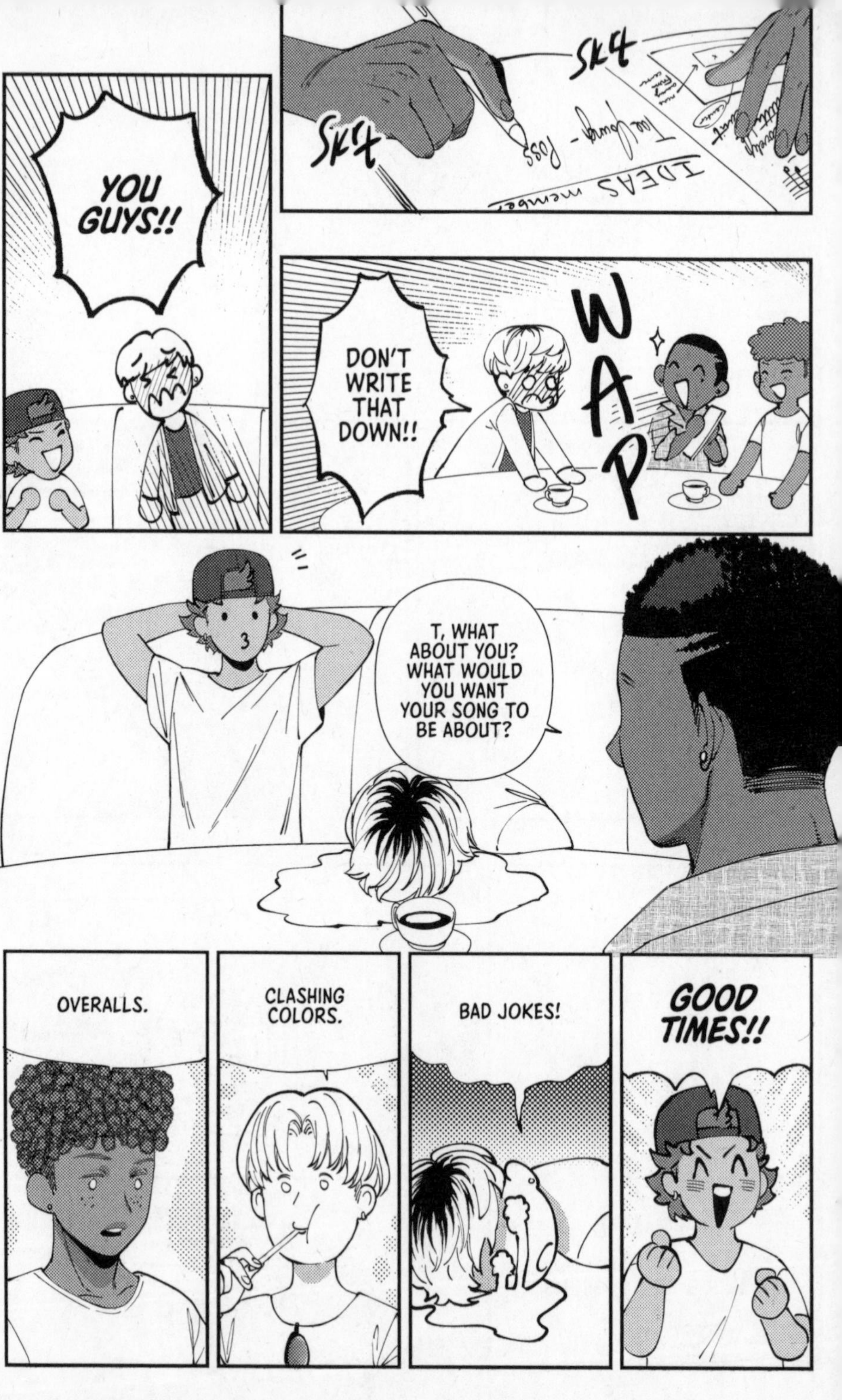
YOU GUYS!!
SK4
SK4
IDEAS
DON'T WRITE THAT DOWN!!
WAP
T, WHAT ABOUT YOU? WHAT WOULD YOU WANT YOUR SONG TO BE ABOUT?
OVERALLS.
CLASHING COLORS.
BAD JOKES!
GOOD TIMES!!

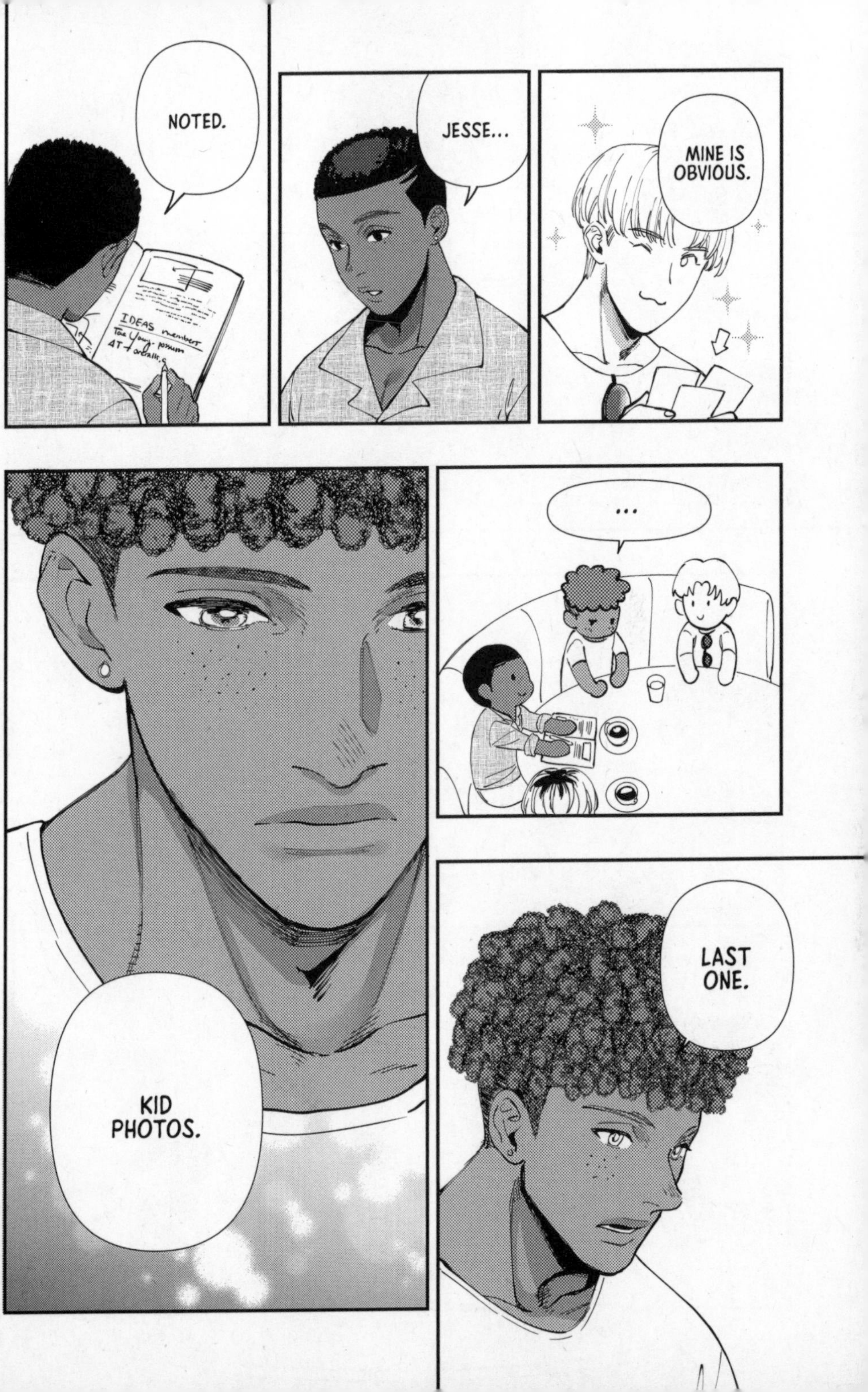
NOTED.
JESSE...
MINE IS OBVIOUS.
KID PHOTOS.
...
LAST ONE.

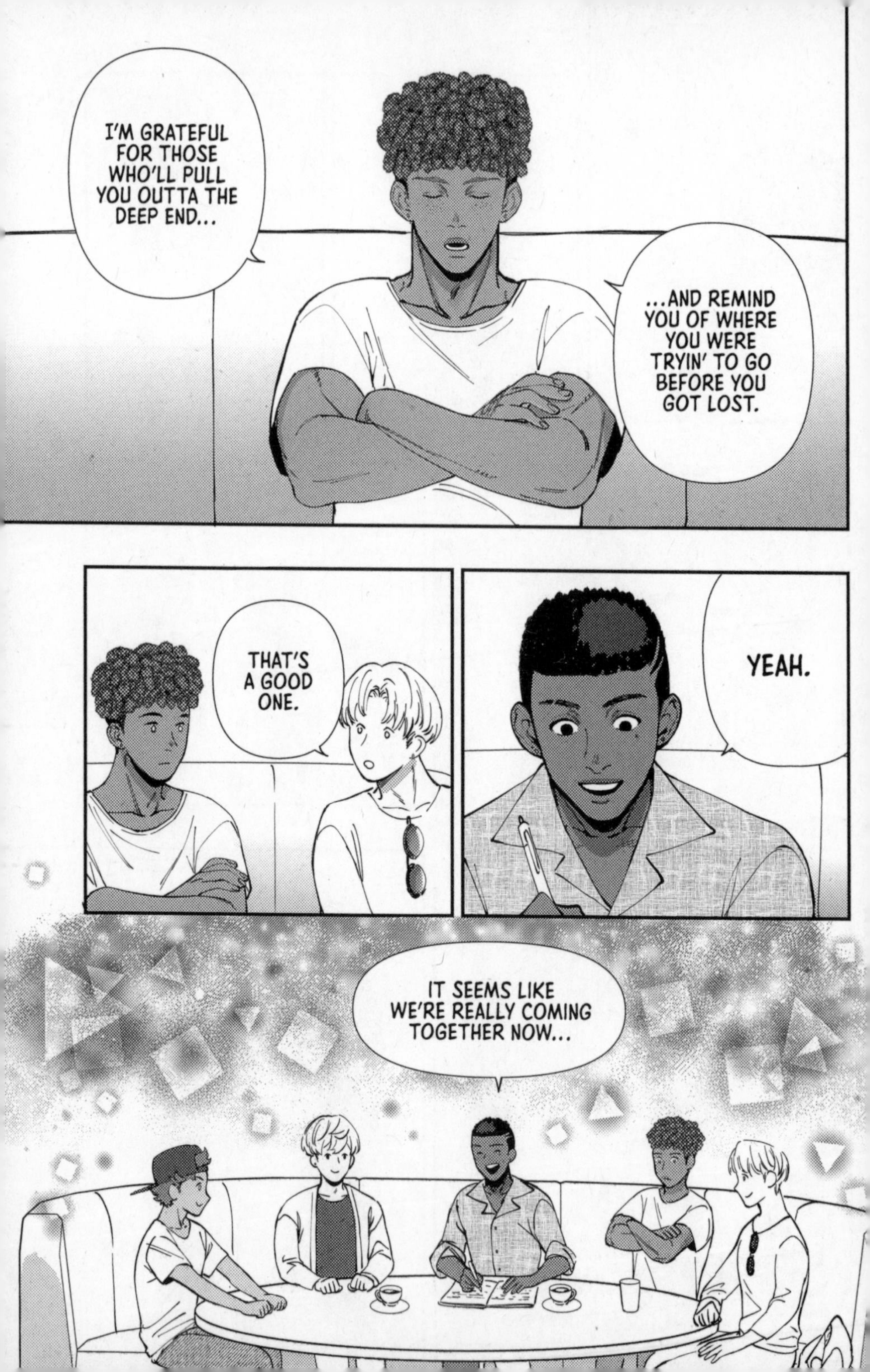
I'M GRATEFUL FOR THOSE WHO'LL PULL YOU OUTTA THE DEEP END...
...AND REMIND YOU OF WHERE YOU WERE TRYIN' TO GO BEFORE YOU GOT LOST.
THAT'S A GOOD ONE.
YEAH.
IT SEEMS LIKE WE'RE REALLY COMING TOGETHER NOW...

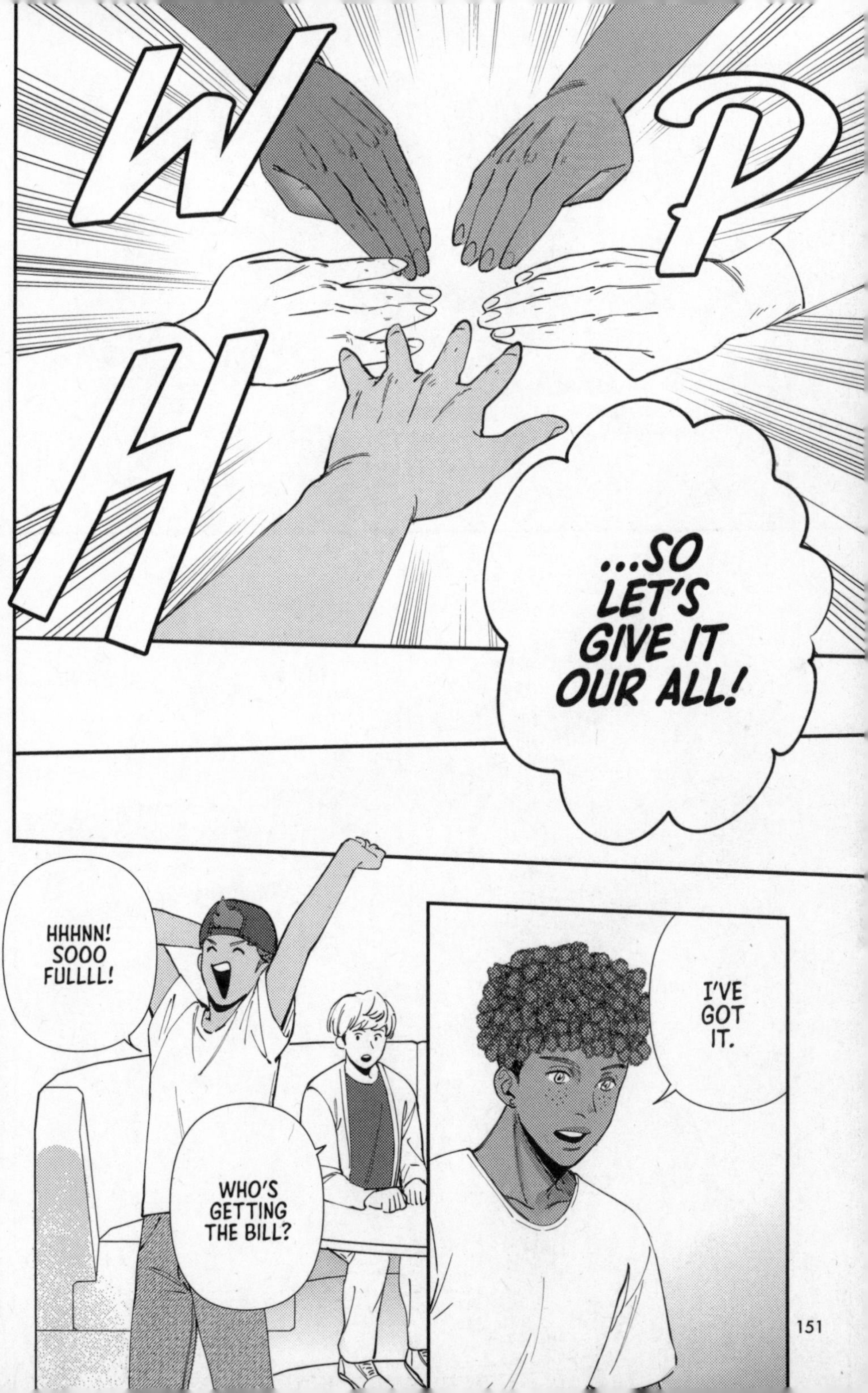
WHP
...SO LET'S GIVE IT OUR ALL!
HHHNN! SOOO FULLLL!
WHO'S GETTING THE BILL?
I'VE GOT IT.

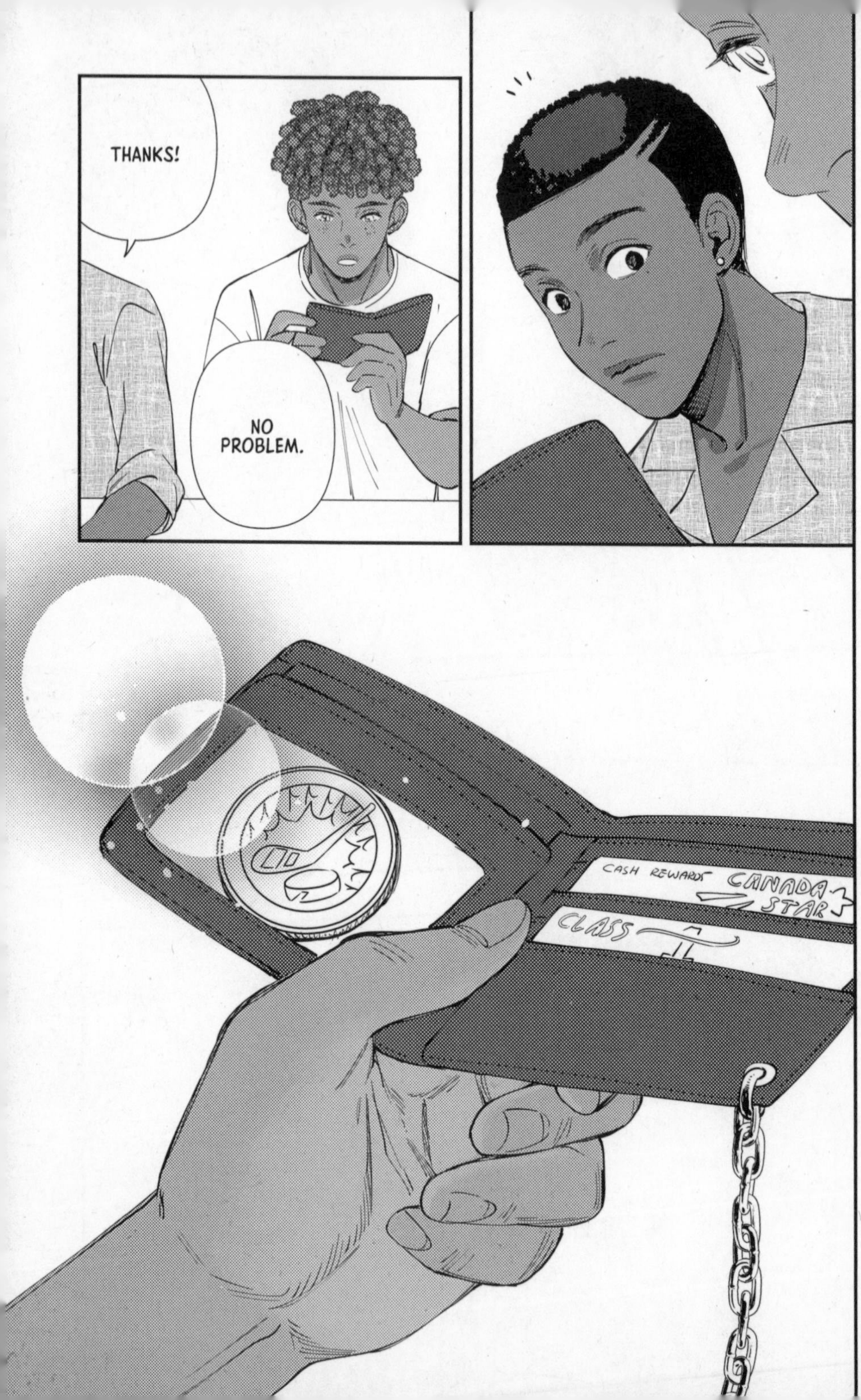
THANKS!
NO PROBLEM.
CASH REWARDS
CANADA STAR
CLASS

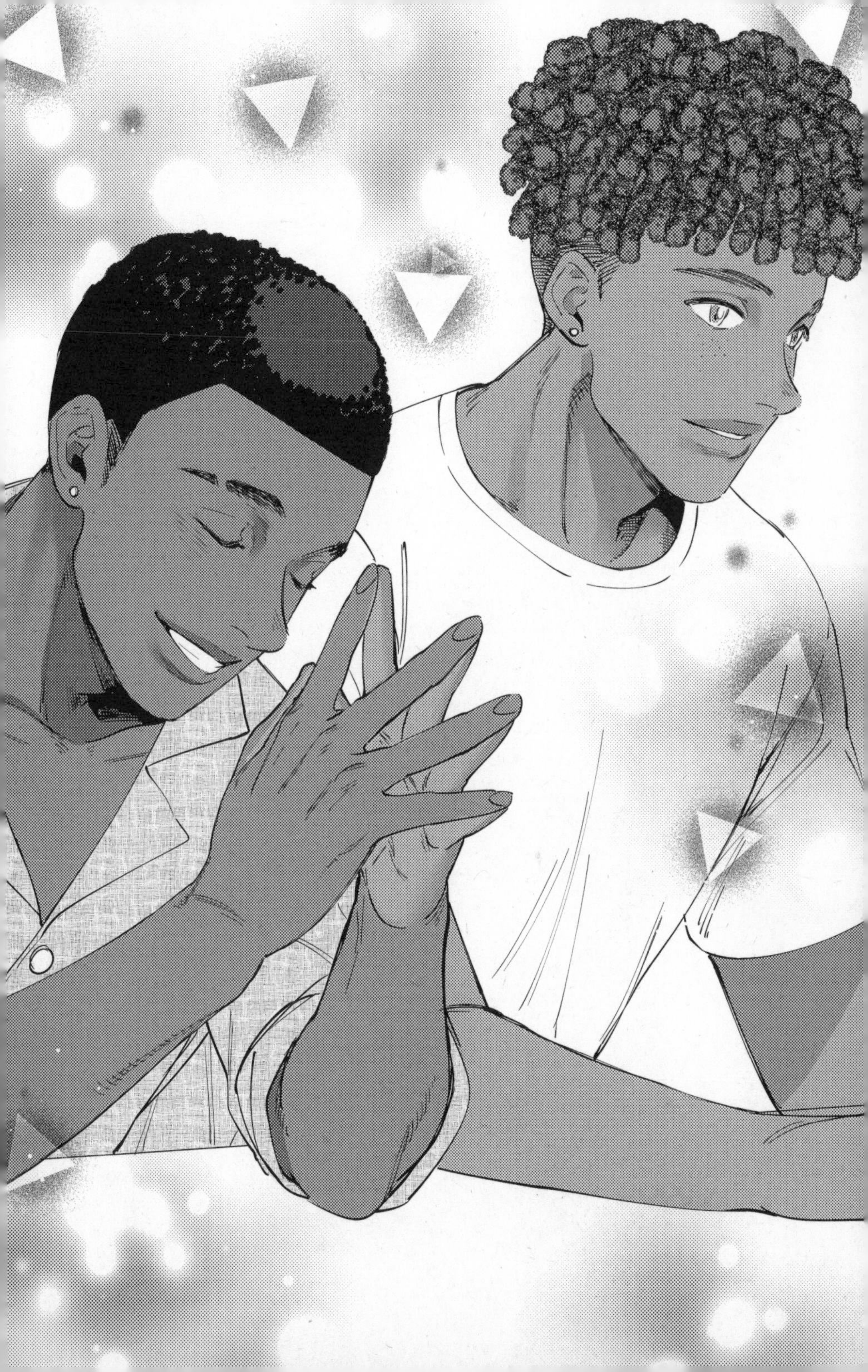

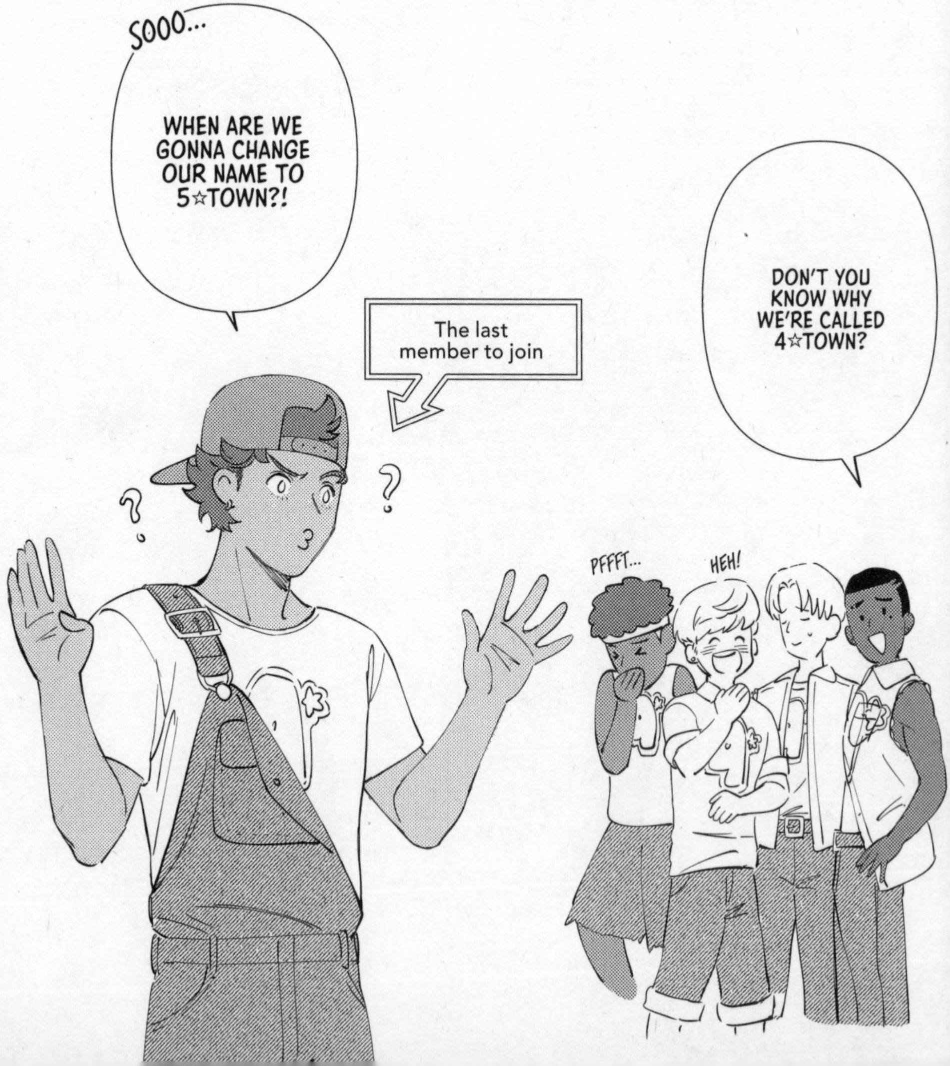
SOOO...
WHEN ARE WE GONNA CHANGE OUR NAME TO 5☆TOWN?!
The last member to join
DON'T YOU KNOW WHY WE'RE CALLED 4☆TOWN?
PFFFT...
HEH!

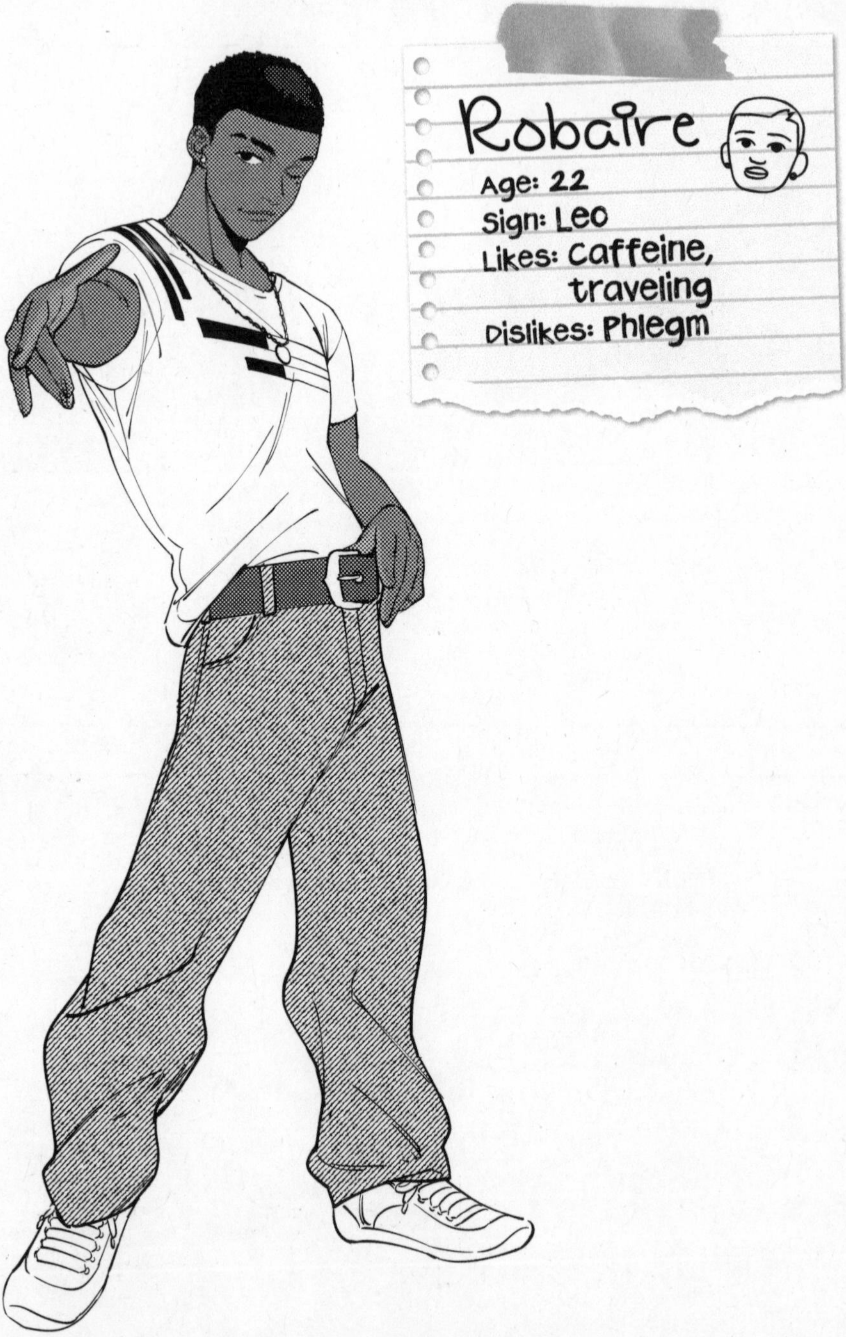
Robaire
Age: 22
Sign: Leo
Likes: Caffeine, traveling
Dislikes: Phlegm

Robaire l'Extraordinaire

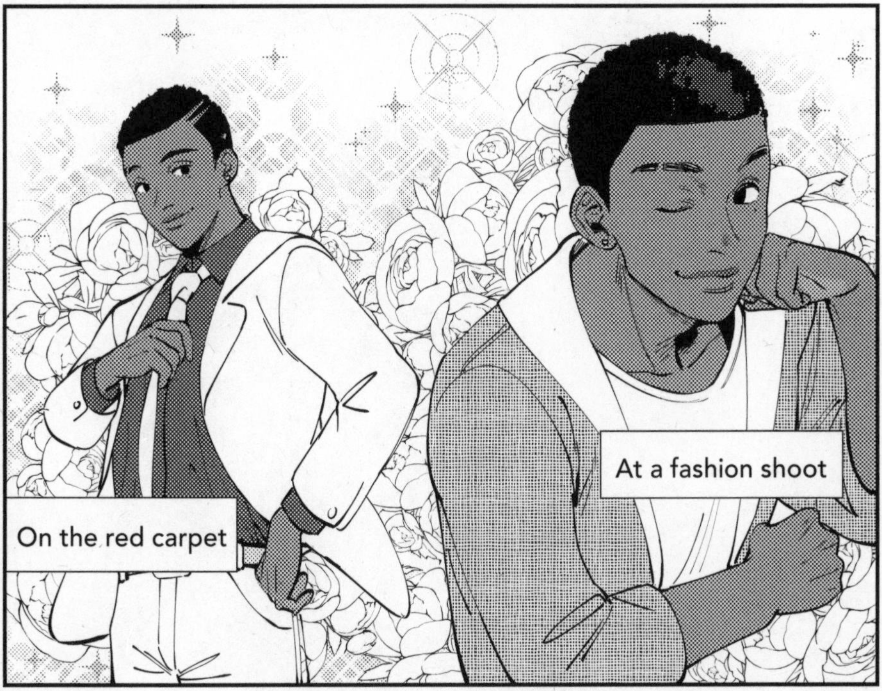
On the red carpet
At a fashion shoot

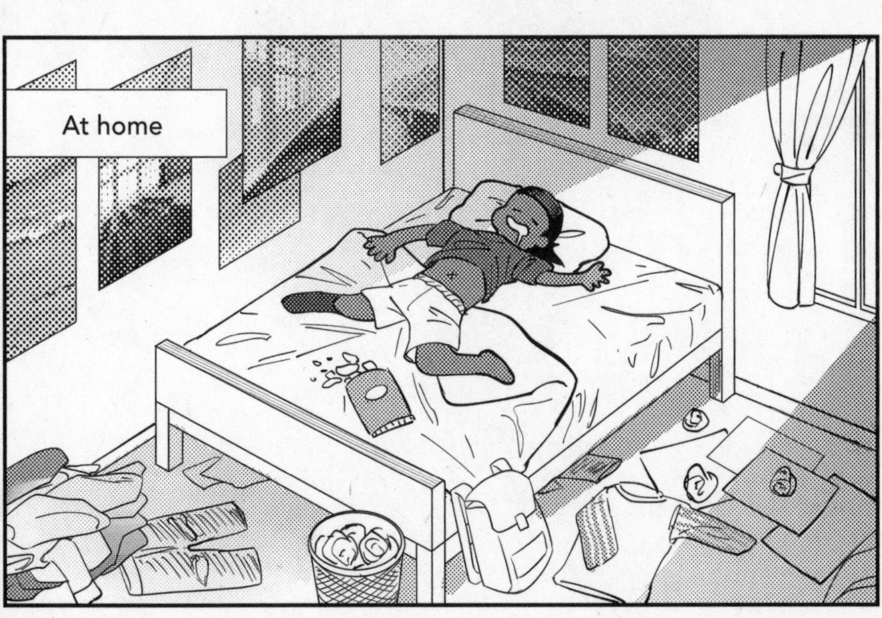
At home

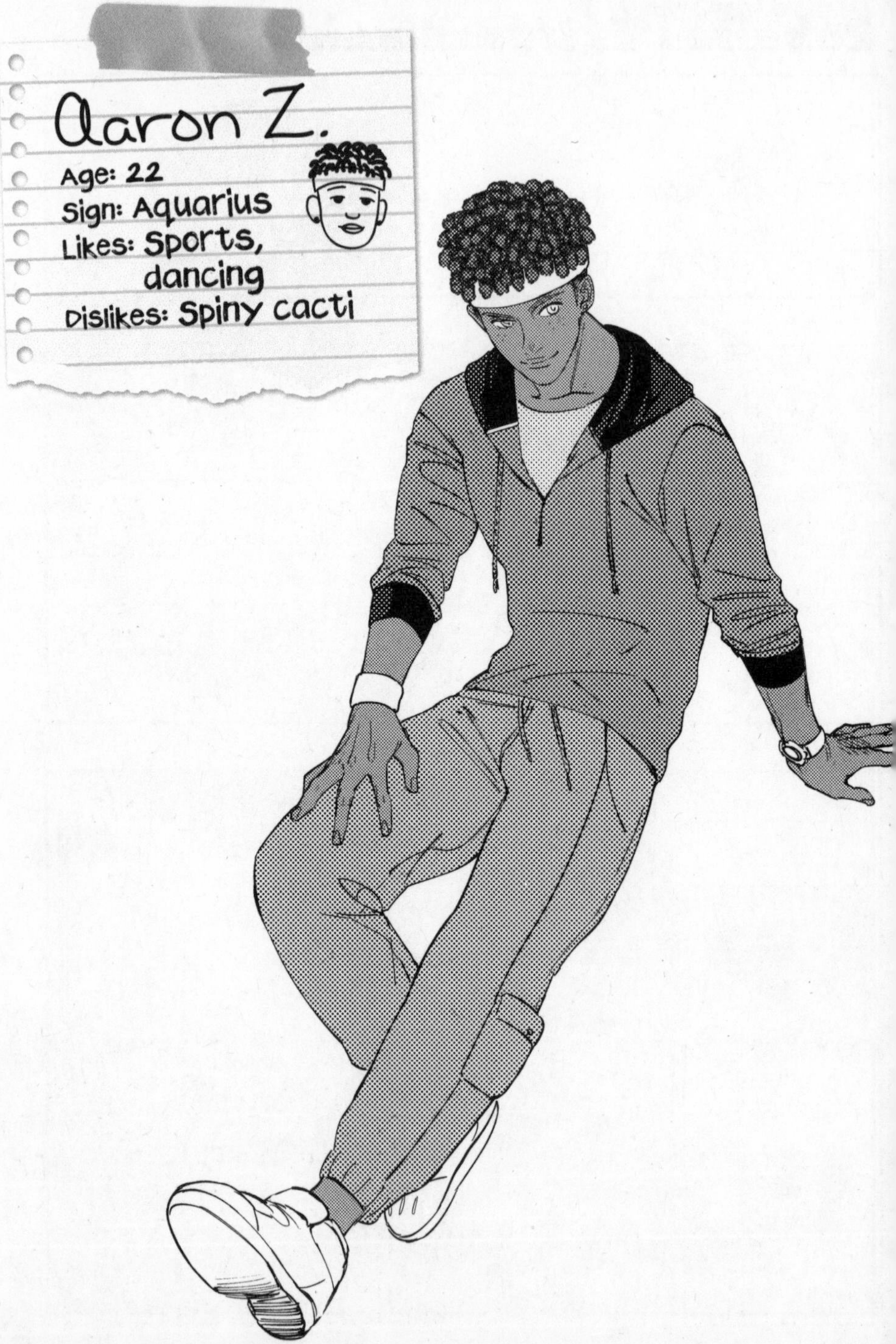
Aaron Z.
Age: 22
Sign: Aquarius
Likes: Sports, dancing
Dislikes: Spiny cacti

Nightmare Z

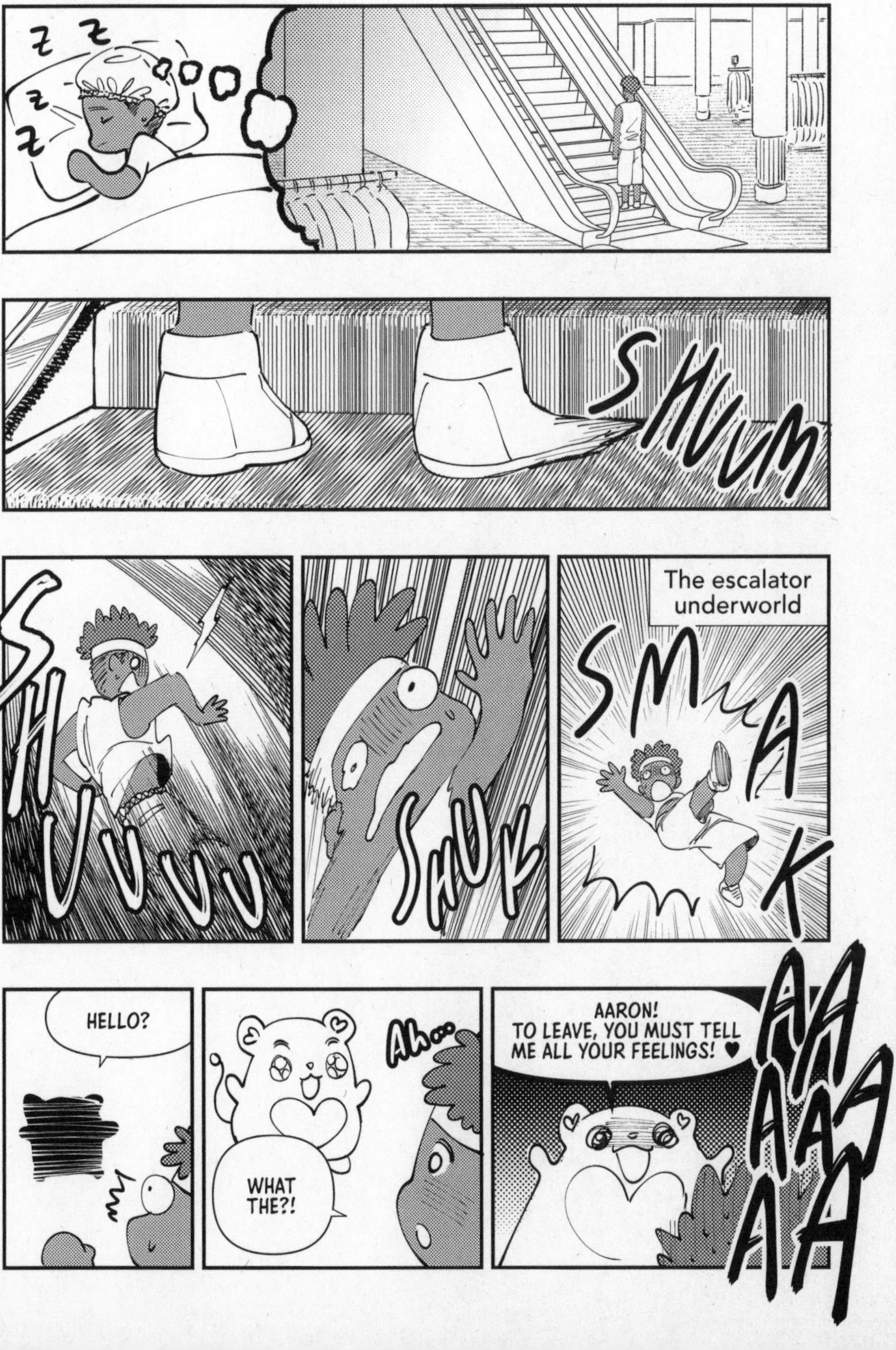
Z Z Z Z
SHUUM
SHUUUUU
SHUK
The escalator underworld
SMAAK
HELLO?
WHAT THE?!
Ah...
AARON! TO LEAVE, YOU MUST TELL ME ALL YOUR FEELINGS! ♥
AAAAAAAA

Tae Young

Age: 18
Sign: Libra
Likes: Wildlife, spicy food
Dislikes: Overcooked noodles

Love Dove

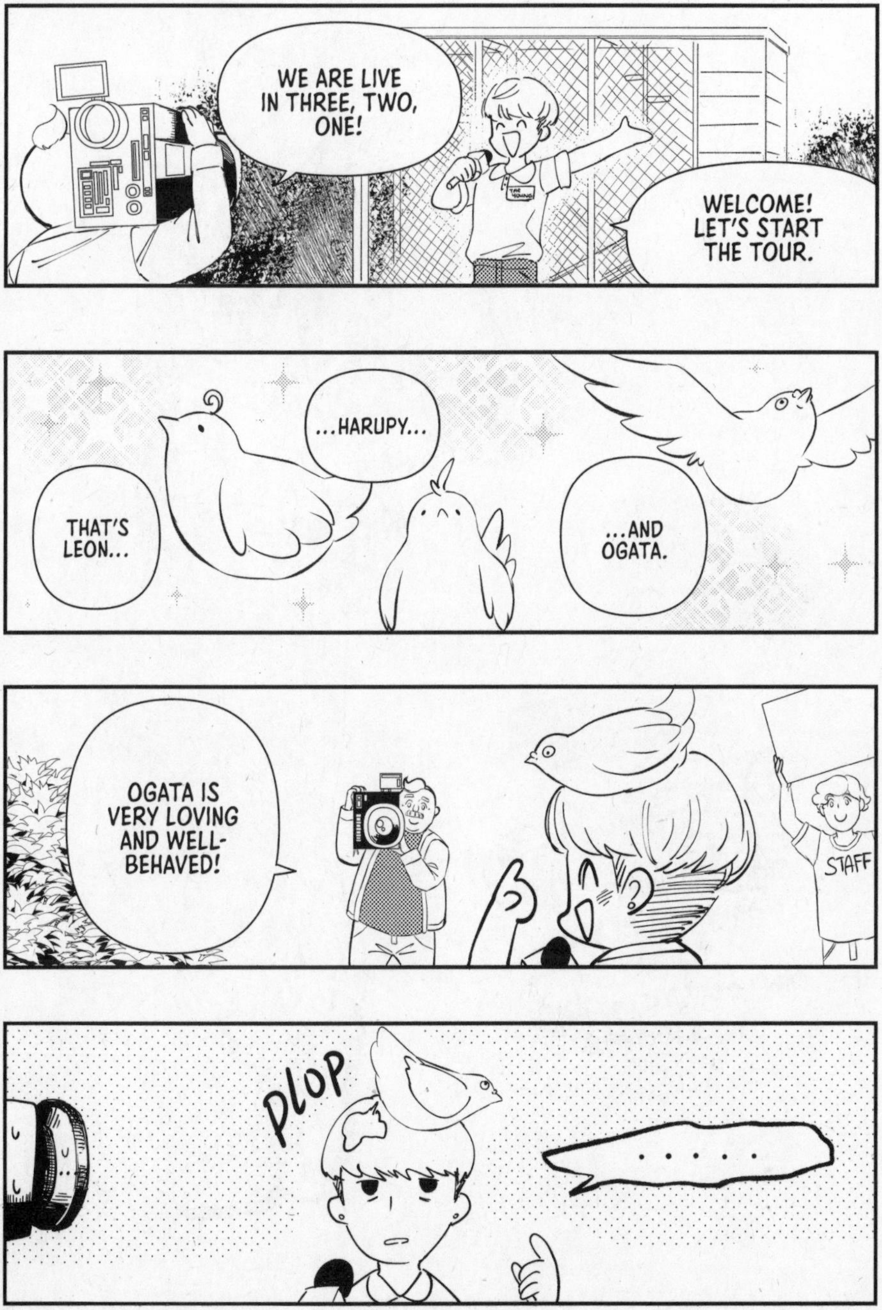
WE ARE LIVE IN THREE, TWO, ONE!
WELCOME! LET'S START THE TOUR.
THAT'S LEON...
...HARUPY...
...AND OGATA.
OGATA IS VERY LOVING AND WELL-BEHAVED!
STAFF
PLOP
......

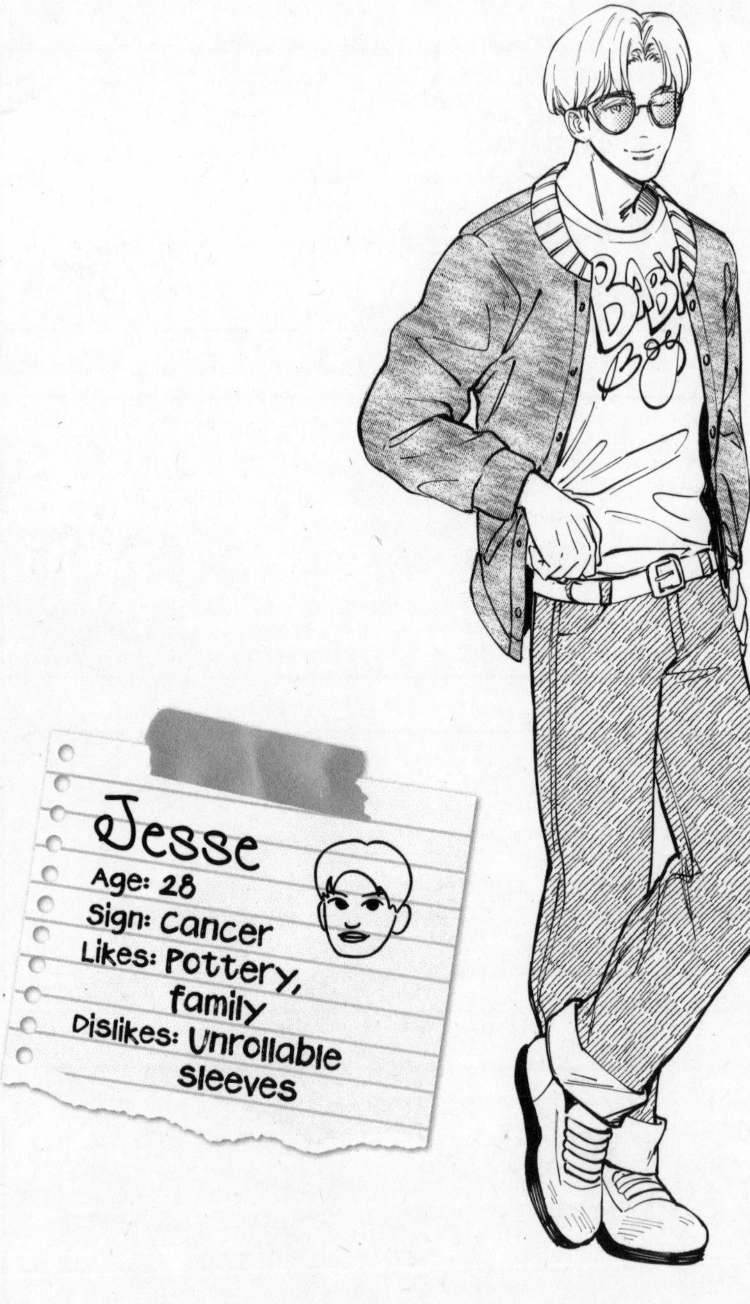
BABY BOY
Jesse
Age: 28
Sign: Cancer
Likes: Pottery, family
Dislikes: Unrollable sleeves

Muscles

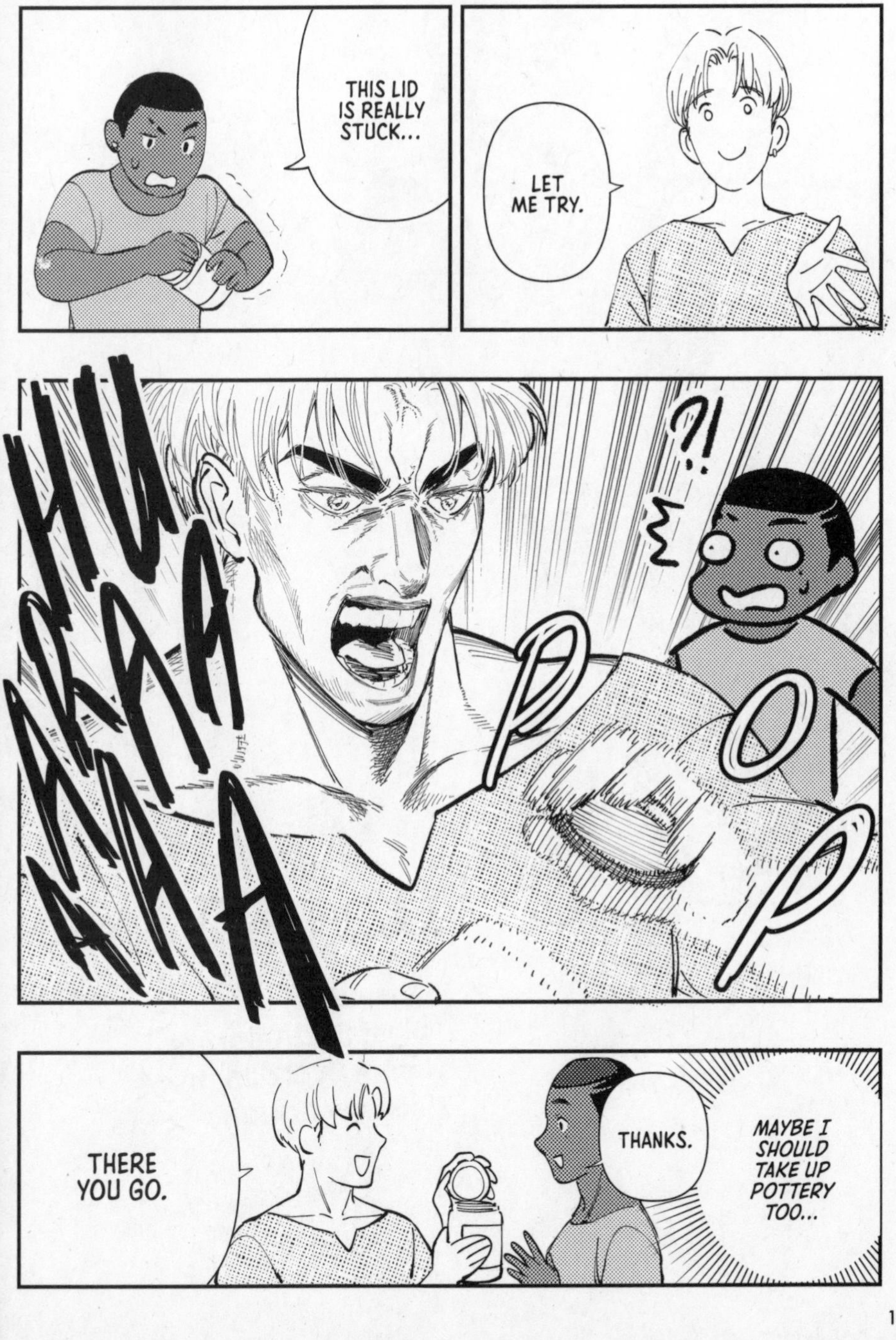
THIS LID IS REALLY STUCK...
LET ME TRY.
?!
POP
THERE YOU GO.
THANKS.
MAYBE I SHOULD TAKE UP POTTERY TOO...

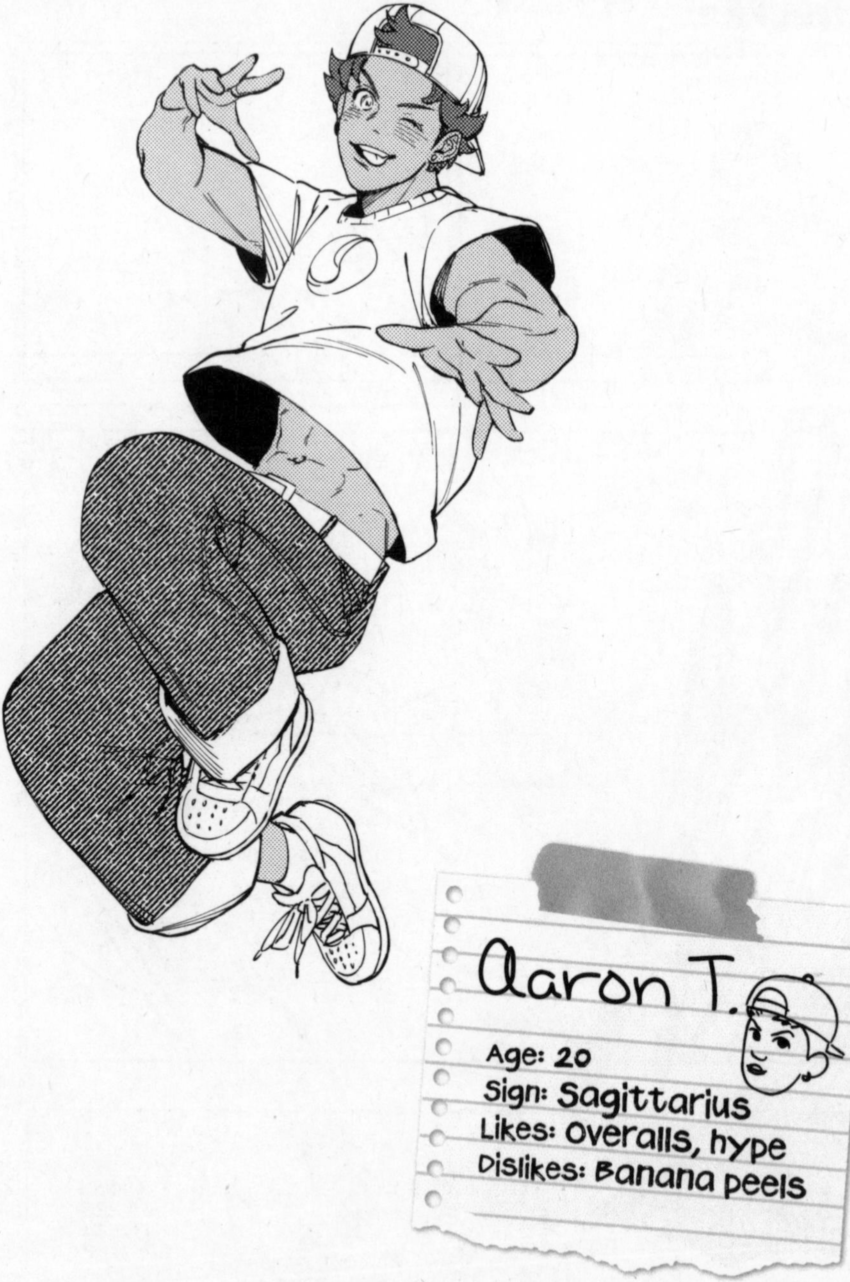
Aaron T.
Age: 20
Sign: Sagittarius
Likes: Overalls, hype
Dislikes: Banana peels

Personal Stylist

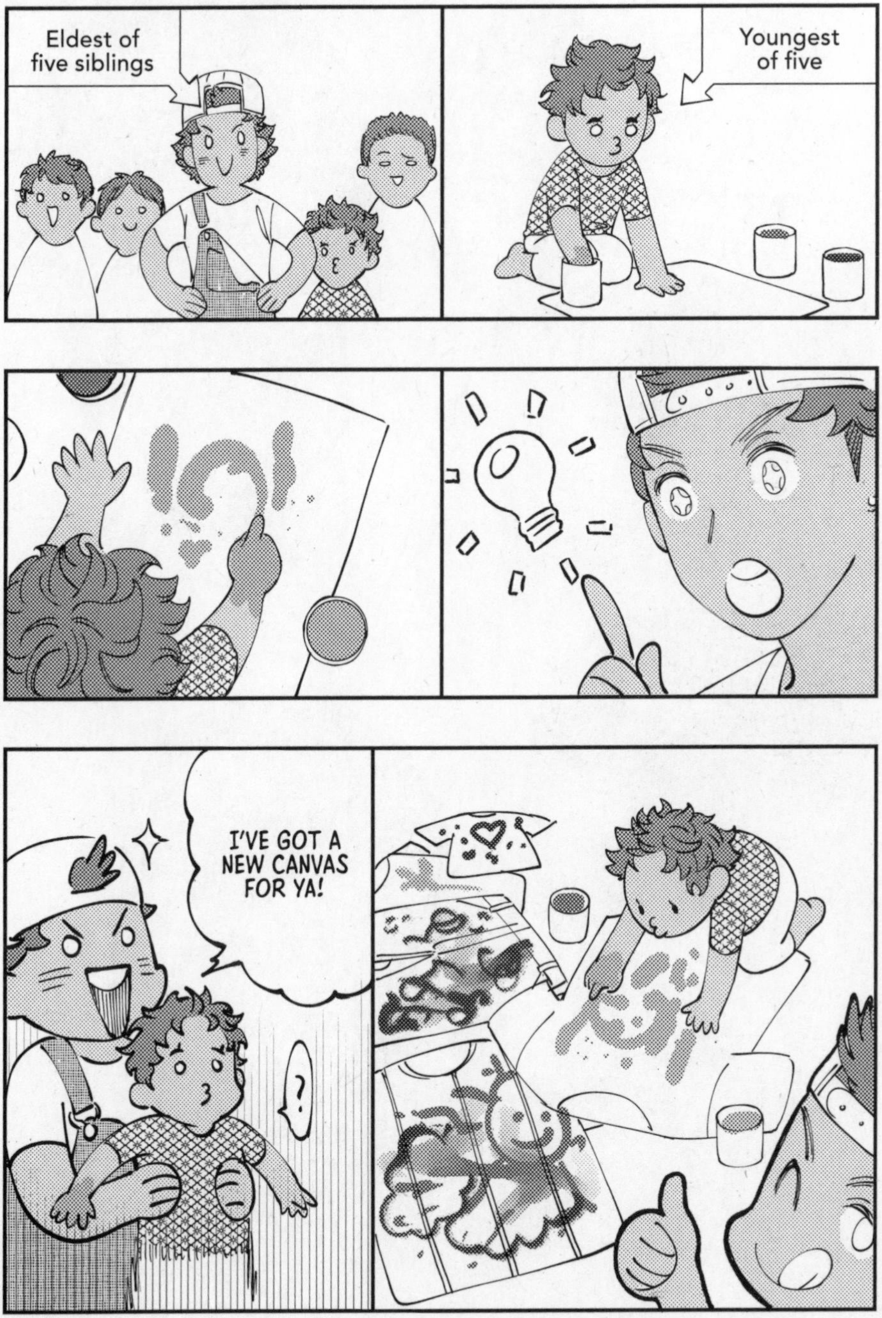
Eldest of five siblings
Youngest of five
I'VE GOT A NEW CANVAS FOR YA!
?

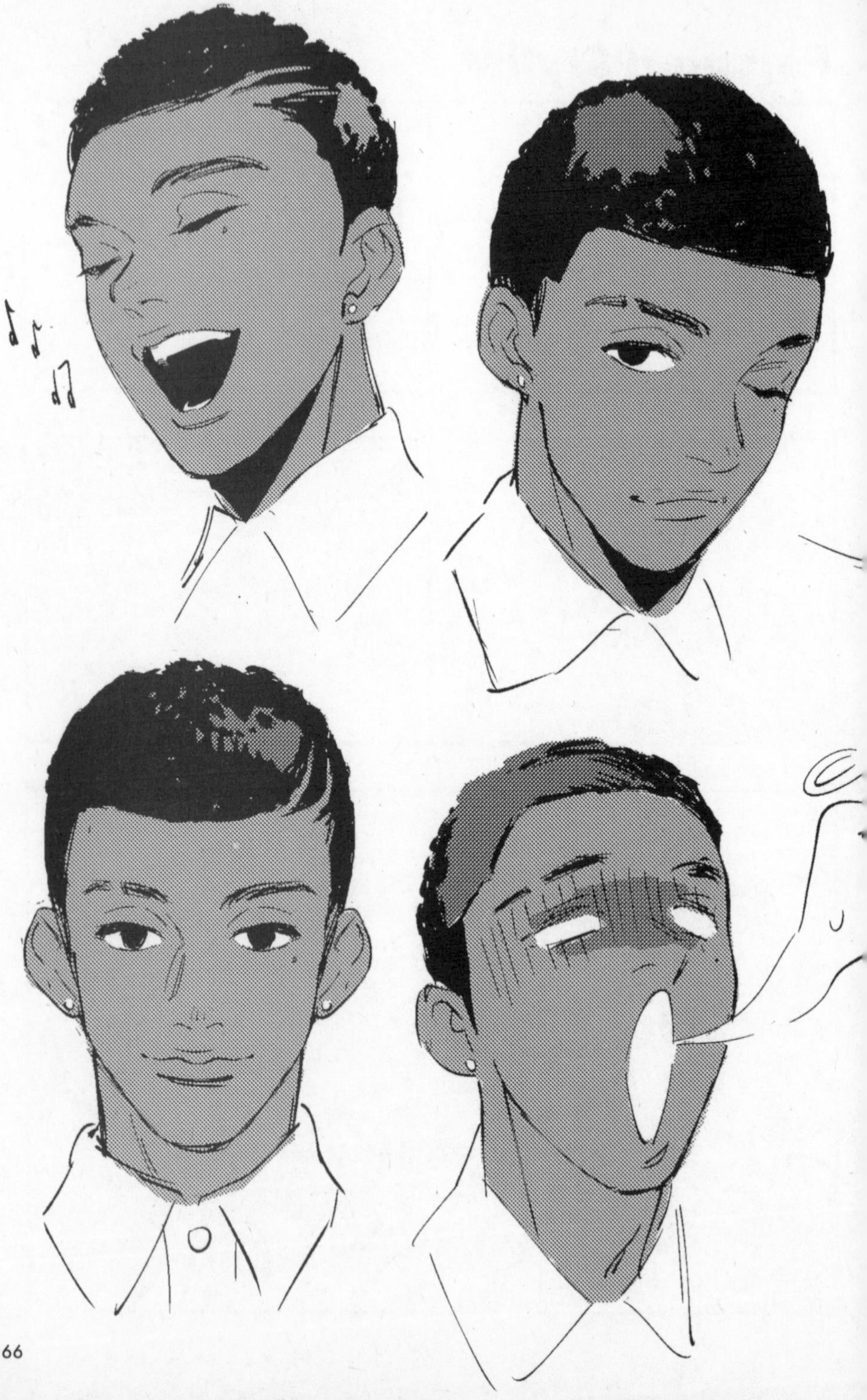

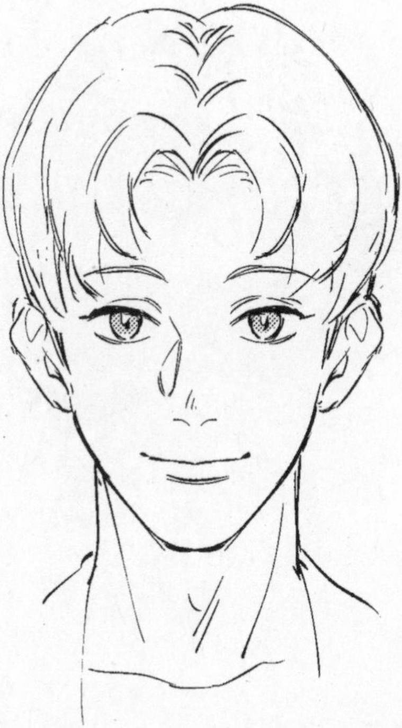

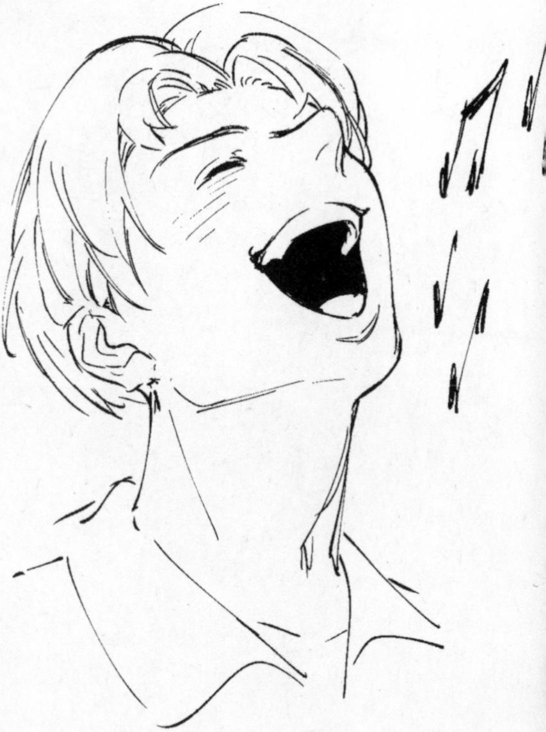

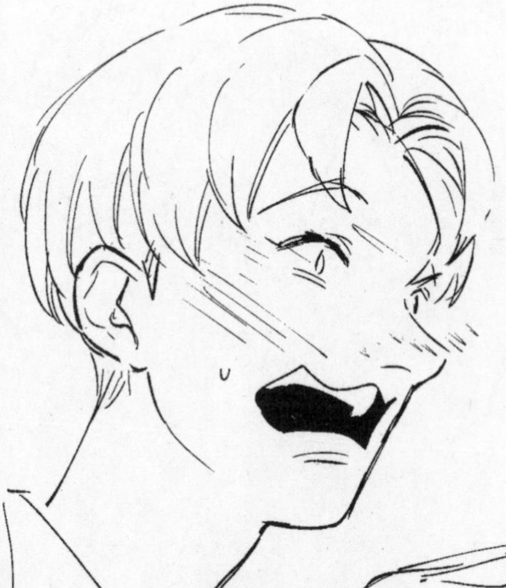

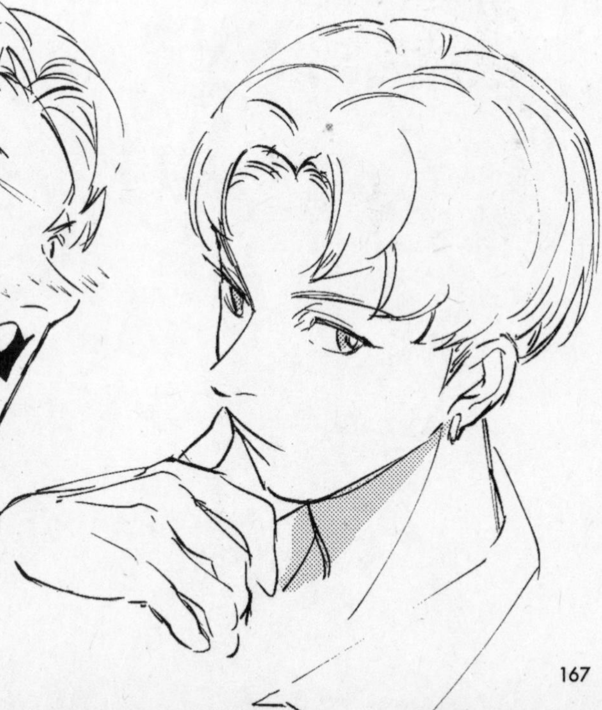

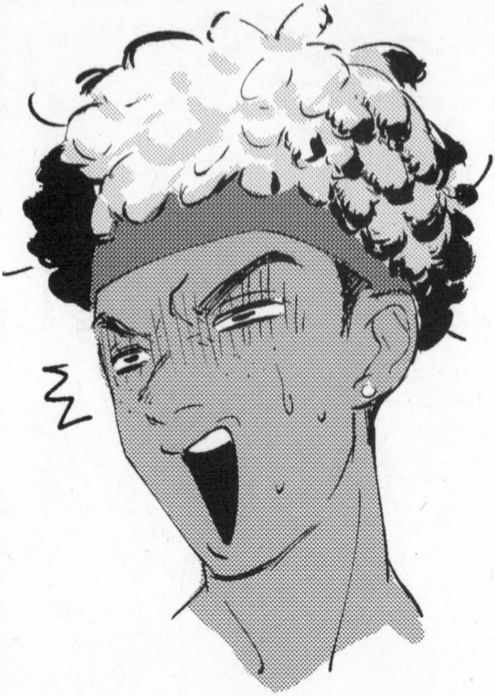

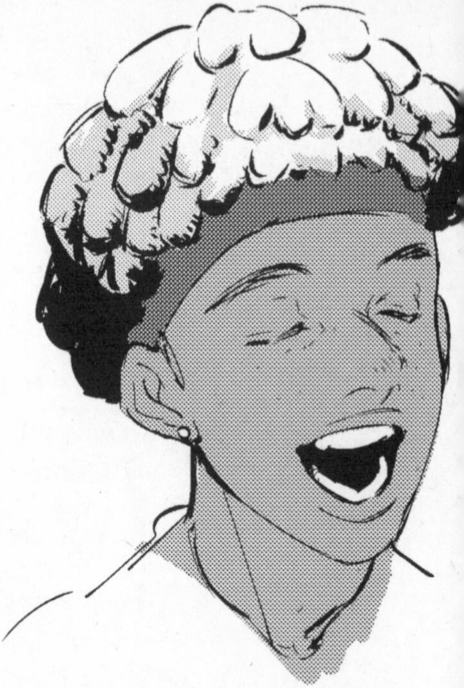

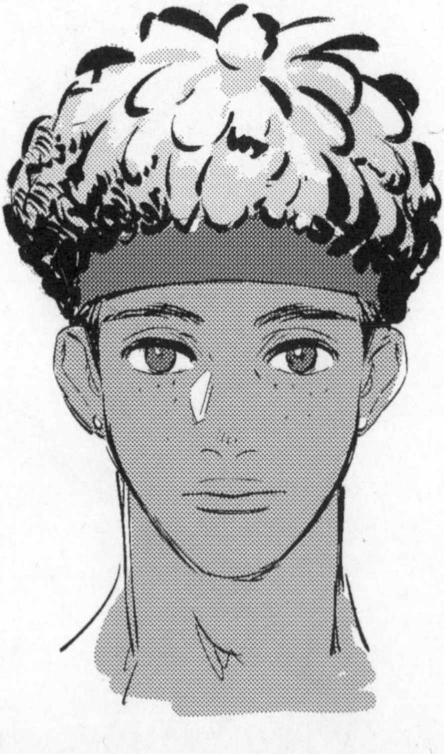

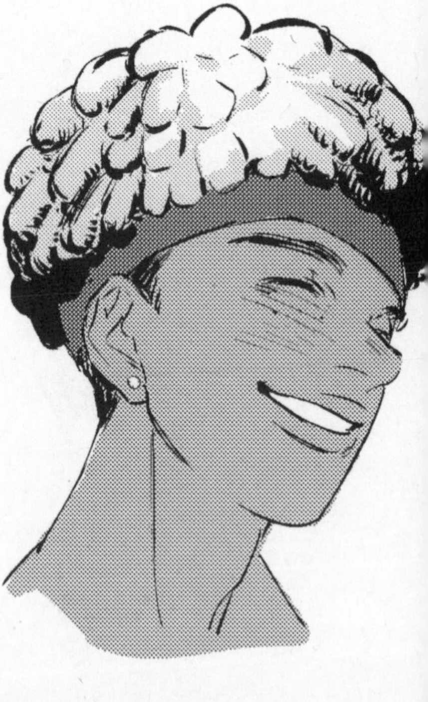

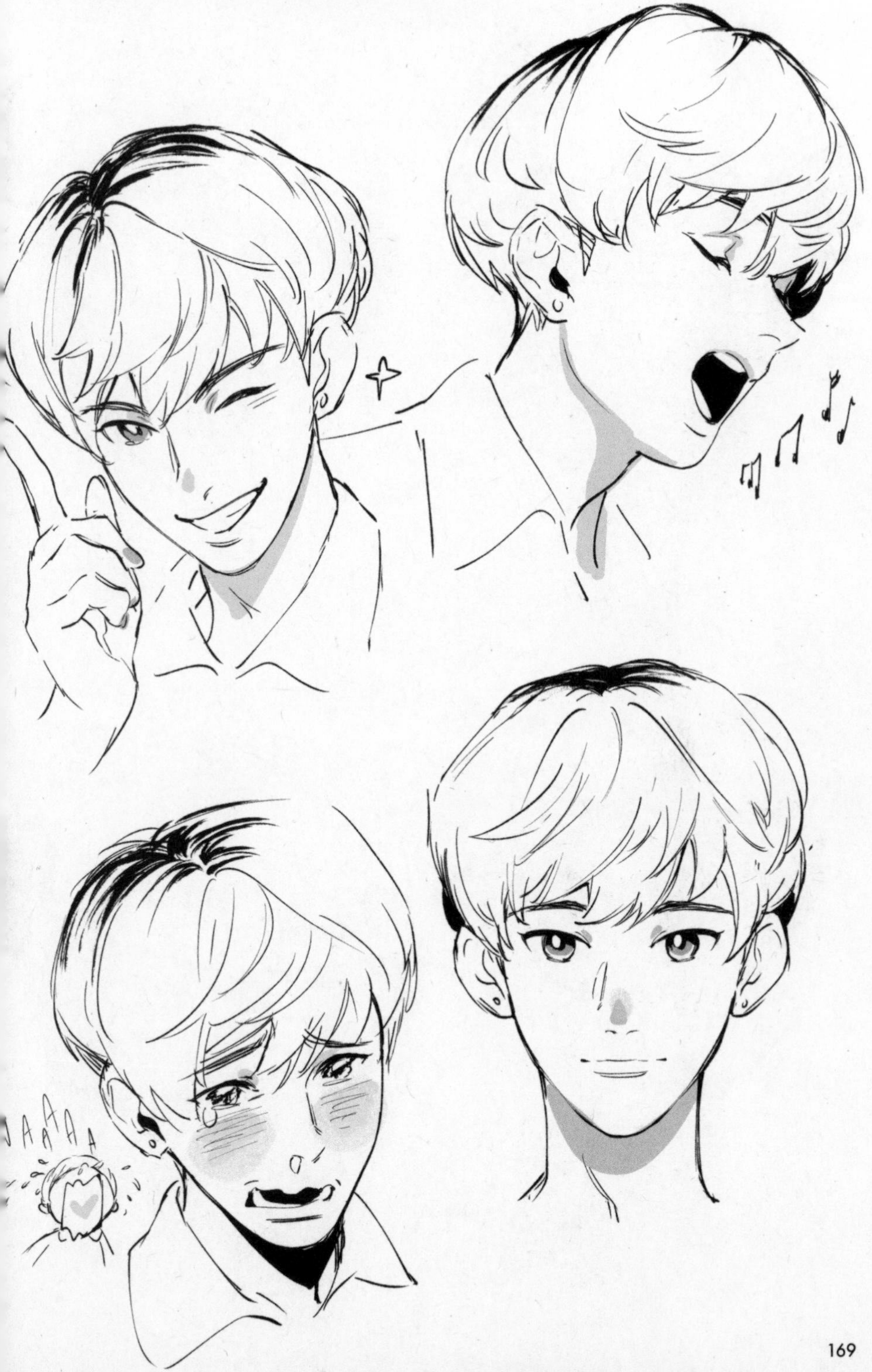
AAAAA

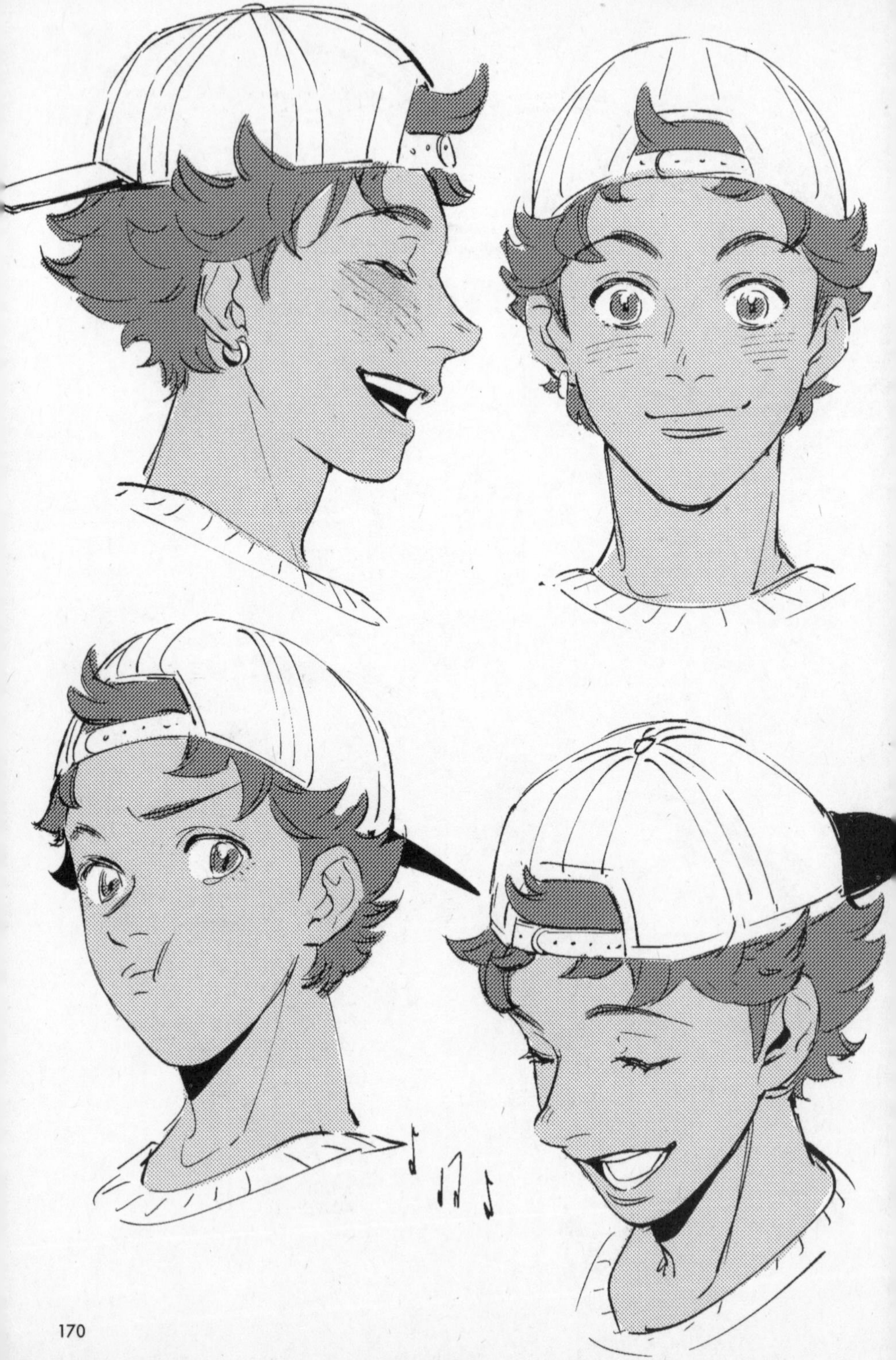

40 TOWN

REUNION IN 2022

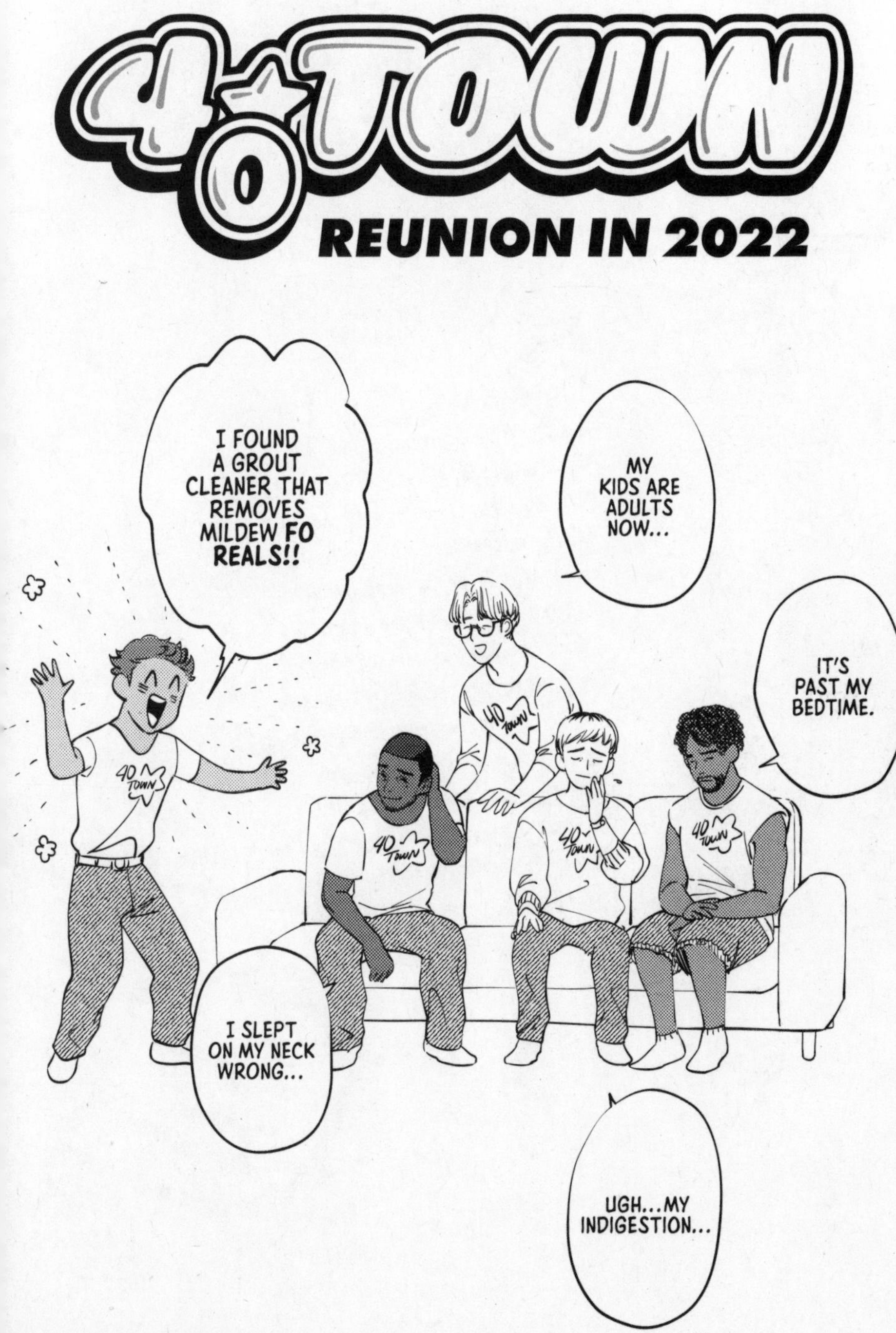
I FOUND A GROUT CLEANER THAT REMOVES MILDEW FO REALS!!
MY KIDS ARE ADULTS NOW...
IT'S PAST MY BEDTIME.
I SLEPT ON MY NECK WRONG...
UGH...MY INDIGESTION...

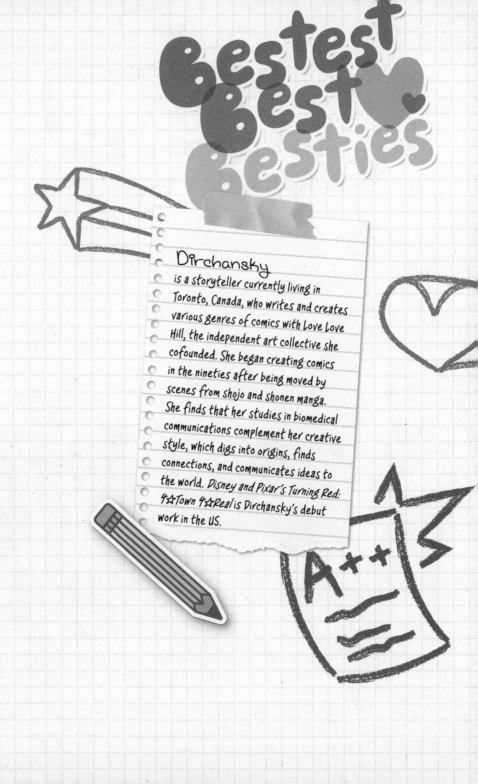

Bestest Best Besties

Dirchansky

is a storyteller currently living in Toronto, Canada, who writes and creates various genres of comics with Love Love Hill, the independent art collective she cofounded. She began creating comics in the nineties after being moved by scenes from shojo and shonen manga. She finds that her studies in biomedical communications complement her creative style, which digs into origins, finds connections, and communicates ideas to the world. Disney and Pixar's Turning Red: 4☆Town 4☆Real is Dirchansky's debut work in the US.

A++

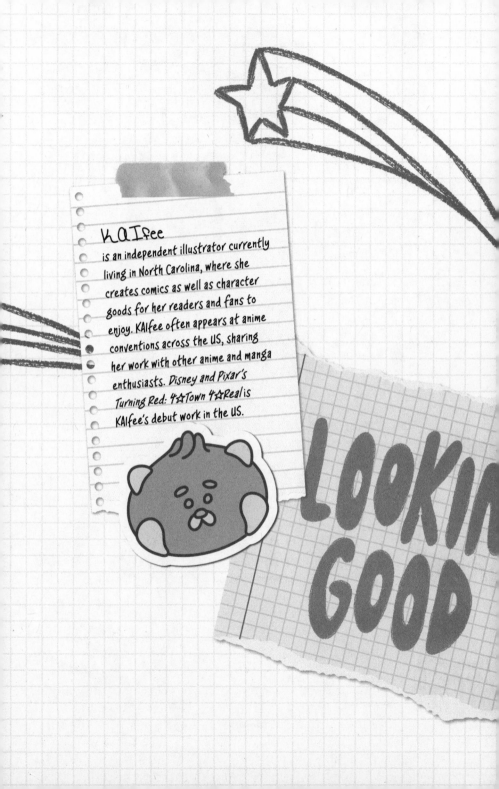

KAIfee

is an independent illustrator currently living in North Carolina, where she creates comics as well as character goods for her readers and fans to enjoy. KAIfee often appears at anime conventions across the US, sharing her work with other anime and manga enthusiasts. *Disney and Pixar's Turning Red: 4☆Town 4☆Real* is KAIfee's debut work in the US.

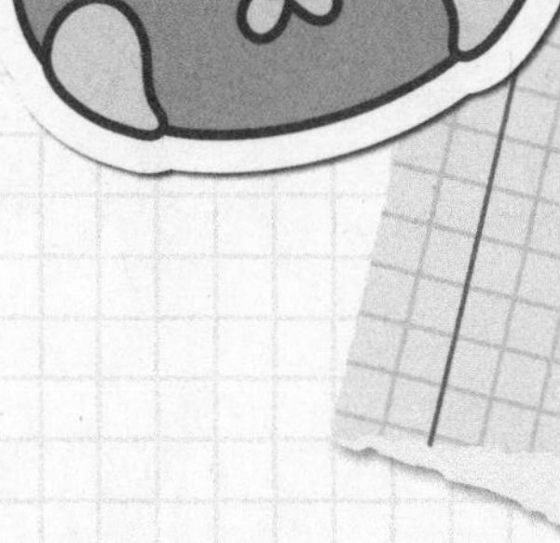

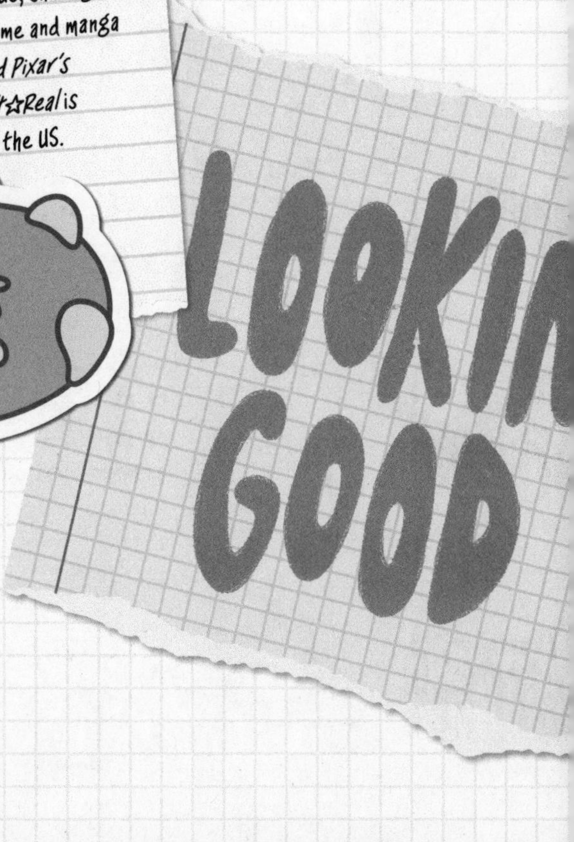
LOOKIN
GOOD

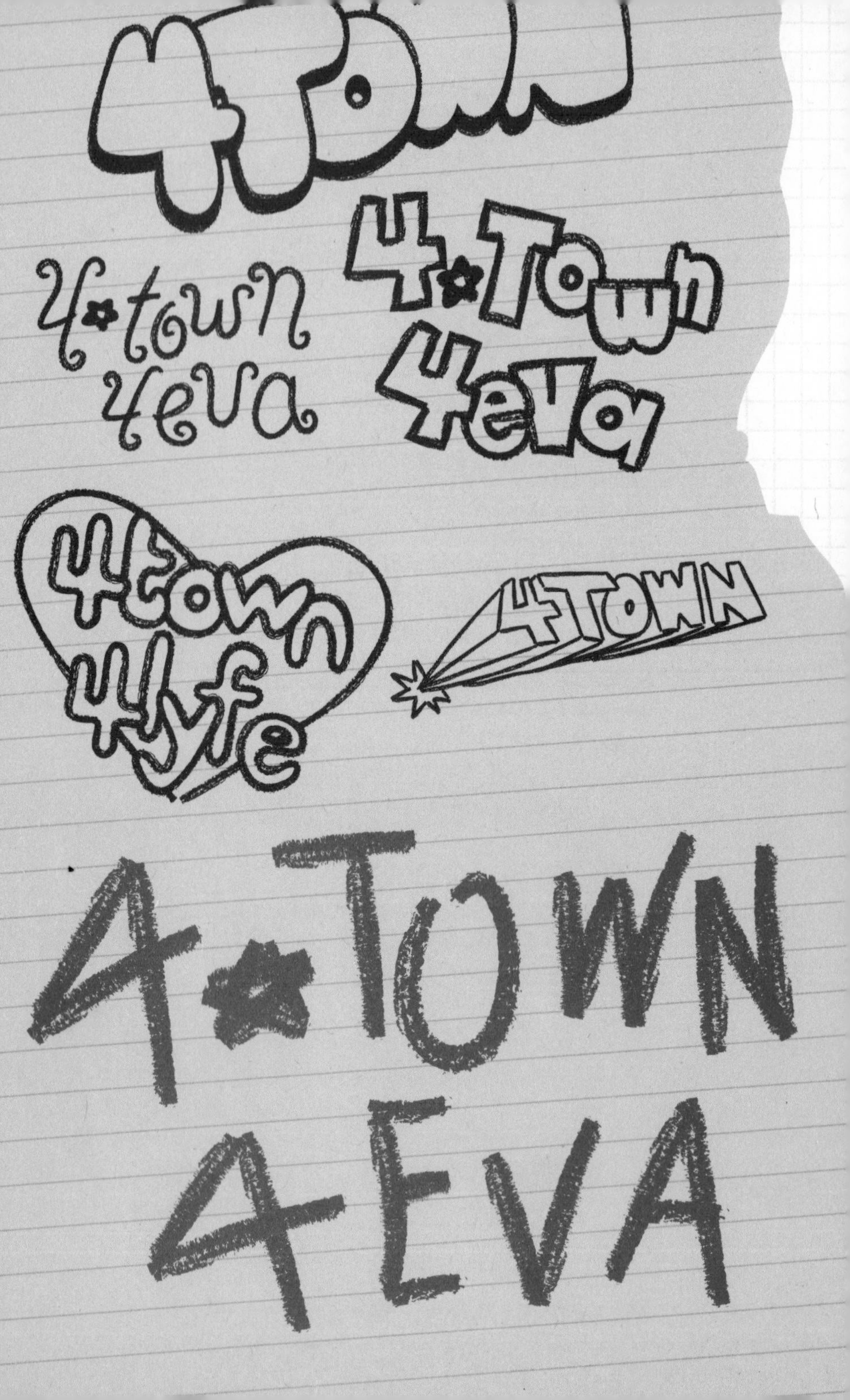
4TOWN
4*town 4eva
4*Town 4eva
4town 4lyfe
4TOWN
4*TOWN 4EVA

Disney · PIXAR

TURNING RED

4☆TOWN 4☆REAL

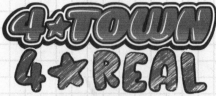

VIZ Media Edition

Story by Dirchansky
Art by KAIfee
Pinup illustration by Bill Presing

Special thanks to Domee Shi, Bill Presing, Behnoosh Khalili, Samantha Keane, Kevin Pearl, and Eugene Paraszczuk

Lettering ★ Erika Terriquez
Cover & Interior Design ★ VIZ Media
Editor ★ Fawn Lau

Printed in the U.S.A.

Published by VIZ Media, LLC
P.O. Box 77010
San Francisco, CA 94107

10 9 8 7 6 5 4 3 2 1
First printing, April 2023

ratings.viz.com
RATED T TEEN

PARENTAL ADVISORY
DISNEY AND PIXAR'S TURNING RED: 4☆TOWN 4☆REAL is rated T for Teen and is recommended for ages 13 and up.

Disney · PIXAR VIZ MEDIA
viz.com

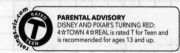

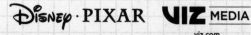

WITHDRAWN